The In
in the "A

STUDIEN ZUR GEWERBE- UND HANDELSGESCHICHTE DER VORINDUSTRIELLEN ZEIT

Vormals Göttinger Beiträge
zur Wirtschafts- und Sozialgeschichte
— — — — — — — — — — — — — — — — — — — —

Begründet von
Wilhelm Abel und Karl Heinrich Kaufhold

Herausgegeben von
Karl Heinrich Kaufhold und Markus A. Denzel

Redaktion:
Hans-Jürgen Gerhard

Nr. 29

Ian Blanchard

The International Economy in the "Age of the Discoveries", 1470–1570

Antwerp and the English Merchants' World

Copy-editing by
Philipp Robinson Rössner

Franz Steiner Verlag Stuttgart 2009

Bibliografische Information der Deutschen Nationalbibliothek
Die Deutsche Nationalbibliothek verzeichnet diese
Publikation in der Deutschen Nationalbibliografie;
detaillierte bibliografische Daten sind im Internet über
<http://dnb.d-nb.de> abrufbar.

ISBN: 978-3-515-09329-3

CONTENTS

TABLES

FIGURES

MAPS

PREFACE (by Ian Blanchard)

One of my colleagues once wrote, "history is a co-operative and kindly profession." I can think of no better proof of the validity of her statement than the present study. It forms part of a wider analysis of early sixteenth-century commerce and involves in particular an investigation of the nature of contemporary mercantile informational systems; a study of the access gained by English merchants to them and an inquiry into the business strategies they evolved on the basis of the information they obtained. The debts incurred in its completion are legion. To the custodians of the archives in which I worked, a thousand thanks are due for their hospitality and kindness, which made research a pleasure. To friends, both in Great Britain and abroad, and in particular, Ekkehard Westermann and Reinhard Hildebrandt, who first set me thinking about the subject of this study, and latterly Erich Landsteiner for maintaining my ongoing interest, my debt is immeasurable. To my colleagues at Edinburgh who have had to live with this study for a very long time, I also offer thanks for both their patience and encouragement. My greatest debts of gratitude are to Herman van der Wee and Peter Earle who gave unstintingly of their time and placed unreservedly at my disposal the fruits of their own researches. My debt to John Munro and Pamela Nightingale must also be recognised for sympathetic discussions on the methodology employed. Finally, I should like to express my debt to the late E. M. Carus-Wilson who originally answered all my queries about cloth production from her unrivalled knowledge of the subject and who has remained a constant guide and inspiration in my work.

Implementation of the research would have been impossible, however, without the generous financial support provided during 1982–5 by the ESRC (Grant HR8205/1, "The Anglo-Netherlands Bill Market and English Export Finance. A Pilot Study") which is gratefully acknowledged. This allowed the development of a RAP-PORT-data base system for the computer storage and manipulation of data contained in mercantile account books and the national customs records. This system was subsequently up-graded to an INGRES-data base system and employed in a second stage of the research programme, again funded by the ESRC, which has been undertaken under my direction (Grant R 000 23 2851: "England and the International Economy, 1544–1561") during the period 1991–1993. By utilising these data-base systems, it was possible to provide the statistical framework for this study and to prepare a series of initial working papers. These were presented at the Workshop on Quantitative Monetary History (Brussels 1982); the Research Seminar of the Monetary History Group (London, 1989); the International Urban History Group seminar on "Cities of Finance" (Amsterdam 1991)[1]; the Mackie Lectures (Aberdeen, 1992)[2]; the confer-

---

1   I. BLANCHARD, Credit and Commerce: From the Mediterranean to the North Sea Economies in the Early Sixteenth Century, in: H. DIEDERIKS / D. REEDER (eds.), Cities of Finance: Proceedings of the Colloquium (Amsterdam, May 1991), Amsterdam 1996, pp. 21–33.

2   ID., Northern Wools and Netherlands Markets at the Close of the Middle Ages, in: G. G. SIMPSON (ed.), Scotland and the Low Countries 1124–1994, East Linton 1996, pp. 76–88.

ence on "Finances publiques et finances privées au bas moyen âge" (Gand, 1995)[3] and the 4e Journées Braudèliennes. NIAS-MHS seminar on "Early modern capitalism", (Wassenar, 1997). I should like to express my gratitude to all present at these seminars for their helpful comments and to all those who have communicated with me on other publications deriving from this work.[4]

The success of this ESRC-funded research group, before its untimely demise in 1993/4, however, was not simply a function of fund-availability but owed much to the efforts of my collaborators to whom I perhaps owe the greatest debt of all. The commitment, dedication, enthusiasm and intellectual stimulus provided by Jennifer Newman and the post-graduate students attached to the group – Evan Jones and Martin Rorke – is gratefully acknowledged. Indeed if this study has any virtues, they derive from discussions with them. I willingly accept responsibility for its weaknesses.

Newlees Farm, Christmas 1998   Ian Blanchard

---

3   ID., English Royal Borrowing at Antwerp, 1544–1574, in: M. BOONE / W. PREVENIER (eds.), Finances publiques et finances privées au bas moyen âge. Actes du colloque tenu à Gand le 5–6 mai 1995, Leuven / Apeldoorn 1996, pp. 57–74.

4   ID., The Continental European Cattle Trades, 1400–1600, in: Economic History Review, Second Series, XXXIX, 3 (1986), pp. 427–460, reprinted in: D. IRWIN (ed.), Trade in the Pre-Modern Era, 1400–1700, Oxford 1995; ID., International Lead Production and Trade in the "Age of the Saigerprozess," 1460–1560, Stuttgart 1994; and ID. / H. VAN DER WEE, The Habsburgs and the Antwerp Money Market: the Exchange Crises of 1521 and 1522–3, in: I. BLANCHARD et al. (eds.), Industry and Finance in Early Modern History: Essays Presented to George Hammersley on the Occasion of his 74th Birthday, Stuttgart 1992, pp. 27–56. Professor Van der Wee provided some of the materials concerning exchange rates for this article.

FOREWORD (by *Philipp Robinson Rössner*)

This book is the unaltered version of a pre-publication copy of a monograph originally entitled "The International Economy in the 'Age of Discovery', 1470–1570, Volume 1: The English Merchants' World", finished by the author in Christmas 1998. Accordingly the thematic approach, its scope and bibliography reflect the 1998 current state of the art in the subject. Only slight editorial alterations were made to the text, references and bibliography (July–December 2008) where appropriate, so as to transform the manuscript into print-ready proof copies.

It is a great pleasure for the writer of these lines that Professor emeritus Ian Blanchard kindly agreed in 2008 to publish the manuscript as a one-volume monograph in the *Studien zur Gewerbe- und Handelsgeschichte der Vorindustriellen Zeit*, ed. by Karl Heinrich Kaufhold and Markus A. Denzel. Even ten years after it was written, the book closes an important gap in early modern European financial, monetary and commercial history, in the same way as it contributes to the discussion of the global contingencies of European silver, lead and tin mining around 1500. In fact Ian Blanchard represents a rare case of an historian capable of writing "big" history by teasing out the global patterns and contingencies of events, situations, trends and structures, which at first sight – or to the uninformed reader – may appear local or regional phenomena at best. Blanchard is thus able to link the fortunes of the "tinners of Devon and Cornwall" with those of the Saxon tin miners of Altenburg (chapter 16); the English lead mines of Bere Ferrers, Devon, with the fortunes of the central European, Thuringian and Saxonian silver producers (chapter 15) without ever losing track of the real significant patterns. One of these would clearly be the strong connection, perhaps even inverse correlation, between the output and productivity record of central European (Tyrolean and Saxon mines, Thuringian *Saigerhütten*) silver production areas on the one, and the movement of interest rates on the Antwerp money market during the first quarter of the sixteenth century on the other hand, and the way they influenced the financing and organization of the intra-European commodity trades, 1470–1570. Only few economic historians are capable of such tasks and the present author is convinced that Ian Blanchard has achieved this by a remarkable bundling of personal qualities and qualifications. His general openness for a multitude of academic disciplines and scientific approaches, his willingness and ability to achieve command (at least in reading) of several Germanic, Romanic and Slavic languages, as well as his general open-mindedness, both private and academic, have provided Ian Blanchard with the unique opportunity to study the working mechanisms of the sixteenth-century European economy *en detail*. Never, however, and this comes across very clearly in the present monograph, has he lost sight of the academic discipline which he was originally trained in – monetary economics. His deep sensibility for the working mechanisms of medieval and early modern society and economy, however, have successfully prevented him from falling into an only too familiar trap, which most of the current or "younger" academics studying the financial markets nowadays probably would, i.e. to produce a – superficially scientific – study in the econometrics of the Antwerp and London stock exchanges, 1500–1570, without having a firm grip on the period studied, the people involved, their motivations, fears, inclinations and, above all, ways of reducing the transaction costs of foreign trade.

Very special thanks are due to the editors, Professor Dr. Markus A. Denzel (Leipzig / Bolzano, Italy) and Professor emeritus Dr. Karl Heinrich Kaufhold (Göttingen) for inclusion of this monograph in their *Studien zur Gewerbe- und Handelsgeschichte der Vorindustriellen Zeit*. Very special thanks are due to the publisher, in particular Dr. Thomas Schaber (Stuttgart), for assistance in the printing process.

Leipzig, December 2008   Philipp Robinson Rössner

INTRODUCTION

THE INTERNATIONAL ECONOMY IN THE "AGE OF THE DISCOVERIES", 1470–1570

Those who today have only latterly come to enjoy the pleasures of supping Antipodean wines with meals that include such items as Alicante melons, Argentinean beef or New Zealand lamb and Israeli strawberries or who have only recently been able to pleasure themselves by dressing in Italian shoes, Taiwanese or Hong Kong shirtsblouses and French over garments would perhaps be surprised at the variety of such exotic wares which were available to their forebears. Yet almost half a millennium ago the men and women of early sixteenth-century England were no less familiar with such products obtained on a world stage. One, albeit substantial, Derbyshire peasant of the 1470s, for instance, wore chemises of Brabantine linen, trimmed his home-spun coats with braid of Italian (and even Asiatic) silk and protected his head from the rain with a Flemish felt hat. The food on his table might be home-produced but it was spiced with the exotic wares of the East Indies and if he or his family were taken ill they could dose themselves with drugs of similar provenance. For such a man's lord the range of such wares that were available was far greater: Netherlands tapestries to hang on the walls of his chamber, jewels from the Hindu Kush set into clasps of Spanish gold to adorn his hose which had been made of Chinese silken fabrics, African apes for the amusement of his lady... In early sixteenth-century England all members of lay and ecclesiastical society from the king right down the social scale to the members of the upper echelon of peasant society enjoyed access to wares obtained from the four corners of the known world. In the new-fashioned shops of the metropolitan centres or from the stalls located at the long-established annual or bi-annual fairs, such individuals were able (if they had the necessary cash) to obtain a wide range of wares from merchants involved in an international economy of truly global dimensions.

The nature of such an international economy, characterised not only by spatial but also by religious, cultural and political divisions, is today difficult to comprehend. In order to undertake this study it has been necessary to formulate a new conceptualization divorced from the anachronistic perceptions of the modern age and embodying both spatial and temporal dimensions of varying extent and duration (Figure 1). Thus in this volume an attempt has been made to examine the world of those English merchants who first accessed the international economy in order to distribute the produce of the realm and secure such goods as were required by the nation's consumers. That the access point is England has no special significance. It could as easily be Venice or Alexandria, Ormuz or Malacca. The only reasons for choosing this particular point of access reside in the author's knowledge of Anglo-Netherlands commercial documentation and in the particular richness of those sources. This richness of documentation is of great importance, however, with respect to this study of the "Merchants' World" for in trying to understand how these traders operated within the bounds of this international economy it is necessary, both in terms of time and space, to concentrate on the *durée courte*.

Figure 1: Schematic Representation of the International Economy, 1470–1570

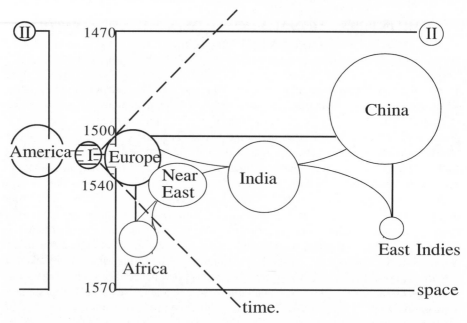

For most English merchants, during the first twenty years of the sixteenth century, their "world" was spatially encompassed within the inner-city bounds of the twin cities of London and Antwerp. There in the winding streets and vennels they could gain first-hand knowledge of everything that might concern their businesses. Daily those members of English mercantile society who were resident in the great western metropolis of Antwerp made an almost ritualistic pilgrimage from their lodgings to the Exchange. There they carefully recorded the quotations and diligently gathered any news of wars, bankruptcy or monetary disorder which might upset the delicate balance of rates at that institution. On returning home almost their first act was to compose succinctly this varied information into an epistle to their masters or agents who eagerly awaited news of the day's events. The singular importance attached to this intelligence by the international merchant community is not hard to understand, for, in large measure, upon the movement of the Antwerp exchange depended the fortunes of their trade through that city. Dear money augured badly for commerce. Those merchants who borrowed money to buy wares would find their costs enhanced. Fearing lest their goods be overpriced on distant markets, they would cut back on their purchases. In such circumstances the mart was likely to be slack and those bringing their wares thence would not easily vent them. Cheap money, on the other hand, opened up the prospect of buoyant business. By reducing the foreign exchange price of commodities at their final point of sale, it increased their competitiveness and sales potential. Merchants thus flocked to buy such wares at the mart where sellers found plentiful takers for their produce. Throughout the years 1470–1570 mercantile correspondence passing between Antwerp and London revealed the intimate connection between the price of money at the western metropolis and the level of commercial activity there. Moreover, with finance costs comprising in normal circumstances ten to twenty per cent of the final wholesale price of commodities even relatively small movements in interest rates on the exchange could significantly affect prices. In the highly competitive markets of the international economy such price movements could make or mar sales of a particular product. Merchants at Antwerp thus watched every movement of the exchange with interest, for upon it depended their very livelihood.

They also listened attentively for those rumours of apocalyptic disaster – war, famine and disease – which perennially circulated on the commodity exchanges. These not only augured an enhancement in finance costs, as monarchs were forced to raise money to deal with the effects of such catastrophes. They also heralded major changes in conditions on those markets where the commodities they traded were ultimately sold or acquired and signified enhanced transportation costs as carriers were forced to seek alternative routes or pay protection money to ensure safe passage. Within the narrow confines of the two north-western European commercial metropolises, where the English merchants worked and played in a space no larger than a fair-sized village, they thus gained access to an extended world of knowledge encompassing information garnered from the length and breadth of a commercial system of global dimensions. Here they heard rumours of Chinese famines or of civil wars in central Asia which, circulating amongst the Arab, Greek or Persian traders at Alexandria or Caffa, were overheard by Italian merchants resident in those cities. These merchants immediately sent the news to Venice or Genoa. From thence it was passed rapidly by pony-express riders to Antwerp. They also appraised themselves of how Sicilian and Neapolitan silk producers were responding to the resultant cessation of eastern supplies and accordingly were able to assess the likely impact of these changes on the prices they would have to pay for the silk desired by peasant and lord alike in England. It was here also that during the years ca. 1500–1520 they received the first news each year of the number of gold-ladened ships which had arrived in the Guadelquavir from the recently discovered Americas. This news not only portended the success of sales of their goods in Spain but forewarned them of the potentially disruptive impact of these specie flows on international monetary systems. Every day such items of mercantile gossip circulated on the Antwerp bourse to become part of that informational flow which would be transmitted by the English residents of that city to their masters and agents across the Channel in the city on the Thames. Sifted, structured and layered from a functional as well as a spatial perspective these fragments of information were gradually formed into a corpus of knowledge. This was then combined with further news, gleaned from traders visiting their counting houses or the various cloth halls of commodity supply conditions, to allow the merchants to formulate their business strategies. Yet encyclopaedic as it was, this information suffered from the fact that it had been gathered from within a temporally and spatially extended trade network. By the time news reached London from distant lands it had passed through numerous hands. Each person along the way perceived and interpreted it in terms of his own particular religious, political and economic pre-conceptions, until it perhaps bore no more than a passing relationship to reality. Such distortions were an inevitable

consequence of the temporal and spatial dimensions of the merchants' extended informational network. They were also an integral and very real element of his world
view.

Nor in the 1530s, when these English merchants for the first time began to establish their personal presence within the interstices of this world commercial system, did
this situation change. During that decade, "direct" English commerce began to establish itself as a permanent feature of the nation's trade. Merchants certainly for the first
time in half a century started to locate branches of their businesses at the markets
where the commodities they traded were ultimately sold or acquired. On this occasion,
moreover, such activities were not confined to continental Europe. Following in the
wake of the original explorers and the South German and Netherlands merchants trading to the new worlds, they also trans-shipped on Spanish and Portuguese vessels to
the Americas and India. As a result of this spatial extension of the "Merchants'
World" its denizens were thus now able to observe directly market conditions in the
places where their goods were sold to final consumers or where the commodities they
required could be bought from producers. With the publication of the explorers' original journals and the receipt of mercantile intelligence in factors' letters, layer after
layer of misconception about market conditions was removed. Lacking a contextual
framework which would allow them to locate their descriptions of local trading conditions in an analysis of indigenous extra-European commercial systems and business
strategies, however, they merely substituted one body of misinformation for another.
The original rumours which had circulated at Antwerp about extra-European trade
might have been distorted, by both distance and time. Yet they were rooted at least in
the knowledge of Islamic merchants who operated on the basis of advanced business
practices and possessed an intimacy with trading conditions in commercial networks
which extended by land and sea between the Near East and China and from the Tell to
the Bilad-al-Sudan. The new reports, arriving from the extra-European worlds to the
South, East and West, though possessing that veracity born of direct observation in
relation to conditions at the points where the Europeans accessed prevailing systems,
in being conceived in terms of an atavistic cultural viewpoint and lacking in such perspectives, were thus no less distorted. As a result of the "Discoveries" the English
"Merchants' World" may have undergone a process of topographical extension but
their understanding of that world remained as restricted as before and continued to be
limited by constraints of time and space.

To this spatial restriction on their knowledge, moreover, the merchants also
brought another temporal restriction, thereby linking their behavioural patterns with
those of their modern counterparts. Today, in spite of the pseudo-scientific conjectures
of those who assure us of long-term ecological disaster as a result of global-warming,
businessmen continue to perceive their world in terms of the *durée courte*. They respond to short-term stimuli and singularly fail to comprehend long-term trends. Their
early sixteenth-century counterparts were no different. They certainly did not lack
prophets of doom who preached millennial disaster. Like their modern counterparts,
however, they concentrated their attention on those day-to-day occurrences which
might affect their business activities. Their letters, like the present-day commercial
press, reported that news of apocalyptic disaster – war, famine and disease – which
perennially circulated on the commodity exchanges because of the immediate short-
term impact that such events would have on finance, transport and market transactions

costs. In the following pages, therefore, the "English Merchants' World" will be considered from the perspective of the merchants themselves, revealing how they made decisions and operated within the international economy on the basis of their spatially and temporally restricted knowledge of events taking place therein.

PART ONE

FINANCIAL AND MONETARY SYSTEMS: ANTWERP

CHAPTER ONE

THE ANTWERP MONEY MARKET. PRELUDE TO DISASTER, 1513–1521

Daily those merchants resident in the great western metropolis of Antwerp made an almost ritualistic pilgrimage to the Exchange. Here they carefully recorded the quotations and diligently gathered any news of wars, bankruptcy or monetary disorder which might upset the delicate balance of rates at that institution. On returning home almost their first act was to compose succinctly this varied information into an epistle to their masters or agents who eagerly awaited news of the day's events. The singular importance attached to this intelligence by the international merchant community is not hard to understand, for, in large measure, upon the movement of the Antwerp exchange depended the fortunes of their trade through that city. Dear money augured badly for commerce. Those merchants who borrowed money to buy wares would find their costs enhanced. Fearing lest their goods be overpriced on distant markets, they would cut back on their purchases. In such circumstances the mart was likely to be slack. Those bringing their wares thence would not easily vent them. Cheap money, on the other hand, opened up the prospect of buoyant business. By reducing the foreign exchange price of commodities at their final point of sale it increased their competitiveness and sales potential. Merchants thus flocked to buy such wares at the mart where sellers found plentiful takers for their produce. Throughout the years 1470–1570 mercantile correspondence emanating from Antwerp revealed the intimate connection between the price of money at the western metropolis and the level of commercial activity there. Moreover, with finance costs comprising in normal circumstances ten to twenty per cent of the final wholesale price of commodities even relatively small movements in interest rates on the exchange could significantly affect prices and in the highly competitive markets of the international economy make or mar sales of a particular product. Merchants at Antwerp thus watched every movement of the exchange with interest, for upon it depended their very livelihood.

During the years to 1526 the all pervasive *leitmotif* running through the operations of that market was the intimate relationship between the central European silver producers of the Alpenland, Thuringian and Slovakian mining complex and the great southern German merchant finance houses, discernible in the events of 1527/8. For more than a quarter of a century after 1500 silver production in this important mining region of central Europe expanded rapidly. Only briefly and sectorally interrupted in 1509–12, 1514–5, 1519–23 and 1525, the boom continued unabated, reaching a peak in 1526 (Figure 1.1).

Figure 1.1: Central European Silver Production, 1470–1570

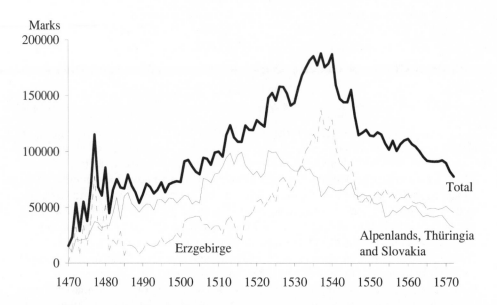

From the Tyrol and Carinthia, Slovakia and Thuringia, a seemingly never ending flood of silver[1] flowed into the coffers of the great South German financiers, continually replenishing their cash reserves and allowing them to expand the credit base of their operations.[2] With their new found wealth they could fund the ever increasing circulating capital requirements of their industrial enterprises; underwrite the burgeoning volume of their exchange dealings, finance their growing involvement in international trade and even satisfy the voracious appetite of the Habsburgs for loans – at a falling rate of interest.

Yet whilst this latter demand was never to stem the decline in medium-term rates

---

1   The place of the Alpenland, Thuringian and Slovak mining complex in the development of the Euro-American industry is briefly considered in H. VAN DER WEE / I. BLANCHARD, The Habsburgs and the Antwerp Money Market: the Exchange Crises of 1521 and 1522–3, in: I. BLANCHARD et al. (eds.), Industry and Finance in Early Modern History, Stuttgart 1992, pp. 27–56.

2   The literature on the integrated operations of the South German houses is immense and a study dealing in part with this subject is currently in preparation. The Fugger Inventory of 1527, however, provides a marvellous insight into the varied activities of one such house in its prime. G. von PÖLNITZ, Anton Fugger, Tübingen 1958, Vol. I, pp. 113–4, p. 453, n. 137 and p. 454, n. 138; J. STRIEDER (ed.), Die Inventur der Firma Fugger aus dem Jahr 1527, in: Zeitschrift für die gesamte Staatswissenschaft, Ergänzungsheft XVII (1905). On the relationship of mining activity to their financial and commercial operations see e.g. E. FINK, Die Bergwerksunternehmungen der Fugger in Schlesien, in: Zeitschrift des Vereins für Geschichte und Alterthum Schlesiens, XXVIII (1894), p. 312; F. DOBEL, Ueber den Bergbau und Handel des Jakob und Anton Fugger in Kärnten und Tirol, 1495–1560, in: Zeitschrift des historischen Vereins für Schwaben und Neuberg, IX (1882), pp. 196, 202; M. WOLFSTRIGL-WOLFSKRON, Die Tiroler Erzbergbaue, 1301–1665, Innsbruck 1903, pp. 52–6, and J. VLACHOVIC, Slovenská Med v 16 a 17 storoci, Bratislava 1964, pp. 37–53.

("credit until the next fair", i.e. trimestrial) or short-term ("at usance", i.e. monthly) interest rates during the years to 1521 it was increasingly becoming – in 1513, 1516/7 and 1521 – a major influence in the market, and a dominant one thereafter (Figures 1.2–3).[3]

1513. The effects of imperial borrowing in the German-dominated Antwerp money market were first felt in this year when the long period of peace and neutrality, which had characterised the opening years of the century, was brought to a close by war against Gelderland and by Maximilian's Venetian campaign.[4] Imperial indebtedness rose to 57,000 livres artois in a market which was still suffering from the effects of central European mining disorders. Interest rates on government loans, which had stabilized at 19.5 per cent during the peaceful quinquennium 1504–1508 and had risen to 20 per cent in 1511–1512, now reached 29 per cent on the outbreak of war.[5] The crisis was, however, an ephemeral one. With the liquidation of the floating debt, following the cessation of hostilities, interest rates fell to 19.25 per cent during 1514–1515, fractionally below the level prevailing during the first decade of the century. Peace had returned and with it easy money, but it was to prove merely an interlude.

---

3   Figure 1.2. On levels of Habsburg indebtedness and interest rates on their medium-term borrowing see F. BRAUDEL / G. BELLART, Les emprunts de Charles Quint sur la place de Anvers, in: Charles Quint et son temps. Colloques internationaux du centre national de la recherche scientifique, sciences humaines (Paris 30. 9.– 3. 10. 1958), Paris 1959, pp. 191–201 and H. VAN DER WEE, The Growth of the Antwerp Market and the European Economy. Fourteenth – Sixteenth Centuries, The Hague 1963, Vol. I, App. 45–2, p. 527. Both studies are based on the accounts of the recette generale des finances de Flandres (Archives departmentales du Nord, Lille. Serie B, 1878–2706) which have, for the relevant years 1515–1540 (ibidem, 2224–2351, 2357–2430, 2436, 2442), also been examined in order to elucidate the market behaviour of individual finance houses in their dealings with the Habsburgs. Bill rates given in Figure 1.3 have been calculated from exchange materials collected by Professors van der Wee and Blanchard, utilising the data base systems developed at Edinburgh during the years 1982–1985 and 1990–1993 with financial assistance provided by the ESRC (Project HR 8205-1/B-0023002-1and R 000 23 2851: Final Reports, which are lodged in both the British Library and the library of the ESRC). Such contracts were negotiated at the Netherlands fairs which began at the following times: Paasch Mart, 3rd week of April; Sinxen Mart: 2nd week of June; Bamus Mart: 3rd week of September; Cold Mart: In this instance the official opening was largely irrelevant to the English, trading operations beginning in January. Details of the provenance of these materials and of the methodology employed may be obtained from the collaborators in this work. For a study of the analogous effects of the arrival of American silver on interest rates at Medina del Campo during the last quarter of the sixteenth century see F. RUIZ MARTÍN, Lettres marchandes échangées entre Florence et Medina del Campo, Paris 1965, pp. lxxxv–lxxxvi.

4   VAN DER WEE, Antwerp, II, p. 141.

5   The size of the floating debt was calculated from data concerning interest charges (ibid.) and the prevailing rate of interest (Figure 1.2).

Figure 1.2: Imperial Indebtedness, 1510–1540

A. Netherlands government floating (3-6 months) debt. In 10,000
   livres artois. B. Interest on 3-month loans. Per cent a year

The resumption of hostilities in the Friesian war again led to increasing Habsburg borrowing, the floating debt rising from negligible levels in 1515 to 380,000 livres artois
in mid-1517 and 430,000 a year later. Unprecedented demands were being placed on a
market which had only recently assumed the mantle of Bruges and it was not found
wanting. Interest rates rose, but even during the siege of Dokkum in June 1517 they
never reached the levels of four years earlier.[6] Indeed, the market was so buoyant that,
after the initial rise which carried interest rates to 28.5 per cent in the summer of 1517,
the Habsburgs managed to undertake a major debt conversion operation, increasing
their nominal indebtedness but restructuring their loans at a much lower rate of interest. From 1517–1518 through the intermediary of the town of Antwerp, on the Emperor's behalf, they successfully issued fixed interest loans secured on the *aides*
granted by the estates. The prices they obtained for these *rentes,* which bore interest at
the rate of "le denier 16" or 6.25 per cent, are sadly unknown. It seems probable, however, that they managed to raise some 150,000 livres artois which were used to pay off
those medium-term merchant debts (*finances*) which fell over the same period to
176,000 livres artois. Interest rates on such paper fell, reaching an all-time low of 15.5
per cent in the summer of 1518. A debt of 380,000 livres artois, bearing interest
charges of ca.76,000 livres artois (20 per cent) was thus converted into a bi-partite
structure of 254,000 livres artois at 6.25 per cent in *rentes* and 176,000 livres artois at
15.5 per cent in *finances*. The imperial debt was thus nominally much larger –
430,000 livres artois – but bore interest payments of only 43,155 livres artois (ten per
cent). Abundant fund availability was allowing the market to equilibrate, during the
years 1517–1518, at lower levels than earlier in the century and the Habsburgs took
full advantage of the situation. Their financial operations, which ultimately in 1520

---

6   VAN DER WEE, Antwerp, II, p. 142, n. 164.

allowed them to borrow on *finances* at 13 per cent, were not carried through, however, without difficulties. During 1517/8, as the conversion operation allowed the liquidation of medium-term debts interest rates on government paper had fallen. From the Bamus mart of 1518, however, participants in the market for such securities began to show signs of unease as first news of political uncertainties in Flanders shattered their mood of euphoria and then rumours of their sovereign's intention to be crowned emperor sent them into a panic.[7] The first of many battles between the newly crowned kings of France and Spain was about to be fought out, not on the battle fields of Picardie and Artois, but on the money markets of Antwerp, Lyons and Genoa. The hapless denizens of those markets now had real cause for alarm.

Figure 1.3: Antwerp Interest Rates at Three-month Term, 1513–1540

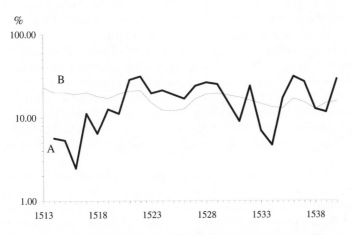

A. Short-term commercial paper. B. Medium-term government loans

During the summer of 1518 the principal focus of activity, in relation to the forthcoming election of the emperor, was Spain. Here a special ambassador, de Courteville, prepared to depart for Maximilian's court with instructions to support the efforts of the Emperor on his grandson's behalf with money and promises, and a sum of a hundred thousand guilders in letters of exchange – which in the event was to prove but a pourboire in the game to be played. Even before his arrival the rules of play had

---

7   The beginnings of the new crises at the Bamus mart of 1518 were signalled by the government's inability to vend hereditary annuities at that time and by the behaviour of the merchant financiers at the mart who suddenly, having granted a loan of 25,057 livres artois at 16 per cent, withdrew from the market and refused to lend at less than 24.3 per cent (VAN DER WEE, Antwerp, II, p.141s). The subsequent events surrounding the imperial election of 1518–1519 are outlined in the following four paragraphs on the basis of materials contained in L. P. C. VAN DEN BERG, Correspondance de Marguerite d' Autriche avec ses amis sur les affaires des Pays Bas, La Haye, two vols., 1842–1847; LE GLAY, Correspondance de l' Empereur Maximilien Ier et de Marguerite d' Autriche sa fille, Gouvernante des Pays Bas, 2 vols. Paris 1845; E. DE QUINSONAS, Materiaux pour servir a l'histoire de Marguerite d' Autriche Duchesse de Savoie, Regente des Pays Bas, Paris 1860.

changed as the seven electors became aware that beside Charles, in his capacity as king of Aragon and Castile, Francis I also wished to sue for the highest dignity in Christendom. They resolved, accordingly, to sell the throne of Charlemagne to the highest bidder. In such circumstances the bills brought by de Courteville, which were to be paid to the electors only after the imperial election, were so much worthless paper for, as Maximilian reported to his grandson, those gentlemen had already accepted considerable sums from the French king and would only be satisfied with cash in hand. How difficult it would be to collect this cash in sufficient quantities now became only too apparent. The effort of Francis to raise large sums by way of loans from the bankers of Lyons and Genoa failed. Only his doting mother, Louise of Savoy, seems to have been prepared to lay her fortune in the balance for the pleasure of seeing her spoilt son crowned Emperor. For Charles too, far away in Aragon, the problem of how to come by sufficient money also posed considerable problems not only in the collection but also in the transmission to Germany. Every source of revenue was surveyed and the capacity of the exchange to transfer large sums examined. Even when all these factors were taken into account, however, the human element remained. Payments to the electors still had to pass through Maximilian's hands and in the process some would almost certainly adhere to his fingers. More reliable intermediaries were required with abundant resources at their disposal and an effective exchange system at hand. The choice, perhaps inevitably, was the Emperor's daughter – Margaret of Savoy. She was brought back from the political wilderness and given charge of the finances with which the coming battle would be fought. Only the official title of Regent was withheld – perhaps as a spur to her endeavours and as a promise to bind her to her nephew's interest.

Thus in the autumn of 1518 were the Netherlands and the Antwerp money market brought into the great game. Margaret once again found herself in the thick of a European war, waged this time not with weapons but with ducats and gold écus, against that ancient enemy of the Burgundian royal house – France. The first campaign of the war, moreover, was already in progress. In August, the emperor had convened a meeting of the Diet in Augsburg. At this meeting he could personally bring pressure to bear upon the electors. His success was overwhelming. De Courteville wrote excitedly to Madame that all was going well. Five of the seven electors were committed to Charles and the two others could be dispensed with. The cost of apparent victory, however, had been high. The Elector of Brandenburg sold his vote for a life annuity of a hundred thousand gulden and a similar sum in cash on the day of the election. In addition, the infant Catherine, Charles' youngest sister, whose marriage to the Elector's son was also part of the deal, was to bring with her a considerable dowry. The three archbishops – of Mainz, Trier and Cologne – were no less rapacious. Mainz was to receive a yearly stipend of ten thousand gulden and another thirty thousand in cash as soon as the other electors committed their votes. Cologne got the promise of an annuity of six thousand gulden and twenty thousand in cash. The Count Palatine demanded no less than a hundred thousand gulden and a yearly stipend of twenty thousand for his brother. Then there were the presents and pensions to friends and members of the family, even to secretaries and servants of the covetous cabal. The total of Maximilian's commitments at Augsburg came to 514,000 gulden.

Charles, shocked at such reckless expenditure on his grandfather's part, made use of a picturesque metaphor in his correspondence with Margaret on the matter. The horse upon which his aunt would like to see him ride was a very expensive one, the young would-be Emperor declared. Margaret had to admit as much. She thought it, however, a horse that its purchaser could easily acquire at the price, and now that it was trained to Charles's hand she was of the opinion that he must not let it escape, whatever it might cost him.

However, the bargain was not yet struck. The Pope, who in the long run would have to crown Charles emperor, fearful of Habsburg influence in Italy, began to procrastinate and began to search for reasons to invalidate Charles' candidature. Francis rapidly took up the cry and then amidst all the uncertainties, on the 12th January 1519, Maximilian died. The game, so recently seemingly in Charles' court, was thrown wide open. Francis doubled his bribes, multiplied his intrigues ten-fold. His ambassadors made no secret that their king would get himself elected, by influence, money or force. They travelled through Germany with a train of mules laden with gold. Because the Fugger would accept no French bills of exchange it was said in Germany that the French transported their gold in Rhine ships in total secrecy. Margaret, to whom all these reports came, now had to act. With the experience of the previous winter behind her when the resources of Antwerp had already been heavily committed to Maximilian's expensive intrigues, she probably regretted her grandiose words to her nephew. Yet she now held the threads of intrigue firmly in her own hands and only one way seemed open: no empty promises, but to give with both hands "*qui faisait avoir le precheur bon credit*". Thus, whilst Francis intrigued in Hungary, Poland and Bohemia, in Rome and even in Spain in the entourage of his rival, Margaret sent her private secretary to the empire with new promises and new bribes, and to lend additional strength to all this activity the merchants of Antwerp were forbidden to lend money to any other foreign power, so that all their wealth could remain at Charles' disposal. The principal result of all these intrigues, however, was that the electors raised the price of their votes. Charles had to hand over more than a million gulden to secure the votes which Maximilian had already bought for him. Gold, gold and yet more gold was required as the struggle for the imperial crown continued, holding all Europe in suspense. Towards the end of February 1519 the confusion was so shocking, the position of the electors so enigmatic, that Margaret, considering Charles' cause lost, counselled retreat. Charles, however, would have none of it. The struggle continued with money and promises, warnings and threats until the very day of the election approached, when the news flashed across Europe that the French king had gone to Lorraine. Would force now prevail where money had not? The German cities armed. Charles, having promised to protect the electors, threw a cordon of mercenaries about the electoral city. This last measure settled the matter. On the 17th June 1519 the Diet met at Frankfurt. On the 28th June, at seven o'clock in the morning the electors betook themselves to the church of St Bartholomew and four hours later Charles was elected king of the Romans by a unanimous vote.

Perhaps the most eventful year in the history of the young Antwerp money market thus drew to a close and it had acquitted itself well. After the first turmoil, occasioned by the annuities fiasco at the Bamus mart of 1518 when rates rose to 24.3 per cent, it had met the almost limitless demands placed upon it with ease. Interest rates remained high until the Sinxen mart of 1519 but never attained the levels of two years earlier. Even amidst the turmoil of the electoral game money had been relatively cheap. Then as the conversion operation, temporarily in abeyance over the winter and spring of

1518/9, was resumed it became absolutely so. During the summer of 1519 annuities sold readily and as the medium-term debt continued to be reduced *finances* could be contracted at rates as low as 15 per cent. By the autumn the costs involved in the great venture begun a year before – the quantities of gold expended, the machinations and plots, the base behaviour which made both bribers and bribed blush with shame – were all but forgotten. Charles was emperor and money was cheap. Nor was this heady atmosphere of financial optimism seemingly to be disturbed as the logical implications of the imperial victory were played out. Charles' victory had made the breach between Valois and Habsburg final and irrevocable and ushered in a new era of imperial finance. By the beginning of 1520 the conversion operation begun in 1517/8 was brought to a close and, in preparation for the inevitable war, borrowing began on all fronts. Once again the town of Antwerp was called upon to raise a loan, of a hundred thousand livres artois, through the sale of annuities – only now the funds raised were not destined for the repayment of existing *finances*. Indeed, new demands were placed upon the merchant community who bore the full brunt of the new policies. They responded, however, with an eagerness which is hard to explain. Interest rates whilst rising marginally at the Cold mart of 1519/20, thereafter rapidly subsided, reaching their lowest point yet at the Sinxen mart of that year – when government loans could be floated at the phenomenally low rate of 13 per cent. A curious euphoria born upon a flood of silver continued to pervade the market which even the avaricious demands of the Habsburgs could not dispel. Yet this was merely the lull before the storm. The gods first blind those they wish to destroy.

If the burgeoning flood of silver prior to this year had paved the way for easy money on the Antwerp bourse then the cessation of that flow, caused by the contemporary Central European mining crisis, reversed that trend and brought a new reality to the market place in the autumn of 1520. The merchant community now no longer found their depleted coffers miraculously replenished. The Imhoff, for instance, whose assets had increased at a rate of 9.5 per cent a year to 1520, now in 1520/1 experienced only a 3.5 per cent annual capital growth. Nor were they exceptional.[8] Amongst the merchant community at Antwerp, which included the Fugger, the Florentine Philip Gualterotti, George van Dorch, Christopher Herwart of Augsburg, Erasmus Schetz, Ambrose Hochstetter, the Affaitadi and a host of lesser luminaries, there was a shortage of funds which resulted in a certain cautiousness in their dealings. Interest rates, accordingly, stabilized and for the first time in three years the Habsburgs felt the full impact of market constraints. Thus when during that winter, due to the exigencies of the uneasy armed peace, they once again began to borrow heavily, pushing up their debts beyond the half million level, interest rates rose sharply and showed no signs of faltering. Caught unawares, the authorities responded by withdrawing from the market. Debts were reduced and interest rates dutifully fell back – to slightly over 16 per cent. As border incidents proliferated and Francis I assumed an increasingly belligerent stance over the Easter of 1521 the Antwerp money market achieved a new equilibrium, in conditions of specie shortage, at a prevailing rate some three points higher than before. It was now clear to Charles that the days when debts could be built up at falling rates of interest were, at least temporarily, over. Henceforth, there

---

8   R. EHRENBERG, Das Zeitalter der Fugger. Geldkapital und Creditverkehr im 16. Jahrhundert, reprint Hildesheim 1963, Vol. I, pp. 227, 237–8.

would be no miraculous silver wand to banish financial difficulties. War, if it was to come, would have to be conducted on terms of strict cost accounting.

Such a situation was hardly likely to gladden the Emperor's heart during the difficult months to follow. In spite of economic circumstances, events had a certain momentum of their own. During May and June, as the English ambassadors at the Valois and Habsburg courts tried to placate the protagonists, matters turned for the worst.[9] Francis, having put his army in order and organized his finances at Whitsun, now stepped up the pressure throwing his support behind the young son of the king of Navarre in his attempt to regain his patrimony. He also assembled troops on the borders of the Low Countries in a show of force on behalf of his client, Robert de la Marck. Charles, in response, placed his army in readiness and called up reinforcements. Brinkmanship was once more the order of the day. Yet the fragile peace was not destroyed. By the beginning of July both sides began to stand down. The great game had once more been played and for Charles at least within the financial constraints imposed during the previous year.

Then, suddenly and unexpectedly, the rivals blundered into war as an impetuous Alençon crossed the Meuse to prevent Nassau's chastisement of the rebellious le Marck clan. At last the long awaited war had come to fruition – in the most unpropitious of circumstances. Yet, in spite of the previous winter's harbinger about the possible financial effects of such an entanglement, a spirit of buoyant optimism pervaded the imperial camp. Even as war broke out it was being confidently asserted that there would be no lack of money. Nor was it idle chatter when members of the Council claimed that an army of 30,000 foot and 10,000 horse would be put in the field by the twenty-fifth of July to join Nassau's troops on the frontier for an invasion of France at the beginning of August. On the nineteenth of July the estates, gathered at Ghent, granted the funds for just such an army, and by the ninth of August Burgundian troops, with a series of successful engagements behind them lay on French soil. For a moment, at least, it seemed as though the war could be constrained within the financial allocations set by the estates. Yet such an impression was illusionary and even as Nassau's troops, reinforced with Francisco's band, pursued the line of the Meuse taking Moisson and laying siege to Masiére the situation was changing. As early as the eighteenth of the month Charles was secretly gathering intelligence for a much greater adventure – the taking of Tournai. Thus even as the full army was engaged before Masiére a change in policy was afoot which would require the deployment of resources far beyond those already committed. At the front, however, during the first week of September such alterations in the basic strategy were not yet apparent. The primary objective seemingly still remained Masiére where 26,000 foot and 8,000–9,000 horse were committed and some 18,000 infantry were held in reserve. But quietly and unobtrusively the build up before Tournai was taking place. Already a thousand horses had

---

9   The cold war of the summer of 1521 and the subsequent financial and military situation during the hostilities of 1521–1523 have been described below largely on the basis of the correspondence listed in note 4 and from the correspondence emanating from the English diplomatic agents in the Low Countries – Sir Robert Wingfield and Thomas Spinelli – and France – Sir William Fitzwilliam – calendared in J. S. BREWER (ed.), Letters and Papers, Foreign and Domestic, of the Reign of Henry VIII. Vol. III, parts 1–2 and IV, part 1, London 1867–70 and henceforth referred to as L&P., III–1 and 2; IV–1, to which the reader is referred for further details.

been withdrawn from Nassau's forces and 4,000 men from Flanders and Hainault diverted to the new objective. The commitment of the estates was clearly being exceeded. Worse, new troops from Germany and artillery were being bought. A simple
count of heads made clear that grandiose stratagems were being formulated. But the
full impact of Charles' grand design only became apparent on the twenty-ninth. On
that day both Moisson and Masiére were abandoned and the expeditionary force was
recalled to Tournai. The Emperor intended to besiege the city, not with the 12,000
troops mooted during the first weeks of the month, but with over 60,000 men. The
war was no longer going to be fought within the financial constraints imposed by the
grants of the estates. Indeed Charles had never intended it to be. Even as the Council
had talked blithely of the adequacy of funds, some three months earlier, the Emperor
had already been laying his own plans for financing his grand design. The task had
certainly not been an easy one. Faced with falling domestic revenues in Spain, due to
the revolt of the *comuneros*, and declining shipments of New World gold, he was
forced to cast about for new sources of funds to pay his troops gathering before Tournai. Not unnaturally therefore he turned to local sources of funding. Antwerp and
other Netherlands towns were persuaded once more to raise money by the sale of annuities. Whilst this yielded, however, almost a quarter of a million livres artois it
stretched municipal finances to their limit, so that when further demands were made
upon this source it was declared that the towns, and particularly Antwerp, were "so
charged that" they "have no more credit."[10] Nor was the situation more promising
amongst the merchant community. Over the summer of 1521 they had been cajoled
into lending an extra 300,000 livres artois, but their reluctance was only too clear. After that dreadful summer even the Fugger, when approached on the Emperor's behalf,
declined to lend. During the course of the Sinxen mart the Emperor had managed to
double the standing debt, which on the eve of the next fair stood at almost a million
livres artois. Yet this had only been achieved at the cost of alienating the merchant
community and driving interest rates up to the exorbitant level of 21.5 per cent. The
lesson of the previous year was now rammed home with a vengeance. There was to be
no new flood of silver to dispel the gloom. War was becoming an expensive pastime
and there were few at Michaelmas 1521 who seemed to share the Emperor's eclectic
taste for the pursuit – particularly as now the grand design began to fall apart.

Even as the *grande armée* withdrew from Masiére in the direction of Tournai it
was beginning to disintegrate. Its victualling train disrupted by de la Marck's harriers,
it was short of food, and disease, reputedly the flux, was rampant in the camp. Worse,
the commanders were at variance. Nassau only reluctantly followed the orders of his
sovereign. Within three weeks little of it remained. On the 21st October it was reliably
reported that two-thirds of the Germans were missing. Only 8,000 remained of whom
many were sick, and but 3,000 remained of the 9,000 cavalry. Moreover, even this
sorry band could not be brought to Tournai for it had to be deployed to repel French
incursions on the frontier. The problems which, for everyone except the Emperor, had
seemed insurmountable at Michaelmas now paled into insignificance. Instead of being
required to maintain an "existing" army of 60,000 men before Tournai, the Emperor
was now requesting the levying of an extra 40,000 troops. The demand was totally

---

10   The towns were "si chargees parcquoy icelles villes n'avoient plus de credit", ADN, Serie B, RGF,
     2309, quoted in VAN DER WEE, Antwerp, II, p. 147, n.28.

unrealistic. He was assailed on all sides with pleas to desist from such folly and conclude a truce. The Regent, writing to her nephew on the 14th of October, perhaps put it most simply when she declared that, "unless the truce is concluded before the imperial forces enter on another month, you will be ruined."[11] In conditions of acute specie shortages, occasioned by the contemporary mining crisis, with the overt hostility of the financial community, and faced with an implacable phalanx of opposition amongst his advisers Charles could do little but retreat and as the Bamus mart opened debts were reduced and interest rates fell.

The Habsburg eagle had thus once again in 1521, as in 1513 and 1517, cast its shadow over the Antwerp money market causing, in the prevailing conditions of illiquidity, an acute *strettezza* to reign therein. Yet for the moment at least whilst interest rates rose sharply the structure of that market was unaffected. The days of cheap money might be past but traditional market relationships remained intact. Within the money market, at least until the Bamus mart of 1521, the complex system of intersectoral rates retained its pre-existing form. During these years, merchants borrowing on the exchange had been confronted with a schedule of interest rates which displayed a marked temporal ordering. At one week or sight (i.e. ten days) money could be obtained at rates which could only be regarded, even by contemporary standards, as astronomic – 1.25 to 3.75 per cent (6–15 per cent per month). Subsequent lengthening of terms, however, brought a pro-rata reduction of rates until at usance or one month they stood at 2–5 per cent and at three, four or five months term bill finance could be obtained at a monthly interest rate (ca. 0.4–1.0 per cent) which placed it at a marked discount on government paper of similar term which paid at a rate of between 1.4/1.6 and 1.6/1.9 per cent per month. In the balmy days before the Bamus mart of 1521 commercial credit was cheap.

The years preceding the crisis of 1521 thus witnessed, within a money market which remained structurally intact, a marked fall in interest rates. Born upon a seemingly never ending flood of silver, merchant-financiers were able to extend the credit base of their operations and offer medium-term government loans at progressively cheaper interest rates which slowly closed on commercial paper rates of similar duration. Only occasionally did government intervention in the market – in 1513, 1517(1518/9) and 1521 – disrupt this trend. On these occasions government borrowing, by increasing interest rates on *finances* and causing a shift of funds from short- to medium-term loans, brought a sympathetic response in the bill market thereby precipitating a general enhancement of rates. Such phenomena were, however, for the moment ephemeral and, in spite of closing intra-market differentials, they in no way disturbed the *relative* cheapness of commercial credit which for the moment characterised the market – though not for long. 1521 saw the first breach in this system and ushered in an era of endemic government interference with the Antwerp money market. For the next five years, 1521–1526, the Habsburg presence dominated the operations of the Bourse, affecting not only the level of interest rates but the whole structure of markets.

11   L&P. III-2, Nr.1679. Margaret of Savoy to Charles V. Bruxelles, 14 October 1521.

CHAPTER TWO

THE ANTWERP MONEY MARKET. THE EXCHANGE CRISES AND
THEIR AFTERMATH, 1521–1526

The autumn of 1521 had been a gloomy one for Charles V. Forced by the financial community, his own Council and his allies to retreat, his own ambition and the exigencies of war impelled him ever on. Yet his sources of finance were clearly inadequate. By late November his situation was desperate. The money he had remaining in hand was only just sufficient to pay the army and if dispensed to this end would leave him with nothing to meet the 200,000 florins a month required to finance the frontier garrisons. Worse, that venal condottiere Franz von Sickingen, who was owed 75,000 florins for his services during the previous campaign, was already making overtures to the French king and threatened to make war on the empire unless he was paid. Yet there seemed no way out of the impasse. Both the *aides* and *les deniers de domaine* were already anticipated for two years to come, and creditors daily demanded money of the cities of Malines and Antwerp, threatening to arrest the merchants if they were not paid. The key to the whole system of imperial war finance was imperilled. Without these sources of revenue not only were current sources of funding curtailed but the very basis of the credit system was threatened. Accordingly, the towns, whose annuities were secured on the *aides*, had to be placated and over the winter of 1521 debts to them were gradually liquidated. To achieve this objective, however, the Emperor was forced to borrow from the merchant community who had forgotten nothing and as attempts were made to compensate for the decline in municipal loans by increased borrowing from amongst their ranks interest rates again shot up to crisis levels. The Emperor was simply juggling his sources of funding, substituting expensive debts for cheap ones, but in no way resolving the basic problem of finance. The situation, indeed, had become so dramatic that even a massive sale of domains, towns and counties in the kingdom of Naples was, for a moment, envisaged. Then suddenly, relief came from a somewhat unexpected quarter. Having been approached for a loan, Spanish merchants, after many difficulties, agreed to conclude an *asiento* for a hundred thousand livres artois – but only on the condition that the money be taken up on the exchange for payment in Spain.

A new source of funds had been discovered and the sanctity of the bill market had been violated. With the intervention of the Habsburgs on the exchange at the Cold Mart of 1521 a new chapter in the history of imperial finance had begun and the market had been thrown into turmoil. At the opening of the fair interest rates rocketed up and commercial paper, far from running at a discount, could only be floated at an excess rate in relation to government issues. The plundering had begun. The imperial authorities, unable to obtain money elsewhere, now pursued a hand to mouth existence taking up money by exchange at colossal rates of interest. Trimestrial commercial paper, which only three months earlier during the Bamus Mart of 1521 commanded interest at the modest rate of one per cent a month, now at the following Cold Mart of 1521/2, where it could be obtained, was available at 12.6 per cent (four per cent per month) and the market was shortening. In a state of acute uncertainty and with rumours circulating of further intervention, the merchants, fearing the worst, panicked. Mid-term, accordingly, found no one who would lend for three months, few for six weeks. The median loan period settled at ten days to two weeks at the enhanced rate of 9.5–10.2 per cent (21–31 per cent a month), until the Emperor's intentions became clear. They did not have to wait long.

In fact during the months of October and November 1521 Charles had been carrying through a carefully controlled gamble with a sense of purpose which was frightening. With the expensively won money he steadily built up his forces before Tournai. Already by the second of November twenty thousand troops were said to have been sent thence and by the twentieth he had 34,000 foot and 500 horse there and on the frontier. The build-up was relentless and seemingly nothing could deflect him from his objective – not even the wholesale destruction of the surrounding provinces for, freed from interference, the French king wrought havoc in Artois and Picardie. Commencing at the end of the third week in October in the region about Valencienne his troops systematically set about burning the standing crops in the granary of the Netherlands, "so that next year they (the Burgundians) would cry for mercy."[1] The devastation was frightful and by the end of November the prospect for the coming year looked bleak indeed, but Charles was single-minded and by this time he had his forces in place. Accordingly, on the thirtieth his reinforced artillery was brought to bear on the walls of the city and next day Tournai surrendered to the Emperor.

Charles had gambled and won, for nothing succeeds like success. With the news of victory his financial situation was transformed. The estates who only two months before had been so resistant to imperial demands and who had witnessed in horror the burning of their grain supplies now fell over themselves in their eagerness to serve their Sovereign. By the 9th of December the members of Flanders had sent a delegation to the Emperor at Oudenarde to congratulate him and to make "large offers for the continuance of the war," offers, moreover, which they turned into grants at the general meeting of the estates convened at Ghent a week later.[2] Nor was Flanders alone in this patriotic fervour. Both Brabant and Holland granted monies at a subsequent meeting held at Brussels in January 1522 whilst Zealand undertook to provision the fleet then being prepared in its harbours. The crisis, which had seemed irresolvable the previous Michaelmas, was over and the linchpin of the imperial financial system was once more firmly in place. On the basis of the *aides* granted over the winter of 1521/2 Charles could now negotiate with his creditors from a position of strength and the New Year, accordingly, witnessed a complete restructuring of his credit position. Secure in the knowledge of obtaining repayment out of the new grants, the financiers

---

1   L&P. II–2, Nr. 1727 (British Library, London Caligula D.VIII fol. 163). Worcester, West and
     Fitzwilliam to Wolsey. Sandemoone, 1 November 1521.

2   L&P. III–2, Nr. 1848 (British Library, London Galba B.VII fol. 167). Sir Robert Wingfield and
     Thomas Spinelli to Wolsey. Oudenarde, 9 December 1521.

were once more prepared to underwrite imperial loans on reasonable terms. As me-
dium- term rates thus fell, from 20.75 per cent prevailing during the Cold Mart of
1521/2 to some 19 per cent six months later, the volume of such loans doubled, pushing medium-term indebtedness beyond the million-mark. The increase in the volume
of outstanding loans was, however, illusory for, with military action confined to frontier forays, the Emperor was able to utilize the funds so obtained to pay off the short-
term debts incurred during the eventful Cold Mart of the previous year. Indeed, even
before the close of that winter fair merchants were beginning to feel the benefits of the
new situation. They, accordingly, once again began to lend on longer terms. The median loan period, which had shortened to seven to ten days at the height of the crisis,
extended to three weeks at the close of the Cold Mart, a month at Easter and two
months at Whitsun 1522. The rate at which they would lend, moreover, began to fall
from 10.75 to 9.5 and finally to 9 per cent usance (even 8 per cent to first class borrowers such as the Greshams) over the same period. By the summer of 1522 it seemed
as though the exchange was returning to normality with two-month paper costing 8
per cent (3.9 per cent per month). As the Emperor prepared for his departure to Spain
that summer, therefore, it was beginning to appear as though the imperial intervention
on the exchange during the Cold Mart of 1521/2 was but a passing interlude. Bill
rates, although still at an excess on those for medium-term loans, were rapidly falling
towards pre-intervention levels whilst the game of war-finance was once again being
played by the old rules within a structure restored to its traditional basis.

Charles' legacy to the Regent that summer was not, however, a straight-forward
one, for whilst he might thus have re-established orthodox war finance during the
spring of 1522, passing on to his successor a large volume of *finances* and *rentes* contracted on the security of the *aides* granted after the glorious victory of Tournai, during the previous winter he had also sown the seeds for its destruction. With his single-
mindedness and determination to take Tournai and his refusal to deploy his troops to
any other end during October and November 1521 he had given Francis, as has been
shown, a free hand to wreak devastation through the granary of the Netherlands so
that by the end of November the prospect for the coming year looked bleak. Before
the next month was out it looked nothing short of disastrous as the Baltic grain fleet,
which could have provided succour for the maritime cities, failed to arrive in the
Scheldt due to the financial disorders occasioned by Charles' intervention on the exchange which made payment for the Easterlings' wares uncertain. Without any doubt
1522 was going to be a difficult year and even as he departed from his Netherlands
possessions during that summer the results of his earlier actions were becoming clear.
Amidst general conditions of acute shortages, in Louvain, Malines and Vilvoorde,
women plundered the granaries of convents whilst burgesses and merchants created
such unrest that the government was obliged to send five hundred troops to prevent
the situation deteriorating. In Ghent the tension was so great that, in order to head off
trouble, the city council purchased grain to sell there at subsidized prices to the poor.
At Antwerp the grain market was attacked and farmers were robbed of the produce
they brought for sale. Charles had sown the wind. Margaret now reaped the whirl-
wind.

Her problems, moreover, were now compounded by the activities of the French
king. True to his word, in this environment of disorder in the Low Countries, Francis,
anticipating that the Burgundians "would cry for mercy" began in May 1522 to muster

troops in Picardie for a major offensive, sending out at the beginning of that month the first parties to raid in the vicinity of Gravelines. Thereafter, the military build-up continued apace and incidents began to proliferate. In June, with 20,000 troops in the field, skirmishes began before Tourneham. In July, with Swiss troops diverted from the Italian campaign rapidly moving up to reinforce the main army, the French burnt Montreuil and encamping between Arde and Guisne they threatened the English Pale. In such circumstances Margaret could not but respond – and in strength. Accordingly, an army of 60,000 troops were put in readiness and by the third week of August 10,000–12,000 were ready to resort to the frontier. Within the context of the financial system bequeathed her by Charles her costs were rising. Yet not all of this increased expenditure was attributable to the enemy who did not warrant this show of strength. Rather it was due to the re-emergence of that dualism of interest which had characterised the previous year's campaign. For Margaret and her Council the primary objective had to be the defence of the frontiers and the engagement of the French which meant, in the view of the military, a direct thrust towards Amiens where the French camp lay. Yet they were constrained by the agreement between the Emperor and his English allies which, as in the previous year, aimed at territorial acquisition – this time the taking of Boulogne. The Regent thus had to prepare for two wars, each with its own protagonists in her Council, each demanding totally different supply requirements. For Isselstein and the "Emperor's party" the principal need was for artillery and a not inconsiderable army of 18,000–20,000 infantry to join Surrey's expeditionary force. For the "young bloods" of the "Burgundian party" the path to glory required the provision of a force, containing a large element of cavalry, to match the French. The costs and logistical supply problems were enormous and involved a commitment of resources similar to that which had almost bankrupted Charles the year before. The outcome was inevitable. Even as the imperial army encamped at Arde in the first week of September 1522 shortages of funds were wreaking dissension in its ranks. Twice in that week the Spanish troops mutinied for lack of pay. The existing burdens just could not be supported.

Thus began an extremely trying week for the Regent when problems, previously avoided, had to be faced. If two separate strategies could not be maintained which was to be given precedence? The answer was soon clear. In the absence of Isselstein, whose illness prevented his attendance at the critical strategy meetings of the 3rd–6th September, the "Emperor's party" represented by Hesdin and Westnore was cast aside and the "Burgundians" – de Beures, Reux, de Croy and de Gaure – were given a free hand to persuade Surrey to abandon the proposed siege of Boulogne and to adopt their strategy of a strike towards Amiens. Burgundian interests were clearly, in the field of military strategy, going to be put before those of the Emperor. Yet even this pruning of military expenditures did not greatly assist the Regent in her financial dilemma and the week about to begin witnessed Margaret engaged in a desperate battle to ensure financial solvency. The estates would grant no money and the bankers, seeing existing revenues already heavily encumbered, declined to lend. Her position was, accordingly, desperate and it is thus hardly surprising that on the 6th September one observer noted that she seemed greatly perplexed. New things were springing up every day. Franz von Sickingen, who had been bought off the previous winter with a promise of payment of his arrears in two instalments, was back claiming some 50,000 florins and, with 7,000–8,000 men at his back, declared that if he was not paid he would wage war in Luxembourg. The Archbishop of Mainz and the Count Palatinate were once again demanding their pensions granted in 1519. On the 9th September the bailiff of Brabant arrived requesting money for the army and especially funds to ensure the quietude of the Spanish and German troops. At last on the 11th September the crisis broke. In the council meeting held that day, with the "Emperor's party" heavily represented, the veneer of normality was still preserved: the members were regaled with a letter from Charles' confessor on the happy state of Spain since the Emperor's return. In private, however, she was forced to admit to the English ambassador the reality of her predicament and the difficulties she was having, within the framework of the imperial system, in providing money for the army. Simply the Treasury was empty and the hope of pursuing "Burgundian" military objectives was forlorn. In desperation she assured him that

> she was fain to lay out two thousand florins of her own, intended for her servants [...] and would pledge her jewels, if only she knew to whom[3],

but this was little more than a childish gesture, and not surprisingly over the next fortnight the military campaign simply fizzled out, serving little military purpose, bringing misery to hundreds of innocent peasants as the unpaid troops rampaged through the Boulonnais, and consuming large amounts of money. Margaret would now have to account. Having inherited a seemingly sound financial system she had failed to sustain her "Burgundian" policies and had wrecked the Emperor's grand design.

In these circumstances, remembering the lessons of the previous year, she gambled. Instead of retreating she stood her ground, reasserted the correctness of her policies and staked all on the taking of Therouenne by Christmas. Isselstein, though retaining the nominal office of captain-general, was set to one side and a small force under the command of de Gaure was despatched at the end of November to accomplish the task. The necessary money, as during the previous year, was obtained on the exchange which once again during the Bamus Mart of 1522 felt the full impact of Habsburg borrowing. The market accordingly shortened to one month and interest rates at usance rose first to 10.9 and then 11.4 per cent. Those merchants visiting the exchange during these troublesome months must have experienced a feeling of deja vu. By the end of November it looked as though the game was going to be played out in exactly the same way as in the previous year – a short and effective campaign, a glorious victory and, to the sound of bells, a meeting of the estates which would sweep away all the financial problems – but it was not to be.

In the first place Margaret had neither the military acumen nor that judgement of commanders possessed by her nephew. De Gaure was no Isselstein. The campaign started off well enough but ultimately came to nothing. During the first week of the enterprise the prospects seemed promising. On the 30th November a troop of Burgundian horse, in advance of the main army, encountered foragers before the walls of Therouenne, slew several and took eight or nine prisoners. Subsequently over the week-end Spanish troops were quartered on neighbouring villages, thereby tightening the Burgundian grip on the town. On the following Thursday a further party of Span-

---

3   L&P. III–2, Nr. 2534 (British Library, London Galba B.VII fol.319). Sir Robert Wingfield to Wolsey, Antwerp, 11 September 1522.

iards were sent to intercept a victualling train of three hundred carts gathered at Hesdin to provision the city before the siege became complete. A quick victory seemed in
sight and the ebullient Fiennes, Count de Gaure, was reported as being in good hope
of intercepting supplies and compelling the surrender of the town. Even the hostile
Hesdin, in the optimistic atmosphere prevailing during that week, grudgingly admitted
that

> Therouenne is in great need of victuals and other things, and if the horse and foot on the fron-
> tier are careful to prevent its coming, some good will come of it [...].[4]

Yet more than five weeks later, on 15th January 1523, the situation was unchanged.
The main army, of a thousand horse and eight hundred foot, with its commander still
lay at Ayre, though many now considered "its cost forlorn".[5] The Spanish contingents,
at the end of their contracts, still remained grouped about Therouenne. The French
garrison, numbering two hundred lances and two thousand foot, still held the town and
daily awaited the lifting of the siege. The enterprise had run out of steam and, after a
number of brief skirmishes, on the 5th February Fiennes finally withdrew his forces to
engage in a general frontier war which had been going on since the beginning of the
year. Having planned on a quick thrust for glory, the Regent now found herself embroiled in a series of protracted melees, which engendered a steadily rising financial
commitment on her part.

Nor in these circumstances were the estates, unimpressed by her martial prowess,
predisposed to afford her the assistance they had granted Charles a year before. At the
general meeting called at Malines, during the week beginning the 11th January 1523,
they were said to be disposed to grant money if only "so the poor tylmen" may be
"saved uneaten."[6] Promises were one thing, however, reality quite another. The story
of the diet was one of continual delay and procrastination. Initially Brussels stood
aloof. When it agreed with the rest, moreover, the meeting was put off until the 15th
February with a special preliminary policy meeting on the sixth before the general
assembly. The spectre of the "Emperor's party" raising difficulties at that meeting,
however, once more caused delays and it was not until the 24th February that the general assembly was finally called – only to reconvene itself on the 16th March. Margaret was now intent on bringing the matter to a conclusion and in the fortnight before
the revocation all the major members of the "Burgundian party" were sent to bring the
estates to hand. On the 4th March Hoogstraten was said to have "those of Holland in
good train"[7], whilst Fiennes was scurrying to Flanders and Berghes to Antwerp to
effect the same result. Yet once again the redoubtable Fiennes bungled the matter and
on the 23rd the estates of Flanders had not yet come to the meeting, at which Margaret
was said to be no little bit surprised. Nor was the matter to be resolved rapidly: whilst
the other estates twiddled their thumbs at Malines for another week, Fiennes cajoled

---

4   L&P. III–2, Nr. 2698. De Hesdin to Wolsey. Antwerp, 3 December 1522.

5   L&P. III–2, Nr. 2776 (British Library, London Galba B.VII fol.214). Sir Robert Wingfield to Wol-
       sey. Malines, 15 January 1523.

6   Ibid.

7   L&P. III–2, Nr. 2869 (British Library, London Galba B.VII fol. 251). Sir Robert Wingfield to
       Wolsey. Malines, 4 March 1523.

and pleaded with the recalcitrant Flemings, promising with his usual unwarranted optimism that they would be at the *Kaiserhof* by the thirtieth. Yet even when this was achieved the delegates from Brabant raised even more obstacles and it was only after a hard day's bargaining on the thirtieth that the grant, first promised three months earlier, was finally made. By this point, however, it was almost irrelevant for the bankers would no longer accept such *aides* as collateral for medium-term loans and had, anyway, since the previous September, been pulling out of the market for *finances* exchanging, as they fell due, their medium-term loans for short-term ones.

Lacking either current funding or access to medium-term credit, Margaret, accordingly, had been forced into an ever-increasing indebtedness to the denizens of the exchange in order to meet rapidly rising military expenditures during December 1522-February 1523. Having shown, at the end of the previous October, considerable concern over her involvement in such transactions and having intended, at the beginning of December, to undertake a brief commitment to such borrowing, thereafter she found it her sole source of financial support and during the Cold Mart of 1522/3 the bill market was revolutionized. Interest rates at usance, which during the previous fair had reached 11.4 per cent, now rose to 12.0, but few would lend at that term. The median loan period was shortening. Money could only be obtained at half usance (at 10.0–10.9 per cent or 21–23 per cent a month) or sight (at 8.4–10.0 per cent or 27–33 per cent a month). The autumn and winter of 1522/3 thus did not simply witness a rerun of the events of a year before. In fact a fundamental change had been wrought in the fabric of imperial finances which made borrowing on the exchanges an integral rather than a peripheral part of that structure.

For Margaret the situation was disastrous but when called to account for her actions, with an obdurateness characteristic of those who do not wish to see, she explained her predicament in a manner which was both simple and disarmingly direct: her explanations, like her policies, focused essentially on short-term phenomena. She was, as she recounted to her nephew, simply the victim of circumstances outside her control. After all, government revenues could no longer be relied upon to serve as adequate security for loans as in 1522 they were in a state of total disarray – due to the disastrous famine of 1521/2. In other words, although she was too tactful to point it out, the fault was not hers but Charles'. With his single-mindedness and determination to take Tournai in the autumn of 1521 he had left the field free for the French to burn the crops. Worse, his manipulations of the exchange during the winter of 1521/2 had deflected the grain fleet from the Scheldt and, accordingly, had precipitated the acute shortages of 1522. The resultant disorder and incursions of the French, to take advantage of the situation, had increased expenditures, whilst revenues had fallen as the dreadful famine wrought havoc in the Netherlands economy. The resultant industrial and commercial malaise had fundamentally undermined toll receipts. As the Emperor willingly acknowledged, in relation to his aunt's defence, "it is clear and evident that during the war the said tolls of Brabant and Zealand are worth little." Nor could he refute the fact that rural and urban impoverishment, arising from that famine, had caused important delays in the payment of the *aides* which had been granted by the estates. At the door of the famine must be laid the blame for the shortage of funds and credit which made her resort to the exchange. With that careful combination of deference and authority, learnt during her long guardianship over her sovereign, the wily Margaret thus successfully implanted in the Emperor's mind the importance of the famine of 1520/1 in the shaping of events. Such an explanation, moreover, had many advantages. Responsibility for the famine could certainly not be placed at her door, and perhaps was better not sought.

The reality of the situation, however, was otherwise. The crisis, far from residing in the short-term impoverishment of the Netherlands economy, rested on a collapse of confidence amongst the financial community – and Margaret knew it. Indeed, in a moment of great distress, she admitted as much when she indiscreetly confided to the English ambassador that

> although there apears to be PLENTY OF MONEY IN THESE PARTS which the owners would employ because money is so dear, no-one will take here the treasurers for sureties [...].[8]

Poverty was certainly not the primary cause of her troubles in 1522 – rather that resided in the fact that no-one any longer regarded the *aides* as suitable collateral. However much money was collected, the creditors had ceased to believe that they would be paid.

Even before Charles departed from the Netherlands in the summer of 1522, the root causes of the problems to come were already apparent. At the general meeting of the estates, held at Ghent in December 1521 in the aftermath of the glorious victory, they had appeared only too clearly. The members of Flanders, whilst only too willing to make substantial grants to their sovereign, respectfully requested that "the money be paid to the troops by men appointed by themselves and not to the *financiers*, lest it be converted to other objects."[9] The result of this request was an immediate uproar, arising from those who administered the revenues, who declared that "the Emperor by doing so would deprive himself of his power and give it to his subjects." The *financiers*, in the desire to protect their "rights" to plunder imperial revenues, were more concerned to safeguard the Emperor's prerogatives than he himself was. For the moment, however, their limitless greed could be restrained and kept under control. In response to his subjects' pleas Charles simply declared that he "would regard the members' contentment and thus without resolution remain this reasonable request."[10] With one simple act of royal will he cut through the encrusted layers of Burgundian bureaucracy and retrieved the funds from the venal officials' hands. Now he set about ensuring that they would never return there, carrying through with a firm resolve and intense energy a complete reorganization of the fiscal administration. In order to keep his Low Countries' subjects from "oppression, and also to recover the lands, seignories and profits taken and detained from the Emperor by diverse persons having the administration of the revenues of his sacred Majesty imperial [...] and his predecessor," he swept away the officers of finance and shut down, in Flanders, Brabant and Holland, the Chambers of Account.[11] In their place he appointed new officials

---

8   L&P. III–2, Nr. 2515 (B.L., London Galba B.VII fol.314). Sir Robert Wingfield to Wolsey. Antwerp, 6 September 1522.

9   L&P. III–2, Nr. 2776 (B.L., London Galba B.VII fol.214). Sir Robert Wingfield to Wolsey. Malines, 15 January 1523.

10 L&P. III–2, Nr. 2215 (B.L., London Galba B.VII fol.306). Thomas Spinelli to Wolsey.

11 Ibid.

(Receivers) responsible to the Council through a single Receiver-General whose accounts were to be audited annually at Lille. Thus it was felt, "the moneys with which the financiers enrich themselves will come to the Emperor."[12] Whilst Charles remained, therefore, a new order seemed to have dawned, and confident in obtaining monies secured on the revenues, the merchant community was only too willing to lend.

With his departure for Spain, however, the carefully laid plans became so much chaff on the wind. The ingrained venality amongst those who administered the system ensured that, in the absence of a strong hand, the old ways would once more reassert themselves within the portals of the new edifice. Henceforth, under the ineffectual tutelage of the Regent, men like the Receiver of Flanders behaved exactly as had their predecessors, running rough shod over the privileges of the estates and leaving men to wonder what had happened to the monies raised on the Emperor's behalf. In such circumstances, accordingly, it is hardly surprising that the confidence, created by the charismatic Charles during the early months of 1522, melted away like the morning mist before the summer sun, and that the financial communities, intent on protecting themselves, adopted new strategies. Against a general background of disillusionment, the crisis came in that eventful second week in September 1522 when Margaret once again approached the estates for money. Their responses revealed all. The members remained firm in their willingness to help the Emperor, and evinced a sadness at seeing his affairs behindhand for lack of money but would not provide the required cash for, with the bureaucracy unchained, they could not be contented "but always find matters to the financiers," speaking "much of their sumptuous buildings and large purchases."[13] Nor were the bankers any happier and Margaret could find no-one who will take here the treasurers as sureties. Yet presented with this clear and unequivocal expression of grievances, Margaret, with that obdurateness which has already been noted, refused to acknowledge what she did not want to see. Her subjects were merely unreasonable, seeing "that they had been plainly shown that the Emperor had only had from these countries, since he came from Spain, 8,000 or 9,000 florins and his charges had mounted to 2,000,000."[14] Even the English ambassador, however, regarded this as merely "a well framed excuse for the *financiers*." Yet there was no better explanation on offer. All the "Burgundian" members of the Council were in accord on the matter, agreeing on the soundness of the existing financial system and on the unreasonableness of the estates. Indeed on the 9th September, only three days after the revolt of the estates, Hoogstraten went so far as to declare that "the finances could not be administered in a surer way than in these countries."[15] Not even the collapse of the whole financial edifice on the eleventh could shake this belief in the fundamental soundness of the system. To de Berghes and the treasurers the problems, which erupted on that day, were simply logistical ones and, on their advice, Margaret asserted that whilst, for the moment, money was not available "she had no doubt" that, given time, "a sufficient

---

12 Ibid.

13 L&P. III–2, Nr. 2515 (British Library, London Galba B.VII fol.314). Sir Robert Wingfield. Antwerp, 6 September 1522.

14 Ibid.

15 L&P. III–2, Nr. 2527 (British Library, London Galba B.VII fol.317). Sir Robert Wingfield to Wolsey. Antwerp, 9 September 1522.

sum might be procured."[16] Margaret and the "Burgundian" cabal, who dominated the Council thus continued to cling to the illusion of normality, blaming their misfortunes on extraneous factors such as the famine or the unreasonableness of the populace.

Others, however, thought differently. For the bankers and the estates a new awareness of the realities of their situation emerged out of the traumatic week in September 1522. The estates, rebuffed on that occasion, were no longer willing to grant money simply to fill the receivers' pockets and, as has been shown, when recalled in January 1523 they simply procrastinated, creating innumerable subterfuges in order not to make a grant. The bankers, similarly lacking any belief that they would be able to obtain repayment of *finances* secured on the *aides* due to the prevailing conditions of endemic bureaucratic venality, were no longer prepared to regard the grants as suitable collateral for loans and from September 1522 withdrew from the medium-term money market. Nor was this a capricious whim on their part, a passing mood conditioned by ephemeral circumstances as Margaret hopefully suggested to her nephew. The endemic problem of bureaucratic venality under her administration ensured that the withdrawal of the great merchant-finance houses, begun that autumn, would remain a permanent feature of operations on the Antwerp money market for many years to come. Relentlessly over the winter of 1522/3 and through 1523 and 1524 they refused to renew *finances* as they fell due for repayment. Outstanding debts owing them by the Habsburgs were thus reduced; they fell from in excess of 700,000 livres artois to a mere 100,000 in the autumn of 1524. Balances in the hands of the bankers increased, and, reflecting these changes, interest rates fell. At first, in the tight money conditions occasioned by the contemporary mining crisis, the decline was slight, but, as news broke on the exchange at Whitsun of mining recovery, the decline was rapid until at the Bamus Mart of 1524 they reached their lowest point yet in the sixteenth century – twelve per cent per annum on medium term paper. Nor was the situation significantly altered during the next eighteen months (Bamus Mart 1524–Easter 1526) when the bankers, attempting to hedge against inflationary pressures occasioned by bimetallic disorders, first stabilized and then enhanced rates. Resolutely they continued their withdrawal until by the summer of 1526 merchant debts had been all but eliminated – only some 4,300 livres artois' worth of paper remaining due – and outstanding Habsburg medium-term debts, amounting to ca. 400,000 livres artois, comprised predominantly *rentes* at 6.5 per cent. Between 1522–1527, by their withdrawal from government financing, the bankers had thus once more built up their cash reserves and, in the context of renewed growth in Central European silver production during 1523–1524 and 1526–1527, had once more established interest rates on that path of long-term decline which could be traced back a quarter of a century and more.

They had also totally transformed the environment for imperial war finance and henceforth, from September 1522, the medium-term rate no longer reflected the primary cost of government borrowing, as the Habsburgs at first became temporally dependent on short-term borrowing and then, with merchant withdrawal from medium-term money markets at the Cold Mart of 1522/3, absolutely dependent. Short-term financing which in the latter days of Charles' personal rule and in the first months of Margaret's regime had only been a temporary expedient now, from September 1522,

---

16   L&P. III–2, Nr. 2534 (British Library, London Galba B.VII fol.319). Sir Robert Wingfield to Wolsey. Antwerp, 11 September 1522.

became the cornerstone of imperial war finance. Old *finances* as they fell due where replaced by short-term bill finance. New loans were contracted in the same way. As the medium-term debt was reduced after September 1522 the short-term one grew. Whatever her illusions, Margaret was being inexorably drawn into a new structure of indebtedness dominated by short-term holdings at high interest rates. The result was disastrous. By Easter 1523, with interest rates on new borrowing at in excess of thirty per cent per month, comparable with the crisis rates of the Cold Mart of 1521/2, the whole edifice of imperial finance seemed ready for collapse.

In spite of Margaret's unwillingness to perceive the realities of her situation, from September 1522, she had been forced into a new market situation. The estates were no longer prepared to accede to making grants which would end up in the pockets of the receivers. Even if they could be cajoled into making such a grant, moreover, the bankers were no longer prepared to make loans on the basis of such security and, accordingly, short-term bill finance, which Margaret continued to perceive, as Charles had in the winter of 1521/2, as a temporary expedient, now had become her sole source of financial support and an integral part of imperial war finance requiring its own careful management. Yet as long as she perceived it as a temporary expedient this was not possible. Accordingly, over the winter and spring of 1522/3, short-term indebtedness rapidly increased both as a result of new borrowing, to support de Gaure's abortive venture, and to pay off the bankers as they withdrew from the market, and, interest rates rocketed up, attaining such disastrous levels that Charles was once more forced to assume the centre of the stage.

Under Charles' influence, at the Easter Fair of 1523, one may perceive a subtle change of direction, as the participants in the drama groped towards a new realism. In part at this time old political forms were again revived and old economic strategies replayed as, to restore financial orthodoxy, Charles attempted to relocate the linchpin of the traditional system – the *aides* – by re-establishing confidence in the administration. To this end Charles, far away in Spain, had to be seen to be in charge and, accordingly, the "Emperor's party" in the Council, comprising Florys d'Egmont, Buren and Hesdin, had to be restored to power. This group, who had spent the previous September organizing a smear campaign against their opponents, and much of January arranging a counter-coup to wreck the policy meeting arranged for the 6th of February, was suddenly, under imperial pressure, restored to the fold. On the 4th of March it was rumoured to the surprise of many, that de Buren would be at the meeting of the estates then planned for the sixteenth and dutifully, when the meeting was actually held on the thirtieth, he was there. Almost miraculously at that meeting the previously intensely hostile factions combined and, by show of unity said to be "lately repaired amongst the great men," the day was carried.[17] Imperial authority had been restored and Easter saw members of the unholy alliance at work putting matters in form. As during the winter of 1521/2 the Emperor had his money but in the transformed situation of 1523 he had little else. Due to the prevailing crisis of confidence in financial circles and the withdrawal of the bankers it would have to be spent as the estates dic-

---

17   L&P. III–2, Nr. 2919 (British Library, London Galba B.VIII fol.24). Sir Robert Wingfield to Wolsey. Malines, 31 March 1523.

tated, blocking any attempt at a conversion operation such as had saved the day during the winter and spring of 1521/2.

Superficially the Emperor had attempted a re-run of the policies which had proven successful during the winter of 1521/2 and had failed, being forced by the combined might of the estates and bankers to adopt a narrowly constrained policy with regard to the disbursement of the funds granted him which precluded their use for the repayment of his short-term debts. Yet such an interpretation of events would be very far from the truth for, long before the meeting on the 30th of March, he had accepted responsibility for an independent management of short-term debts. Indeed, even as he engineered the restoration of the imperial faction to the Council, he had despatched a hundred thousand ducats' worth of bills of exchange to the fair at Antwerp, reserving a further million and a half for the use of his agents should they require them. Easter 1523 had in fact seen, under Charles' influence, the institution of an entirely new policy and had witnessed the emperor accept responsibility for the independent management of debts in BOTH medium- and short-term markets, now pursuing a consistent policy with regards to his dealing on the exchange. The implementation of this new policy was not, however, without its difficulties. Initially, as the first funds were disbursed amongst the dealers, rates merely stabilized at the levels of three months earlier, but at least terms lengthened and money could be obtained at usance even if at the advanced rate of 12 per cent. In the tight money conditions prevailing at the Easter Mart of 1523 the first steps towards normality had been made. As soon as the reserves were deployed and the first news of mining recovery in Central Europe broke on the exchange, the situation was transformed. Interest rates began to tumble. At usance even before the close of the Easter Mart they had fallen to 9 per cent and thereafter the decline was relentless: 8 per cent at Michaelmas and 7.6 per cent at Christmas. Even more significantly, by the autumn fair the merchants were prepared to tender five-month bills at a mere 10.6 per cent (or 2 per cent per month).

By the institution of new policies at the Easter Mart of 1523 the Emperor had brought the crisis, which had attained disastrous proportions during the winter and spring of 1522/3, to an end. He had also implicitly recognized the place now occupied by the imperial authorities in both medium- and short-term money markets and had acknowledged the necessity for a careful management of resources within these markets. As a result, by a careful management of operations on the exchange, the Habsburgs now participated in the fall in bill rates through 1523–1524. Yet still they had to pay an excess on such paper in relation to the rates on medium-term loans of similar duration. The Habsburgs, from Easter 1523, might have learnt to master the intricacies of operations on the exchange but since the winter of 1521/2 that market had been transformed. Commercial paper which until that date had run at a discounted rate in relation to government medium-term script of comparable duration, thereafter, due to the Habsburg's "crowding out" of other takers, consistently paid an excess, setting a pattern which would plague denizens of the exchange for years to come.

In the aftermath of the crises, during the years from 1523 to 1526, dealers on both medium and short-term markets operated in a completely new environment. The withdrawal of big firms from the finance market, which had begun over the winter of 1522/3 remained a permanent feature of operations on the Bourse until the autumn of 1524 when the level of outstanding merchant loans amounted to no more than 100,000 livres artois and medium-term interest rates reached their lowest point yet during the sixteenth century – twelve per cent. Nor did the situation significantly alter during the next eighteen months when financiers, attempting to hedge inflationary pressures, first stabilized and then increased rates. Redemption operations continued in spite of the changed circumstances, as *rentes* were contracted to replace those *finances* which fell due. By the summer of 1526, accordingly, merchant debts had all but been eliminated – only some 4,300 livres artois' worth of paper remaining due – and outstanding Habsburg medium-term debts, amounting to 400,000 livres artois, comprised pre-dominantly *rentes* at $6^{1/2}$ per cent. 1526 thus seemingly witnessed the culmination of a trend established a quarter of a century and more before. Rising silver production, interrupted only 1509–12, 1514–5, 1519–23 and 1525, had afforded merchants, during the years to 1526, the opportunity to provide loans at a steadily falling rate of interest. With an increasing efficiency they managed to underwrite an ever growing Habsburg demand for medium-term (*finances* and *rentes*) loans on progressively cheaper terms. Only occasionally, in 1513, 1517 and 1521–3, were they found wanting, when the excessive demands of the Emperor cast an, as yet fleeting, shadow over the market. In 1526, however, such inroads into the market for medium-term finance were things of the past. Medium-term government debts, amounting to about 400,000 livres artois, bore interest charges of 26,000 livres artois or $6^{1/2}$ per cent, where only six years earlier a similar volume of indebtedness had born interest at 10 per cent. That curious euphoria born upon a flood of silver, which had characterised the medium-term money market during the late-1510s, had seemingly returned.

Not all borrowers, however, were so lucky. For those seeking commercial finance on the exchange the situation was very different. Until 1521 they too had shared in the benefits derived from falling interest rates, obtaining loans in that year at rates as low as one per cent per month, but the events of the Cold mart 1521/2 put an end to all that and ushered in a new age of dear money on the Antwerp exchanges. Henceforth Habsburg intervention on the exchange remained an endemic feature of imperial finance and the structure of interest rates, first imprinted on the market during that traumatic winter fair, remained intact. Thus although commercial paper shared in the fall in interest rates between 1523 and 1526, at the latter date the bill rate still stood some five points higher than at the beginning of the decade and takers were forced to pay a premium on the rate for government paper of similar term. Long after others had forgotten the traumatic events of 1521 and 1522–3, participants in the mercantile credit market retained an awareness of the baleful effects of Habsburg interventionism which resulted in a marked upward equilibration in rates as a result of the continuing Habsburg presence on the Exchange, "crowding out" private borrowers.

Even if those seeking commercial credits thus continued, some five years after the first Habsburg intervention onto the Antwerp bill market, to possess an appreciation of the baleful effects of such government behaviour, however, such knowledge must not have impinged greatly on their consciousness for, throughout most of the period from 1523–1526 as rates on both short- and medium-term loans fell in a restructured An-glo-Netherlands money market, they were called upon to deal with far greater problems as that institution experienced the full impact of an acute monetary crisis. From ca. 1524–early 1527 as gold prices rocketed ever upwards a trade in specie began to rival their trade in goods and the merchant wishing to borrow money on the exchange to finance his commodity trade had to compete with that man so hated by Renaissance princes, the exporter of bullion, who he had to outbid for the money he required. At this time on the London and Antwerp exchanges, there existed a system of bi-metallic premiums: surcharges which the merchant had to pay above the prevailing falling bill rate in order to induce his financier not to export bullion.

CHAPTER THREE

BI-METALLIC DISEQUILIBRIUM AND MONETARY DISORDER, 1525–1527

Moneys and gold are now at a higher price than at which they were valued (3 August 1515)

There was published at Mons an ordinance[1] revaluing the gold pieces, which have been enhanced by too great an amount [...] but the said ordinance was ineffectual and afterwards everything was dearer than before (15 December 1525)

Because of the great disorder to which the merchants and other persons have been subjected and which daily grows due to the enhancement, day by day, of the moneys [...] the Emperor and his Council, seeing this disorder, were advised[2] to place an order and price upon each piece [...] (1 January 1527)[3]

In such a manner did Antoine de Lucy, burgess of Mons, express his growing concern about a phenomenon which, since the second decade of the sixteenth century, had become a permanent feature of everyday life – the enhancement of gold – for if the fifteenth century may be described as the age of the silver crisis, the sixteenth seems to justify the label of the century of the gold crisis.[4] Year by year the price of gold rose in the Netherlands and with it the price of the internationally traded currencies which circulated therein.[5] Yet the experience of the Low Countries was not unique. Throughout Western Europe there was a similar series of debasements of gold resulting in a weakening of the notional moneys of account in terms of that metal.[6]

---

1   I.e. the ordinance of 25 November 1525.

2   On the basis of this advice the ordinance of the 10 December 1526 had been formulated.

3   A. LOUANT (ed.), Le Journal d' un Bourgeoisie de Mons, 1505–1536, Bruxelles 1969, Nr. 176, p. 79; Nr. 631, p. 257 and Nr. 646, p. 264.

4   A. M. WATSON, Back to Gold – and Silver, in: Economic History Review, Second Series, XX, 1 (1967), pp. 31–34.

5   C. CAU (ed.), Groot Placaet-Boek vervattende de Placaten, Ordonantien ende Edicten vande Door-luchtige, Hoogh Mog. Herren Staten Generael [...], 's Gravenhage 1658, Vol. I , 2609s. for the 1520 and subsequent ordinances. H. VAN DER WEE, The Growth of the Antwerp Market and the European Economy. Fourteenth–Sixteenth Centuries, 3 Vols. The Hague 1963, Vol. I, Table XVI, pp. 133–4 provides an overview of free market gold price movements in the Netherlands.

6   For a survey of monetary changes in western Europe see the now somewhat dated study of W. A. SHAW, The History of Currency, 1252–1894, London 1895, pp. 79–82.

When this rise in the price of gold was coupled with a relative stability in the price of silver, leading to a relative strengthening of gold in relation to that "pale and common drudge" of the European monetary system, moreover, the latter was subjected not only to an endemic state of debasement but also to a chronic condition of bi-metallic imbalance which afforded merchants opportunities to profit from trade in that most valuable of all commodities – bullion. Trade in specie competed with trade in goods. The merchant wishing to borrow money on the exchange to finance his commodity trade found a rival in that man so hated by Renaissance princes, the exporter of bullion, who he had to outbid for the money he required. Thus there existed, within each European financial centre, a system of bi-metallic premiums: surcharges which the merchant had to pay above the prevailing bill rate in order to induce his financier not to export bullion.

The Antwerp bourse during the 1520s was particularly plagued by the problem of these premiums. Even at the beginning of the decade the rise in Netherlands gold prices, which had resulted in a devaluation of the *livre gros* in terms of all currencies save those of the eastern Baltic, had caused an enormous rift in that bi-metallic equilibrium from which Antwerp had drawn its strength during the opening decade of the century.[7] A state of growing bi-metallic imbalance had emerged during the years 1515–1522[8] between Antwerp and her principal trading partners[9], Spain and Central Europe, causing the emergence of premiums on exchange dealings with these countries. The only compensation for the merchants who frequented the Antwerp Bourse was the corresponding equilibrium established through 1519–1522 with England, where since the beginning of the century gold had been grotesquely over-valued[10],

---

7   During the years 1500–15 the potential profitability of bullion transfers between the major continental European centres had been slight and usually below the prevailing rate of interest. Antwerp offered the lowest interest rate in Europe, as for instance in 1515 (Lyon 18.6 per cent; London 5.4 per cent; Antwerp 3.2 per cent *usance*). The Lyon rate has been taken from data contained in K. D. MÜLLER, Welthandelsbräuche, 1480–1540 (=Deutsche Handelsakten des Mittelalters und der Neuzeit, Vol. 5), Berlin 1934, p. 70.

8   During this first stage of the devaluation, which continued until November 1525, the Flemish pound (which since 1435 had amounted to 1.5 pounds of Brabant groats, thereby making it possible only to refer to the one unit) weakened most against the strong English, Spanish and Central European currencies (Frankfurt-on-the-Main, Augsburg, Speyer etc.), with major secondary weakening against the Florentine and Ottoman ones. Parallel devaluations in France and Venice muted the effects, whilst in the eastern Baltic the rapid debasements of the Riga-Lübeck marks and the Danzig *Groschen* against the gulden were of such a magnitude that they resulted in the appreciation of the pound groat in terms of these currencies. W. A. SHAW, op. cit., pp. 301–423. M. J. EL-SAS, Umriss einer Geschichte der Preise und Löhne in Deutschland, 3 Vols. in 2, Leiden 1936–40, I, pp. 118–122; IIA, pp. 3–10. O. BARKAN, Les mouvements des prix en Turquie entre 1499 et 1655, in: Mélanges en l' honneur de Fernand Braudel: histoire économique du monde mediterranéen, 1450–1650, Toulouse 1973, pp. 71–72; J. PELC, Ceny w Gdansku w XVI i XVII wieku, Lwów 1937, pp. 2–3; G. MICKWITZ, Aus Revaler Handelsbüchern. Zur Technik des Ostseehandels in der ersten Hälfte des 16. Jahrhunderts, Helsingfors 1938, pp. 83–85.

9   In 1522 the bi-metallic ratios in Spain and Imperial Germany were 10.26 and 11.2:1 respectively, and at Antwerp the ratio had risen to 12.17:1, thereby yielding a potential profit from bullion export to Spain of 13 and to Germany of 5.5 per cent. With bill rates of 8.4–10 per cent, premiums of 3–4.6 per cent would accordingly have to be paid on exchange dealings to Spain.

10   The English bi-metallic ratio of 12.08:1 overvalued gold by as much as 33 per cent in comparison with most European currencies in 1500. A. E. FEAVERYEAR, The Pound Sterling: A History of

and with the Anglo-centric financial network which on occasion during the second decade of the century had come to include France and the Levant (from 1512) and Venice (from 1517).[11] This equilibrium, however, was of but scant significance as long as the Antwerp market was wracked by the financial crises of 1519–1522, and with the return to cheap money in the course of 1523 the continuing rise in the price of gold led to the emergence of premiums on ALL of the Antwerp exchanges.[12]

In 1523–1524, the initial effect of increased premiums was slight, for although some business was deflected to Lyon and Frankfurt, the lure of cheap money continued to attract most merchants, including those of London, to the towns of the Scheldt estuary.[13] When, from the Cold Mart of 1524/5, Anglo-Netherlands gold prices began to rise rapidly, however, the cost of exchange dealings between London and Antwerp and the rest of Europe became extremely expensive. Trade declined and the commerce in bullion displaced that in goods.[14] In November 1525 the Netherlands authorities reacted. By enhancing the price of silver relative to that of gold they succeeded, ephemerally, in re-establishing a bi-metallic ratio of 10.9:1 and in reducing premiums on many of the Antwerp exchanges, but not with England where the prevailing bi-metallic ratio of 12.03:1 caused the emergence of sizeable premiums on the London–Antwerp exchange.[15]

Monetary stability, however, was not so easily achieved. In the Netherlands through December 1525, as de Lucy noted in his diary, gold once more began to rise in price.[16] In England the process was stayed for a while, as high interest rates on the exchange impeded specie exports whilst the decline in the import trade encouraged an

---

English Money, Oxford 1931, pp. 346–7, and SHAW, History of Currency, pp. 40, 69. Amongst this group of currencies the premium was lowest on the Anglo-Venetian and Anglo-Florentine exchanges, amounting to 3–6 per cent on an interest rate of 5 per cent. For example the profit on Anglo-Florentine export of silver (the respective ratios were 12.08 and 10.46:1) was 13.4 per cent which, after transport costs (empirically derived) have been deducted, amounted to 10.8 per cent net. The premium is, accordingly, 10.9 less 5 per cent prevailing interest rate: 5.9 per cent. The rise in gold prices at Antwerp, however, gradually brought the two currency systems into equilibrium. At some time between the first and second semester of 1522 (bi-metallic ratio at Antwerp: I-1522, 11.94:1; II-1522, 12.4:1) the transition was completed.

11 Gradually over the period 1500–1522 the enhancement of gold in these countries brought their bi-metallic ratios into line with that of England. At Venice, for instance, the bi-metallic ratio rose from 10.97–11.32:1 in 1516/7 and again to 12.04:1 in 1519. Premiums could not exist, therefore, on these exchanges. This was of but scant significance, however, when the Antwerp market was operating normally, for the cost of money (i.e. bill rate plus premium) at Antwerp was still lower than at London. Only when bill rates were markedly enhanced at Antwerp did it become cheaper to raise money at London for trade with these countries.

12 Chs. 1, 2 above.

13 On this occasion, moreover, the English came by choice for, even with a premium amounting to three per cent on the eve of the monetary reform of November 1525, the monthly interest rate on dealings via Antwerp was still one point below the cost of those financed solely at London.

14 The outflow of gold from Germany to England and the Netherlands, for instance, attracted the attention in 1524/5 of no less a person than Martin Luther: G. FABIUNKE, Martin Luther als Nationalökonom, Berlin 1963, p. 114.

15 On the edict of November 1525 and the discussions pursuant upon its formulation see VAN DER WEE, Antwerp, II, p. 148.

16 See above.

inflow of bullion into the realm[17], but by the spring of 1526 the situation existing before the attempted reform had been re-established and throughout 1526 gold prices
again rose rapidly, causing Antwerp to become a magnet, drawing to itself the supplies of all of Europe. From England, France, Germany and even from far away Venice there was a steady, if illicit, flow of gold towards the Low Countries. The monetary systems of these countries were accordingly thrown into disarray as gold appreciated in terms of the money of account. In Venice the shortage of good ducats was such
that they rapidly began to appreciate in terms of bank or 'nominal' money. In the
spring of that year the latter were already at a discount of six per cent or more. By July
1526 the rate of discount had risen to fourteen per cent and in October the situation
had become so bad that it was rumoured that one banker at least had died "from mel-
ancholia of the bank" caused by the depreciation of his assets.[18] Similarly in London
and elsewhere 'nominal' or bank money depreciated against gold and, as men became
unwilling to hold paper debts, interest rates rose.[19] An acute monetary tightness
reigned throughout the financial centres of Europe. Moreover, as long as Netherlands
gold continued upon its inflationary path, attempts to resolve these monetary problems
were to prove at best ineffectual, at worst damaging to the economies concerned.

During July and August 1526 in England the government reacted to the crisis developing in the City by markedly enhancing the price of gold, a procedure which,
apart from setting merchant against merchant and bringing the exchanges to a halt,
was to prove remarkably successful – for about a month. From the 22nd August it was
no longer attractive to export gold. Indeed, its price was now so high that the precious
metal flowed towards England. One anonymous contemporary observer declared to
Wolsey, that since the proclamation[20], he knew personally "of an import of ten thousand crowns and ten thousand pounds of gold" to London.[21] As supplies increased
domestic gold prices stabilised. Silver, now the prime exportable metal, on the other
hand, increased in price as enhancement in the Netherlands, which made groats "that

---

17   Ch. 8. On the decline of the import trade: G. SCHANZ, Englische Handelspolitik gegen Ende des
      Mittelalters, Leipzig 1881, Vol. II, p. 86.

18   F. C. LANE, Venetian Bankers, 1496–1533, in: Journal of Political Economy, XLV (1937), re-
      printed in Venice and History. The Collected Papers of Frederick C. Lane, Baltimore 1966, p. 84.

19   Ch. 7.

20   On the crisis of July and August 1526 see ch. 5. The mint ordinance of the 22 August is printed in
      L & P., Henry VIII, VI (2), Nr. 2423 and the reaction of the merchant community to the monetary
      reform is graphically described in a letter written in the period immediately following the procla-
      mation. "[…] nuper sunt aliquas controversias in civitate londoniensis. inter mercators anglios, ita-
      los, flandrensis et hispanos post publicum edictum aestimationis auri, circa muyuas et reciprocas
      solutiones debitorum, sunt enim multi qui sic interpretantur quam debitum contractum ante pro-
      clamationem, nominatum videlicet libras sterlingorum, marcas et nobiles, debeat post proclama-
      tionem solui a debitoribus, creditori, computando libram debitam, viginti duas solidas, et marcam
      solidas quatuordecim, et demarios quatuor, et nobilem, solidas septem et denarios quatuor, sive so-
      lutio fiat in argento sive in auro... mercatores quoque omnes in hac ambiguitate abstinent a Cam-
      biis, que ante solebant exerceo […]." (extended transliteration, original grammar and punctuation
      retained from The National Archive, Kew (formerly Public Record Office, Chancery Lane, hence-
      forth referred to as TNA), SP1/55 fo. 184. The letter is undated, but it is clear from the above ex-
      tract that it must have been written in the period immediately following the proclamation of 22
      August 1526.

21   TNA, SP1/55 fo.184, lines 21–2.

were want to go here (in 1524/5) for 5d ob and 6d, now […] go for 6d ob and in som-wher for 7d.," drew up prices in England.[22] The English bi-metallic ratio which had risen to 13.2:1 in August, was closing, falling to 13.1:1 in September and 12:1 in Oc-tober and the government accordingly prepared to encapsulate the new metallic price relationship in an ordinance.[23]

Yet before pen was even put to paper the decree was obsolete. Our anonymous observer, even as he watched the gold inflow, was sufficiently aware of the continuing pressure on English gold to be somewhat trepidous of its fate, counselling Wolsey that it "would be exported unless care is taken"[24] and recommending that "the searchers be warned to attend to their duty"[25], to prevent such a turn of events. Throughout the first three weeks of September the relatively high export price of silver (32.5 s.Fl.) pre-vented this occurring[26] but the continuing rise in gold export prices was ominous. On the 14th September Netherlands merchants "would accept the angel-noble at 11s.3d.Fl. or 67 ¹/² plaks."[27] By the 18th September if some merchants would accept this price, others wanted more. Hacket wrote, "mone wylbe ryssyng here everyday […] angellettes […] be want now here 11s. 4d. flemys."[28] By the 30th September gold export prices once more exceeded silver, triggering off at least one illicit outflow of the metal from England, for a report is extant of a rumour, current in Brussels on that day, of a hoy of Antwerp coming from London which had been lost on the coast of Zeeland carrying a pack of kerseys in which an Italian had secreted £1,600 in rose nobles and angelets.[29] The continuous rise in Netherlands gold prices had totally ne-gated the impact of the attempted reform, so that when on the 5th November the long awaited monetary ordinance, carefully prepared to avoid a repetition of the September dislocations, was published it passed for naught.[30] Merchants continued, in spite of the exhortations of both king and emperor, to ship gold to Antwerp in order to take advan-tage of the enhanced price there.[31]

What royal ordinances could not achieve, however, market forces did. The devel-oping *strettezza* on the London market forced up interest rates to such a level by the

---

22 BL Galba B IX fo.29. Hacket to Wolsey, 18 September 1526, wherein he also reported that the Welser had declared that because of this enhancement silver exports yielded them an extra 4 per cent over the London-Antwerp bill rate of 8 per cent.

23 I. e. in the ordinance subsequently formulated on 30 October and published on the 5 November.

24 TNA, SP1/55 fo.184, lines 23–4.

25 TNA, SP1/55 fo.184v, lines 14–5.

26 It seems unlikely that the export price of silver went much above 32.5s fl., for in spite of the sub-sequent enhancement of silver in the Netherlands referred to in Hackett's letter of the 18 Septem-ber (BL. Galba B IX fo.29), rising English domestic prices (amounting to an enhancement of ten per cent before silver ceased to be an exportable metal, Howell's Ledger, fo. 37) led first to a sta-bilisation of, and then a fall in the external value of English silver to 29.5s fl. at the time of the second monetary ordinance.

27 L&P., Henry VIII, IV (2), Nr. 2485.

28 L&P., Henry VIII, IV (2), Nr. 2492; BL. Galba B IX, fo. 29.

29 TNA, SP1/39 fos. 251–2. The angelet was a gold coin of 23ct. 3.5 gr. fineness and 40 gr. Troy weight; the rose noble was of the same fineness, but weighed 120 gr. Troy.

30 L&P., Henry VIII, IV (2), No. 2609.

31 Ibid., nr. 2609, 2628.

third week of November (16.5 per cent usance), that, even with a gold export price of 34. 39s. Fl., the outflow was stayed.[32] For an instant hope returned to the market as gold prices stabilized.[33] Interest rates in the bill market held steady at their enhanced levels and clothiers at Blackwell Hall once more tentatively advanced sales credits to their customers.[34] Normality was returning to the market as the monetary stabilization seemingly held firm.

Yet for how long could this situation prevail when across the Channel the "coy-ness […] rynys […] abow all rayson" because of "the enhancement, day by day, of the moneys"?[35] The English stabilization was not a week old when premiums once again began to appear on the exchange. How far the situation changed at this time is clearly revealed by the negotiations between Hacket and the German finance houses of Welser and Höchstetter over transfers of money to Hungary. On the 21st November, after consultation with the principal merchants about the Exchange, Hacket declared, "the merchants would be glad to give 2 or 3 per cent to take gold out of the realm," for that was the profit they could make by such an operation over and above the prevailing bill rate.[36] Three days later the situation had deteriorated as the bi-metallic ratio in the Low Countries reached 13.6:1. After further consultation with the principal merchants of Germany he now found only the Welser prepared to come to terms, undertaking to transfer funds to Nuremberg at 16.4 per cent (i.e. formal 9 per cent plus 4 per cent premium on the London-Antwerp exchange, together with an incremental 3.4 per cent premium on the Antwerp-Nuremberg exchange).[37] A mere two or three days after stabilization premiums had once more begun to appear on the exchange and on the 29th November the London market again collapsed. Sales at Blackwell Hall declined and the credit network, so recently re-established therein, disintegrated into atomistic anarchy.[38] As long as the Netherlands currency thus remained unreformed attempts at stabilization in England proved at best ineffectual, at worst disruptive.

Elsewhere they were totally destructive. In Venice, for instance, the Senate, by operating upon the symptoms rather than the cause of the disorders, precipitated an acute crisis. On the 6th November it prohibited the selling of bank money at a discount and ordered payment in (appreciated) coin. A perhaps not unexpected run on the banks developed. By the 5th December the Molini partners had to appeal to the chiefs of the Ten to come to the Rialto to restore order amongst depositors. On the 7th December the da Molin went into liquidation to be followed by Andrea Arimando. By the end of the year a major sector of the Venetian banking system was in ruins.[39]

An effective reform of the various European currencies and the re-establishment of commercial credit systems could thus only begin once monetary stabilization in the

---

32 See ch. 7.

33 On conditions during the week beginning 18 November see BL. Galba B IX. fo. 35; TNA, SP1/40 fos. 6–7.

34 See ch. 7.

35 TNA, SP1/40 fo. 7, and LOUANT (ed.), Journal, Nr. 646 as quoted above.

36 BL. Galba B IX , fo. 35.

37 TNA, SP1/40 fo. 21

38 See ch. 7.

39 LANE, Venetian Bankers., pp. 84–5.

Netherlands had been achieved. The first stage of such a stabilization came on the 10th December 1526 when the Council, to use the lowly Mons burgess' words, "wishing to have the best gold and money" set down "the best order and price of each piece which [...] was to run until the end of February", when the second stage of the reform was to be implemented and "all would be reduced and set at the price prevailing in 1520."[40] In response to these manoeuvres a completely new situation emerged on the Antwerp bullion market. Anticipating the impending return to the monetary standard of 1520 no-one would now buy gold at the previous inflated price level and holders of the yellow metal in their haste to unload their hoards depressed prices on the private bullion market, closing the price differential between it and the Antwerp mint. In January 1527 the two were not yet in equilibrium but by the fourth of that month the differential was no more than six per cent, private bullion prices having fallen by almost a fifth during the preceding four weeks.[41] Seven weeks later, on the 20th February 1527, the first stage of the reform had been completed, enabling Hacket to write, in a somewhat more cheerful vein than usual, that "the publication of gold and silver [...] is here well Intertenyd and substance kepte [...]."[42] The second stage was now merely a formality. From 1st March 1527 the standard of 1520 was restored and the equilibrium between private and public bullion prices re-established.

Where Antwerp led London followed. The decline in Netherlands gold prices, due to the successful implementation of the Low Countries' monetary reform, eliminated the excessive premiums on the Antwerp exchanges. From a level of 10.8 per cent premium on a London bill rate of 9 per cent immediately before the proclamation of the 10th December it had fallen to 3 per cent on 8 at the turn of the year and on the 4th January the Welser, in renewed negotiations with Hacket, were prepared to undertake the transmission of funds to Hungary at the prevailing bill rate, leaving the money within the realm. Premiums on the London-Antwerp exchange had, at long last, been eliminated as they were to be subsequently on many of the other Antwerp exchanges, thereby removing the incentive for the previously active trade in specie.[43] The London bullion market price for gold, some 5.5 per cent above the mint price at the end of November 1526, accordingly, stabilized at that level to January 1527 and then began to fall.[44] By March the English monetary ordinance of the previous October, abortive at its inception, became effective.[45] Over the winter of 1526/7, therefore, English monetary stabilization, so elusive during the previous year, was achieved and the

---

40 LOUANT (ed.), Journal, Nr. 646, p. 264, and present chapter above.

41 The Netherlands price of gold 0.0306 grams per Flemish groat at the end of November (TNA, SP1/40 fos. 21–2) fell to 0.0362 grams per Flemish groat on the 4 January, or somewhat above the mint price of 0.0384 grams per Flemish groat (BL. Galba IX, fo. 38). For the mint price see VAN DER WEE, Antwerp, I , table XV, p. 128.

42 BL, Galba B VI , fo. 4.

43 In the negotiations with the Welser in January 1527 there is no mention of a premium on the London-Antwerp exchange, the respective bi-metallic ratios at that date – 11.4 and 11.6:1 respectively – yielding an insufficient profit in relation to the prevailing bill rate of 8.66 per cent *usance*. See BL Galba B IX, fo.38. A similar effect of falling gold prices was felt on the Antwerp exchanges with France, Germany and Central Europe during the opening months of 1527.

44 TNA, 1/40 fos. 21-2 and BL. Galba B IX , fo. 38.

45 Cf. present chapter above.

credit system began to recover. Already before Christmas 1526 interest rates in the bill market had begun to fall.[46] The sales-credit network, after the turmoil which had prevailed during the first fortnight of December, began to operate normally once more from the third week of that month.[47] By March 1527 the monetary reforms in both the Netherlands and England had been completed and normalcy had returned to their respective money markets. Potential margins on specie export had been reduced and trade in goods replaced trade in bullion. That trade, however, now took place in an entirely different environment from that which had existed before the tumultuous events of 1525–1527.

Where the rise in Netherlands gold prices had led to devaluation and weakening of the pound groat during the years to 1526 in all areas save the Baltic, revaluation in 1526/7 had the opposite effect, especially where it took place in an environment of international debasement. The Reform of 1526/7 ushered in a "hard money" era in the monetary politics of the Low Countries during which every attempt was made to maintain the monetary standard of 1520 in the face of internationally rising gold prices.[48] For more than a decade the reformed Flemish pound strengthened steadily against most other currencies.[49] The effect was most dramatic in relation to the eastern Baltic currencies. Already weakening before 1525, their continued decline now coincided with the Flemish revaluation, leading to an acceleration in the rate of appreciation of the latter currency. Within a decade of the Reform the Flemish pound commanded almost forty per cent more Riga marks than in 1520. Yet the strengthening of the Flemish pound was now also felt in most other markets with heavy appreciation in terms of the French, English and Central European currencies and modest gains against the Rhenish, Italian and Levantine ones.[50] Only one market area maintained the stability of its currency: Spain, where inflows of American gold ensured the integrity of the ducat and actually led to its appreciation after 1537.[51] In terms of the reformed currency Netherlands goods were now expensive on European markets, though least so to the south and east, and it is thus perhaps not surprising that a new era was dawning for Antwerp, one dominated by the "overwhelming importance of trade to the south, linked with the close Hispano-American relations and the expansion of the Levant trade"[52], particularly as other forces inherent in the process of monetary change tended to reinforce these trends.

---

46   Interest rates at 16.5 per cent *usance* during the third week of November 1526 had fallen to 11.7 per cent a month later and 8.66 per cent at the beginning of January.

47   See ch. 7.

48   VAN DER WEE, Antwerp, II, p. 163.

49   As the effects of the 1526/7 Reform weakened during the late 'thirties, a new series of monetary ordinances were enacted from 1538–1540 to re-establish the standard of 1520.

50   The pound groat appreciated by 27–33 per cent in terms of the first group of currencies and by 15–24 per cent in terms of the second.

51   Present chapter, n. 9.

52   VAN DER WEE, Antwerp, II, p. 163.

In terms of the Anglo-Netherlands bi-metallic equilibrium the reform completed in March 1527[53] re-established the situation of 1520 with regards to the London-Antwerp exchange. With the rest of Europe, however, it did not. The English bi-metallic ratio was now closer to that of most European states, apart from Spain, than the reformed Antwerp one. Premiums were thus abolished on many of the London exchanges and for more than a decade the barriers to the operation of the London bill market, with one exception, were removed.[54] The exception was brought about by the Venetian and Florentine monetary reforms of 1527–31 which established their bi-metallic ratios at 10.5 and 11.1:1 and caused a realignment of these currencies, which had previously been closely related to sterling, back into Antwerp's monetary net-work.[55] The once almost unitary European monetary equilibrium, in relation to which England stood on the periphery, was now split asunder.[56] Out of the turmoil of 1525/6 two distinct spheres of monetary influence, centred on the London and Antwerp exchanges, had emerged, divided by a barrier of bi-metallic premiums but within each of their respective fields of influence characterised by an absence of such financial impedimenta.

Thus from Easter 1527, free from the effects of those bi-metallic disorders which for two years (1524/5–1526/7) had disrupted operations, the pre-existing pattern of financial dualism once more came to characterise activity on the Antwerp Bourse. The differentiated movement of short- and medium-term interest rates now, however, took place within an entirely new market system characterised by the "overwhelming importance of trade to the south, linked with the close Hispano-American relations and the expansion of the Levant trade." The great South German finance houses, who were the principal participants in the medium-term loan market, were awash with money. Having withdrawn from financing the Habsburgs over the winter of 1522/3 and having successfully secured repayment on their outstanding debts during the years 1523–6 they found their cash balances rapidly growing. As the silver boom in the Alpenland, Thuringian and Slovak mining complex reached its peak in 1526/7 and a flood of silver poured forth from the mines, their investments in the workings yielded them record dividends and yet again augmented their reserves. In the medium-term money market funds were plentiful and interest rates reflected the abundance. During the summer and autumn of 1525 interest rates had edged upwards in response to inflationary pressures but with the implementation of the Netherlands monetary reform of December 1525 they stabilized in time for the Cold Mart and by Easter 1526 were once more poised to fall to the 12 per cent level of a year before – and perhaps even beyond. Medium-term government loans could still during the brief period of monetary stabilization (November 1525–June 1526) seemingly be floated with ease and the

---

53   In England the ordinance of October/November 1526, once it had become effective, by spring of 1527 re-established a bi-metallic ratio of 12:1 which greatly overvalued gold in relation to the Netherlands, where a ratio of 10.9:1 prevailed.

54   England: 12:1, France: 11.76, North Germany: 11.96, East Baltic: 11.3-11.7, Central Europe: 11.5-11.8, Venice (to 1527): 12.04.

55   Netherlands: 10.9:1 and Spain: 10.3:1.

56   In ca. 1500 the English currency had over-valued gold by as much as a third in relation to most European currencies.

issue of *rentes* at this time at the extraordinary rate of 6.5 per cent reflected the state of buoyant optimism which pervaded the market.

For those seeking commercial finance the situation was somewhat different. They too in 1526 experienced the phenomenon of RELATIVELY cheap money. Bill rates had followed the general trend in interest rates over the years 1523–6 until during the period November 1525-June1526 money at usance stood two points below the level of two years before. Commercial funds were thus relatively cheap, but at 5.6 per cent the bill rate, as a result of the continuing Habsburg presence on the Exchange "crowding out" private borrowers, was still considerably higher than at the beginning of the decade. Participants in that market thus, whilst revelling in the availability of relatively cheap money, retained a certain awareness of the baleful effects of Habsburg interventionism. Whilst money was cheap, therefore, a basic underlying dualism in early-1526 characterised the Antwerp money market distinguishing the financiers, who were the principal participants in the medium-term loan market, from the merchants, who operated on the exchanges.

Yet for the moment in 1526 such distinctions remained buried deep below the surface and when John Hacket[57] arrived at Antwerp early that summer to take up his post as royal agent the Bourse displayed an outward calm. Both gaudily attired imperial agents, tendering government bonds, and more soberly garbed merchants, hawking their bills of exchange, basked for a moment in an atmosphere of buoyant optimism which seemed indestructible. Even disturbing rumours, which travelled from Spain with the alacrity reserved for ill-tidings, that "the Emperor has ordered the hundred thousand ducats in Fernando de Beruny's hands to be appropriated. One half to pay his men of war in 'Duchland', the other to be delivered at the king's pleasure" left the worthy financiers, who subscribed to imperial loans, unperturbed.[58] Medium-term interest rates edged up marginally. Only merchants on the exchange reacted and their response may have been more related to the re-emergence of monetary problems than to the news from Spain. Interest rates, which had settled at about 5.6 per cent usance during the early-summer, rose rapidly thereafter to 8 per cent at the Bamus mart and, as the news from Spain broke amidst conditions of monetary chaos in November, to 13 per cent. Yet this was only a foretaste of events to come. With the Netherlands reform of the 10th December the monetary element in the crisis was eliminated and over that winter bill rates at both London and Antwerp became set on a downward path. At London where the rate on commercial paper had attained 16.5 per cent in late November 1526, a month later it stood at 11.7 per cent and in late January 1527 it amounted to only 8.66 per cent at which point it stood at par with the Antwerp rate. With the return to monetary stability over the winter of 1526/7 the underlying trend in Anglo-Netherlands bill rates was clearly downwards. Yet at Antwerp the rumours from Spain

---

57   Wingfield, then resident in the Low Countries, first recommended Hacket, an Irishman living in Middelburg, to Wolsey in December 1521 and again brought his name before the Cardinal in 1522 and 1523 when he suggested him as a replacement for the Spinelli, who were then acting as royal agents in the Netherlands. It was not, however, until May 1526, after the Irishman had enjoyed a brief sojourn in England, that he was appointed to the post amidst the turmoil of the contemporary monetary crisis within which he acted as both a participant and observer. L&P, Henry VIII, III , Nos. 2833, 3366; IV, No. 2161.

58   TNA, SP1/40 fo. 21v.

which had circulated in November continued to trouble the merchants' minds and when the arrival of the fleet from Andalusia in early January provided confirmation of the news they panicked. The Cold Mart of 1526/7 thus closed in conditions of total financial disarray. Anticipating the worst, merchants at first would only proffer bills at the incredible rate of 22 per cent usance and although subsequently the market returned to normality, the rate finally settling at 8.66 per cent at the close of the fair, participants therein were clearly jumpy.

Their premonition of disaster, moreover, was to prove only too accurate. When the Habsburg eagle once more spread is wings casting deep shadows over the Bourse and the new techniques of forced interest-free loans were extended at the Easter fair of 1527 to Antwerp, the realities of their predicament were brought forcefully home to all denizens of that institution. Medium-term interest rates now also rose rapidly, settling at 18 per cent and thereafter subsiding slowly as the Emperor fell back from the attack. Retreat, however, came too late for at the Bamus mart chaos once more reigned on the Bourse when news from Leipzig of events on the Rammelsberg broke.

CHAPTER FOUR

THE ANTWERP MONEY MARKET. THE EFFECTS OF THE CENTRAL EUROPEAN MINING CRISIS, 1527/8[1]

1527 summer. A sergeant in the service of Duke Henry the Younger of Brunswick led his company of troops against the city of Goslar. It may be wondered whether he any more than Shaw's anonymous "gentleman in London" realised the full implications of his actions.[2] Yet the shots fired that summer on the Rammelsberg, as a minor aristocrat tried to enforce his obscure claims over a half-forgotten mortgage on the citizens

---

1 Historians have long considered the events of 1527/8 as of major importance in the evolution of the Antwerp money market. R. EHRENBERG, Das Zeitalter der Fugger. Geldkapital und Creditverkehr im 16. Jahrhundert, 2 Vols., Frankfurt-on-the-Main 1896, Vol. I, p. 385, placed 1528 alongside 1562 and 1575 as one of the periods of "great crisis" in the sixteenth century. J. STRIEDER, Studien zur Geschichte kapitalistischer Organisationsformen, Munich / Leipzig 1914, almost twenty years later examined some of the organizational ramifications of the crisis. Latterly, E. WESTERMANN, Das 'Leipziger Monopolprojekt' als Symptom der mitteleuropäischen Wirtschaftskrise um 1527/8, in: Vierteljahrschrift für Sozial- und Wirtschaftsgeschichte, 58/1 (1971), pp. 1–23, having analysed the origins of the mining crisis at the centre of the Central European disorders of 1527/8, has seen in these events a major turning point for European commercial activity. He discusses on pages 22–3 of that article the impact on the contemporary cattle trade. The question of the effects of the 1527/8 crisis on the European cattle trades has been taken up subsequently in E. WESTERMANN (ed.), Internationaler Ochsenhandel (1350–1750). Akten des 7th International Economic History Congress (Edinburgh, 1978), Stuttgart 1979, and by I. BLANCHARD, The Continental European Cattle Trades, 1400–1600, in: Economic History Review, Second Series, XXXIX, 3 (1986), pp. 435–9, text and n. 40, 42 and 46, where the impact on specific cattle markets is considered. On pp. 10–12 of WESTERMANN, Das 'Leipziger Monopolprojekt' and pp. 254–9 of ID., Der Goslarer Bergbau vom 14. bis zum 16. Jahrhundert, in: Jahrbuch für die Geschichte Mittel- und Ostdeutschlands, 20 (1971), pp. 254–60, Westermann examines the relationship between the crisis of 1527/8 and the structural transformation of the European lead trade. Further consideration of changes in the international lead trade at this time is given in I. BLANCHARD, International Lead Production and Trade in the 'Age of the Saigerprozess', 1460–1560, Stuttgart 1994, pp. 121–146. Finally in G. VON PÖLNITZ, Jacob Fugger, Tübingen 1951, Vol. II, p. 532 and ID., Anton Fugger, Tübingen 1958, Vol. I, pp. 57, 102–4, 131–4, 144–6, 156 and 159–64 the question of the Höchstetter bankruptcy and its relationship to the crisis is considered. Yet much remains obscure, particularly with regard to the role of the 1527/8 crisis in the broader framework of financial and monetary disorders, which beset the Antwerp money market during the 1520s, described by H. VAN DER WEE, The Growth of the Antwerp Market and the European Economy. Fourteenth–Sixteenth Centuries, 3 Vols., The Hague 1963, and with regard to the impact of these dislocations on long-term changes in the patterns of European commerce.

2 B. SHAW, 'The Devil's Disciple' from 'Three Plays for Puritans', The Bodley Head Bernard Shaw. Collected Plays and Prefaces, Vol. II, p. 131.

of the imperial city, were to echo throughout the financial centres of Europe, for the devastation amongst the Harz forests temporarily destroyed a key supply centre of the Central European silver industry – the Goslar lead mines.[3]

The collapse of mining at Goslar in the summer of 1527 and the ensuing transformation of the Central European lead market dealt a major blow to the *Saigerhändler* of Thuringia and a mortal one to those of Saxony, for, in spite of their frantic efforts to reorganize their sources of supply, the quantities of the all-important smelting material available to the *Hüttenmeister* (*literally: "hut masters"*, i.e. entrepreneur smelters running the Saiger huts, P. R.) fell catastrophically during the closing years of the 1520s.[4] A crisis was thus precipitated in these silver and copper producing centres.[5] The intermittent mining boom which since the great mining crisis of 1486–1492 had continually replenished the bulging coffers of such Leipzig merchant-*Saigerhändler*[6] as Wolf Wiedermann, Lucas and Hans Straube, Hans Leimbach or Ulrich and Hieronimus Rauscher, came to a halt causing an acute shortage of funds, such as had plagued the Saxon orientated houses like the Lintacher for some years past. Cash became tight and those merchants who had backed their commercial paper with anticipated revenues now found themselves in difficulties. The moment of truth came at the Leipzig autumn fair when the bills handed over at Frankfurt for the cloth

3   The literature on the dispute and its consequences is not inconsiderable but see, F. ROSHAINER, Die Geschichte des Unterharzer Hüttenwesens, in: Beiträge zur Geschichte der Stadt Goslar, XXIV (1968), pp. 90–5; F. GUNTER, Die älteste Geschichte der Bergstadt St. Andreasberg, in: Zeitschrift des Harzvereins für Geschichte, 1909, p. 191; H. BOYCE, The Mines of the Upper Harz from 1514–1589, Menasha, Wisconsin 1920, pp. 28–9, 49–50; U. SCHMID, Die Bedeutung des Fremdkapitals im Goslarer Berghau um 1500, in: Beiträge zur Geschichte der Stadt Goslar, XXVII (1970), pp.136–40 and W. HILLEBRAND, Der Goslarer Metallhandel im Mittelalter, in: Hansische Geschichtsblätter, LXXXVII (1969), p. 33.

4   On the Saigerprozess see L. SUHLING, Die Seigerhüttenprozess. Die Technologie des Kupferseigerns nach den frühen metallurgischen Schriften, Stuttgart 1976, and I. BLANCHARD, English Lead and the International Bullion Crisis of the 1550s, in D. C. COLEMAN / A. H. JOHN (eds.), Trade, Government and Economy in Pre-Industrial England. Essays presented to F. J. Fisher, London 1976, pp. 21–22. On the reorganization of central European lead markets, see WESTERMANN, Monopolprojekt, pp.38–43 and ID., Der Goslarer Bergbau, pp. 254–60.

5   Silver production only briefly stayed in 1499–1511, 1516/8–21, 1524–5, but expanded during the course of the second great production cycle (1492–1526) to 1526/7, before being displaced to more easterly locations, the crisis of 1527/8 marking not only a short-term fluctuation in output but also the beginning of a period of long-term decline in existing production centres (see ch. 1, Figure 1.1). It is curious that whilst short-term politically induced crises have been studied in depth (for example I. MITTENZWEI, Der Joachimsthaler Aufstand 1525, Seine Ursachen und Folgen, [Berlin, 1968]) the causes of the general mining crises have been the subject of only one study: E. WESTERMANN, Die Bedeutung der Thüringer Saigerhandels für den mitteleuropäischen Handel an der Wende vom 15. zum 16. Jahrhundert, in: Jahrbuch für die Geschichte Mittel- und Ostdeutschlands, XXI (1972), pp. 89–90.

6   *Saigerhändler*: Merchant-capitalists and financiers involved in the *Saiger* trades (P. R.). On the activities, financial, commercial and industrial, of these Leipzig families, see T. G. WERNER, Das fremde Kapital am Annaberger Bergbau und Metallhandel des 16. Jahrhundert, Neues Archiv für Sächsische Geschichte und Alterthumskunde, LVII (1936), pp.125–6, 158, 165n, 144, 166; Ibid., 58 (1937), pp. 23–4. WESTERMANN, op. cit., pp. 75–79. G. FISCHER, Aus zwei Jahrhunderten Leipziger Handelsgeschichte, 1470–1650, Leipzig 1929, pp.108–10, 135–41, 148–59, and E. WESTERMANN, Das Eislebener Garkupfer und seine Bedeutung für den europäischen Kupfermarkt, 1460–1560, Cologne 1971, pp. 103, 118n, 440–1, 281–3, 311, n. 4.

and other Anglo-Netherlands wares which formed the staple of their trade, fell due. Speculation and rumour ran riot and when the house of Lintacher defaulted on its paper unease turned to panic.[7]

All along the great trade route which stretched from London via Antwerp and Frankfurt to Venice men found themselves holding bills of exchange for which they could not secure payment. A state of acute illiquidity prevailed in mercantile circles, cash was at a premium and interest rates rose. To the south-east at Wiener-Neustadt the small firm of Alexius Funck, which had quadrupled the size of its bill and other obligation holdings between 1516–1527, now set about retrieving its liquidity by calling them in.[8] At Venice, an already developing crisis in which the da Molin and Arimando banks had collapsed now turned for the worse as State intervention in the market brought down the mighty house of Pisani and caused the virtual suspension of commercial credit in the city.[9] Gloom and despondency hung over the *palazzi* of the city, as they did also over the gabled merchants' houses of the western financial metropolis – Antwerp – where the same story of credit restriction and bankruptcy may be chronicled. Lesser men, like Edmund Claysson, lacking large cash reserves, were forced to sell off real estate to meet their creditors.[10] Larger merchant-houses, such as the Fugger, Tucher or Welser, no longer extended their holdings but avoided any embarrassment by drawing upon their private fortunes to meet their commercial obligations.[11] Only where reserves were held in the form of not easily realisable assets was the stability of such houses threatened. Yet when this occurred, as in the case of the Höchstetter, the crash was felt throughout Europe. Their involvement in an abortive attempt to create a world mercury monopoly had left them dangerously exposed, holding a large proportion of their assets in stocks of the over-valued metal.[12] When the crisis broke they were soon in difficulties. At the end of March 1528 Wolf Tucher wrote to his father Leinhard from Lyon that

7   On the Lintacher bankruptcy see WESTERMANN, Monopolprojekt, p. 22 and FISCHER, op. cit., p.110.

8   O. PICKL (ed.), Das älteste Geschäftsbuch Österreichs. Das Gewölberegister der Wiener Neustädter Firma Alexius Funck (1516–ca.1538), in: Forschungen zur geschichtlichen Landeskunde der Steiermark, XXIII (1965), p. 404.

9   On the Venetian crisis of 1525–6 see ch. 3 above, whilst the events of 1527/8 are described in F. C. LANE, Venetian Bankers, 1496-1533, in: Journal of Political Economy, XLV (1937), reprinted in Venice and History. The Collected Papers of Frederick C. Lane, Baltimore 1966, pp. 70–71, 84–6.

10 R. VAN UYTVEN, Een rekening betreffend Edmond Claysson, handelaar te Antwerpen (ca.1518–1520, in: Bijdragen tot de geschiedenis, inzonderheid van het oud hertogdom, Brabant, XLII (1959) as quoted in VAN DER WEE, Antwerp, II, p.146.

11 EHRENBERG, Zeitalter der Fugger [reprint Hildesheim 1963], I, pp.122–35, 219, 226–7.

12 On the Höchstetter attempt to create a world mercury monopoly, see Götz Freiherr von PÖLNITZ, Jakob Fugger, Tübingen 1955, Vol. II, pp. 549s and ID., Anton Fugger, Tübingen 1958, Vol. I, p. 57. R. KLIER, Der Konkurrenzkampf zwischen dem böhmischen und dem idrianischen Quecksilber in der ersten Hälfte des 16. Jahrhunderts, in: Bohemia, VIII (1967), pp. 90–2.

there has been a complete loss of faith in the Höchstetter on the exchange, so that no-one will loan them money […].[13]

Nor were these sentiments confined to the French fair town. The Greshams at Antwerp, so Joachim Höchstetter later claimed,

declared him a bankrupt, which so defamed him that he was obliged to sell a mass of silver at five hundred pounds below its true value to recover his credit by paying ready money […].[14]

If this had been the case then it was money ill-spent, for that year the Höchstetter defaulted, exacerbating the already dangerous crisis. Throughout 1527/8 an acute financial stringency prevailed amongst the merchant community at Antwerp and interest rates rose to levels which Henry VIII's financial agent at Antwerp, John Hackett, regarded as totally prohibitive.[15] Yet whilst the baleful effects of the central European mining crisis of 1527/8 continued to affect commercial activity at the Frankfurt Fairs for many years to come[16], at Antwerp once again, after the immediate impact of the crisis was spent, interest rates fell back during the winter and spring of 1528.

---

13 EHRENBERG, Zeitalter der Fugger [Hildesheim 1963], I, p. 216. The exact dating of this letter is provided by KLIER, Konkurrenzkampf., p. 92, n. 57.

14 TNA, SP1/50 fo. 34r.

15 TNA, SP1/46 fo. 45r.

16 Until at least 1533 recovery taking place at sometime between then and 1545: A. DIETZ, Frankfurter Handelsgeschichte, 5 Vols., Frankfurt-on-the-Main, 1910–1925, Vol. I, pp. 50, 68, 88, 316–323 and 358.

CHAPTER FIVE

THE ANTWERP MONEY MARKET. THE CONTINUING CRISIS,
1526–1540

At Antwerp, for merchant and financier alike, after the trials and tribulations of 1527, the relatively calm conditions prevailing during the spring of 1528, in spite of the outbreak of war, must have provided balm for their troubled minds. They may not even have noticed that during the intervening months rising imperial indebtedness had caused a three point rise in the market for *finances*. If this was the case then the renewed Habsburg assault on the market that summer, which increased the outstanding debt to the financiers from 70,000 to 400,000 livres artois and pushed the total level of outstanding obligations once again over the million mark, must have provided a shattering experience. Moreover, this was only the beginning. During the next eighteen months the imperial bureaucracy deployed every trick in their repertoire until in December 1529 total indebtedness surpassed 1,200,000 livres artois. The market was reduced to a state of utter chaos. Panic swept the city and "an incredible *strettezza* developed on the Antwerp bourse, rates of interest on public loans rising to $21^{1/2}$ per cent through 1528 into early 1529."[1] As during earlier crises declining silver production, rising imperial borrowing and a collapse of confidence all combined to precipitate a severe short-term crisis on the Antwerp money market.

The 1520s thus ended as they had begun in the throws of an acute financial crisis induced by Habsburg intervention on the Antwerp money market. The intervening years had been traumatic ones for the denizens of that city's Bourse. 1521–3 had witnessed momentous changes therein. Having at the Cold Mart of 1521 discovered the key which would open up the riches of the Exchange, the Habsburgs had for the next three years struggled in difficult circumstances to control that market and tap its wealth for the purposes of war finance. By 1523/4 they had proved their mastery of the new game and were able to manipulate successfully the bill market to their own ends. In the process, however, they had effected a total change in conditions for dealers on the Bourse. In the aftermath of the crises, during the years from 1523 to 1526, dealers on both medium and short-term markets operated in a completely new environment. The withdrawal of big firms from the *finance* market, which had begun over the winter of 1522/3 remained a permanent feature of operations on the Bourse until the autumn of 1524 when the level of outstanding merchant loans amounted to no more than 100,000 livres artois and medium-term interest rates reached their lowest

---

1   H. VAN DER WEE, The Growth of the Antwerp Market and the European Economy. Fourteenth–Sixteenth Centuries, 3 Vols., The Hague 1963, II, p. 149.

point yet during the sixteenth century – twelve per cent. Nor did the situation significantly alter during the next eighteen months when financiers, attempting to hedge inflationary pressures, first stabilized and then increased rates. Redemption operations continued in spite of the changed circumstances, as *rentes* were contracted to replace those *finances* which fell due. By the summer of 1526, accordingly, merchant debts had all but been eliminated. That year accordingly seemingly witnessed the culmination of a trend established a quarter of a century and more before. Rising silver production, interrupted only 1509–12, 1514–5, 1519–23 and 1525, had afforded merchants, during the years to 1526, the opportunity to provide loans at a steadily falling rate of interest. With an increasing efficiency they managed to underwrite an ever growing Habsburg demand for medium-term (*finances* and *rentes*) loans on progressively cheaper terms. Only occasionally, in 1513, 1517 and 1521–3, were they found wanting, when the excessive demands of the Emperor cast an, as yet fleeting, shadow over the market. In 1526, however, such inroads into the market for medium-term finance were things of the past. Medium-term government debts, amounting to about 400,000 livres artois, bore interest charges of 26,000 livres artois or $6^{1/2}$ per cent, where only six years earlier a similar volume of indebtedness had born interest at 10 per cent. That curious euphoria born upon a flood of silver, which had characterised the medium-term money market during the late-1510s, had seemingly returned.

Not all borrowers, however, were so lucky. For those seeking commercial finance on the exchange the situation was very different. Until 1521 they too had shared in the benefits derived from falling interest rates, obtaining loans in that year at rates as low as one per cent per month, but the events of the Cold mart 1521/2 put an end to all that and ushered in a new age of dear money on the Antwerp exchanges. Henceforth Habsburg intervention on the exchange remained an endemic feature of imperial finance and the structure of interest rates, first imprinted on the market during that traumatic winter fair, remained intact. Thus although commercial paper shared in the fall in interest rates between 1523 and 1526, at the latter date the bill rate still stood some five points higher than at the beginning of the decade and takers were forced to pay a premium on the rate for government paper of similar term. Long after others had forgotten the traumatic events of 1521 and 1522–3, participants in the mercantile credit market retained an awareness of the baleful effects of Habsburg interventionism which resulted in a marked upward equilibration in rates as a result of the continuing Habsburg presence on the Exchange "crowding out" private borrowers, and which by 1526 had established a new and long-term pattern of dear commercial credit on the Antwerp Exchange.

No less significant, however, for the future of the Antwerp money market were the changes wrought therein during the second half of the decade. Superficially the events of 1525/6 – the monetary crisis – and 1527 – the first wave of Habsburg borrowing and the mining crisis – which have been described above and enhanced medium-term interest rates by some 6–7 points, were traumatic but transitory phenomena. In fact their significance was much deeper than this. 1527, indeed, marked the beginnings of a completely new phase in the evolution of the Antwerp money market. The ill-conceived and poorly timed assault on the market that spring marked the beginning of a phase of endemic Habsburg interference in the market for *finances*. No longer would the government even attempt, as it had in 1515 and 1523–6, to liquidate its outstanding debts to the bankers. Henceforth its level of indebtedness might fluctuate, largely in response to the requirements of war, but even during the intervening periods of peace indebtedness remained high.

Table 5.1 Medium-term interest rates on government loans. Antwerp 1504–1544 (per cent per annum)

PHASE 1 (1504–26)	Peak	Trough	PHASE II (1528–40)	Peak	Trough
1504–8		19.5	1528	21.5	
1513	29.0		1535		12.5
1514–5		19.25	1536	20.0	
1517	28.5		1539		12.0
1520		13.0	1540	19.5	
1522–3	20.75				
1524–6		12.0	PHASE III (1541–44)		
			1541		11.5
			1544	17.0	

In part the reasons were related to the effects of the second crisis of that year, occasioned by the collapse of Central European mining activity, during the autumn. The short-term downswing in silver production in 1527–9, in spite of a brief recovery, henceforth from 1528–1541, in the all important Alpenland-Thuringian-Slovak mining complex, turned into a protracted and severe decline in output (Figure 1.1). Increasing production to 1526 had favoured a long-term decline in interest rates and facilitated the financiers' dealings with the Habsburgs. Declining production now opened up the prospect of a reversal in these trends. With no incremental funding at their disposal they could not easily accommodate Habsburg demands. The market for medium-term finance at Antwerp was accordingly transformed. Financiers, with little incremental funding at their disposal each year, were cautious in venturing new loans. The Habsburgs, denied this source of credit, were forced to deploy limited current revenues to redeem existing debts. Each operated in extremely circumscribed conditions. Gone were the days of rapidly falling interest rates. For more than a decade after 1527/8 the Central European mining crisis left its imprint on the market, the restriction of the credit base enhancing the overall level of interest rates by half to three-quarters of a point and causing them to ossify in a mould cast during the tumultuous days of the 1520s. 1527 thus ushered in an era of dear money in the market for royal and imperial finance, with interest rates sufficiently high to strait-jacket imperial financial officials and to deflect marginal borrowers, like Henry VIII, away from Antwerp.[2]

---

2   During the negotiations of Hacket with the Welser and Höchstetter, which took place during 1526/7, Henry had shown himself to be very interest-rate conscious; see particularly BL Galba B

Only with the recovery of mining production in Thuringia after 1541 was a period of cheap money to be re-established in the market for medium-term government finance on the Antwerp Bourse.

On the Antwerp exchanges, however, the situation was very different. Not for the last time in 1527 the New World was called in to redress the balance of the Old. Thuringian silver might be in short supply on the markets of Central Europe but at Seville cart after cart trundled through the city loaded down with gold, recently trans-shipped from the Indies fleet tied up at the wharves of the Guadalquivir. From the late 1520s the supplies of gold from the New World steadily increased, the stream turning into a torrent with the opening of the Tehuantpec mines in the 1530s. So great indeed was the volume of gold entering the Spanish economy that it saturated the local markets at Seville, Valencia and New Castile, driving down the gold-silver exchange at a time when in the rest of Europe the price of gold was steadily rising and thereby creating forces entirely antithetical to Habsburg bullionist policies.[3] In principal Spain was a closed vase into which the enormous American fortune flowed and came to a halt but the closure was not perfect...[4] In 1527, 1548, 1559 and again in 1562 the Cortès complained about the seemingly never ending outflow of bullion from the realm. A constant, if illicit, stream of gold flowed to Genoa and Italy, Lyons and France.[5] One observer noted that in the years to 1556 an estimated five and a half million écu d'or had passed out of the realm[6], much finding its way into the coffers of the great Italian

---

IX, fo. 38. On Henry's reaction to the post-1544 conditions of "easy" money, see R. B. OUTHWAITE, The Trials of Foreign Borrowing: the English Crown and the Antwerp Money Market in the Mid-Sixteenth Century, in: Economic History Review, Second Series, XIX, 2 (1966), pp. 289–305.

3   F. BRAUDEL, La Méditerranée et le monde mediterranéen à l'epoch de Philippe II, 2 Vols., 2nd ed. Paris 1966, Vol. I, pp. 427–436; E. J. HAMILTON, American Treasure and the Price Revolution in Spain, 1501–1650, Cambridge, Mass. 1934. Unfortunately Prof. Hamilton's figures (Ibid., Table 3 p. 42) are only presented in the form of decennial averages, and it has proven necessary to recalculate the data in quinquennial terms for the 'twenties:

     1511–5   1,195,553   1531–40 1,754,774
     1516–20   993,196   1541–50 3,027,308
     1521–5   134,170   1551–60 5,169,830
     1526–30   976,130

     NOTE: all figures are of pesos' worth of gold at constant 1511–5 gold prices.
     For a more detailed chronology of shipments to Seville during the quinquennium 1526–30 see P. CHAUNU, Séville et l' Atlantique, 1504–1650, Paris 1959, Vol. VIII 2.1, p. 61 which reveals that the peak of the 1522/32 cycle of voyages occurred in 1527–9 for ships returning from the Indies. On the production of gold, see C. H. HARING, American Gold and Silver Production in the First Half of the Sixteenth Century, in: Quarterly Journal of Economic History, XXIX, 3 (1915) and on production at the important Tehuantpec mines during the 'thirties there is the excellent study of J.-P. BERTHE, Las minas de oro del Marqués del Valle en Tehuantpec, in: Historia Mexicana, VIII (1958), referred to in BRAUDEL, Méditerranée, I, p. 429, n. 3.

4   F. BRAUDEL / F. SPOONER, Prices in Europe from 1450–1750, in: E. E. RICH / C. H. WILSON (eds.), Cambridge Economic History of Europe, Vol. IV: The Economy of Expanding Europe in the Sixteenth and Seventeenth Centuries, Cambridge 1967, pp. 374–486, at p. 459.

5   BRAUDEL, Méditerranée, I, p. 433.

6   R. GASCON, Grand commerce et vie urbaine au XVIe siècle. Lyon et ses marchands, Paris 1971, Vol. I , pp. 118–9 on the balance of trade between Spain and Lyons; VAN DER WEE, Antwerp, II,

banking houses– like the Bonvisi, Grimaldi or Affaitadi – who were not slow to seize the opportunities, afforded by the difficulties which beset the southern German financiers, to utilise their newly acquired wealth to establish themselves at the centre of the Antwerp and London money markets.[7]

With the new found source of funding at its disposal the Antwerp market, accordingly, underwent a major structural transformation. Interest rates began to fall from late 1528 but because of the southerners' unwillingness to become as intimately embroiled in financing imperial ambitions as the Germans had been the direct effects were felt almost exclusively on the exchange and the fall was associated with a restructuring of interest rates on the Antwerp Bourse.[8]

When during the years 1528–41, in the market for medium-term government obligations, the Habsburgs, freed from the exigencies of war, set about liquidating their expensive burden of debts (in 1529/30 to 1531–4 and 1536–9) the problems facing them were formidable indeed. Initially, with the cessation of hostilities at the *Paix des Dames* (August 1529), their primary concern was with the excessively expensive structure of their existing debts – *finances* at 20.3/21.3 per cent per annum and outstanding bills at 9 per cent usance – and debt redemption was associated with a restructuring of their obligations. Bills were paid off as they fell due. The level of *finances* was drastically reduced, falling to half their former level by the winter fair of 1530/1, and the unpopular forced loans, which had reached almost 200,000 livres artois at the close of the war, were gradually eliminated. Yet this was only partly achieved by payments made out of current revenues. It also rested on the willingness of the towns to float new *rentes*. When, accordingly, the compliance of the urban elites was terminated in the spring of 1531 a short-term crisis was precipitated and the realities of their predicament were brought home to Habsburg officials. Henceforth no amount of financial juggling could make their task an easy one. Each subsequent redemption operation, in 1531/2–1533/4 and 1536–9, was to prove a long and arduous affair, as resources won by the most frugal financial management were cautiously deployed to eliminate existing loans. The massive operations of previous decades were no longer possible and the effects of the protracted and difficult manoeuvres, undertaken during the 1530s, were strictly limited. In both situations the authorities managed to eliminate the unpopular forced loans but at no time during that decade did the outstanding amount of *finances* fall below 200,000 livres artois, nor the level of total indebtedness decline below three quarters of a million.[9] Even in favourable situations

---

pp. 201–2; R. EHRENBERG, Das Zeitalter der Fugger. Geldkapital und Creditverkehr im 16. Jahrhundert, 2 Vols., Frankfurt-on-the-Main 1896, I , p.136.

7   E. ALBÈRI, Relazioni degli ambasciatori veneti al Senato, II , p.405 as quoted in BRAUDEL, Méditerranée, I , pp. 435–6.

8   On the Italian houses at Antwerp, see EHRENBERG, Zeitalter der Fugger, I, pp. 317–8, 321, 327–34. The English State Papers of the 1530s and 1540s abound with references to the financial relations of these houses with the English Crown (eg. L&P, Henry VIII, VI , Nr. 1603; XI , Nrs. 1419 and 1433; XIII [2], Nr. 924). In the light of this latter evidence, it is hard to accept the views put forward in G. D. RAMSEY, The Undoing of the Italian Mercantile Community in Sixteenth-century London, in: N. B. HARTE / K. G. PONTING (eds.), Textile History and Economic History. Essays in Honour of Miss Julia de Lacy Mann, Manchester 1973, pp. 26–7 in their entirety.

9   See present chapter below.

the government was operating in a financial strait-jacket and inevitably its ability to pay off old debts affected its ability to contract new ones when, as in 1536, times demanded. In such a situation it was confronted with strong resistance from its creditors which pushed up interest rates to the prohibitive levels of the 1520s.[10] The years 1528–41 were to prove difficult ones for those who visited the Antwerp Bourse in search of government finance. The market, constrained in its operations by an acute shortage of funds, was characterised by a rigid and high structure of interest rates, such as pervaded all the German-dominated money markets of Central Europe during these years.

Commercial loans on the other hand, in favourable circumstances, became relatively cheap in relation to those made to public bodies. Even as the market reeled under the shock of the Habsburg onslaught of 1528 those who resorted to the Italians on the Bourse to finance their commercial paper began to benefit from the new conditions. Interest rates on the exchanges might be higher than during the balmy days of 1524–6 but they were never to attain the disastrously high levels attained during the crisis of 1522–3. Moreover, whilst the price of government loans continued to fluctuate erratically about the high levels reached at the Whitsun fair 1528 for another eighteen months, on the exchange interest rates on commercial paper fell progressively over the same period. The short-medium term interest rate differential, established at the eventful winter fair some seven years earlier, was thus steadily, if slowly, whittled away. Rarely during these seven years from 1521–1528 had merchants enjoyed cheap commercial credit. As will be seen from table 5.2 "short-term" mercantile finance had cost at least 9.5 times the price of "medium-term" government loans on an annual basis in crisis conditions, 7.4 times in more normal circumstances – a situation which continued to prevail, in the aftermath of the Habsburg assault, at the Sinxen mart of 1528. As the Italian influence made itself felt, however, at the autumn fair of that year interest rates on commercial paper began to fall closing the pre-existing differential. A new age was dawning under Italian tutelage on the Antwerp exchanges.

---

10   See present chapter below.

Table 5.2: Intra-market Interest Rate Differentials on the Antwerp Bourse, 1521–41

(% p.a., bills at usance divided by % p.a., government loans at three months term)

PHASE I (−1521)	Peak	Trough	PHASE III CONT.	Peak	Trough
1521	1.3		1531		0.9
			1532	8.7	
PHASE II			1533		0.5
(1522–8)			1535–6	8.5–15.8	
1522–3	9.5–14		1539		1.3
1524–6		7.4	1540	10.8	
1528*	9.5		PHASE IV		
PHASE III			(1541–)		
(1528–40)			1541		4.8
1528–9	8.5				

* Sinxen mart only, Bamus mart included in phase III.

With the cessation of imperial intervention shortly after the *Paix des Dames* and the redemption of existing obligations over the winter of 1528/9 the potential of the new situation was fully realised. At the Cold mart of 1529/30 interest rates on bills of exchange declined rapidly, reaching 2.8 per cent usance and falling... With abundant funding at its disposal the market was finding a new equilibrium. Those attempting to float government loans might, even in the favourable circumstances prevailing during the years 1529–30, 1531/2 to 1533–4 and 1538–9, find themselves entrapped in the rigid mould of interest rates first cast in the 1520s. Those tendering commercial paper suffered no such fate. During those years bills of exchange found takers at incredibly low rates of interest, running at or near par with medium term finance. Under the influence of the Italians cheap money had returned to the exchanges in conditions reminiscent of the years before 1521.

In one respect, however, the situation was very different. From the late 1520s Italian involvement in the market took place against the background of a permanent and massive Habsburg presence which, in spite of their aloofness from imperial entanglements, could not but affect them either directly or indirectly. As has already been noted, the size of the government standing debt after 1527 necessitated imperial intervention in the market in the form of protracted redemption operations from 1529–34 and 1536–9. These programmes were not, however, always carried through with complete competence and when, as in 1531 and 1532, they were accompanied by what can only be described as criminal financial mismanagement even the Italians felt the shock which reverberated through the market. Worse were the effects of direct imperial intervention on the exchanges. At the tumultuous Cold mart of 1521/2 the Habsburgs had discovered the key to unlock the riches of the Exchange and for them a lesson once learnt was never forgotten. Inevitably therefore when pressed for money – as in 1536 and 1540 – they again resorted to the Exchange and interventionism became the order of the day. The defences of the Italians were breached and the sanctity of the exchanges violated – with disastrous results. Directly or indirectly, therefore, the

Habsburgs periodically (in 1531, 1532, 1536 and 1540) exercised their influence over the market for commercial credit. Nor were they alone in perpetuating the baleful effects of interventionism. The eruption of municipal rivalries in 1535 similarly caused a major disruption on the exchanges. Interventionism had become an endemic feature of the market, intermittently negating – in 1531, 1532, 1535–6 and 1540 – the beneficial effects of Italian funding.

The first such crisis came in the spring and summer of 1531 when as Stephen Vaughan noted,

> Brabant and Flanders...each offered to pay the Emperor 1,200,000 crowns of four shillings Flemish in six years, if he will require no money in gift in the interim, giving them as surety certain jewels that he has in Spain.

Denied this source of funding, upon which so much reliance had been placed during the preceding eighteen months, the Emperor accordingly made,

> many chevisances and shifts for money by means whereof riseth such interest that ten makes not seven [...].[11]

Vaughan's analysis of the situation, moreover, was completely accurate. The interest rate on government paper, which had fallen from 21.3 to 16.75 percent per annum during the course of the redemption operation of 1529–31, rose at the Sinxen mart to 18 per cent. Even more dramatic was the rise on the exchanges. The bill rate which had attained 3.6 per cent usance at the Easter fair of 1531 now shot up to 5 per cent – 71 per cent per annum. Certainly ten was not making seven. Crisis conditions once more prevailed but not for long. The imperial authorities, aghast at the effects of indiscriminate borrowing, retreated over the winter of that year resuming the redemption operation – but with a new awareness of their predicament.

1532 marked the beginnings of a realistic redemption policy which, with the effects of a marked monetary deflation, served ultimately to establish imperial finances on a firm footing. The path, was to be long and arduous and not without its trials and tribulations. Having resolved the problems of 1531, the redemption operation, initiated shortly after the *Paix des Dames*, was once more in the early part of 1532 in full swing. The amount of outstanding *finances* and *rentes* was steadily, if slowly, reduced. The bill market was calm, and with all impediments removed dealings took place at a mere one per cent usance. By Easter the unpopular forced interest-free loans had been all but eliminated, leaving only some 3,000 livres artois' worth of obligations outstanding. Once more all seemed right with the world.

By Whitsun 1532 the arduous struggle, begun some six months earlier, was clearly beginning to pay off. Yet at that mart a note of uncertainty entered the proceedings as rumours spread of new imperial exactions. On the exchanges of Lyon, Venice and London, accordingly interest rates began to rise until the Emperor's intentions became clear.[12] Then when the news broke, panic spread. Impatient perhaps at

---

11   L&P, Henry VIII, IV (3), No. 246

12   EHRENBERG, Zeitalter der Fugger, II, p. 79 and the evidence of the Tucher letters from Lyon at this time, as quoted in VAN DER WEE, Antwerp, II, p.201, n. 325.

the slow pace of debt redemption, the imperial authorities embarked on a course which can only be described as irresponsible. They decided once more to impose forced interest-free loans upon the merchant community. The amounts involved were negligible. They amounted to perhaps some 27,000 livres artois. The psychological impact of the measures, however, was not. Interest rates rose rapidly over the summer to 7.5 per cent at usance in July and 9.5 per cent in September at which time government loans could not be floated at less than 16.75 per cent per annum or some two points higher than the level of six months earlier. The crisis was, however, as ephemeral as that of a year before. As the imperial authorities, realising their mistake, retreated over the winter of 1532/3 normalcy returned and the redemption operations were resumed with a renewed vigour. By the end of 1532 the events of that autumn, like those of 1531, were banished from men's minds. They appeared as little more than passing distractions, momentarily diverting attention from the unfolding of a grand design.

During the course of 1532/3 the solid achievements deriving from the redemption operations, carried through with such care and diligence over the years 1529–34, were only too clear for men to see. The government, having reduced its medium-term debts to the financiers to below 200,000 livres artois, could now raise loans at rates which would have been inconceivable a few years before. Unfortunately so effective was the redemption operation that no such loans were floated in 1533, and, accordingly, the exact level of medium-term interest rates will probably for ever remain unknown. No such barrier, however, impedes our perceptions of the exchanges. Benefiting fully from the effects of Italian funding and undisturbed by imperial intervention, the market for commercial paper was operating at the Bamus mart 1533 about a previously unheard of level – half a per cent *usance*. For the manipulators of imperial finance self-congratulations were perhaps in order, as a combination of fiscal policies and favourable monetary circumstances paved the way for the re-establishment of Habsburg credit on the Antwerp Bourse. Just how changed the situation was, now was to be revealed. Over the winter of 1533/4 the authorities began testing the market, relentlessly probing to find how far they could exploit the newly established confidence in imperial solvency. Within six brief months they managed to double the volume of their outstanding debts owing to the financiers, the final element being added on the eve of Easter 1534 as an astonished John Coke explained to Cromwell, writing that,

> notwithstanding the mountains of gold found lately by the imagination of the Spaniards the Emperor has not forsaken his old practice, for about eight days ago (i.e. on Saturday 28th March) a finance or shift of £10,000 was made for him here in Antwerp […].[13]

Yet with the volume of outstanding *finances* at half a million livres artois and total indebtedness hovering about the million mark, the financiers were prepared to underwrite this loan at 13.5 per cent – a high but not exorbitant rate. The Habsburgs had found the new market equilibrium they sought. Henceforth, for the next two years (Easter 1534–6) both imperial indebtedness and interest rates fluctuated, within a narrow range of variance, about the level established at the beginning of 1534. Within the

---

13   L&P, Henry VIII, VII , Nr. 440.

constraints imposed on the medium-term money market in 1527, the Habsburgs were benefiting from the fruits of their endeavours, maintaining a high level of public debt at moderate rates of interest. Nor were the effects of the redemption operation confined to the market for government loans. On the exchanges dealers, operating solely on the basis of market forces, set their rates during 1534 at about 1.35 per cent usance affording merchants the benefits of cheap credit, at least until the end of the year.

Then at the Cold mart of 1534/5 things turned for the worst. The circumstances are perhaps best described by a contemporary, who was intimately involved in the events of that winter, who laid the blame on

> the new rule at Antwerp that payments are retarded for three months after the time fixed. So that if a merchant sell at the Sinxen mart at Whitsuntide to be paid at the Bamus mart at Michaelmas he does not get his money until after Christmas. By the time they get to Bergen the Cold mart has begun and because of the short time of the freedom they must return to Antwerp in a fortnight to three weeks [...].

The motivation was clear, for the merchants could

> not spend more than six weeks at both (of the Bergen-op-Zoom) marts, living all the rest of the year at Antwerp to the great decay of one and strength of the other [...].[14]

Yet, aimed to serve the ends of inter-municipal rivalry, the act was to have far reaching consequences. Merchants, forced to lengthen the period of their capital turnover, suffered acute cash flow problems and were forced off the exchange, creating a situation where "ready" money was "scant" and hawkers of bills found few takers.[15] The new circumstances were reflected, accordingly, in high interest rates as the market equilibrated markedly upwards to 6.2 per cent usance where it would remain, save for a brief interruption, throughout the next eighteen months. Stability thus continued to characterise the market after the basic structural re-alignment of interest rates at the Cold mart of 1534/5, but the era of cheap money on the exchange had been brought to a close. For those tendering bills of exchange on the Bourse in 1535 crisis conditions had returned. Yet the events of that year, trying as they might be, would soon seem worthy of only passing note. The denizens of the Bourse had a much greater shock in store.

For those who, during early 1536, followed carefully the business contracted on the Bourse there may have been some precognition of what was to come for in February at the time of the Cold mart the Emperor had taken up large sums on the exchange for transmission to Genoa. Moreover, his feelings of urgency may have been sensed for the operation was bungled. Intervention on the 18th February coincided with heavy borrowing by merchants who were buying wares for the next fair at Frankfurt-on-the-Main, and interest rates, which for a year had remained stable at 6.2–6.3 per cent usance, rose rapidly for a few days (viz. 18–25th February 1536), before once

---

14   BL. Galba B. X, fo. 49.
15   L&P, Henry VIII, VIII , Nr. 197–8.

again falling back to their old level.[16] Few, however, seem to have taken the hint for through the remainder of the winter fair and the ensuing Easter mart rates remained "low." Even the news in April that the Emperor had gone to war passed unnoticed for it was rumoured that "five millions in gold" were "on their way to the Emperor from the New World" and this surely would be sufficient to satisfy his martial ambitions and cover a myriad of imperial indiscretions.[17] Within four months, however, they thought otherwise and probably cursed their lack of foresight. What contemporaries had previously missed, by August they had become only too painfully aware of. At that time the arrival of the news from Seville concerning "the arrival of three ships from Peru with a great substance of gold and silver" had become of but passing interest for it was believed that

> the Emperor's charges are such that it is barely enough to continue the war" so that "great efforts were made to get money for him at twenty per hundred annually" even though "no money was to be had, and what there was, was too little for the Emperor.[18]

The plundering had begun and at the Sinxen mart 1536 all hell broke loose. For the next six months Habsburg pressure was unrelenting. During that fair the volume of new loans from the financiers pushed the level of outstanding debt owing to them ever upwards until it surpassed all previous high points and total debts outstanding even began to approach the two million livres level. Interest rates, accordingly, rose from fifteen to eighteen and finally, as Lok noted, to twenty per cent per annum, but even at that price such money as was available was "too little for the Emperor." The financiers, thus, pushed him over onto the Exchange where rates correspondingly began to rise. If from the 9th–16th August observers had been shocked at the Emperor's inability to raise money on medium-term loans at below twenty per cent per annum, they must now have been appalled as events unfolded. On the 17th August the prevailing bill market rate was 9.8 per cent at usance and two month bills found acceptance at 11.3 per cent (5.5 per cent per month). By the following Monday (21st August), however, the market had shortened to usance and the rate was rising. Having risen to 10.7 per cent on that day, the usance rate continued ever upwards until, almost a fortnight later on 2nd September it stood at 12.6 per cent. Yet even this rate, far beyond any level previously attained, could not choke off imperial demand and, accordingly, creditors, fearful of their money, once again shortened the term at which they would lend. On the Wednesday before Michaelmas money could only be had at sight and then solely if the borrower would pay twelve per cent (40.5 per cent per month). The finely wrought market balance, tended with so much care until June 1536, had been,

---

16 L&P, Henry VIII, X , Nr. 319. This letter sent on the 18th February 1536 by Christoper Mont at Antwerp to Cromwell is very revealing on the relationship between the Antwerp and Frankfurt financial markets at this time. For the reasons given above, as well as for the sake of secrecy, he does not advise sending money to Central Europe via the Greshams at Antwerp or indeed via the Leipzig fair. Rather he suggested that moneys should be sent through the Köln merchants at the Steelyard to be paid at the next Frankfurt fair, for if these merchants were allowed to use the money until then the interest would be small.

17 L&P, Henry VIII, X, Nr. 442 and 565.

18 L&P, Henry VIII, XI, Nr. 254 and 314.

within three brief months destroyed. The edifice of imperial credit, built with such skill during the years 1529–34, lay in ruins.

The immediate problems that winter thus were formidable. Lacking access to even short-term credit at the Cold mart of 1536/7, the Regent was forced to seek sources of current revenue to continue the war, and during the opening weeks of the new year the Council was locked in lengthy discussions over the current fiscal situation. The results of their deliberations were, however, disappointing for they were unable to obtain

> any grant but in Brabant, who have agreed to pay for every chimney a carolus gulden which equals 2s 6d sterling. They hope Holland and Zealand will pay after the same rate. Flanders, however, will give no money, but would rather find men of war and pay them monthly.[19]

The estates were clearly resistant, as also were the English when an attempt was made to tax the profits of neutrality, a five per cent tax being levied on the English carrying trade between the belligerent nations.[20] During the prelude to the spring campaigning season the imperial authorities in the Netherlands thus found themselves in extremely straitened circumstances. Times were bad and they grasped at every straw that fortune threw to them.[21] Yet, at least for the moment, the tensions inherent in mounting an actual field campaign were absent and the authorities, with a resolution forged in the turmoil of the previous autumn's crisis, now set about using the limited funds available to restore their credit by resuming the redemption operation which had been suspended since the previous summer. Over the winter of 1536/7 they restricted new borrowing and assiduously paid off existing debts as they fell due – with dramatic effect. Rates on medium-term government paper, which had edged down to 17 per cent during the Cold mart, fell precipitously to $14^{3/4}$ per cent at Easter 1537. Even more spectacular was the decline in interest rates on commercial bills. Such paper, only obtainable on ten-day term at a rate of twelve per cent during the previous autumn, was available at Easter 1537 on three-month term at a monthly interest rate of only 3.3 per cent. On the eve of the 1537 campaigning season therefore money was once again relatively cheap. Nor were Mary and her advisers prepared to be deflected from their course by the resumption of hostilities during the spring and summer of 1537. Government loans continued to be paid off. At first the process was a slow one but following the Sinxen mart it gathered such momentum that by the autumn total indebtedness was once more at the level of a million livres artois. As a result interest rates on such paper, after rising to 16 per cent at Whitsun in anticipation of new calls being made on the market, fell to a new low of $13^{1/4}$ per cent in the autumn. Similarly in the bill market, whilst there was a brief sympathetic enhancement of rates at the Sinxen mart, by the autumn money could be obtained at three- or four-months term for 2.3–2.5 per cent per month. Viewed in terms of Habsburg credit management, 1537 had been a very successful year. The Regent, by re-instigating the redemption operations which had been suspended in late 1536, had managed to reduce government indebtedness and cause a corresponding fall in interest rates on government paper. By her policy of

---

19   L&P, Henry VIII, XII (1), Nr. 60.

20   Ibid.

21   L&P, Henry VIII, XII (1), Nr. 364.

restoring Italian tutelage in the bill market, moreover, she allowed the latter group to once more re-establish conditions of cheap money on the exchanges, much to the relief of merchants venturing to the autumn fair. Yet what was remarkable about these operations was not only their success but that they had been carried through in conditions of open Valois-Habsburg hostilities. From the spring of 1537 campaigning had been resumed and military action undertaken without government calls being made on either medium- or short-term money markets. That this could be accomplished in part resided in the inactivity of the French king. Given his acute shortage of funds, of which there was much talk at court, and the wide range of territories for him to defend, Francis was quite incapable of making any firm commitment of his forces. Thus having initially decided on a campaign against Savoy and collected some 12,000 Italians in Piedmont to undertake the venture, he failed to send necessary reserves of lance-knights to initiate the action for fear of leaving undefended his northern frontiers. Nor were these fears unfounded, but when the Habsburgs moved in May on St Pol the lance-knights he had withheld proved an insufficient force to mount a counter-offensive and the French king satisfied himself with merely fortifying the town. Accordingly, much to the surprise of an emissary at his court, June found "the French king [...] hunting at Fontainbleau as though there was no war."[22] Yet such blatant inaction, as the Habsburgs were to find, was very much a double-edged weapon. It certainly allowed them to undertake an easy and low-cost offensive. Indeed June saw not only St Pol fall to their forces but also Monstreul, whilst seige was laid to Terrouane. But by being unable to bring the French king to battle the prospect of a long campaign soon loomed large in the minds of the Burgundian commanders and their political masters as did the possibility that the money for such a campaign would fail. By committing herself to the restoration of Habsburg credit on the Antwerp market through the re-instigation of redemption operations, Mary had denied herself access to public sources of funding and had commenced the offensive secure only in the sums which could be raised on the security of such of her notables as the Cardinal of Liège or d'Arschot – and such funds were strictly limited. Accordingly, even as the French king besported himself at Fontainebleau, she was praying that he would join battle "before money fails" and feared great confusion arising from this cause if he did not come.[23] Yet Francis maintained his masterly inactivity and accordingly, fearful that her army would be thrown into disarray, Mary was forced to desist. Military activity in the North-west thus ground to a halt and for the rest of the summer, as the protagonists vied to gain advantage in the negotiations preparatory to the inevitable truce, martial pursuits were confined to maritime actions in which privateering (thinly disguised piracy) was to play a major role. When the ten-month truce was finally signed at the end of July even these actions gradually petered out.

August 1537 thus saw an end of martial activity in the north-western theatre of war but in terms of Habsburg financial policies this was of but passing interest. In respect to these policies the die had been cast long before. In committing herself the previous winter to a thorough-going redemption operation, Mary had set out on a

---

22   BL. Harl. MS. 6989, fo. 74.

23   K LANZ, Correspondenz des Kaisers Karl V, Aus dem königlichen Archiv und der 'Bibliothèque de Bourgogne' zu Brüssel, 3 Vols., Leipzig 1844–1846, Vol. II, p.76.

course of action from which she could not be turned. As has been suggested, even as
the summer offensive ground to a halt she had increased the tempo of her financial
operations, bringing total Habsburg indebtedness down to the million livres mark by
the Bamus mart. During the subsequent winter, accordingly, she merely continued
along a long-established path, so that before the close of the 1537/8 Cold mart Habsburg debts amounted to little more than 900,000 livres artois and interest rates in the
market for government paper settled at about 12 per cent per annum. Subsequently, as
the temporary truce drew to its close and both the French and Burgundians again prepared for war, rates in both the medium- and short-term money markets again edged
upward but with the meeting of Charles and Francis at Nice in June 1538 and the extension and prolongation of the truce – for another TEN YEARS – such preparations
were abandoned and for the Habsburgs at least the redemption operation recom-
menced. Henceforth throughout the remainder of 1538 and the whole of 1539 existing
government loans were paid off, reducing total indebtedness to some 700,000 livres
artois and interest rates on such paper falling to 12 per cent once again. Even more
spectacular were the effects of Habsburg withdrawal from the short-term bill market.
Here, with the market again restored to Italian tutelage, rates fell precipitously to a
mere half a per cent usance in May 1539. Within the mould of money market interest
rates first cast in 1527, Mary of Hungary had learnt to play the game of financial management well and with an exemplary self-discipline she had carried through during the
years 1536–9 an effective redemption operation which once more, after the elimination of the monetary disorders which had plagued the market before the reform of
May 1539[24], allowed government loans to be floated at a mere 12 per cent and permitted merchants to find acceptance for their bills at a rate of only a half a per cent
usance. In extremely difficult circumstances she had in 1539 created conditions of
cheap money on the Antwerp Bourse, conditions which had been singularly absent in
that institution since the eventful days of 1527.

   For some forty years (ca.1500–1540) successive generations of merchants had
diligently watched every movement of interest rates on the Antwerp Bourse, carefully
recording the quotations and diligently gathering any news of wars, bankruptcy or
monetary disorder which might upset the delicate balance of rates at that institution.
Nor during most of the first two decades of the new century were they disappointed at
the news they received. For some twenty years interest rates on short-term commercial
and medium-term government debt steadily fell making the city on the Scheldt the
cheapest financial centre in Europe from whence monies could be transferred the
length and breadth of the continent at minimal cost (chapter 1). Only occasionally did
government intervention in the market – in 1513, 1517(1518/9) and 1521 – disrupt
this trend. On these occasions government borrowing, by increasing interest rates on
finances and causing a shift of funds from short- to medium-term loans, brought a
sympathetic response in the bill market thereby precipitating a general enhancement
of rates. Such phenomena were, however, for the moment ephemeral and, in spite of

---

24   From Whitsun 1538–9 merchants and financiers had hedged inflationary pressures resulting from a
     marked rise in gold prices by briefly increasing interest rates on both government and commercial
     paper, but with the elimination of these pressures by the monetary reform of the 8th May 1539
     market rates once more resumed their downward course.

closing intra-market differentials, they in no way disturbed that *relative* cheapness of commercial credit which characterised the market.

Then at the Cold Mart of 1521 the Habsburgs discovered the key which would open up the riches of the Exchange and for the next three years they had struggled in difficult circumstances to control that market and tap its wealth for the purposes of war finance (chapter 2). By 1523/4 they had proved their mastery of the new game and were able to manipulate successfully the bill market to their own ends. In the process, however, they had effected a total change in conditions for dealers in commercial paper as, against a background of a protracted if erratic decline in medium-term interest rates, the bill rate was enhanced. Consistently at a discount in relation to government skrip of similar term before 1521, after that date it commanded a premium. The Antwerp mercantile credit market was thus from 1521 transformed as it was subjected to a marked upward equilibration in rates as a result of a continuing Habsburg presence on the Exchange "crowding out" private borrowers.

This long-term enhancement in the level of bill rates was reinforced from 1527/8, moreover, as the long-term effects of the Central European mining crisis made themselves felt on the Antwerp market (chapter 4). The mining crisis marked the end of that production-cycle upswing of 1492–1526 which had raised the Thuringian-Slovak-Alpenland mining complex to a position of central importance amongst European precious metal producers. For some thirty years silver production from this mining complex had expanded rapidly, an expansion only briefly interrupted in 1509–12, 1514–5, 1519–22 and 1525 before it reached a peak in 1526/7. A seemingly never ending flood of the precious metals had flowed from the mines into the hands of the great South German merchant-financiers, continually replenishing their cash reserves, allowing them to expand the credit base of their operations and permitting them to proffer loans on the Antwerp market at a steadily falling rate of interest. In 1527/8 this process came to an end. Production in the previously important mining complex began to decline relentlessly, subsequent crises in 1530/1 and 1536–8 pushing output in existing production centres to lower and lower levels before the production-cycle drew to a close in the acute crisis of 1541–2. The liquidity of the German houses was compromised. All seemed set for a stabilization if not an enhancement in interest rates. Yet not for the last time the New World was now called in to redress the balance of the Old. As medium-term loan rates proffered by the Germans stabilized, a flood of Central and South American specie allowed a group of Sevillian-Italian merchant-financiers to guide the Antwerp bill market once more into an epoch of cheap money. The trend of falling interest rates thus continued, but the fiscal crisis of April 1527–March 1529 coupled with the mining crisis of September 1527/8, shattered the old symbiotic relationship between Antwerp and Frankfurt-on-the-Main, which had placed the South German houses at the centre of a European-wide financial network. In its place a new relationship arose, based on American gold rather than Central European silver which linking Antwerp to the ascendant star of Medina del Campo via the intermediary of Luccese and Genoese finance houses. Yet whilst under Italian tutelage the Antwerp bill market from 1528 thus once more experienced the benefits of cheap commercial credit the new financiers were no more than their German predecessors able to avoid imperial entanglements which (in 1528, 1532 and 1533/4, 1535/6 and 1538–40) negated their endeavours. From 1521, as a result of both imperial inter-

ventionism and mining disorders, Antwerp had ceased to be a source of cheap commercial credits.

As a result of the monetary crisis of 1525–6 and the Netherlands monetary reform
of the winter of 1526/7 (chapter 3), moreover, its sphere of financial influence had
become more spatially restricted. From that time Antwerp was displaced from its position of supremacy in the hierarchy of financial centres. Henceforth, behind a barrier of
bi-metallic premiums, it was restricted to servicing the financial requirements of the
trades to Spain and Italy and even in this capacity, because of Habsburg intervention
in the money market and the effects of the central European mining, its services did
not come cheap. In these circumstances merchants, accordingly, began to avoid the
city and its Exchange: they took new routes to their markets and after selling their
wares, put out their money at financial centres elsewhere. In such a manner, during
successive Antwerp crises London dealers experienced the availability of cheap
money, intermittent activity by alien merchants operating in Lombard Street before
1541 thereafter giving way to a permanent presence. Continuing Habsburg intervention on the Antwerp Exchange following the first assaults in 1521 and 1522–3, by
"crowding out" private borrowers and enhancing bill rates, had made the city an expensive source of commercial credit and had resulted in a financial diaspora from
which other centres, such as London, now benefited.

PART II

FINANCIAL AND MONETARY SYSTEMS: LONDON

CHAPTER SIX

LONDON 1528: FROM PAROCHIAL BACKWATER TO INTERNATIONAL FINANCIAL CENTRE

Information concerning conditions in the London bill market during the opening decades of the sixteenth century is almost entirely derived from a very scanty collection of accounts and commercial correspondence recording exchange transactions. Limited as this information is, however, it does reveal a market which down to the twenties at least was not markedly dissimilar to that described in the Cely letters some fifty years earlier.[1] It continued to engross both the mercantile balances of the London community and the funds made available, through an elaborate sales-credit network, by a multitude of petty merchants, manufacturers, yeomen and graziers.[2] In normal circumstances exporters of wool, cloth or metals were able to finance their trade on the basis of the credit extended to them by their suppliers, only finally settling their outstanding debts after they had disposed of their wares and remitted the proceeds on the exchange to England. Whilst they were thus inveterate users of the Antwerp-London exchange such was not the case with regard to reciprocal dealings at London on Antwerp. Their use of these facilities, available from Italian houses operating in Lombard Street, was

---

1   H. E. MALDEN (ed.), The Cely Letters, London: Camden Society, 3rd Series, I, 1900; A. HANHAM (ed.), The Cely Letters 1472–1488, London 1975, and ID., The Celys and their World. An English Merchant Family of the Fifteenth Century, Cambridge 1985, particularly part II, pp. 109–254. It should be noted that the terms of credit noted by E. POWER, The Wool Trade in the Fifteenth Century, in: Id. / M. M. POSTAN (eds.), Studies in English Trade in the Fifteenth Century, London 1933, pp.56–7, are somewhat abnormally generous, due to the contemporary depression in the export trade.

2   The statements concerning the changes in terms of sales-credits referred to here and in subsequent pages, are based on an analysis of some 350 agreements entered into by clothiers (predominantly from Suffolk, Kent and Wiltshire) during the period 1514–1538 and recorded in the account books of Thomas Howell (preserved in the muniments of the Draper s Company) and Sir Thomas Kitson (Cambridge University Library, Hengrave Hall MSS, 78/2). This material, together with additional data for the period 1538–1552 derived from the account books of Thomas Gresham (preserved in the muniments of the Mercer's Company), and John Smythe (preserved at the Bristol Record Office amongst the Ashton Court MSS., AC/B63 and published as J. VANES [ed.], The Ledger of John Smythe 1538–1550, London 1974]) was extracted, manipulated and analysed using the new RAPPORT-computer data-base system developed during 1982–5 and upgraded and converted to an INGRES-data base system in 1990–1993 with the financial assistance of the ESRC (Project HR 8205–1, B–0023002–1 and Project R 000 23 2851).

confined to emergencies which created delays in their normal pattern of operations. The London bill market was accordingly characterised by a certain thinness and volatility whilst the credit system as a whole was both narrow and parochial, remaining isolated from those forces which during the years 1492–1526 were transforming Antwerp into the financial metropolis of the West.[3] In the movement of interest rates on the "London Exchanges"[4] there is no hint of the great widening of the continental European credit base which had driven down rates at Antwerp, nor indeed is there any sign of the periodic crises which beset the latter structure.[5] It was called upon only to meet the needs of the indigenous mercantile community. The course of trade, not the ambitions of Emperors, provided the *leitmotif* which ran through all dealings therein. Each upswing in trade stimulated the demand for loans and increased interest rates, each downswing resulted in a fall, in which respects the fluctuations moved inversely to those prevailing at Antwerp. Yet even as an instrument of merchants it was an expensive and unresponsive one. Under conditions of unimpeded commercial intercourse the supply of funds forthcoming for mercantile finance at London was sufficiently restricted down to the 'twenties to ensure that the prevailing rate of interest was some six or seven points above that reigning at Antwerp.

Unwieldy and expensive, this structure was, during 1525/6, subjected to marked pressures. Not for the first time during the 'twenties a new pattern of demand, conditioned by the unpredictable vagaries of royal finance, was superimposed upon that of the merchant community.[6] In 1525/6 Henry's forced loans broke on a totally unprepared money market.[7] Bewildered Suffolk clothiers, shorn of their working capital, stoically reported to their workmen that, "our goods have been taken from us", and accordingly "we are unable to set you to work [...]."[8] Production fell, unemployment rose and clothiers, lacking the funds to extend normal trade credits, had to demand cash from their customers on delivery of their wares. Indeed the plight of some East Anglian manufacturers was so parlous that they were forced to put up their stock in

---

3   M. M. POSTAN, Credit in Medieval Trade, in: Economic History Review, First Series, I, 2 (1928), reprinted in E. M. CARUS-WILSON (ed.), Essays in Economic History, London 1954, Vol. I, pp. 61–87, contains much that is relevant to a description of the London money market during the opening decades of the sixteenth century. On the contemporary changes taking place at Antwerp see I. BLANCHARD, International Capital Markets and their Users, in: ID. et al. (eds.), Industry and Finance in Early Modern History. Essays presented to George Hammersley on the occasion of his 74th Birthday, Stuttgart 1992, pp. 13–25.

4   On the informal structure of the early sixteenth-century London money market see A. P. TRAVERS, The Practice of Usury in Mid-Sixteenth Century England, Unpubl. University of Edinburgh Ph.D Thesis, Edinburgh 1975, pp.177–197.

5   See ch. 1 above.

6   In 1522 the crown had attempted to raise two large loans via the Corporation of London; R. R. SHARPE, London and the Kingdom, 3 Vols., London 1894, as quoted in R. B. OUTHWAITE, The Trials of Foreign Borrowing: the English Crown and the Antwerp Money Market in the Mid-Sixteenth Century, in: Economic History Review, Second Series, XIX, 2 (1966), p. 291, whilst in 1523 a lay and clerical subsidy of unprecedented size had been levied. Thereafter royal demands upon the market remained modest, being limited to the raising of the subsidies of 1524/5, until the commissioners went to work in March 1525.

7   J. J. SCARISBRICK, Henry VIII, London 1971, pp. 185–8.

8   E. HALL, Chronicle, London 1809, p. 699.

hand as "gauges" for urgently needed loans.[9] As the volume of sales-credits con-tracted, from March 1525 to December 1526, and exporters were tipped over onto the exchange the crisis spread to the London market which was subject to the same depre-dations. Anger rose to white heat amongst the merchant community and was vented, both on the streets and behind closed doors, against all who wished to appease the crown over the question of the loans.[10] Confidence was shattered, money was tight and accordingly interest rates rose, reaching twelve per cent usance at the height of the disturbances occasioned by the loans. Henry's subsequent retreat might have gone some way to restoring confidence but his singular unwillingness to repay the moneys already raised did nothing to relieve the financial stringency.[11] When, therefore, a new crisis broke on the market in the summer of 1526 it was thrown into utter turmoil.

The origins of the crisis which broke on the London market during the summer of 1526 may be traced back to at least the beginning of the previous year when the mar-ket first felt the impact of monetary instability occasioned by a rise in the price of gold.[12] From June 1526, however, the situation began to rapidly deteriorate, causing merchants like Thomas Howell, to abandon credit dealings and to hold his assets in either coin or plate.[13] Nor did attempts at stabilization in August alleviate the situa-tion, indeed, the uncertainty occasioned by the intervention of the State, according to one anonymous observer, resulted in "controversies in the City of London amongst the merchants" and a virtual suspension of credit dealings.[14] Credit at this time was extremely tight and interest rates rose sharply, reaching 16.5 per cent usance during the third week of November and remaining high until the implementation of the Neth-erlands monetary reform on the 10th December paved the way for a final restoration of the English monetary and credit systems.[15]

Thereafter, over the winter of 1526/7 conditions in the bill market eased but as long as the English sales-credit system remained paralysed it seemed probable that the fall in London bill rates would not be great. Fortunate it was then for the London mer-chant community when, during the second week of the first buying for the Cold Mart

---

9   See for example, Draper's Company, Howell's Ledger, fo. 48.

10   E. HALL, Chronicle, London 1809, p. 699.

11   Howell for instance had not been repaid either the loan of 1522 or that of 1525 at the time of his death in 1528 (Ledger..., fo.86), whilst in April 1528 requests for repayment of the loans became frequent from those impoverished by the famine (L&P., Henry VIII, IV [2], Nr. 4173, 4188.)

12   Ch. 3 above.

13   Howell's Ledger, fos.36-7.

14   TNA, SP1/55, fo. 184.

15   See ch. 3 above for a full discussion of the events of June–December 1526 occasioned by condi-tions of monetary instability at Antwerp.

of 1526/7[16] the sales-credit system began to operate normally once more, even if its operations were constrained within a narrower range of fluctuations than had been the case during the early 1520s due to shortages of cash amongst clothiers induced by the exactions of a rapacious king.[17] Credit availability to exporters once more increased and as they withdrew from the bill market rates therein also declined.[18] Even before the Cold Mart of 1526/7 drew to its close normality had returned to the London market and throughout the following year each trade downswing caused clothiers to lengthen credit to their customers, each upswing resulting in its restriction whilst the movement of interest rates on the exchange resumed its familiar trade-related pattern. Such conditions, however, were not to last long, for the sales-credit system, already operating poorly since the closing stages of the 1527/8 Cold Mart, collapsed once more in the last week of March 1528. The crown, amidst the turmoil occasioned by the famine of 1527/8, in forcing clothiers to retain their workforces under conditions of falling demand for their products precipitated acute internal cash flow problems in many enterprises, resulting once more in a restriction of trade credits.[19]

---

16 From an analysis of prices (see figure 6.1), derived from the same contracts entered into by clothiers at Blackwell Hall referred to above, certain distinctive patterns emerged relating price movements to buying patterns in preparation for the Netherlands fairs. Following an inter-fair slump in prices the first buying began some considerable time before the next fair. Thereafter for some six weeks prices settled down at a high level before the second buying began, normally about three weeks before the opening of the fair.

	First buying	Second buying	Official opening of Fair
Paasche Mart	2nd week February	4th week March	3rd week April
Sinxen Mart	...	2nd week May	2nd week June
Bamus Mart	...	3rd week August	3rd week September.

    With regards to the Cold Mart, the official opening date was largely irrelevant, "because of bad weather and the late arrival of the […] English, the Cold Mart lasted unofficially through January into February […]." F. EDLER, The Van der Molen, Commission Merchants of Antwerp: Trade with Italy, 1538–44, in: Medieval and Historiographical Essays in Honour of James Westfall Thompson, Chicago 1938, pp. 113–4. It is in relation to this unofficial fair that buying patterns developed: Cold Mart   3rd week November   4th week January, the departure of the fleet for the mart following immediately thereafter.

17 It could be that the two phenomena were interconnected, the toughness in the sales-credit system, which persisted throughout the period from March/April 1525, caused by Henry's depredations, being aggravated by a flight into cash amongst the cloth making fraternity during June–December 1526, similar to that which occurred in London. Certainly the conditions of monetary instability prevailing at that time as gold prices rocketed up would do nothing to encourage them to become creditors.

18 Real interest rates, related to the demand for commercial credit, independent of the sums needed to outbid specie exporters fell from 9 per cent usance in November–December 1526 to 8.66 per cent in the first week of January 1527.

19 See ch. 13 below.

Figure 6.1: Intra-annual "Buyings" for the Low Countries Fairs, 1530–4

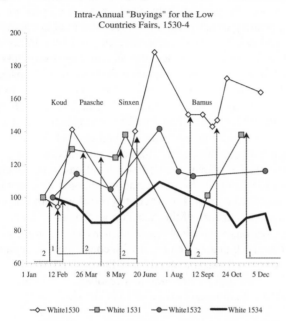

Intra-Annual "Buyings" for the Low
Countries Fairs, 1530-4

Koud   Paasche   Sinxen   Bamus

1 Jan   12 Feb   26 Mar   8 May   20 June   1 Aug   12 Sept   24 Oct   5 Dec

—◇— White1530   —■— White 1531   —●— White1532   ▬▬ White 1534

Note the effects of the "buyings" for the "direct" trades in the summers of 1530, 1532 and 1534

In March 1528 royal intervention thus once more had precipitated an acute short-term crisis in English credit systems but on this occasion conjunctural forces combined with structural ones, symbolised by the famine, to effect a once and for all change in the sales-credit element of the financial system. Henceforth, as that pattern of population growth, which had revealed the inadequacies of the agrarian regime in the famine of 1527/8, undermined the prosperity of the rural population the latter found itself unable to extend financial facilities to its customers and was forced to restrict the granting of sales-credits. Slowly yet relentlessly therefore from 1528 the sales-credit system contracted, until by the 1540s goods were only available from the peasant sector of the economy for cash. All thus seemed set in 1528 for another major dislocation in the London bill market and on this occasion it promised to be one which would pose irresolvable problems for the London financial community.

Yet at the very point in 1528 when the English credit system seemed threatened with collapse a fresh injection of funds, provided as at Antwerp by the Italian banking houses, lessened the pressure and dissipated the tensions.[20] Henceforth the market was transformed and all who visited the porch of St Pauls or Temple Garden in search of commercial loans benefited from the presence of these aliens. The volume of funds available to the market increased, providing it with a previously unknown flexibility in dealing with the needs of both merchant and king.[21] The old passive role of the

---

20   See ch. 5 above.

21   Whilst the Italians limited their involvement in royal and imperial finance it would be hard in the light of the evidence provided by the English State Papers (e. g., L&P, Henry VIII, VI, No. 1603;

London financial community, which in earlier years had merely responded to exogenously determined trade fluctuations, disappeared.[22] In its place the Anglo-Italian financial elite created for itself a positive role, providing a direct stimulus to commercial activity. Each supply-induced downswing in interest rates (in 1528, 1532 and
1533/4, 1535/6 and 1538-40) which occurred when the Italian merchant-bankers
abandoned their cloth export and failed to buy "the commodities of the realm", instead
delivering their "money to other merchants by exchange"[23] carried English trade,
when unimpeded by other influences (as in 1532)[24], to ever higher levels. Each upswing in rates (in 1529–31, 1534/5, 1536–8)[25] caused a retreat.[26] Yet each subsequent
fluctuation left interest rates at a lower and English trade at a higher level than before.
The English market under Italian tutelage, thus, from 1528 came into its own, so that
when in 1541 interest rates, ON AN UPSWING, settled at a level half a percentage
point below those prevailing on the Antwerp Bourse, London emerged as a serious
competitor in the provision of commercial credit for the commerce of western Europe.
1528 thus marked a turning point in the history of the "London Exchange". The Netherlands monetary reform of the previous winter had removed many of the bi-metallic
impediments to its operation. Now the Italians provided it with cheap money, opening
up opportunities for all who wished to raise commercial loans there. The English merchants seized these opportunities – but not before they had resolved the problem of
inflationary pressures occasioned by the monetary crises of 1531–1534.

XI, Nr. 1419, 1433 and XIII [2], Nr. 924) to accept the view put forth in G. D. RAMSEY, The Un-
doing of the Italian Mercantile Community in Sixteenth-Century London, in: N. B. HARTE / K G.
PONTING (eds.), Textile History and Economic History. Essays in Honour of Miss Julia de Lacy
Mann, Manchester 1973, pp. 26–7, of their role in English royal finance in its totality.

22 See present chapter, supra.

23 E. HALL, Chronicle […], London 1809, p. 781.

24 See chapter 7 below

25 Apart from the major fluctuations outlined above there were various intra-annual movements too
numerous to mention.

26 On the course of trade, E. M. CARUS-WILSON / O. COLEMAN, England's Export Trade, 1275–
1547, Oxford 1963, pp. 116–118, 139.

CHAPTER SEVEN

INTERNATIONAL MONETARY SYSTEMS AND IMPORTED INFLATION: ENGLAND, 1531–4

Operating within a system of exchange rates which were kept in a constant state of flux by each variation in bill market interest rates (chapters 1–2 and 5–6), changing mint parities of the internationally traded currencies and bimetallic premiums (chapter 3) it is hardly surprising that merchants, whose finance costs were vitally affected by these fluctuations, followed with an avid interest the daily movement of the exchanges on each of their national bill markets. On the basis of these fluctuations, merchants, like Antoine de Bombergen, formulated their purchase and sales strategies. His correspondence with Antonio Grimani, the Venetian merchant who employed him as his Antwerp agent, reveals the intimate connection which existed between exchange rate movements and the decision making of a European merchant.[1] During the third quarter of 1532, when the surviving correspondence begins, high interest rates at Antwerp (7.5 per cent usance) had depressed the market for English textiles, products for which he declared "there is not much demand", and had repelled the English merchants from venturing thence. Unable to sell either their kerseys or their cloths at the Sinxen mart, it seemed to Antoine, with interest rates continuing to rise (the Venice exchange moved from 66–65.66[2] (7.5–9.5 per cent usance) between July and early September) that they would not come at all to the Bamus mart. Yet whilst van Bombergen lamented the depressive effects of exchange movements on his own trade and the corresponding absence of Londoners at the Brabant fairs, the very favourable rates on the London exchange (1.8 per cent usance), occasioned by his counterparts in England delivering their "money to other merchants by exchange", seem to have persuaded at least some English merchants to venture forth on their own account. In the summer of 1532 they may be discerned lading ships at Southampton for direct trade with the Mediterranean.[3] For a brief moment Antwerp's hegemony in the southern trades, reestablished in 1529, was challenged, but neither very effectively nor for long.[4] From the end of September 1532 through December 1533 the return to normality at Antwerp re-established the market situation of 1529–30. Interest rates fell (late-September

---

1   The following two paragraphs are based upon the van Bombergen correspondence: W. BRULEZ (ed.), Lettres commerciales de Daniel et Antoine de Bombergen à Antonio Grimani1532–43, in: Bulletin de l' Institute Historique Belge de Rome, XXXI (1958), pp. 186–197.

2   I.e. the amount of deniers de gros per ducat at two months term.

3   TNA, E122/143/8.

4   See ch. 3.

1532: 8 per cent, December 1532: 6.75 per cent, February 1533: 1 per cent at usance). The exchange rose and, with the decline in the Venetian price of English wares[5], Grimani again expressed interest in the purchase of these commodities. Nor did van Bombergen consider that there would be any difficulty in satisfying his client's wishes. On the 14th December 1532 he predicted that "the English will certainly come to the Bergen fair (Koud Mart)." On the 31st December his prediction was proven correct and he reported the English have begun to arrive. The return of the Antwerp bill market to pre-crisis conditions had again realigned the trade in English cloth and kersey through that city to the south. Yet in one significant respect conditions had changed.

In his letter of the 20th September 1532 Grimani, anticipating an increased demand for English textiles now that their price at Venice was falling, ordered from Antwerp the traditional wares of his trade – kerseys and Kentish long cloths.[6] Of the former product van Bombergen had no worries. They could be purchased at much the same price as in the pre-crisis years (2–4 livres de gos "according to fineness") and with the Venetian exchange in late 1532 operating on slightly more advantageous rates than in 1528–31 they would probably sell easily.[7] Thus he suggested that Grimani would be advised to "order as many as he wished." The long cloths, however, he regarded as a much more dubious proposition. Throughout November and December he prevaricated, indicating his hope that they might be bought at a reasonable price (ca. £4 Sterling) and exploring the relative advantages of purchasing at the Brabant fairs or directly from England in order to secure the lowest price. In March 1533, even with the exchange at 67.25, he was trepidous of the saleability of his purchases, writing to Grimani, "you desire that I buy long cloths to be sent to Venice for the 10th July; I hope they will prove satisfactory." When his purchases could not be made at less than £5 Sterling, he went further and clearly indicated that he regarded his client's orders as foolhardy. In a letter of 28th March he suggested that rather than pursuing the policy of buying English longs which were rapidly rising in price and were of poor quality, Grimani would be better advised to use the money he had at Lyon to buy Languedoc cloth. Thus whilst the return of the Antwerp bill market to conditions of

---

5   After rising from 8 ducats a kersey in January 1527 to 9.5 in early 1532, prices fell to 9 in late September. I am deeply indebted to Dr Peter Earle for providing me with information concerning cloth prices at Ancona derived from his researches in the notarial archives of that city. This data invaluably supplements that contained in the van Bombergen correspondence and that of the van der Molen which has been consulted from the studies of F. EDLER, The Van der Molen, Commission Merchants at Antwerp: Trade with Italy 1538–44, in: Medieval and Historiographical Essays in Honour of James Westfall Thompson, Chicago 1938, pp. 78–145; ID., Winchcombe Kerseys at Antwerp, 1538–44, in: Economic History Review, First Series, VII (1936), pp. 57–62 and ID., Le commerce d' exportation des says d' Hondschoote vers l' Italie, d' après la correspondance d' une firme anveroise, entre 1538 et 1544, in: Revue du Nord, XXII (1936), pp. 249–266, and the MS collection of their correspondence (Antwerp Town Archives, Fonds Insolvente Boedelkamer, IB 2039), a microfilm of which was kindly obtained for me by Professor Herman van der Wee.

6   For a description of each of the major cloth types referred to in this study see the glossary in the appendix.

7   In March 1531 the Venetian exchange stood at 64.25 (Strozzi MSS, preserved in the Florence archives, a photocopy of which was kindly provided me by Professor van der Wee). In December 1532 it stood at 67.25.

normality might encourage the expansion of English cloth exports through the latter town, for the merchant dealing in "longs", a product whose domestic price increased relative to that of its competitors, there was little benefit to be gained from this overall expansion.

Figure 7.1: Price Statistics 1500–1544

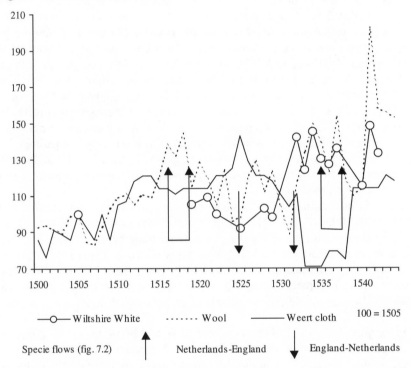

Here then in miniature is the story which has been unfolded in the preceding pages. The van Bombergen correspondence, encompassing a period of eighteen months, reveals clearly how exchange movements could affect the sales price of commodities entering international commerce and accordingly the volume of trade, could induce changes in the patterns of purchasing and even lead to the re-orientation of trade along new routes. Yet equally clearly it shows the important role price variations could play in the process of change. Indeed it is this aspect of the merchants' problems which is particularly highlighted in Antoine's letters, for even as he wrote them the contemporary cloth market was going through the turmoil of a minor "price revolution" (figure 7.1).[8] As may be seen from that figure, however, the phenomenon was, in 1531/2, a

---

8   Sources: Ipswich and East Suffolk Record Office, C13/15/1 fos. 144–6 and C5/12/8. Cambridge University Library, Hengrave Hall MSS, 78/1–2. Drapers Company, Howell's Ledger, 1522–7. Mercers Company, Gresham's Day Book. For wool prices, see P. BOWDEN, Statistical Appendix, in: J. THIRSK (ed.), The Agrarian History of England and Wales, Vol. IV, Cambridge 1967, pp. 840–4. The price of cloth at Antwerp is taken from H. VAN DER WEE, The Growth of the Antwerp

new one for during the period 1500–1529 price changes had played a decidedly subordinate role in comparison with exchange movements in influencing merchant decision making. Both Low Countries and English cloth prices had followed a basically
similar long-run path, rising from 1500/5–1514, stabilizing thereafter to 1523 and then
falling to 1529 when they settled at a higher level than in 1500/5. In terms of long-
term domestic price changes, therefore, both groups of producers lost ground in third
party markets to indigenous producers who could maintain stable prices; whilst neither gained any overall advantage at the expense of the other. In the short-run the
emergence of price differentials might temporarily offset these trends, stemming for
an instant the inflation or swinging the advantage for a brief interval in favour of either the Netherlands (1514–22 and 1526–8) or English (1524–5) product. In both the
long- or short-run, however, the impact of these changes was slight when compared
with that of exchange movements. Any short-term advantage enjoyed by the English
producer before 1526 or by his Low Countries' counterpart thereafter was offset by
the rise and subsequent fall of the English exchange. Any disadvantages both producers might suffer, through domestic inflation, in relation to third party competitors, between 1500/5–1523 was offset (during the years 1500–8, 1515, 1518–9 and 1524–6)
by the fall in the cost of money on the Antwerp Bourse. Exchange influences during
the years 1500–1529 reigned supreme.

Of paramount importance to the merchant communities was the long-term fall in
interest rates from 1492–1526 which, reducing transaction costs and the foreign exchange price of their wares, paved the way for a major trade boom through Antwerp.
Of no less concern were the periodic exchange crises which in 1513, 1517 (1518–9)
interrupted that trade boom and in 1521 and 1522–3, when direct Habsburg intervention into the Antwerp bill market "crowded out" private borrowers enhancing the general bill rate level and increasing the amplitude of crisis-induced fluctuations, crippled
it.[9]

Also in the years prior to 1530 the same merchants had begun to feel the effects of
another source of commercial disorder, far more important than domestic price
movements, as the emergence of bi-metallic disequilibria, by offering financiers an
alternative source of profit, enhanced rates on the exchange. For the first time in a
quarter of a century, during which a state of bi-metallic equilibrium had prevailed in
Europe, 1514/5 marked the beginnings of a protracted phase of disequilibria in international monetary systems. In part these were related to the changing fortunes of silver producers in the Saxon-Bohemian *Erzgebirge* which affected bullion market conditions in the Baltic and eastern Europe introducing alternating phases of stability (in
1460–75, 1492–1514 and 1530–42) and acute instability associated with monetary
debasements (in 1475–92 and 1515–30) and specie imports to the region. Yet these
changes merely had a regional impact within the European economy. Of far greater
significance was a phenomenon which from 1515 became a permanent feature of everyday life – the enhancement of gold – which whilst causing an enhancement in the
price of that metal in terms of the notional monies of account also effected a transfor-

Market and the European Economy. Fourteenth–Sixteenth Centuries, The Hague 1963, Vol. I, p.
271.

9   Chapters 1, 2 above.

mation in its price relationship with silver. Accordingly from 1515 an endemic state of debasement was normally associated with a chronic condition of bi-metallic imbalance which afforded merchants the opportunity to profit from trade in that most valuable of all commodities – bullion. Trade in specie thus competed with trade in goods. The merchant wishing to borrow on the exchange to finance his commodity trade was now forced to outbid a rival who could profit directly from the export of moneys. There thus emerged on the exchanges a system of bi-metallic premiums: surcharges which the merchant had to pay above the prevailing bill rate in order to induce his financier not to export bullion.

In the case of England, as will be seen in figure 7.2, at the beginning of the sixteenth century commerce was particularly affected by such premiums.[10] Due to the grotesque over-valuation of gold they existed on most of the London exchanges, maintaining interest rates at in excess of 8 per cent usance. Gradually, however, the rise in continental European gold prices eliminated them as markets in France and the Levant in 1509–13, Venice in 1516/7 and the Netherlands in 1517–21 entered into a state of bi-metallic equilibrium with England. For the merchants this was largely irrelevant, however, as Habsburg intervention on the Antwerp Bourse in 1517(1518/9) and 1521 autonomously enhanced interest rates above the rate of return from the bullion trade. Such was not the case in 1525–6. On this occasion the crazy increase in Netherlands gold prices rapidly enhanced premiums until they stood at 10.8 per cent on a London bill rate of 9 on the eve of the Netherlands monetary reform of December 1526. Only with the successful implementation of that reform over the winter of 1526/7 were premiums reduced but with re-establishment of the monetary standard of 1520–1 in the Netherlands, although on the London-Antwerp exchange the status quo was re-established, with the rest of Europe it had not. The English bi-metallic ratio was now closer to that of most European states, apart from Spain and from 1531 Venice, than the reformed Antwerp one. Thus from 1527 a prolonged phase of bi-metallic imbalance existed between Antwerp-Spain-Venice and the rest of Europe including England which again created inter-bloc premiums as English interest rates declined.

---

10   The sources for figure 7.2 are the same as those for figure 1.3.

Figure 7.2: Exchange Movements, 1514–1544

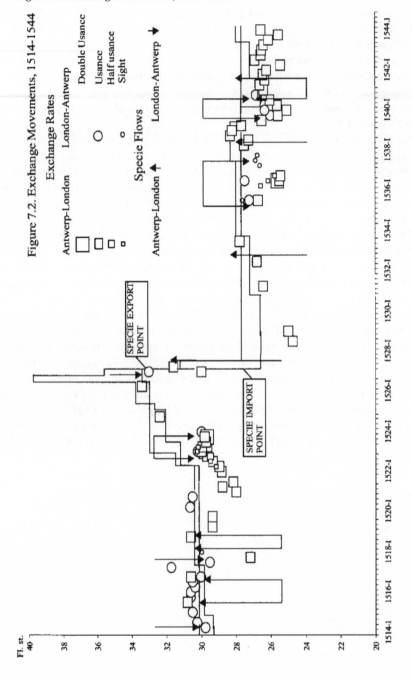

Figure 7.2. Exchange Movements, 1514-1544

Once again therefore monetary disorders, occasioned by bi-metallic disturbances, were predominantly felt by the merchant community through their effects on exchange rates rather than through price changes. Obscured in 1521 and 1522-3 by the effects of the Habsburg intervention in the Antwerp bill market they had first made themselves felt on the exchange in 1525–6 when premiums on bill rates had been markedly enhanced and commerce correspondingly crippled. From 1500–1529 it was exchange movements, resulting from either interest rate movements or the emergence of bi-metallic premiums, which exercised merchants' minds and shaped their business strategies.[11]

Specie flows when, in conditions of bi-metallic disequilibrium, trade was depressed (in 1513, 1516/7–8, 1521–2, 1525/6, 1527–8, 1531/2 and 1533/4, 1535/6 and 1538–40), had in most circumstances no long-term price effect. Their bi-lateral character, whilst creating a short-term alternating pattern of Anglo-Netherlands price fluctuations whose periodicity was related to the duration of the crisis and intensity to the degree of bi-metallic imbalance, ensured that they had no long-term effect on national monetary stocks. Crises on the Antwerp Bourse by enhancing interest rates afforded merchants investment opportunities in depressed trading conditions and caused a flight from short to medium-term paper, increasing interest rates on the exchange and blocking specie exports from the Netherlands. At the same time, however, they depressed English commodity exports, drove down bill rates on the London exchange and, when these fell below the specie export point, triggered a specie outflow. In spite of royal prohibitions and the activities of the searchers, on each of these occasions when the exchange fell below the specie export point merchants like Thomas Kitson abandoned the exchange and exported bullion.[12] Accordingly, a deflationary phase was introduced in England and an inflationary one in the Netherlands which with the cessation of the crisis, as normal trade was resumed, relatively over-priced the Low Countries' products and set the process in reverse until price equilibrium between the two countries was again achieved (see Figures 7.1–2: 1514–5, 1516/7–8 and 1535/6, 1540–1).

Whilst this self-equilibrating mechanism continued to operate throughout the period under consideration, however, the years 1531/2–1534 witnessed a major transformation in market conditions. As Antwerp bill rates, under the influence of American specie supplies and the tutelage of Italian merchant-bankers, equilibrated to a new low level, for the first time during late-1531 crisis conditions saw a rise in interest rates on the exchanges which, whilst depressing trade at Antwerp, was insufficient to stem the outflow of specie (Figures 7.2/7.3)[13] or to halt the resultant Netherlands deflation (Figure 7.1). Nor did the crisis on this occasion precipitate a downswing in

11   The underlying changes in the international precious metal industries which were at the root of the monetary disorders outlined in the previous three paragraphs will be discussed more fully in a study on international mining and metallurgical production, 1460–1560 currently being prepared for publication, whilst evidence concerning the symptoms of these changes is presented in chapter 3 above.

12   See his ledgers preserved in the Cambridge University Library, Hengrave Hall MSS., 78/1–4.

13   The data presented in figure 7.3 is the same as that presented in figure 1.3 but cast in actual rather than three-monthly terms and on a quarterly rather than annual basis to render it compatible with figure 7.2.

English commerce which, expanding[14] sustained the English exchange, prevented the re-export of the imported specie and thereby precipitated acute inflationary pressures within the economy. At this time therefore England became a net importer of specie with resultant inflationary effects.[15] Inevitably, however, as in the course of 1532 inflation worked its way through the economy there was the danger that English wares would be over-priced. Trade, already declining through the winter fair of 1531/2 and the Easter one of 1532 as in the aftermath of the crisis it re-orientated towards Antwerp, would collapse. The exchange would fall. And, indeed, there is some evidence that during 1532 this occurred. During that summer the exchange once more fell below the English specie export point, and as bullion flowed out of the realm inflationary pressures were relieved[16], but not before they had wrought havoc in the English export trades. The embryonic recovery of the previous autumn already loosing its impetus during the following winter and spring as trade re-orientated towards Antwerp, at the Easter fair, turned into a severe depression which prevailed over the summer and caused English trade in 1531/2 to again decline.

---

14   On trends in English commercial activity see figure 8.1. Overall during 1531/2 trade declined as the effects of summer depression in commercial activity offset the effects of the direct trade boom of the winter.

15   As the "hot" money was allowed to circulate in both England and the Netherlands at this time (see C. E. CHALLIS, Currency and the Economy in Mid-Tudor England, in: Economic History Review, Second Series, XXV, 2 (1972), p. 314 and C. CAU [ed.], op. cit., I , 2741s.) the inflows of 1530/1 and 1532 were only partially reflected in mint output which particularly from 1527 had been greatly influenced by the dis-hoarding of plate by merchants see C. E. CHALLIS, The Tudor Coinage, Manchester 1978, appendix II, tables 12–3, pp. 305–8.

16   Direct evidence of specie exports at this time is provided in L&P, Henry VIII, V, No. 1276.

Figure 7.3: Interest Rates on Antwerp Money Market, 1514–1544

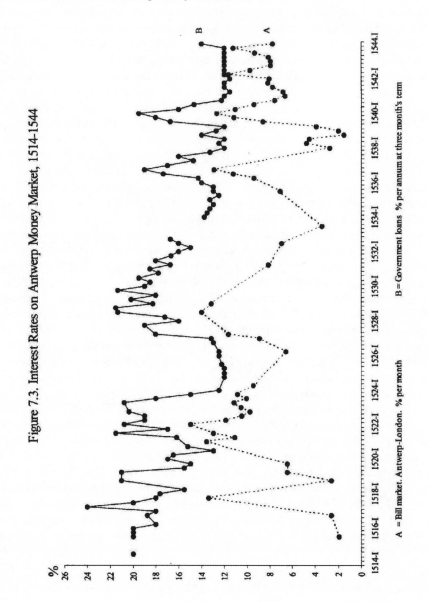

Figure 7.3. Interest Rates on Antwerp Money Market, 1514-1544

A = Bill market. Antwerp-London. % per month   B = Government loans % per annum at three month's term

Nor did it look, at that time, as though the situation would be very different in 1532/3 for during the autumn of 1532 the pattern of the previous year seemed to repeat itself. The continuing rise in interest rates at Antwerp during September, whilst depressing trade through Antwerp, was again insufficient to stem the outflow of specie from the Netherlands or to halt the resultant deflation there. English trade, moreover, as van Bombergen reported, whilst declining at the Brabant fairs, underwent during late-1532 an overall expansion[17], maintaining the exchange and preventing the escape of the specie that flowed in. Prices after a brief respite, accordingly, again over the winter of 1532/3 began to rise to a new, even higher, level.[18] But on this occasion they failed to choke off the trade boom, although, as interest rates at Antwerp fell and from the Cold mart of 1532/3 trade re-orientated itself towards that city, much of the earlier impetus was lost.[19] During 1532/3,therefore, English trade ran its normal course, as at the time of the Bamus mart of 1532 England's "direct" commerce began to push up her overall export trade, whilst through the winter fair of 1532/3 and the Easter one of 1533 it declined as trade re-orientated itself through Antwerp. That year, moreover, saw a repetition of the inflationary situation which had wrought havoc in English commerce in 1531/2. On this occasion, however, rapidly rising price levels singularly failed to influence the course of trade. The reason lay in merchants adjustments to the new situation. As unit cloth prices rose, a shift from the heavy long cloths to the kersey (which itself had undergone a process of technological change) reduced export commodity price levels and allowed trade to follow its "normal" course. Accordingly, the specie imported over the winter of 1532/3 remained in circulation and the general price level in England was maintained at its greatly enhanced level. English commercial activity, which had declined in 1531–2 as a result of inflationary pressures, however, now recovered and gaining strength in late-1532, pushed the nation's exports, for the first time, beyond the levels of 1527/8.

The problems occasioned by inflationary pressures in the economy had been resolved and the course of English trade expansion, first set under Italian financial tutelage in 1529, but briefly interrupted in 1532, now continued unabated. A completely new situation had arisen producing a recurrent behavioural pattern. In conditions of acute bi-metallic disequilibrium, such as again occurred in 1541–2, crisis conditions in the Netherlands, whilst disrupting trade at Antwerp, did not provide a sufficient incentive in the form of high interest rates to prevent an outflow of specie, which entering England did not escape as commerce expanded.[20] Prices rose, but a restructuring of the export commodity mix ensured that the price rise was not passed on to foreign

---

17   See Van Bombergen's analysis of the situation prevailing at the Bamus and Cold marts.

18   See figure 7.1.

19   The recovery at the winter fair described by Van Bombergen and the more robust one at Easter referred to by Chapuys in a letter to Charles V (L&P, Henry VIII, VI, Nr. 351), occasioned by the fall in interest rates at that time, collapsed at the Sinxen mart of 1533 (ibid., VI, Nr. 934), as interest rates once again edged upwards, bringing what had been a very chequered year at Antwerp to a close.

20   As Netherlands gold prices had once more edged upwards between 1534–9 premiums and the incentive to export specie had diminished but once more increased after the monetary reforms of 1538–40.

consumers. The English trade boom thus continued, the exchange was maintained and the general English price level was sustained at its newly enhanced level.

The crises of the 1520s had thus gone a long way to bringing about a complete re-structuring of European financial and monetary systems. From that time Antwerp was displaced from its position of supremacy in the hierarchy of financial centres. Hence-forth, behind a barrier of bi-metallic premiums, it was restricted to servicing the finan-cial requirements of the trades to Spain and Italy and even in this capacity, because of the long-term effects of the central European mining crisis and endemic Habsburg intervention in the money market, its services did not come cheap. Such was not the case with the new London money market which from 1528 came into its own, provid-ing cheap commercial finance within a trade system encompassing northern and cen-tral Europe, France and the Levant. Before this cheap money could be taken advan-tage of, however, one problem still remained to be resolved – that of inflation – which as a result of specie inflows from the "hard" currency areas in 1532 posed a major dilemma for exporters as the new decade began. Nor, as has been suggested, were English merchants slow to come to terms with the new situation. By altering their product mix they were able to offset price increases and, utilising the cheap money available to them, were able to lay the basis for a major trade boom. A new age was dawning. Its form and nature remains to be discussed. The story is a memorial to the ingenuity and skill of early sixteenth century merchants and manufacturers.

PART III

ROUTES, PORTS AND TRAFFIC

CHAPTER EIGHT

ANTWERP AND THE "ALTERNATIVE COMMERCE" 1505–1523[1]

> If English men's fathers were hanged at Andwerpes gates their children to come into that towne
> woulde creepe betwixt their legges.[2]

Thus was encapsulated in a well-known late sixteenth-century proverb, long after the reality had passed, the remembrance of an age when, as in the years immediately preceding the accession of Henry VIII, all paths had led the English merchants to Antwerp. During these years, and particularly during the quinquennium 1505–9 cheap money[3] and security had drawn irresistibly the expanding trade in Anglo-Netherlands produce towards the financial and commercial metropolis of the West from whence these wares were distributed to markets within a European-wide trading system. As in the fifteenth century, the most important of these markets lay in Central Europe. In-

---

1   It must be stressed that the following section deals predominantly with the cloth trade. Changes in the volume and direction of trade described therein may not be applicable to the commerce in other commodities which do not share the same high-value/low-bulk characteristics and high price elasticity as cloth. During the 1530s, for instance, when the sea-borne trade in cloth to Italy declined, displaced by an overland commerce, that to the Levant continued, it was not abnormal for the same vessel to carry wool to Leghorn and then pass on with its cargo of cloth to the Levant. Similarly, when during the first two decades of the sixteenth century, the direct trade in cloth from English ports to Spain gave way to an indirect commerce via Antwerp, this did not mean that ships did not continue to venture thence, only that they did not carry significant quantities of cloth. Indeed, ships bound for Spain seem to have sailed in ballast (grain or lead), returning ladened with Spanish wares. It is thus necessary to distinguish between a pattern of shipping and land transport routes which enjoyed a degree of permanence and its use for the carriage of specific goods which constantly altered. Only a study of each commodity trade – both import and export – in relation to the permanent pattern of shipping routes will ultimately reveal the constantly changing pattern of sixteenth century commerce. As the import trades are not examined in this study such an investigation cannot be undertaken here. Accordingly the modifications to the picture presented below, required to accommodate the trade in lead and tin, may only be tentatively sketched out. In many cases these wares served as ballast for the cloth and wool fleets and thus the picture is clear, but on occasion (in the Spanish trade referred to above or the Baltic trade of the 1530s) they served as ballast in empty ships outward-bound to pick up import cargoes. In such cases it was decisions concerning these import wares (outside the scope of this study) which determined whether they were shipped or not.

2   TNA, SP. D. Eliz. XXXVI, 34 (1565?) as quoted in F. J. FISHER, Commercial Trends and Policy in Sixteenth Century England, in: Economic History Review, First Series, X, 2 (1940) reprinted in E. M. CARUS-WILSON (ed.), Essays in Economic History, London 1954, Vol. I, p.154.

3   See Part I, chapter 1 on conditions in the Antwerp money market at this time.

termediaries in this trade were the merchants of Cologne and Frankfurt who, like Jan Questenborch or the van der Biese, each year either ordered from their London factors or bought at the Brabant fairs the English goods which were the staples of their trade.[4] These wares then passed eastward by cart along the great central European highway, through Cologne and Frankfurt, to be finally distributed to Saxony and the Czech lands through Leipzig, to southern Germany and the Alpenlands from Augsburg and to the lands of the Hungarian crown through Vienna (Map 8.1).[5] Along the way they shared passage with the wares of those merchants who traded to Italy, merchants whose commerce was in the years 1505–9 recovering from the effects of the 1500–3 Venetian financial crisis.[6] At Augsburg the two parted company as the traders bound for Italy continued via the Brenner and occasionally the Rescheneideck passes to Verona and Venice. Thus in 1505–9 both the Italian and Central European trades passed along the same land routes from Antwerp.

---

4   H. POHL, Köln und Antwerpen um 1500. Mitteilungen aus dem Stadtarchiv von Köln: Köln, das Reich und Europa, LX (1971), pp. 477–482, for a description of the Cologne merchants' textile trade at Antwerp as revealed in the *Certificatie-boeken* of 1488–1513. For a critique of the use of these documents, see E. SCHREMMER, Antwerpen als Warenhandelsplatz im 15. und 16. Jahrhundert und seine wirtschaftlichen Beziehungen zu Mitteleuropa, in: Jahrbücher für Nationalökonomie und Statistik, CLXXVIII (1965), pp. 273–8.

5   The information concerning routes used by cloth traders in ca. 1500, 1522 (Map 8.1) and 1529, 1542 (Map 10.1) is largely derived from W. BRULEZ, Les routes commerciales d'Angleterre en Italie au XVI siècle, in: Studi in onore di Amintore Fanfani, Milan 1962, IV, pp. 120–184; R. GASCON, Grande commerce et vie urbaine au XVIe siècle. Lyon et ses marchands, Paris 1971, I, pp. 141–203 and F. BRUNS / H. WECZERKA, Hansische Handelsstrassen, Weimar: Quellen und Darstellungen zur Hansischen Geschichte, NF XIII, 1–3; 1962–8.

6   On the crisis of 1497–1503, which reached its nadir during the years 1500–3, and which paralysed the trade along the Antwerp-Venice land route, see F. C. LANE, Venetian Bankers, 1496–1533, in: Journal of Political Economy, XLV (1937), repr. in: Venice and History. The Collected Papers of Frederick C. Lane, Baltimore 1966 pp. 70–1, 76–80. On the temporary re-diversion of that trade by the sea route to Italy, A. RUDDOCK, London Capitalists and the Decline of Southampton in the Early Tudor Period, in: Economic History Review, Second Series, II, 2 (1949), pp. 141–2 and ID., Italian Merchants and Shipping in Southampton, 1270–1600, Southampton 1951, pp. 221, 236–8.

Map 8.1: Anglo-Netherlands Textile Trade, 1505–22

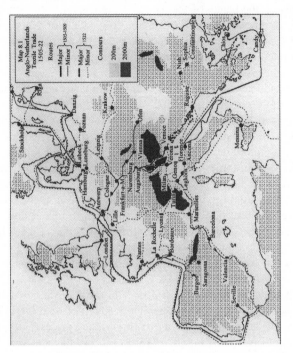

This land route also linked with the main maritime ways of passage at the western metropolis. The ships which carried the goods of men like Questenborch[7] from London to Antwerp, for transmission to Central Europe, after disembarking these wares, then sailed on into northern waters, carrying the same wares to customers in lands bordering the Baltic. Nor were the French and Spanish trades, which as recently as 1502 had enjoyed a flourishing independent existence, immune from the same centripetal forces at work during the years 1505-9.[8] Cheap money and efficient handling facilities at Antwerp irresistibly drew Exeter merchants like John Greenway and John Coleshill to London in order to trade with that city.[9] Equally inevitably these same forces caused Breton and Spanish merchants to bring their wares to the Brabantine

---

7   On the purchases of the Cologne merchants, like Questenborch, of cloths in London, see POHL, Köln und Antwerpen, p. 478, n. 42; for their shipment in Danzig vessels from London: TNA, E122/80/2 and for their subsequent transmission to Central Europe: POHL, Köln und Antwerpen, p. 478. In the same ships cloths of Danzig merchants were carried, which subsequently passed through the Sound. Rigsarkivet, Copenhagen, Sundtoldregudkab 1503 fos. 7, 12–4, 21. All the documents referred to above refer to the year 1502/3.

8   E. M. CARUS-WILSON, The Expansion of Exeter at the Close of the Middle Ages, Exeter 1963, pp. 10–16, and ID., The Overseas Trade of Bristol, in: E. POWER / M. M. POSTAN (eds.), Studies in English Trade in the Fifteenth Century, London 1933, pp. 219–220; G. CONNELL-SMITH, Forerunners of Drake: A Study of English Trade with Spain in the Early Tudor Period, London 1954, pp. 208–210.

9   E. M. CARUS WILSON, The Expansion of Exeter at the Close of the Middle Ages, Exeter 1963, pp. 28–9.

city for distribution, the years 1500–9 witnessing the establishment of Breton and Spanish mercantile colonies on the banks of the Thames and Escaut.[10] In return they carried Anglo-Netherlands commodities south to Rouen, Rochelle, Bordeaux and the Iberian ports. Thus in the year that the young king ascended the English throne his nation's trade was concentrated almost exclusively on Antwerp and the towns of the Scheldt estuary.

Whenever, during the troubled years that followed, the Antwerp market operated under conditions similar to those prevailing in 1505–9 this pattern of commerce, with one notable exception, repeated itself. As interest rates on the Antwerp Bourse fell through 1514–5 and 1518–9, moreover, trade passing through that city expanded, at first slowly and then in 1518–9 more rapidly (Figure 8.1).[11] The initial cause of retardation in 1514–5 lay in the rise in domestic prices, but even this was insufficient to totally eliminate the impact of cheap money at Antwerp. Foreign currency prices of Anglo-Netherlands wares fell, if slightly, and production and trade in these products increased. With the removal of these impediments to growth, in England due to the fall in domestic prices; in the Netherlands due to the fall in export prices caused by the debasement of the *livre de gros*, production and trade expanded through 1518–9. By the latter date, the trade was far larger than in 1509 but still retained, with one exception, the characteristic features of the earlier period.

The exception was the trade to the eastern Baltic. The rapid devaluation of the Riga mark and Danzig groschen after 1515 led to an appreciation of both the Flemish pound and sterling in terms of these currencies. Foreign currency prices[12] of Anglo-Netherlands products, falling from 1515 through 1518-9 in most other markets, actually increased by some 12.5 per cent at Riga. This posed major problems for exporters. The average price of their commodity mix was too high and only by its reduction did trade continue.[13]

---

10   J. FINOT, Relations commerciales et maritimes entre la Flandre et l' Espagne au Moyen Age, in: Annales du Comté flamand de France, XXIV (1898); J. A. GORIS, Etude sur les colonies marchandes méridionales à Anvers, 1477–1567, Louvain 1925, and Z. W. SNELLER / W. S. UNGER, Bronnen tot Geschiedenis van den Handel met Frankrijk, s' Gravenhage (=Rijks Geschiedkundige Publicatien G. Ser. LXX. 1930–42), I, Nr. 415s.

11   Sources. Zeeland water toll: W. S. UNGER, De Tol van Iersekerood, 1321–1572 (=Rijks Geschiedkundige Publicatien, Kl. Ser. XXIX), s'Gravenhage 1939, pp.156–162. Brabant water toll, H. VAN DER WEE, The Growth of the Antwerp Market and the European Economy. Fourteenth–Sixteenth Centuries, 3. Vols. The Hague 1963, Vol. I , Appendix 43/1, pp. 510–6. Brabant land toll, ibid., Vol. I, Appendix 43/2–3, pp. 517–9. English cloth exports E. M. CARUS WILSON / O. COLEMAN, England's Export Trade, 1275–1547, Oxford 1963, pp. 111–9. Rupelmonde toll: J. A. VAN HOUTTE, Quantitative Quellen zur Geschichte des Antwerpener Handels in 15. und 16. Jahrhundert, in: H. AUBIN et al. (eds.), Beiträge zur Wirtschafts- und Stadtgeschichte. Festschrift für Hektor Ammann, Wiesbaden 1965, p. 198.

12   G. MICKWITZ, Aus Revaler Handelsbüchern, Helsingfors 1938, pp. 100–1; M. J. ELSAS, Umriss einer Geschichte der Preise und Löhne in Deutschland, 3 Vols. in 2, Leiden 1936–49, Vol. I, pp. 498–9.

13   On the general method employed and its specific application in this instance, see chapter 12 below.

Figure 8.1: Netherlands Commercial Activity, 1490–1542

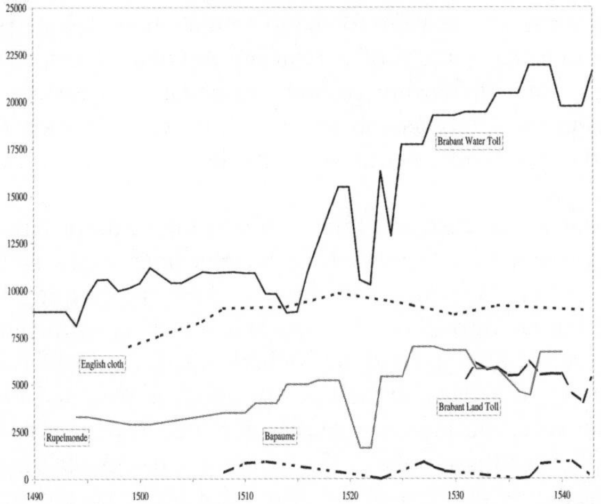

Tolls in livres artois. English cloth to Antwerp in '0 cloths measured, for reasons given
in text, between fluctuation peaks to 1526 and troughs thereafter.

Yet if the conditions giving rise to changes in export commodity mixes were exceptional during the years of Antwerp's supremacy, they were certainly not unfamiliar to
the merchants who plied the trade routes of Europe during the second and third decades of the sixteenth century. Over and over again during those years the Habsburg
rape of the Antwerp money market (in 1509–13, 1516–7 and 1520–3) threatened the
very foundations of that city's commercial supremacy. Interest rates rose and for those
merchants who maintained their commitment to trade at the Brabant fairs costs increased. In an attempt to soften the impact of rising export prices they were forced to
adopt the practices familiar to Baltic traders, altering their product mix in an effort to
reduce its price. Yet their efforts at product diversification seem to have been largely
in vain, for as foreign currency prices of their wares increased so the merchants' trade
declined, both individually and collectively, at Antwerp (Figure 8.1).

Many merchants, however, did not maintain their allegiance to Antwerp and, during these crisis years, in transferring their trade to new commercial and financial centres they brought into existence an "alternative commerce", thereby altering the whole
trade map of Europe (Map 8.1).The commercial houses of southern Germany seized
the opportunities, afforded by the rise in prices in the London/Antwerp trades to Cologne and Danzig, to re-forge links between Anglo-Netherlands producers and their
customers in Central Europe and the Baltic which had lain dormant during the years of
Antwerp's supremacy. Centring their trade on Frankfurt they revitalised these old
routes carrying their wares northward via Lunenburg to Lübeck for distribution to the
ports of the Baltic littoral.[14] Eastward their routes passed via Leipzig, Kraków and

14 H. WITTHÖFT, Das Kaufhaus in Lüneburg als Zentrum von Handel und Faktorei, Landfracht,
    Schiffahrt und Warenumschlag bis zum Jahr 1637, Lüneburg 1962.

Poznan to Poland, Lithuania and the Ukraine.[15] Yet such trades were expensive in comparison with that through Antwerp during the heyday of its mercantile activity and in their commerce the German merchants were forced to emulate their counterparts in the western metropolis, altering their pattern of purchasing to reduce the foreign exchange prices of their wares, but still loosing ground, particularly on eastern Baltic markets, to indigenous producers. Thus as the trade of Antwerp declined that of Frankfurt grew[16] but not without difficulties occasioned by the over pricing of western European wares.

The story is not dissimilar in the case of France. During the years of Antwerp's supremacy French and Breton ships had crowded the Scheldt anchorages and innumerable carts had passed north via Bapaume and Arras to Antwerp carrying French wares to that city for distribution throughout Europe and returning with, amongst other products, the commodities of England and the Netherlands. When, however, this trade was disrupted by financial disorder and the price of goods transmitted via Antwerp to the French consumer rose, the incentive existed for French merchants to establish direct links with suppliers of these wares.[17] They responded with alacrity and it is surely no coincidence that during the first of the crises that broke on the Antwerp money market, between 1510–5, the Lyon market finally emerged as a major financial centre.[18] The finance houses there now seized their opportunity to establish a network of correspondents in Spain, Italy and England, swelling the volume of credit dealings and affording financial facilities to merchants who now built completely new trading systems about the French fair town.[19] During each crisis at Antwerp (1509–13, 1516–7, and 1520–3) Breton shippers, when not impeded by the outbreak of Anglo-French hostilities (as in 1512–3 and 1521–2), abandoned the Scheldt and flocked in increasing numbers to the English south coast ports.[20] Their French counterparts, during the same years, expanded their trade to London creating a large, if unpopular, colony there.[21] Similarly in the trade to the Netherlands, when not obstructed by Habsburg-Bourbon hostilities, Lille gained by the diversion of the French trade from Antwerp.[22]

15 H. SAMSONOWICZ, Über Fragen des Landhandels Polens mit Westeuropa im 15. und 16. Jahrhundert, in: K. FRITZE et al. (eds)., Neue Hansische Studien, Berlin 1970.

16 A. DIETZ, Frankfurter Handelsgeschichte, 5 Vols., Frankfurt-on-the-Main 1910–1925, Vol. I , pp. 67–8, 316–58 and P. JEANNIN, Les relations économiques des villes de la Baltique avec Anvers au XVIe siècle, in: Vierteljahrschrift für Sozial- und Wirtschaftsgeschichte, XLIII, 2 (1956), pp. 193–5.

17 Z. W. SNELLER / W. G. UNGER, Bronnen tot de Geschiedenis van den Handel met Frankrijk (=Rijk Geschiedkundige Publicatien, G. Ser. LXX), s'Gravenhage 1930–42, I, pp. 639–41; J. FINOT, Etude historique sur les relations entre France et la Flandre au Moyen Age, Paris 1894, pp. 67, 69.

18 F. C. SPOONER, L' économie mondiale et les frappes monétaires en France, 1493–1680, Paris 1956, p. 281.

19 On conditions on the finance market of Lyon at this time see, M. MOLLAT, Affaires et infortunes de Gaspar Centurione en Normandie, 1522–32, in: Mélanges en l' honneur de Fernand Braudel: histoire économique du monde mediterranéen, 1450–1650, Toulouse 1973, p. 432.

20 H. TOUCHARD, Le commerce maritime breton à la fin du moyen age, Paris 1967, table 18; pp. 401–4.

21 E. HALL, Chronicle […], London 1809, pp. 586–90.

22 E. COORNAERT, Le draperie-sayetterie d Hondschoote, XVI–XVIIe siècle, Paris 1930, pp. 487–9.

French merchants, like their German counterparts, thus seized the opportunities, afforded by financial crises at Antwerp, to establish direct links with their suppliers.

As in the German trades, however, the opportunities opened up for the enterprising merchants were wider than merely supplying their domestic markets and extended to the possibility of penetrating third party markets. Increasing costs and rising prices in the trade via Antwerp to Spain or Venice and the Levant provided just such openings for merchants to establish lower cost links between producers and their customers in these markets. The commercial houses of the Florentine dominated emporium of Lyon were not slow to exploit such openings, establishing a series of financial and commercial agencies to service the needs of a new commercial network linking Lyon to suppliers in England and the Netherlands and to markets in Spain, Italy and the Levant.[23] It merged with the domestic supply network for English goods at Nantes and La Rochelle. Many of the cargoes, either bought by Breton merchants in English south coast ports or despatched by London factors of French mercantile houses, never found their way to French consumers but passed directly from the ports via either Limoges or the Ponts-de-Cé to Lyons for re-export. At St Quentin the network merged with the domestic supply system for Flemish wares, a proportion of which passed each year by cart via Troyes and Chalon-sur-Saone to Lyon, again for re-export.[24] In 1522–3, 238 bales (each of 10 cloths) of English textiles and 46 of Flemish were transported in such a manner to Lyon for transportation elsewhere.[25] Southwest, pack trains carried them from the gate of St Juste via Bayonne to Spain. Southward, along the banks of the Rhone, four mule trains each year linked the fair town to Marseilles, from whence northern produce was channelled into the great Florentine route which extended from the wool ports of eastern Spain via Livorno to Florence and from thence via Ancona and Ragusa to Constantinople and the lands of the Ottoman Empire.[26] Eastward from Lyon these same markets were attained by way of the *chemin de Piedmont* to Turin, Milan and Ancona. By a multiplicity of routes northern goods thus found their way to the French and, via Lyon, the Mediterranean market. Compared with the trade via Antwerp, during the hey day of its mercantile prosperity, however, this was an expensive commerce and only by altering export product mixes to offset enhanced costs could the French and Italian merchants involved ensure that trade boom which carried Lyon to its highest RECORDED point of commercial activity in 1522–3.[27] Within continental Europe, as Antwerp was, in 1509–13, 1516–7 and 1520–3, beset by financial crises and trade declined through that city, new financial centres – Lyon, Frankfurt and Leipzig – emerged, providing facilities for an expanding "alternative commerce". But neither the development of these "direct" trades nor the changes by mer-

---

23 R. GASCON, Grand commerce et vie urbaine au XVIe siècle. Lyon et ses marchands, Paris 1971, I , pp. 68–74.

24 Ibid., I, p. 156.

25 The low level of Netherlands imports (ibid., I, p. 69), was due to Habsburg-Bourbon hostilities which interrupted trade. At Bapaume the toll collector recorded that year, "est ledit droict de péaige non valloire à cause de la guerre qui est entre l' Empereur nostre dit sire et le Roy de France." FINOT, Etude historique, p. 69.

26 P. EARLE, The commercial development of Ancona, 1497–1551, Economic History Review, Second Series, XVII, 2 (1969), p. 34.

27 GASCON, Grand commerce, Vol. II , p. 597.

chants in their export-commodity mixes to foster their growth were sufficient to compensate for the decline in the old traffic via Antwerp and in aggregate commercial activity declined.

Nor was the situation different in England. Here a similar process of diversification away from Antwerp may be discerned, although due to the system of bi-metallic premiums on the London exchanges which was only gradually rendered inoperative, English merchants were slow to establish direct trade links with other nations. During the first Antwerp crisis (1509–13) the scope for diversification was limited to the founding of direct trades to France and the Levant. Yet limited as the opportunities were, London merchants responded readily. In 1511 and 1512 they freighted "diverse ships of London" to sail to "Sicily, Candy, Chios and sometimes to Cyprus, as also to Tripoli and Beirut and Syria."[28] More mundane perhaps, but quantitatively probably more significant, were the activities of men like Kitson, who contributed a vessel to the small fleet of English ships which sailed in consort during each year of the first Antwerp crisis (save 1512–3) to Bordeaux, in order to sell English goods and to acquire wines which in more settled times had been obtained from Antwerp.[29] These were the pioneers who ventured first into trades which were to become permanent features of English commerce when crisis conditions beset Antwerp. During each succeeding Antwerp crisis they were joined by others who, like Henry Tooley, abandoned their Low Countries' connections to trade in 1516–7 and 1520–2 at Bordeaux.[30] During each crisis at Antwerp, therefore, when not hindered by war, English merchants abandoned that city to venture forth to France and the Levant. From 1516–7 Venice was added to their destinations and in 1521–2 the whole of Europe was thrown open to the English cloth merchant.[31] Throughout the latter year a spirit of adventure pervaded the ports. Before the outbreak of Anglo-French hostilities large fleets ran the gauntlet of French corsairs to trade with Bordeaux.[32] London merchants, like Thomas Howell, and their provincial brethren, whose export trade to Spain in previous years had been of negligible proportions, sent large consignments of English wares to Biscayan and Andalusian ports.[33] Others freighted vessels for Venice and the Levant.[34] Others again made up shipments to the Baltic.[35] Diversification was the order of the

28   R. HAKLUYT, The Principal Navigations, Voyages, Traffiques and Discoveries of the English Nation, 3 Vols. in 2, London 1599–1600, Vol. I, p. 96.

29   Cambridge University Library, Hengrave Hall MSS., 78/1.

30   J. WEBB, Great Tooley of Ipswich. Portrait of an Early Tudor Merchant, Ipswich 1962, pp. 4, 28. On his appointment of a temporary factor – Simon Cowper – to transact his business at Bordeaux from 11 July 1520–3 June 1522, see ibid., pp. 29–30.

31   See ch. 3 above, n. 11.

32   L&P, Henry VIII, III (2), Nos. 1533, 1544, 1558.

33   On provincial shipments during the years to 1521, see CONNELL-SMITH, Forerunners of Drake, pp. 211–2, revealing a pattern of ships sailing to Spain in ballast, which repeated itself from 1523 to late 1526. On the heavy purchases of London merchants engaged in this trade in 1522, see Drapers' Company, Howell's Ledger, fos. 13–14 (1518–21), fos. 14, 18 and 25 (1522), fos. 39s. (1522–7).

34   RUDDOCK, Italian Merchants, pp. 241–2 (1516/8), 228–30 (1521/2).

35   Archiwum Gdanskie, customs accounts of Danzig 1519, 1522–4. I am grateful to the late Professor A. Maczak for aiding me in the acquisition of micro-films of these documents.

day but diversification had its costs. It might prove cheaper than trade via Antwerp, where during successive crises the average monthly cost of finance rose by between 2 and 10 per cent, but it was still expensive. For the merchant trading direct from England to distant markets financial oncosts increased (in relation to "normal" Antwerp rates) by between 1.5 and 7 per cent and, even allowing for reductions in freights negotiated on outward-return carriages, the costs involved in such enterprises were not cheap. Merchants, like their continental European counterparts, were thus forced to diversify their export mix but whilst this facilitated an expansion in England's "direct" trades this in no way compensated for the decline in the traffic through Antwerp and in aggregate English trade declined (Figure 8.1).

Thus as long as peace and security prevailed at Antwerp (1500–9[36], 1514–5 and 1518–9), trade expanded. When, however, that city's money market was disturbed by the impact of Habsburg borrowing (1509–13, 1516–7, 1520–2), trade passed elsewhere, to Lyon, Frankfurt and London, bringing into existence an "alternative commerce". But the new system was a poor substitute for the old and with rising costs the onus was thrown on merchants to diversify their export-commodity mix in order to offset the effects of increased costs on the foreign currency price of their wares. On no occasion, however, were they able to effectively reduce the price of their wares enough to eliminate the effects of increased transaction costs and trade declined.

---

36 Save in the Italian trade.

CHAPTER NINE

CRISIS AND THE OLD ORDER, 1523–8

As the 1520s opened few merchants at Antwerp could have anticipated the trials and tribulations, opportunities and possibilities to come. With the ending of the 1520–2 crisis for many the time must have seemed ripe for the resumption of old habits and for the re-establishment of old trading patterns. Nor were their expectations to remain entirely unrealised. Trade in 1523–4 once more began to assume many of the features which had characterised Antwerp's commerce during its heyday.[1] The lure of cheap money again irresistibly drew the commodities of Europe to the still undisputed financial and commercial metropolis of the West for distribution through the known trading world. London merchants, who had withdrawn from the Brabant fairs in large numbers during the preceding crisis, once more flocked to the towns of the Scheldt estuary.[2] English exports rose, as the traditional trade reasserted itself, almost, but not quite, re-attaining in 1524 the previous high level achieved before the crisis of 1520–2 (Figure 8.1 above). The products of the English sold readily at the Bergen and Antwerp fairs to the Cologne merchants who once more traversed the great Central European highway to Frankfurt, from whence their wares passed via Leipzig to Saxony and the Czech lands, to Augsburg, supplying the Alpenland and South Germany, or to Vienna for distribution to Hungary. As in an earlier age along the way they shared passage with those merchants who carried similar wares, via the Brenner or Rescheneideck passes, to Verona and Venice. 1523–4 thus witnessed the reestablishment of one major element in Antwerp's traditional commercial network – the trans-continental trade to Central Europe and Italy. Yet even amongst all the bustle occasioned by the return of the English there were signs that times were changing as at the Cold mart of 1523/4 rising bi-metallic premiums deflected the French from returning to the Bergen fair. The impact of this change on the aggregative level of mercantile activity to the Scheldt town, however, was obscured at this time by the increasing activity of the Merchant Adventurers at the Fair. From 1523 and throughout 1524 English exports rose and merchants, like Kitson, achieved in 1524 their highest ever recorded level of exports.[3]

---

1   By this is meant the periods (1500–9, 1514–5 and 1518–9) when cheap money and security placed the city at the centre of a European-wide trading system.

2   In 1523–4 the English, moreover, came to Antwerp for clear financial reasons: even with bi-metallic premiums rising to three per cent between 1522 and the monetary reform of November 1525, the monthly interest rate on dealings via Antwerp was still one point below the cost of those financed solely at London.

3   Cambridge University Library, Hengrave Hall MSS, 78/1.

Far more ominous than the French episode, however, was the effect of the emergence of sizeable premiums on the exchanges with the Baltic and Spain which undermined that other major element in Antwerp's commercial economy – the maritime trades. Spanish and Portuguese ships, which had vacated the Scheldt anchorages in 1521–2, at no time during 1523–4 returned because of the rise in premiums on the Antwerp-Medina del Campo exchange.[4] When at the Cold mart of 1523/4 the Baltic grain fleet again failed to arrive, as in 1521 precipitating famine conditions in the Netherlands[5], Antwerp s maritime commerce was in total disarray. Business at the Bergen fairs declined and the revenues of the Zeeland water toll, already declining through 1520–2, continued to fall (Figure 8.1).[6] The continuing rise in Netherlands gold prices through 1523–4, thus precipitated a sectoral crisis in Antwerp's trade which otherwise, under the influence of cheap money, was returning to normality.

When, from the Cold Mart of 1524/5, Anglo-Netherlands gold prices began to rise rapidly, however, the sectoral crisis turned into a general one.[7] During that winter the first ominous signs of recession began to appear as merchants, like Kitson, began to react to the re-emergence of premiums on all exchange dealings between London-Antwerp and the rest of Europe. His shipments which had reached their highest recorded level in 1524 began to falter and in response to enhanced financial cost he began to diversify his export-product mix to reduce the foreign currency price of his wares.[8] Currency instability and tight money on the London market thus combined, from Christmas 1524, to cause the beginnings of the first of the crises which were to plague Anglo-Netherlands commercial relations during the coming quinquennium. The attempts of the Netherlands authorities almost a year later, during November 1525, to halt the rapid rise in gold prices and restore the bi-metallic equilibrium of an earlier age, by raising the price of silver, moreover, merely served to ossify the "crisis situation" on the English exchange. High interest rates at London, by preventing an outflow of specie, might ensure monetary stability but continuing high potential prof-

---

4   See ch. 3 above, n. 11 and H. VAN DER WEE, The Growth of the Antwerp Market and the European Economy. Fourteenth–Sixteenth Centuries, 3 Vols., The Hague 1963, Vol. II, p. 144. On the role of the Spanish at the Bergen fairs see F. EDLER, The Van der Molen, Commission Merchants of Antwerp: Trade with Italy, 1538–44, in: Medieval and Historiographical Essays in Honour of James Westfall Thompson, Chicago 1938, pp. 116–7, whose description of their trade is confirmed by the Welser letters quoted in VAN DER WEE, Antwerp, II, p. 177.

5   Judging by the data presented by Professor VAN DER WEE, Antwerp, I, Appendices 1–2, pp. 177, 181 by June 1523 Netherlands producers were already anticipating the withdrawal of the Germans and estimated prices at the forthcoming harvest far above the current level and very much in line with what they subsequently turned out to be.

6   On the importance of the Bergen fairs – the Koud or Cold mart held officially at the end of October but extending unofficially into February with fair payment days in that month and the Paasche or Easter fair beginning before Good Friday and ending ten days before Pentecost with four payment days in the week before Pentecost – to the French and German trades, see VAN DER WEE, Antwerp, II, p. 165. On the withdrawal of the merchants at the winter fair of 1523/4 and Easter fair of 1524, their return at Easter 1525 and during the winter of 1525–6 and their subsequent abandonment of the Bergen fairs from Easter 1526–7, see K. SLOOTSMAN, Brabantse kooplieden op de Bergse jaarmarkten, in: Oudheidkundige Kring "De Ghulden Roos" Roosendaal, Jaarboek, XXIII (1963), p. 48.

7   Chapter 3.

8   Cambridge University Library, Hengrave Hall MSS., 78/1.

its on specie dealings meant a prolongation of high finance costs. Thus trapped within a bi-metallic prison and burdened with the high cost of commercial credit the English merchant found no relief from the continuing crisis.[9] Many merchants accordingly succumbed. English trade continued to decline and in the period down to the suspension of shipments at the Bamus mart of 1526 those that remained made a concerted, but futile, attempt to reduce prices through product diversification. All was in vain, however, and as trade contracted unemployment in the export industries increased.[10]

Yet whilst the Netherlands monetary reform of November 1525 exacerbated the already developing crisis in English trade, contributing to the state of commercial and industrial decay which prevailed throughout 1525 and 1526, at Antwerp it paved the way for the return of the Germans and Spaniards. Business at the Bergen fairs, declining since 1521/2, recovered at the Cold mart of 1525/6 and when in the spring of 1526 a Spanish fleet of no less than fifty ships entered the Scheldt estuary the gains of the previous winter were consolidated.[11] From November 1525 through to the late spring of 1526 the Netherlands economy enjoyed a high, if ephemeral, level of commercial and industrial activity.

As de Lucy noted, however, this situation was not to last. As early as December 1525 it was clear to him that the monetary ordinance of the previous November had failed to stay the rise in Netherlands gold prices.[12] When, therefore, at the Easter and Sinxen marts of 1526 the situation of monetary instability and bi-metallic imbalance existing before the attempted reform was re-established, the trade depression, which had continued in England through 1525 and 1526, accordingly became more general and deepened, whilst unemployment and bankruptcy amongst manufacturers spread from England to the Low Countries.[13] From April to December 1526 continental European commerce suffered a prolonged malaise, as the trade in goods was displaced by a trade in specie, and English trade thence ground to a halt from the Bamus mart of 1526.[14] Nor, at least until the ephemeral stabilization of the London money market in October–November, were English merchants, because of high interest rates, able to diversify their trade. Commercial activity thus relentlessly declined and, as Netherlands gold prices continued their dizzy flight, their seemed no hope of relief. It was thus an act of desperation, the resort of drowning men grasping at straws, when, with the brief stabilization of conditions at London in October–November 1526, merchants of that city first attempted to revive the "alternative commerce". During the last quarter of the year, as the Antwerp bill rate at usance rose from 13 to 22 per cent whilst London rates briefly stabilized at the former level, goods were once more despatched to Spain, Italy (via Lyon) and to the Levant, but it was a passing interlude and with the collapse of the London market in December few would, for the moment, venture their

---

9   Chapter 3.

10   See chapter 13 below.

11   SLOOTSMAN, Brabantse kooplieden, p. 48, and VAN DER WEE, Antwerp, II, p. 177.

12   A. LOUANT (ed.), Le journal d' un bourgeoise de Mons, 1505–1536, Bruxelles 1969, No. 631, p. 257 as in the introductory quotes to chapter 3 above.

13   VAN DER WEE, Antwerp, II, p.146.

14   Chapter 3 above.

capital in such a manner.[15] Only monetary stabilization in the Netherlands could seemingly save the day.

This occurred during the Cold Mart of 1526/7 with the Netherlands monetary ordinance of the 10th December, which ushered in what was to prove perhaps the last important year of English commerce through Antwerp. From December to the completion of the monetary reform on 1st March 1527 interest rates fell on both the London and Antwerp money markets and premiums disappeared on their respective exchanges.[16] By March the problems which beset the Anglo-Netherlands monetary and financial systems seemed well on the way to being resolved, and, although interest rates at that time remained considerably higher than during previous periods of Antwerp's prosperity, thereby encouraging a resumption of England's "alternative commerce" through December 1526–March 1527, all augured well for a return to normal trade at Antwerp by the latter date. The market in 1527 was, however, a very different one from that which had existed before the crisis of 1525–6. The Netherlands monetary reform of the winter of 1526/7 together with the Venetian one of 1527 established Antwerp's future pattern of financial influence. The bi-metallic equilibrium now existing between the Spanish, Venetian and Netherlands currencies facilitated inter-market monetary transfers in the southern trades. The old European-wide hegemony, already crumbling in 1523–4, was replaced by a more limited financial function – the servicing of Ibero-Mediterranean commerce. In the city's adaptation to this new role, however, the path was smoothed by the pattern of international debasements which began to emerge during these years and which became more pronounced as time passed.[17] The slight extent of Italian and Ottoman debasements and the stability of the Spanish monies in comparison with the changes in the currencies of the rest of Europe ensured that these southerly markets were the cheapest and most expansive in Europe. Trade was thus, in 1527, in the process of reorientation from northern and central Europe towards the Mediterranean and the south and the Antwerp merchant was ideally placed to benefit from this transition. The same reforms which thus concentrated the activities of the Antwerp financial and mercantile community on southern trade, however, equally served to isolate that sector of European commerce from the rest which, during 1524–7 had become increasingly dependent on London. In 1527 the city on the Thames stood at the centre of a bi-metallic system encompassing the markets served

---

15   See Howell's Ledger, fos 39, 44–7, 51–2, 54–6 for cloth exports October 1526–March 1527. It seems probable that some of this cloth sent to Spain was subsequently re-shipped to Spanish America (G. CONNELL-SMITH, The Ledger of Thomas Howell, in: Economic History Review, Second Series, III, 3 [1951], p. 368 and ID., Forerunners of Drake: A Study of English Trade with Spain in the Early Tudor Period, London 1954,. pp. 74-5) where, as the colony entered on a phase of expanding economic activity, English textiles enjoyed a certain popularity: R. PIKE, Enterprise and Adventure: The Genoese at Seville and the Opening of the New World, Ithaca / New York 1966, p. 210, n. 26. From March 1527, however the direct trade from England declined (see Howell's Ledger, fo. 47 which reveals no further shipments of cloth) and Spain and its colonies obtained supplies of the English product via Antwerp (see chapter 13 below). On the Levant trade at this time see Cambridge University Library, Hengrave Hall MSS, 78/1, whilst P. EARLE, The Commercial Development of Ancona, 1497–1551, in: Economic History Review, Second Series, XVII, 2 (1969), p. 35, n. 4 provides evidence of shipments via Lyon to Ancona.

16   Chapter 3.

17   Chapter 3.

by the maritime traffic traversing northern seas.[18] Two distinct spheres of commercial and financial influence thus came into existence in 1527: one to the south which was buoyant and expansive, serviced by the Antwerp merchant community and the other, fraught with difficulties since its inception, which drew upon the financial and commercial resources of London.

If the new situation thus made the adjustments required of the Netherlands merchant relatively easy, however, for manufacturers times were more difficult. High interest rates prevailing at both London and Antwerp during 1527, by enhancing export prices, posed difficulties for both Netherlands and English producers.[19] For the latter the impact of dear finance was offset, however, by the devaluation of sterling and falling domestic prices which resulted in a fall in foreign currency prices of the English product on third party markets.[20] Such was not the case in the Netherlands where stable domestic prices and revaluation enhanced product prices abroad. In 1527 the English manufacturer thus came into his own. In both spheres of commercial activity his products enjoyed a superior position. Long before the mining crisis of 1527/8, therefore, a new pattern of European commercial and industrial activity had begun to emerge. Yet many problems still remained to be resolved before the new structure was to emerge in its totality in 1529.

At Antwerp the first stage in the emergence of the southern-orientated commercial network began during the winter of 1526/7. Falling interest rates encouraged merchants to establish a connection, through that city, between suppliers of cheap English wares and the expanding markets of southern Europe. Spanish ships, absent since the previous year, once more returned to the Scheldt and throughout the year January 1527/8 the Iberians were active buyers at the Low Country fairs.[21] Cologne and Italian merchants, similarly absent since the previous year, also returned in the spring of 1527 eager to buy the English product for transmission along the central European highway to the South.[22] Trade, which had been slack during 1526, began to recover and rose to such a frenzy during the spring of 1527 that Netherlands production declined in the face of this onslaught which at the time of the Cold and Easter marts channelled al-

---

18 I.e. the traffic traversing the Channel, North Sea and Baltic.

19 Chapter 6.

20 For domestic prices see Figure 7.1, the sources for which are detailed in chapter 7, n. 8 above. For foreign currency prices at Frankfurt a. M. see M. J. ELSAS, Umriss einer Geschichte der Preise und Löhne in Deutschland, 3 Vols. in 2, Leiden 1936–49, Vol. II/A, pp. 498–9. Riga: G. MICKWITZ, Aus Revaler Handelsbüchern, Helsingfors 1938, pp. 100–1. Ancona, notarial records of Antonio Stracca and Antonio Pavesi (Archivio di Stato, Ancona II, ASA. 17–8, 21 and ASA 11 respectively). Information kindly provided by Dr Peter Earle.

21 L&P, Henry VIII, IV (2), No.4404. The Andalusian fleet carrying fruit and oil normally arrived in January, the Biscayan fleet with wool in June.

22 M. UNGER, Die Leipziger Messe und die Niederlande im 16. und 18. Jahrhundert, in: Hansische Geschichtsblätter, LXXXI (1963), pp. 21, 25–6 and 29. It seems probable that the low interest rates on the Frankfurt and Leipzig Exchanges, occasioned by the silver boom of 1526/7 (see ch. 1) offset the impact of bi-metallic premiums between these centres and Antwerp in early 1527 and encouraged trade via that city to Central Europe rather than a direct trade such as emerged during 1528–30 (present chapter below).

most 20,000 kerseys and an indeterminate number of English cloths to Venice.[23] The boom was halted in April with the financial crisis at Antwerp, occasioned by the Habsburg imposition of forced loans on the hapless denizens of the money market, but although this led to the collapse of the "second buying" at London during the first week of that month it afforded no relief for the Netherlands producer. Also the crisis was short lived and with the recovery of the market in time for the Sinxen mart all seemed set for a renewed English onslaught. In the event, however, the Netherlands producer found an odd ally in Henry VIII who in July attempted to divert the resurgent English trade from the Brabant fairs to Calais during the prelude to open Habsburg-Bourbon hostilities.[24] The indignation of the Italians, Spaniards and Flemings, who had flocked to the fairs that summer to acquire the English product, can be imagined. Hacket reported the openly hostile attitude of those who regaled him with complaints about the interruption of commercial intercourse.[25] Feelings were probably no less intense in London. Merchants who had flocked to the "first buying" for the Sinxen mart in mid-May subsequently abandoned the cloth halls, which remained deserted through the rest of the summer. The English producer's loss, however, was his Netherlands counterpart's gain. Protected by the ineptness of Henrican policy, Netherlands producers now found a ready vent for their wares at the Sinxen mart, occasioning an expansion in output and heavy imports of Spanish and other wools.[26] If Netherlands industrial prosperity in the summer of 1527 was predicated on English governmental blunders, however, the local magistrates were intent on ensuring that the boom would not be as ephemeral as the policies. With the reversal of Henrican policy in time for the Bamus mart, therefore, and the resurgence of English exports ordinances were passed, operative from the second week of September, "that no-one should admit any English cloths".[27] The English export boom, following the reversal of Henry's ill-judged policy, which had pushed up cloth prices at Blackwell Hall to enormous levels in late August, collapsed. The Netherlands boom, which had brought prosperity to the Flemish producer over the summer, after a brief interruption during August, continued. All seemed set for an expansion of the trade in Netherlands goods southward when the news from Leipzig, of the chaos in the central European mining industry, broke.[28]

Michaelmas 1527 witnessed the traditional supply route which linked Antwerp via Frankfurt to Venice cut and through the autumn and winter of 1527/8 a financial crisis developed on the Antwerp money market of such severity as to deter merchants from visiting that city. The buoyant traffic which had been carried via Antwerp to the south in 1527 was now in full retreat. Already declining through the winter of 1527/8, the restraint imposed by Margaret of Austria on Anglo-Netherlands commerce in January

23   On changes in Netherlands textile production at this time see chapter 13 below. On the transit trade in kerseys see the report of the Venetian Senate of 30 August 1527 as quoted in BRULEZ, Les routes commerciales, p. 129 n. 21.

24   L&P, Henry VIII, IV (2), Nr.3262.

25   Ibid., Nr. 3313.

26   TNA, SP 1/44 fo. 99v.

27   Ibid., fo. 99r.

28   Chapter 4.

1528 brought the English export trade thence to a complete halt.[29] Thus whilst Baltic grain ships, deflected from the Scheldt, arrived in English ports and Gonson's men o' war vigilantly patrolled the Channel, protecting English and French shipping from "Dutch" privateers – "those unthrifty braggarts of war" – and solicitously "wafting" their charges into the Thames, commercial intercourse with the Low Countries was at a standstill.[30] From January to the end of May Netherlands hoys were held in English ports and English ships and goods were arrested in Low Country towns.[31] Nor did the lifting of the restraint (22nd May) or the formal truce (15th June) markedly alter the situation.[32] The continuing financial crisis at Antwerp ensured that the recovery of Anglo-Netherlands commerce, so hoped for by both Wolsey and Margaret, would fail to materialise. In spite of rushing through the publication of the truce so that merchants might have a market at the Synchyeme mart for their cloth, sales at the Antwerp fair were slight.[33] Nor was the Bamus mart any better. On the 7th August Vaughan wrote from Antwerp that trade remained slack: a product of dear money and the Gelder War which had cut the road to Cologne.[34] A week and a half later, at the close of the fair, the situation had not improved. Sir John Stiles reported to Wolsey that the merchants "have had a very slack market at Antwerp. Their cloth, lead and tin remain yet unsold. After All Hallows (1st November) the mart at Barrow (Bergen-op-Zoom) will begin to which they will repair."[35] Yet once again hope remained unfulfilled. The Cold mart of 1528/9 was a failure.[36] Only an abatement of the financial crisis at Antwerp could lead to a resumption of Anglo-Netherlands trade and a re-establishment of the trading patterns of 1527.

The time had come for a recall of the "alternative commerce". If financial chaos reigned on the money markets of Antwerp, Frankfurt and Venice alternative sources of funds, no more expensive than those available in 1527, existed at London and Lyon. The bi-metallic equilibrium between these centres and Florence, moreover, ensured cheap monetary transfer, unimpeded by the existence of premiums, all along the route, used during previous Antwerp crises, from the south of England, through the

29 O. DE SCHMEDT, De Engelse natie te Antwerpen in de XVIe eeuw, 1496–1582, Antwerp 1950–4, Vol. I, pp. 139–141.

30 L&P, Henry VIII, IV (2), Nr. 4018, 4065-6, 4193, 4217, 4244, 4286, 4330.

31 Ibid., Nr. 3958, 4009, 4071, 4147.

32 L&P, Henry VIII, IV (2), Nos. 4256 (the commission of Margaret of Savoy, given at Malines on 12 May to conclude a mercantile peace) and 4280 (commission of Henry VIII on 19 May to a similar end). On the 22 May report of a proclamation by Margaret that no-one shall trouble the English by land or sea (L&P, Henry VIII, IV (2), No. 4286). On the continuing difficulties for English merchants from both the French and Netherlanders (see L&P, Henry VIII, IV (2), Nos. 4286, 4330, 4369) during the period from 22 May to 13 June. For the truce of 15 June see L&P, Henry VIII, IV (2), No. 4377.

33 L&P, Henry VIII, IV (2), Nos. 4389, 4432.

34 L&P, Henry VIII, IV (2), No. 4613. At this time Stephen Vaughan, who was subsequently to replace Hacket as financial agent for the English crown in the Low Countries, was just beginning his career, see W. C. RICHARDSON, Stephen Vaughan, Financial Agent of Henry VIII. A Study of Financial Relations with the Low Countries, Baton Rouge 1953.

35 L&P, Henry VIII, IV (2), No. 4638.

36 SLOOTSMAN, Brabantse kooplieden, p. 48.

Florentine and Luccese dominated emporium of Lyon, to Ancona and the Mediterranean. If the South German and Venetian intermediaries in Antwerp's trade were financially embarrassed, others were only too happy to take their place in transmitting goods southwards. In the three months from September 1527 until the imposition by Margaret of Austria of the restraint on Anglo-Netherlands trade in January 1528 finally put an end to the dwindling London-Antwerp commerce, some 4,000 kerseys and an indeterminate number of short cloths were shipped, predominantly by Italian houses like the Bonavisi, from London via Lyon to Ancona.[37] From January to September 1528 this trade continued, the number of kerseys passing along the "new" overland route (Map 8.1) to the south amounting to some 6,000.[38] Antwerp had been displaced in the trade to the Mediterranean and would remain so as long as high interest rates prevailed in that city. Yet Lyon was to prove as poor an alternative as it had been in earlier years and as trade declined the Italians bought little of the "commodities of this realm."[39]

Nor is the story different in the Spanish trade. Crisis conditions at Antwerp during the winter of 1527/8 deterred the return of the Andalusian fleet to the Scheldt and encouraged London merchants, like Howell, and their provincial counterparts to prepare for direct voyages to the Peninsula. From October–December 1527 they avidly bought up cloth on the depressed textile markets for the January shipping, but before the vessels could depart the news of the Habsburg–Tudor breach and the arrest of English goods in Spain became public.[40] From January to June 1528 the trade was accordingly at a halt. With peace and continuing high interest rates at Antwerp, which kept the Iberian merchants away from the Low Country fairs, however, the direct commerce from England to Spain was resumed. On the very day the truce was signed (15th June) Howell ventured a cargo in the *Peter of London*, which sailed in company with other ships, to Seville.[41] Antwerp was once again displaced as English merchants carried their wares direct to Spain, but again it seems probable that this "alternative commerce" was to prove a poor substitute for the previous "indirect trade" via the city on the Scheldt. As during previous crises at Antwerp, the decline in commerce through that city in 1527/8 led to an emergence of an "alternative commerce" to Iberia and the Mediterranean, but expansion in the "direct" trades to Spain or the indirect commerce via Lyon to the Mediterranean was never sufficient to counteract the effects of the collapse of Anglo-Netherlands commerce to the South.

English merchants thus in 1527–8, as during previous crises at Antwerp, looked elsewhere and working within the unified bi-metallic system bequeathed to them from Antwerp's previous European-wide financial network by the Netherlands monetary

---

37   TNA, E122/83/6 of receipts of a levy of 4d on each kersey exported from London, Michaelmas 1527–8 and on the arrival of these kerseys at Ancona, see: EARLE, Commercial Development, 1479–1551, p. 35, n. 4.

38   TNA, E122/83/6.

39   See chapter 6, n. 23 above. During the year August 1526/7 far in excess of 20,000 kerseys had been exported from London to Venice alone (present chapter, n. 23). From September 1527–8 only 10,000 kerseys were exported from London to all markets including the all important Italian one (chapter 10 below).

40   L&P, Henry VIII, IV (2), Nr. 4404; Howell's Ledger, fos. 56, 75.

41   Howell's Ledger, fo. 85.

reform of December 1527 the London merchant communities, together with their provincial counterparts, forged, in collaboration with continental European merchants, direct links with markets in the Baltic, the Levant, France and Central Europe and were even prepared when interest rates on the London market were low enough to venture to parts unknown. A new spirit was stirring in England perhaps best epitomised by these latter ventures, cryptically described by Hall:

> This same month the king sent two fair ships, well manned and victualled, having in them diverse cunning men, to seek strange regions, and so forth they set, out of the Thames the twentieth day of May (1527).[42]

This was the icing; however, the cake had more substance. In the Baltic new links were forged with Danzig (Gdansk), resuming an earlier pattern of intermittent voyages to that port. Each summer through 1527–9 a small fleet of Newcastle and Hull ships, usually sailing in twos and threes, departed from England for the northern sea.[43] Initially few in numbers, during 1528, twenty-nine English ships passed through the Sound.[44] The Levantine connection, resumed during the ephemeral period of stabilization on the London bill market after October 1526 but subsequently abandoned during the following spring and summer of 1527, also flourished from Michaelmas of that year and grew to a position of such importance that early in 1530 a consul, one Denis Harris, was appointed to handle the affairs of the English merchants who flocked to Candy.[45] Again in the French trades, the irregular visits of merchants, like Tooley, during the second and third decades of the century, continued through 1527–8.[46] During these years ships again crowded the harbours of Rouen and Bordeaux, a number servicing French domestic needs, although many more at this time again carried goods en route for southern climes via Lyon.[47] Moreover, for the first time during the years 1527–8, a "direct" commerce with Central Europe was established. The pattern of commercial activity which had emerged at the Cold mart of 1526/7, whereby German merchants acquired both their produce and finance at Frankfurt and Antwerp, continued until Michaelmas 1527, when the news of the Central European mining crisis broke.[48] Thereafter this trade declined and the merchants who remained, because of

---

42 E. HALL, Chronicle […], London 1809, p. 274. See also R. HAKLUYT, The Principall Navigations, Voyages and Discoveries of the English Nation, London 1589, p. 517.

43 A. H. JOHNSON, The History of the Worshipful Company of Drapers of London, Oxford 1914–22, II, pp. 251–2; I. BLANCHARD, Commercial Crisis and Change: Trade and the Industrial Economy of the North-East, 1509–32, in: Northern History, VIII (1973), pp. 74–5.

44 N. E. BANG / K. KORST (eds.), Tabeller over Skibsfart og Varetransport gennem Øresund 1661–1783 og gennem Storebælt 1701–1748, Copenhagen / Leipzig 1939–1945, I, pp. 2–6; Rigsarkivet, København, Sundtoldreguskab 1528, fo. 18 lines 1–2, 4, 15–6; fo. 21 lines 17–8, 25; fo. 22 line 12; fo. 23 line 19 and fo. 28 line 2 for individual English vessels sailing eastward through the Sound.

45 Cambridge University Library, Hengrave Hall MSS, 78/1; L&P, Henry VIII, IV (3), Nr. 6357.

46 J. WEBB, Great Tooley of Ipswich. Portrait of an Early Tudor Merchant, Ipswich 1962, p. 37; P. BOISSONNADE, Le mouvement commerciale entre la France et les îles Britanniques, in: Revue Historique, CXXXV (1920), p. 18.

47 Present chapter, above.

48 Chapter 4.

high finance costs, were forced to rapidly diversify their product mix in an attempt to reduce the price of their wares.[49] The crisis of 1527/8, however, shifted the main channels of trade elsewhere. Hanseatic and English shippers established new links to Hamburg.[50] The Hamburg *Wantsinder* then blazed new trails via Erfurt to Nuremberg and Central Europe[51], establishing a path along which English kerseys and "whites" dyed in Hamburg passed to consumers in South Germany and the Hungarian lands.[52] Once again in late 1527 and 1528, as during previous Antwerp crises in 1509–13, 1516–7 and 1520–3 and the winter of 1526/7, English merchants, in common with many of their continental European counterparts, had diverted their commerce away from that city towards the paths of the "alternative commerce".

In one respect, however, conditions were very different in 1527–8 from before, when the shift in trade towards the channels of the "alternative commerce" had resulted in an aggregative decline in English trade, for now English trade expanded rapidly. Initially in 1527, because of the continuing high cost of finance, the progress of the independent "direct" trades had been slight, but when in 1528 the Italians, because of the interruption of their southern trades, failed "to buy the commodities of this realm" and instead "delivered their money to other merchants by exchange" interest rates fell and commerce boomed.[53] Over two hundred English ships and an unknown number of foreign ones departed from England in 1528 for Baltic and North Sea ports (apart from Scotland and Iceland).[54] Others sailed to France and the Levant. English exports, in spite of the decline in the southern trades, expanded rapidly during the year September 1527/8 almost reaching 100,000 "cloths" – the highest point yet attained in the sixteenth century.[55] Times were changing as in 1528 the English merchant, for the first time, came into his own.

In terms of the route networks through which merchants distributed their wares, the crises of the 'twenties had wrought no great changes to the commercial patterns established during the previous two decades. When untroubled by financial or monetary disorders – in 1505–9, 1514–5, 1518–9, 1523–4 and 1527 – Antwerp, by the availability of cheap money on its Bourse, continued to draw to itself, by land and sea, the merchants whose wares were subsequently redistributed throughout a commercial system which was of European-wide dimensions. When, however, crisis conditions prevailed at Antwerp – in 1509–13, 1516–7, 1520–2, 1525–early 1527 and late 1527–

---

49   L&P, Henry VIII, IV (2), Nr. 4662/1–7.

50   In 1530 Hamburg and English merchants brought craftsmen, at first dyers and finishers, from Antwerp to Hamburg (from the reference in R. EHRENBERG, Hamburg und England im Zeitalter der Königin Elisabeth [Jena 1896], p. 78). It seems probable that their trade to Hamburg had continued for some time prior to this date.

51   BRULEZ, Les routes commerciales, pp. 178–181.

52   G. SZÉKELY, Niederländische und Englische Tucharten im Mitteleuropa des 13.–17.Jahrhunderts, in: Annales Universitatis Scientiarum Budapestinensis de Roland Eötvas nominatae. Sectio Historica. VIII (1966), pp. 33–5.

53   Chapter 6.

54   L&P, Henry VIII, IV (2), Nr. 5101.

55   E. M. CARUS-WILSON / O. COLEMAN, England's Export Trade, 1275–1547, Oxford 1963, pp. 111–6 on the overall expansion of English commerce during 1528. The decline of the southern trades is dealt with on pages 114–115 (ibid.).

1528 – merchants (save during the years 1525–6) diverted their commerce away from that city towards the paths of an "alternative commerce". Drawing on the resources of new financial centres - Lyon and London (throughout the period) and Frankfurt (until 1520–2) – they created an alternative commercial system. As far as London was concerned, however, this process was a lengthy one. Only gradually were the bi-metallic impediments to the operation of its money market removed as first (in 1509–13) France and the Levantine ports and then (between 1516/7 and 1520–2) Venice were drawn into its high-cost, alternative financial network. Indeed it was only in the 'twenties that London largely freed itself of such impedimenta, allowing, in 1520–2 and 1527–8, a free transfer of funds within a system of truly international dimensions. Nor even then, before 1528, was it, any more than Lyon, a cheap source of funds. In terms of the route systems serving the requirements of European commerce the twenties thus saw things continue much as before.

In terms of the traffic passing through these systems it was otherwise. During the years 1505–9, 1514–5 and 1518–9, as a result of steadily falling interest rates on the Antwerp Exchange, trade through that city had expanded to a high point at the latter date and English exports, still at that time overwhelmingly destined for the Brabant fairs, followed a similar course. During the 'twenties, however, this trend was reversed as from 1521 a general enhancement of interest rates on the Antwerp bill market increased the finance costs of merchants visiting that city and from 1522 a bi-metallic realignment of the Netherlands currencies created an endemic condition of premiums on its exchanges, deflecting merchants from visiting the towns on the Scheldt. Thus in 1523–4, as the English trade recovered from the previous years crisis, dear money and the withdrawal of the Spaniards, Hansards and French, which undermined commercial activity at the Bergen fairs, aborted the export boom, causing trade to stabilize at a lower level than before (viz. in 1518–9). Nor was the situation different in 1527. In spite of the competitive advantage enjoyed by English producers over their Netherlands counterparts at this time, English trade, still tied to the Brabantine fairs, failed to recover beyond the level previously attained in 1523–4. The trade boom which had characterised English commerce, both at Antwerp and in general, during the first two decades of the sixteenth century, was over. During the 'twenties whenever the English were active at the Low Counties fairs (in 1523–4 and during the summer of 1527), due to high finance costs and an absence of many of their customers, trade stagnated at a new low-level equilibrium, slightly below the peak of 1518–9.

The 'twenties also marked a distinct break with the past with respect to the volume of trade passing through the channels of that "alternative commerce" which emerged whenever crisis – in 1509–13, 1516–7, 1520–2, 1525–early 1527 and late 1527–1528 – beset the Antwerp market. During the years 1509–13, 1516–7 and 1520–2 this had proven a poor substitute for trade through Antwerp and whilst on these occasions "direct" English commerce to new markets had expanded, aggregate English trade had markedly declined. Again, however, this situation began to change during the 'twenties, on this occasion the crisis of 1525–early 1527 marking the turning point in the trend. Few, however, could have anticipated this when the crisis first broke and the acute bi-metallic disequilibrium between England and the Netherlands crippled commerce with that country whilst the dislocation of sales-credit systems and Henrican depredations, in enhancing domestic interest rates, prevented a revival of England's "alternative commerce". Yet when in late-1526 the domestic situation eased for a moment and the "alternative commerce" again revived, the strength of the "direct" trade boom was such as to significantly support the aggregate volume of English commerce in that year. Certainly the strength of this boom is not explicable in terms of low interest rates on the London exchange. Indeed these remained inordinately high at this time. Yet that rate now prevailed within a financial network which thanks to the bi-metallic realignment of European currencies 1515–1526 was of truly international dimensions. Over the winter of 1526/7, therefore, there was a widening if not a deepening of commercial activity within the network of England's "direct" trades. Moreover, when those trades were resumed after Michaelmas 1527 it looked as though this pattern would repeat itself, after the Antwerp boom of the summer, the direct trades growing and aggregate English trade declining but the downswing now being only of modest proportions (in comparison with 1509–13, 1516–7 and 1520–2). The London bill market, servicing an extended financial system, was still, like Lyon, not a cheap source of funds. Then in 1528 when the Italians, because of the interruption of their southern trades, failed "to buy the commodities of this realm" and "instead delivered their money to other merchants by exchange", interest rates fell, the "direct" commerce expanded rapidly and aggregate English trade, instead of falling, actually increased – to its highest point yet in the sixteenth century.

The 'twenties had thus seen dramatic changes in the position of the English merchants. From 1521–2, whenever they were active at the Low Counties fairs (in 1523–4 and during the summer of 1527), due to high finance costs and an absence of many of their customers, their trade stagnated at a new low-level equilibrium, slightly below the peak of 1518–9. When, however, they were forced to abandon that trade, because of financial and monetary crises at Antwerp (in 1525–early 1527 and late 1527–1528), and, over the winter of 1526/7 and in 1527/8, adopted once more the paths of the "alternative commerce" they found their position ameliorated. Initially, because of continuing high finance costs on the London bill market, overall trade still declined on these occasions but when in 1528 finance costs there were reduced, the independent trades increased sufficiently to raise the overall level of English commerce. In the events of 1528, however, two forces combined to promote the expansion of English commerce. First, the boom was a product of the application of cheap money to trading activities within a new Anglo-centric financial and commercial system operating since 1527 independently of Antwerp. Second, the boom resulted from the emergence of interest rate differentials between London and crisis-torn Antwerp which led the Italians to fund their trade to the South through other centres than the city on the Scheldt. It thus remained to be seen what would happen when trading conditions at Antwerp returned to normal, interest rates at that city fell and the Italians resumed their trade through that city to the South.

CHAPTER TEN

ROUTE REALIGNMENT AND ENGLISH TRADE EXPANSION IN CONDITIONS OF PRICE INSTABILITY, 1529–1544

During 1529 Antwerp's trade recovered and the fate of England's "alternative commerce", formed during the previous crisis year, hung in the balance. Over the winter of 1528/9 there had been an abatement of the financial crisis at the western metropolis. Medium-term rates on government paper stabilized at slightly below the crisis levels of the previous summer and almost imperceptibly edged downward over the following year. Commercial paper rates, on the other hand, under Italian tutelage, fell heavily along that path which ultimately in early-1531 would once again bring cheap money to the Antwerp Exchange.[1] Already by Easter 1529 the fall in the bill rate (to 10 per cent usance) was sufficient to effect a revival of trade at that fair. On 21st March strange news arrived at London from Calais of a Spanish fleet of some 120 ships standing off Nieuport.[2] Late perhaps, the Spaniards had returned to the Scheldt. The same fair saw a return of the Italians. Yet one problem, a legacy of the mining crisis of 1527/8, remained before the southern trades could once more, as in 1527, become the central element in Antwerp's commercial empire. The crisis at Frankfurt, occasioned by the mining disorders of the previous year, which crippled the South German financial houses and depressed the trade of that city into the early thirties, prohibited the use of the central European highway to the South.[3] New sources of finance and new routes had to be found. The source of funds, as has been shown, was provided by the Italians and particularly the financiers of Lucca and Genoa – the Bonavisi, Grimaldi and Affaitadi.[4] They also pioneered the new routes (Map 10.1) which linked England via Antwerp to Cologne and from thence either by way of Basle and the St Gothard Pass to Milan, Brescia and Genoa or by way of Mainz, Augsburg, Salzburg and the Tavern Pass to Venice.[5] Whichever route was taken Frankfurt was by-passed[6] and its trade declined whilst that passing along the new route expanded, as

---

1   See Ch. 5.

2   L&P, Henry VIII, IV (3), Nr. 5395.

3   A. DIETZ, Frankfurter Handelsgeschichte, 5 Vols., Frankfurt-on-the-Main 1910–1925, I, p. 68.

4   Ch. 5 above.

5   W. BRULEZ, Lettres commerciales de Daniel et Antoine de Bombergen à Antonio Grimani 1532–43, Bulletin de l' Institute Historique Belge de Rome, XXXI (1958), pp. 120–184.

6   On the recovery of the Adventurers' trade at Antwerp which had begun tentatively at the Cold mart of 1528/9 when they were said to have sold their cloths better at this mart than they did (L&P, Henry VIII, IV [3], Nr. 5171) see for instance Hengrave Hall MSS., 78/1 which illustrates

English wares were transported by Italian merchants to customers in southern climes. Antwerp during 1529 thus resumed its role in the expansive Italian and Spanish trades and the commercial map of Europe was redrawn.

Map 10.1: Anglo-Netherlands Textile Trade 1530–42

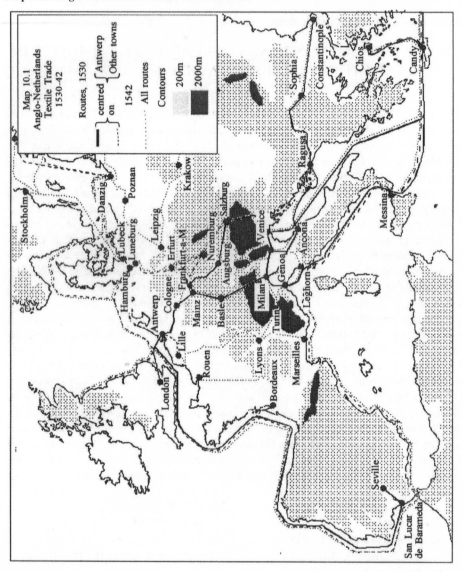

the recovery of the English cloth trade through 1529 of one shipper at least who had been absent from the fairs since the Cold mart of 1526/7.

Certain elements of London's "alternative commerce" were thus now wrenched from its grasp as in 1529 commercial activity re-centred on Antwerp. The London agents of such Italian merchant-finance houses as the Bonavisi, who in 1527/8 had trans-shipped cloth via Lyon to the Mediterranean, abandoned that trade and dispatched their wares to the Brabantine fairs for reshipment South. In the Spanish trades merchants, like Howell, who in 1527/8, when unimpeded by restraints on trade (January–June 1528), had pursued an active export trade to the Peninsula, abandoned their "direct" commerce with the return in March 1529 of the Spaniards to the Scheldt. From that time English exports were despatched to Spain, as in 1527, by way of Antwerp. Occasionally this "indirect" commerce, which was dependent on the safe arrival of the Spanish fleets in the Scheldt, was interrupted by French naval action in the Bay of Biscay and at such times the occasional English ship was despatched to Spain.[7] Such influences were during 1529 ephemeral, however, and from the Easter fair of that year there was a general resumption of the Anglo-Netherlands-Spanish trade. Henceforth, England's exports to Spain, as to Italy, would pass via Antwerp.

Whilst the Iberian and Italian trades thus in 1529 passed back into Antwerp's sphere of influence others, however, maintained their allegiance to the English "direct" commerce. That year saw a distinct "Baltic Interest" formed by merchants whose previous intermittent voyages were now displaced by a permanent trade to the ports of the northern sea. Throughout the following decade these merchants pursued a regular commerce, their shipping needs being catered for by English skippers, like John Hughes of Yarmouth or the Newcastle masters John Keswick and John Brokers, whose vessels may be discerned regularly passing through the Sound and unloading at Danzig; or again by Hanseatic ships, like the *John of Danzig* or the *Esyll of Danzig* whose captains, Jacob Slaggart and Herman Hasse, regularly visited such east coast ports as Hull.[8] Year after year these "stationed" ships, like their Dutch counterparts, plied a regular and growing traffic between their home ports and the Baltic[9] but when crisis conditions prevailed at Antwerp and interest rates on the London exchanges fell (in 1532 and 1533/4, 1535/6 and 1538–40) they were joined by many other vessels seeking alternative employment. Indeed, such were the numbers of ships that sailed for the Baltic on these occasions that they aroused protectionist sentiments amongst the merchant communities of the Hanseatic towns which became an endemic element of Anglo-Hanseatic relations, sometimes, as in 1532–4, invoking such dramatic measures as the closing of the Sound but more often, as in 1535/6, resulting in a low-level state of clandestine guerrilla warfare between Hansard and English merchant. On that occasion the first signs of the impending politico-economic crisis began to emerge during the early summer of 1535 when rumours circulated that the Lübeckers had seized a Scots ship[10] and were fitting out vessels against the Dutch.[11] It was at this

---

7   G. CONNELL-SMITH, Forerunners of Drake: A Study of English Trade with Spain in the Early Tudor Period, London 1954, p.78

8   Rigsarkivet, København, Sundtoldreguskab 1528, 1535–44. Wojewódzdkim Archiwum Pánstwowym w Gdansku, 300/19 Nr.11. TNA., E122/64/15–6 and 99/27, 31.

9   From 1536 this pattern is clearly revealed in the Sound Toll Registers: N. E. BANG / K. KORST (eds.), Tabeller over Skibsfart og Varetransport gennem Øresund 1661–1783 og gennem Storebælt 1701–1748, Copenhagen / Leipzig 1939–1945, I, pp. 2–6.

10   BL. Royal MS. B 18 VI, fo. 30.

moment, moreover, that the English merchants first became entangled in the web of subterfuges and deceits which characterised the new Hanseatic protectionism.[12] In early May, "certain English ships bound for Livonia and Prussia" were taken into "protective custody" at Copenhagen by the Duke of Oldenburg (on behalf of Christian [III] and the Duke of Mecklenberg) to prevent their being seized by the Lübeckers who stood at the very gates of the city. What their fate would have been is uncertain because the ships were released before the city fell to the Lübeckers in the second week of the month, but with the arrival of the next English vessel at Copenhagen after that event (viz on the 15th May) something of the complexity of the emerging situation is revealed. Again, after paying toll at Elsinor on the 17th May, the ship was seized and held by the Danes for some three weeks, whilst it was stripped of its ordnance, but on this occasion it was through the mediation of the Burgomaster of Lübeck that it was released and in resuming its voyage to Danzig it sailed not in fear of the Lübeckers (from whom its predecessors had been "protected") but rather of the Swedes. It sailed, moreover, in the certainty that as long as the Lübeckers held the Sound it would be able to return unmolested. The merchants' problems seemed to be over. Yet on arriving at Danzig another dimension of the political situation in the Baltic and of intra-Hanseatic relations was revealed. The merchants, like those who had already arrived, were met by Hans von Werd, who as head of the Danzig merchant community, greeted them with "fair words", assured them that they would be well treated "so that the King would know the Danzigers were his friends" and then by various subterfuges delayed their departure for some seven weeks.[13] The reason resided in events taking place further west for that August Christian was busy retrieving Copenhagen from the Lübeckers whose friendly relations with the English merchants had, since the latter's departure in June, blossomed into a full-blown political alliance with their king. It was thus not until Christian (in alliance with the High Master of Prussia) was actually once more in control of the Sound and the Lübeckers had withdrawn to Varberg, that the English ships departed from Danzig – straight into a trap. At one fell swoop on the 29th August all 13 or 14 vessels that had sailed from Danzig were seized by Swedish men o' war and carried into Copenhagen. The political strategies behind the arcane game of cat and mouse were now at long last revealed. Arrayed in open conflict was Lübeck, allied with the English crown (represented by Bonner and Cavendish who arrived at Varberg aboard the *Minion* on the 26th August), who stood in opposition to an alliance which, in spite of their fair words, linked the fortunes of Danzig to those of the Danish "king". With the English ships in their hands, moreover, neither Christian nor the Danzigers had any further need for subterfuge. The English captives were accordingly regaled with the boasts of a Danish captain

---

11 L&P, Henry VIII, VIII, Nr. 760.

12 The following account is based on three sets of sources, all of which are included in the collection L&P, Henry VIII, Vols. VIII–IX : the mercantile correspondence between merchants involved in the events and their masters in England (ibid., IX , Nrs. 246, 323); the official correspondence of Henry VIII and members of his council with both the English merchants and Christian, elect III and his officers (ibid., VIII , Nrs. 1170–1; IX, Nrs. 285, 290–1, 831 and 1019/6) and the political intelligence of the course of events in London sent by Chapuys to Charles V (ibid., IX , Nrs. 356, 434, 594, 732, 776 and 861). Of these the first is by far the most useful.

13 Ibid., IX, Nr. 291.

who had already openly taken an English crayer and hoy and threatened shortly to be once more in England to "fetch 4–5 more ships".[14] Their king was treated in no lesser manner. In a missive to him Christian seemingly declared that the seizure of the English ships was "but the assay of the wine they intended to have" and that "in the spring they would come and drink of it at the place."[15] Nor was this braggadocio rooted in the insecurities of weak men for in September, even as Henry ordered the sequestration of Hanseatic goods in England[16] and prepared to despatch two vessels ladened with men, munitions and money to join the *Minion* at Varberg[17], Christian carried forward his final campaign and on the 25th it was reported that Varberg had fallen and rumours even circulated at London that the king's envoys to the Lübeckers had been taken. In the event it was not so but the envoys now had little more to do than make peace. Through October and November negotiations continued but it was only on the 21st November, long after the shipping season had closed, that eight of the captured ships returned to England whilst, humiliatingly for the English crown, four were retained in Denmark in the service of the Danish king. Yet peace had returned to the Baltic trades and as economic condition at Antwerp ameliorated during the next year and fewer vessels frequented these northern waters there was no repetition of these events. Yet a pattern had been set. From 1529 a distinct "Baltic Interest" had emerged as an important element in the new English "direct" commerce to continental Europe. Its trade, moreover, had rapidly expanded. The tempo of expansion, however, was irregular and was most pronounced when dislocations of the Antwerp market (in 1532 and 1533/4, 1535/6 and 1538–40) deflected trade from that city and caused a host of "irregulars" to join the ranks of the permanent group of Baltic traders, thereby posing a major threat to Hanseatic commerce. The nature of that threat was revealed by the Hanseatic reaction to the alien invasion of its preserves. Lübeck secure, on such occasions, in obtaining overland supplies of those South German goods which previously had been trans-shipped to the Baltic from Antwerp by Dutch and Scots merchants, did not feel threatened. Danzig, on the other hand, seeing her position in the all-important *Englandfahrer* challenged, did, and consistently during this period and after[18] the city led the opposition in the Hanseatic Diet to that growing English threat which had first materialised with the creation of the English "Baltic Interest" in 1529.

The Levantine trade, which had continued intermittently during the winter of 1526/7 and throughout the year 1527/8, also flourished and acquired a new permanence in 1529–30, attracting the attentions of substantial London merchants whose agents arrived at Candy in such numbers during these years that a permanent consul, one Dennis Harris, was appointed to handle their affairs.[19] It was a complex business involving the integration of the English firms into the existing labyrinthine shipping

---

14   Ibid., IX, Nr. 323.

15   Ibid., IX, Nr. 594.

16   Initially from the 13 October–6 November the sequestration extended to the goods of all Hanseatic merchants but from the latter date it was restricted to the goods of the Danzig merchants, ibid., IX, Nrs. 594, 732 and 776.

17   A 200-ton vessel and its 60-ton tender carrying munitions and money and a levy of 100 troops of whom Chapuys wrote that "there was never such a sorry sight", ibid., IX, Nr. 356.

18   In 1542–3 and 1550–4.

19   L&P, Henry VIII, IV (3), Nr. 6357.

and trading networks of the Ibero-Italian merchant houses – an operation which was not without its own particular difficulties. When John Gresham's factor in Candy, William Heath, despatched a cargo to England worth 12,000 ducats aboard the Portuguese ship the *San Antonio* he embroiled his master in a frenetic search during 1531 as the latter attempted to retrieve his goods which, following their despatch from the eastern Mediterranean, had been high-jacked by the ship's captain, Diego Perez, and secreted in some Portuguese haven.[20] Such "misunderstandings" were not unusual in the dealings between the English "Levantine merchants" and the Ibero-Italians with whom they "collaborated". The voyage of the *Mary Plantagenet* in 1533 was plagued by them. Even as it sailed south via Cadiz news filtered back to Southampton of troubles between the supercargo, John Cheriton, and the master and Italian merchants aboard. Matters came to a head at Messina and were only finally resolved when Cheriton sold the ship at a loss of some 600 ducats to those who he claimed "had wrought" him "all the mischief they can". Nor were Cheriton's problems over with the departure of the vessel, under new owners, for Candy. Having unloaded the ship's ordnance at the Sicilian port he trans-shipped it to Leghorn aboard a vessel whose captain on being retained by the Duke of Florence surrendered his charge into the hands of his new master. The summer of 1533 was thus a busy one for the supercargo who now domiciled himself at Pisa and threw himself into the task of retrieving the artillery and repairing his fortunes. To this end he entered into relations with the Florentine merchant house of Capone and through their mediation obtained both the return of the ordnance and a loan which he invested in a cargo of silks, camlets, alum and galls worth some 1,300 ducats. Early in the new year he freighted these goods and a package of silks, bought with the sale money from the ship, aboard a Portuguese vessel bound for Marseilles – which was cast away between Savona and Genoa. He thus arrived in France, where he was committed to invest funds for the Capone in Gascon woad, once more destitute and "in trust" to the Italians. His letters in February and March 1534 to his master Lord Lisle, written as he undertook his work for the Italians at Bordeaux and Toulouse, reveal a pathetic individual and he must have cut a pitiful figure on his return to Portsmouth where he was forced to await the arrival of a 200 tun cargo of wine, which he had freighted from France on Breton ships, for some eight months, possibly pondering ruefully on what had been a disastrous year.[21] The Levantine trade, for those who collaborated with the Ibero-Italians was not an easy one. Nor was

---

20 R. HAKLUYT, The Principal Navigations, Voyages, Traffiques and Discoveries of the English Nation, 3 Vols. in 2, London 1599–1600, II, p. 96. Gresham's agent in this search was John Ratcliffe who was despatched to Portugal with a letter of introduction from the king dated 15 October 1531.

21 The account of Cheriton's adventures may be pieced together from the Lisle Correspondence preserved in the State Papers: L&P, Henry VIII, VI, Nrs. 1147, 1353, 1462; VII, Nrs. 191, 233, 274, 428, 436, 461, 587/23; VIII, 83 and 88 subsequently edited by M. St. C. BYRNE (ed.), The Lisle Correspondence, 6 Vols., Chicago / London 1981. During 1534–6, as Lisle despatched a new venture to the Levant, Cheriton tried to re-ingratiate himself with his master by attempting to retrieve the ordnance left in the hands of the Capone. On his continuing adventures during these years see ibid., VIII, Nrs. 1051; X, Nr. 538. It is possible that Lisle was a marginal shipper, enticed into the trade of the regular "Levant merchants" by the fall in interest rates on the London exchanges in 1532 and 1533–4. Certainly for its voyage to the Levant the *Mary Plantagenet* was diverted from more mundane employment in the local commerce of the West Country and the Irish Sea, an employment serviced by Lisle's galliots during the years 1532–4.

it any less troubled for those English merchants who ventured cargoes on English ships, such as the *Holy Crosse*, the *Mathew Gonson* or the *Trinity of Erith*, which, year after year, conducted a regular trade to the isles of the eastern Mediterranean.[22] At best they might, in the manner of Dennis Harris (who on surrendering his office as consul at Candy to the Genoese merchant Benedict Justiniani in October 1531[23] had resumed his service with the London Adventurer William Castelayn), become embroiled in the net of Iberian mercantilist legislation.[24] At worst they might suffer the fate of the crew of the *Trinity of Erith* who in 1536 were betrayed by a Genoese pilot and forced to turn back from Messina, leaving their captain, James Romney, "abed naked with a harlot".[25] Exotic certainly, profitable possibly, the Levantine trade, which had continued intermittently during the second and third decades of the sixteenth century, from 1529 became a important accretion to England's commercial empire whose permanence was attested by the appointment of a whole series of successors to Harris as consul/factors at Chios (Benedict Justiniani, 1531–3; William Eames, 1533–44 and Robert Bye, 1544–).

More mundane, but almost certainly more significant, was the establishment of a permanent Anglo-French "direct commerce". Here, as in the other trades, the irregular visits of merchants to Bordeaux and other French ports, carrying goods for that market as well as for re-export through Lyon, during the second and third decades of the century, were replaced from 1529 by a regular commerce. Few henceforth, before 1535, carried goods for transhipment via Lyon to the Mediterranean but, year after year, merchants, like Tooley, regularly plied their wares on the Bordeaux market. Symbolic perhaps of this new permanent commerce is his renting of a house in the parish of St Remi, but surer evidence lies in the voyages of his ship the *Mary Walsingham*, once or twice a year, in company with others to Bordeaux during the years down to 1540.[26] From the perspective of English exporters this commerce to Bordeaux was of paramount importance, constantly exercising the mind of merchant and royal adviser alike in an age of mutual suspicion between Tudor and Valois courts, but it was only one element in a complex pattern of Anglo-French commerce which, on occasion, was very far from mundane. Thus when over the winter of 1536/7 we have revealed to us the activities of a Parisian jeweller trading at London[27] we are afforded a brief glance of a trade normally lost to view amongst the hurly-burly of Anglo-French trade but one which was, as, if not more important than the every-day traffic in cloth or lead, wine or woad. The story is that of Jehan Lange, a Parisian jeweller, who over that winter was in London acting for a syndicate of French merchants and jewellers.[28] His

---

22 HAKLUYT, Principal Navigations, II , pp. 96–9.

23 L&P, Henry VIII, IV (3), Nr. 506/3.

24 Ibid., VII , Nr. 938.

25 Ibid., X, Nr. 538.

26 J. WEBB, Great Tooley of Ipswich. Portrait of an Early Tudor Merchant, Ipswich 1962, p. 48; Ipswich and East Suffolk Record Office, C13/15/1 fo. 131 together with the un-foliated sheets of voyages of the *Mary Walsingham*.

27 His correspondence is preserved amongst the intercepted letters in State Papers: L&P, Henry VIII, XI, Nr. 47/1–19.

28 These comprised Cardin de la Londe, a jeweller living at Paris near Chatelet; Jacques Poullain, merchant, Jehan Lorens, jeweller, Thibaut Comtet and Robert Ronnell, all living "under the Pont

stay was not an unpleasant one and whilst travelling with the court between Westminster and Greenwich he made "good cheer" and sold to the King many of his wares – various images; a gown and hose of Jacques Poullain which Henry declared he was too old to wear and immediately bought for 4000 crowns; a mirror of Thibault Comtet and a hat of M. Caillot worth 200 crowns, and a collar and "visor", a martin and various linens of Jan de Gram worth 400 crowns – for a total of some 5,000 crowns. Other goods, such as a "St John" and another image enriched with a sapphire belonging to Jehan Lenfant, he sold to a gentleman for 70 and 20 crowns a piece. Then began the business of settling the affairs of the syndicate, paying the debts due in London by Cardin de la London and visiting a whole host of French merchants in London both to gather monies in and to arrange for the transmission of funds on the exchange to his correspondents in Paris. In all bills worth some 2,000 crowns were dispatched to members of the syndicate in Paris – but never arrived.[29] Exceptional perhaps, this trade was certainly one which would have benefited (had the letters and bills arrived safely) from the new conditions of cheap money on the London-Paris exchange. Lange's activities putting out money on the exchange, moreover, reveal the presence in London of many more Frenchmen, engaged in more mundane trading activities perhaps, but still involved in an Anglo-French commerce which since 1529 had assumed a permanent place in English mercantile activity.

If the English commerce via Hamburg to Central Europe, which also continued through the 1530s, is also added to this list then it may be seen that from 1529 a totally new pattern of European trade had emerged.[30] From that date Antwerp's European supremacy had become a thing of the past. Her merchants and financiers now performed a more limited function within European trade. Behind a barrier of bimetallic premiums they serviced, when unimpeded by financial crises, the needs of the buoyant trades to Spain and Italy. The corollary of these changes was the emergence of a sphere of commercial activity independent of Antwerp, engrossing markets in northern and central Europe, France and the Levant, within which London acted as one of the principal nodes. For the first time in 1529, freed from distortions created by financial dislocations on the Antwerp money market, a new pattern of European trading networks had emerged.

Within those networks, moreover, trade now followed a completely new course. Henceforth, for more than a decade, it was to be by the endeavours of English merchants in fostering their direct trades that English trade expansion took place. From 1528 each downswing in interest rates on the English exchanges (in 1528, 1532 and 1533/4, 1535/6 and 1538–40), which occurred when the southern trades handled by the Netherlands-Italian houses at Antwerp were in abeyance, carried English trade to ever higher levels as denizens utilised the money released by the Italians to expand their direct trades. Each increase in interest rates (in 1529–31, 1534/5 and 1536–8),

du Change"; Allart Ploumyer, living under the Pont de Notre Dame "à l' image de St George" and Jehan Lenfant, living on that Bridge; Jacques Caillou, resident in the Rue de la Savonnerie, and Guion de Nesme, in the Rue St Dennis near St Katherine, as well as Jahan de Gram, Nicholas Mabre and Francis Leschasier, merchants and goldsmiths, all domiciled in Paris.

29   On suspicion of Lange being a spy the letters and bills were intercepted and thus to this day remain amongst the State Papers.

30   See ch. 6 above.

which occurred when the trade via Antwerp was resumed, witnessed a retreat in English commercial activity, as the "direct" trades, starved of funds, declined and trade through Antwerp stabilized at, and then after 1535 fell from the low equilibrium levels of the 1520s. Yet each subsequent fluctuation left interest rates on the London exchanges at a lower, and English trade at a higher level than before as the long-term rate of growth in the "direct" trades contrasted with the slowly declining English commerce through Antwerp.[31]

1529 thus marked the beginnings of a new age in the history of English commerce but before the new trends would become fully apparent one problem remained to be resolved, namely that created by inflationary pressures within the economy in 1532. Prior to this date the new mechanisms had operated in the manner first established in 1528–9. Whilst crisis conditions had prevailed at Antwerp in 1528 the Italians had abandoned their cloth export and failed to buy "the commodities of the realm", instead delivering their "money to other merchants by exchange."[32] English trade, guided by these "other merchants" expanded – to its highest point yet in the sixteenth century. With the abatement of the Antwerp crisis over the winter of 1528/9, however, this mechanism was thrown into reverse. Interest rates on commercial paper at Antwerp again fell and from the Easter mart of 1529 the Italians once more resumed their trade to the South either buying their wares through their factors at London, who again "bought the commodities of the realm", or from English merchants who flocked to the Brabant fairs. In these circumstances money was scarce on the London money market, interest rates there rose, and both the "direct" trades and the total volume of English commerce declined. Moreover, the more bill rates at Antwerp fell (from 10 percent usance at Easter 1529 to 4 per cent during the period Whit 1529–30 and then to 3.6 per cent at Easter 1531) and the more Antwerp's trade expanded, so the more English bill rates rose and the deeper the English trade depression became.

Then at the Sinxen mart of 1531 crisis conditions returned to Antwerp. The interest rate on government paper, which had fallen from 21.3 to 16.75 percent per annum during the course of 1529–31, rose at the fair to 18 per cent. Even more dramatic was the rise on the exchanges. The bill rate which had attained 3.6 per cent usance at the Easter fair of 1531 now shot up to 5 per cent. Crisis conditions once more prevailed at Antwerp, trade through that city declined but aggregate English commerce increased, although not for long. The imperial authorities, aghast at the effects of indiscriminate borrowing, retreated over the winter of that year. The amount of outstanding *finances* and *rentes* was steadily, if slowly, reduced and bills of exchange were redeemed as they fell due. By Easter government paper could be floated at 15 per cent and the bill market was again calm: with all impediments removed dealings there took place at a mere one per cent usance.[33] Accordingly, from the winter fair of 1531/2 English trade once again re-orientated itself through Antwerp and such was the intensity of the subsequent boom through the city during the winter of 1531/2 and spring of 1532 that protectionist sentiments began to spread amongst the denizens of the Netherlands cloth making districts. As early as December 1531 Stephen Vaughan en route to meet-

---

31   This paragraph is based on the analysis undertaken in ch. 5 above.

32   E. HALL, Chronicle […], London 1809, p. 781.

33   See ch. 5 above.

ings at Brussels heard at Bergen-op-Zoom rumours "that the Hollanders had banished English cloth." Subsequent enquiries amongst the authorities at Brussels yielded him no information but on returning to Antwerp before the end of the month he learnt that the report was common.[34] It was not until the second week of February, however, that he was able to lay hands on a copy of the ordinance for dispatch home and by then it was too late.[35] As a result of these measures the English trade at the Cold mart was a total failure and already five weeks earlier he had been forced to report that "less cloth by one half have been shipped to this mart."[36] Yet if the situation at the beginning of January was bad, as interest rates tumbled during the course of the fair they looked as though they could get far worse. By the third week of February he reported that similar sentiments to those of the Hollanders were also felt amongst the Flemings and with the opening of the Easter fair sentiment turned to action.[37] With interest rates on the exchanges as low as one per cent usance all seemed set for a major boom in the English cloth trade through Antwerp and the Flemings knew it. Vague hostility thus turned to action. Flanders, like Holland, banished English cloth and the Flemings "spitefully burnt all that they can find."[38] During the course of 1531/2, therefore, the new trade mechanisms once more revealed themselves: at the time of the Sinxen mart of 1531 trade through Antwerp declined and England's "direct" commerce began to push up her overall export trade. Through the winter fair of 1531/2 and the Easter one of 1532 trade reoriented itself through Antwerp providing the one positive element in an overall trade depression. Even this element was threatened, however, by its own success as protectionism began to emerge in the Netherlands clothing districts. Not surprisingly, therefore, Stephen Vaughan, who the previous autumn had been dilatory in the extreme in meeting imperial demands for a commercial diet, during the following winter and spring came with a sense of urgency to the negotiating table.[39] Bluff

---

34 BL. Galba X, fo. 24. Stephen Vaughan to Cromwell, 30 December 1531.

35 Ibid., fo. 3. Stephen Vaughan to Cromwell, 14 February 1532. In a subsequent letter dated the 20 February 1532 he refers to the despatch of this document with Thomas Sutton, mercer.

36 On 3 January 1531/2 Vaughan had written to Cromwell from Bergen-op-Zoom that "[l]ess cloth by one half have been shipped to this [Cold] mart", L&P, Henry VIII, V, Nr. 1531. On the 11 January Chapuys reported that the English have "great fear of the ordinance" which may have extended also to finishing, L&P, Henry VIII, V, Nr. 707.

37 BL. Galba X, fo. 3. Vaughan to Cromwell, 14 February 1532.

38 BL. Galba X, fo. 4. Vaughan to Cromwell, 16 March 1532 where it was remarked "[h]ow Flanders, which receives more profit from us than (from) any other country as our merchants buy linen cloth, St Thomas worsted, says, buckrams, Bruges satens and other things for ready money has banished our cloth and spitefully burnt all they can find [...]. The Merchant Adventurers and clothiers should be asked on occasion to remember this and how Holland banishes our cloth."

39 The instructions, dated the 31 October 1531, to Chapuys stressing Charles V's sense of urgency in obtaining the commercial diet promised after the Peace of Cambrai are preserved in BL. Additional MS. 28173, fo. 242. Preliminaries concerning such a diet were the matters which caused Vaughan to visit the court at Brussels in December where he sensed that the Amsterdam ordinance against English cloth had Charles' hand behind it and was designed to bring the English to the conference table. BL. Galba X, fo. 24. He seems, however, to have underestimated its possible impact for he remained as inactive as before, waiting until he secured a copy of the ordinance to dispatch home (on 14 February 1532) before doing anything more. In the interim, however, the Adventurers' trade at the fair had collapsed and Charles' Council, seemingly much more cognizant of the course of events unfolding, were busy organizing for the diet. Indeed, it was only as the Eng-

and counter-bluff, threat and counter-threat became the order of the day until even as
the diplomatic crisis reached its height during the first two weeks of March 1532 a
new element entered into the equation – with the Netherlanders complaint that the
English products were "falsely wrought" – which signalled that the terms of the great
game had been changed.

The new element was the emergence of inflationary pressures in the English
economy which during the course of 1532 removed the English threat which had previously hung over Netherlands cloth producers. As has been shown, at the Sinxen
mart of 1531, for the first time, the rise in interest rates on the Antwerp exchanges,
whilst sufficient to depress trade through the city, was insufficient to stem the outflow
of specie from the Netherlands or to halt the resultant deflation there. English commerce expanding at this time, moreover, sustained the English exchange, prevented
the re-export of the imported specie and thereby precipitated acute inflationary pressures within the economy. Thus England became a net importer of specie with resultant inflationary effects. Inevitably, however, as in the course of 1532 inflation
worked its way through the economy and manufactures, trying to economize on more
expensive raw materials, "falsely wrought" their cloths there was the danger that English wares would be over-priced, the remaining, already declining trade would collapse and the exchange would fall. Indeed, there is some evidence that during 1532
this did occur. During that summer the exchange once more fell below the English
specie export point and as bullion flowed out of the realm inflationary pressures were
relieved.[40] The inflationary crisis was thus by late 1532, for the moment, over, but not
before it had wrought havoc in the English export trades. The embryonic recovery of
the previous autumn already loosing its impetus during the following winter and
spring as trade re-orientated towards Antwerp, at the Easter fair, turned into a severe
depression which prevailed over the summer and caused English trade in 1531/2 to
again decline.[41]

---

lish merchants prepared for the "first buying" of the Paasche mart that one may sense a feeling of
urgency in his actions as his reports reveal his (largely ineffectual) political manoeuvrings. Charles
was clearly packing the commission with "protectionists" and gathering information to support
their case and Vaughan's belated attempt in the third week of February to use the lord of Bergen to
secure the appointment of someone more amenable to the English cause was at this stage a futile
gesture (BL. Galba X, fos. 3 and 4). Thus at the beginning of March as the intensely hostile imperial commissioners received their instructions and prepared to come to the conference table an intense and ill-prepared body of correspondence passed between London and Antwerp as the English
still attempted to appoint and brief their commissioners (BL. Additional Ms. 28173, fo. 258 and
Galba B X, fos. 4 and 34^v). Nor at this point did the rush have very much point for as the news of
Netherlands complaints about "cloths falsely wrought" arrived, the game for the English was already lost (BL. Galba X, fo. 34^v). The production of such cloths was symptomatic of rising wool
prices in England which, leading to an over-pricing of English cloths, removed the basis of the
English trade boom through Antwerp and the corresponding English threat to Netherlands producers. Thus whilst the diet was finally assembled in April, just in time to wreck the English sales at
the Easter fair, and reconvened in June, in time to have the same effect at the Whit fair, the English
threat to Netherlands producers had long before been removed (L&P, Henry VIII, V, Nrs. 946,
1056, 1090–1).

40   Direct evidence of specie exports at this time is provided ibid., V, Nr. 1276.
41   This paragraph and the next are based on the analysis undertaken in ch. 7 above.

Nor did it look, at that time, as though the situation would be very different in 1532/3 for during the autumn of 1532 the pattern of the previous year seemed to repeat itself. The continuing rise in interest rates at Antwerp during September, whilst depressing trade through Antwerp, was again insufficient to stem the outflow of specie from the Netherlands or to halt the resultant deflation there. English trade, moreover, as van Bombergen reported, whilst declining at the Brabant fairs, underwent during late-1532 an overall expansion[42], maintaining the exchange and preventing the escape of the specie that flowed in. Prices after a brief respite, accordingly, again over the winter of 1532/3 began to rise to a new, even higher, level.[43] But on this occasion they failed to choke off the trade boom, although, as interest rates at Antwerp fell and from the Cold mart of 1532/3 trade re-orientated itself towards that city, much of the earlier impetus was lost.[44] During the course of 1532/3, therefore, the new trade mechanisms yet again revealed themselves. At the time of the Bamus mart of 1532 England's "direct" commerce began to push up her overall export trade, whilst through the winter fair of 1532/3 and the Easter one of 1533 it declined as trade re-orientated itself through Antwerp. That year, moreover, saw a repetition of the inflationary situation which had wrought havoc in English commerce in 1531/2. On this occasion, however, rapidly rising price levels singularly failed to influence the course of trade. The reason lay in merchants' adjustments to the new situation. As unit cloth prices rose, a shift from the heavy long cloths to the kersey (which itself had undergone a process of technological change) reduced export commodity price levels and allowed trade to follow its "normal" course. Accordingly, the specie imported over the winter of 1532/3 remained in circulation and the general price level in England was maintained at its greatly enhanced level. English commercial activity, which had declined in 1531–2 as a result of inflationary pressures, however, now recovered and gaining strength in late-1532, pushed the nation's exports, for the first time, beyond the levels of 1527/8. The problems occasioned by inflationary pressures in the economy had been resolved and the course of English trade expansion, first set in 1529, but briefly interrupted in 1532, now continued unabated.

England's export trade, already in 1532/3 increasing in an unpropitious commercial situation, now, as this situation ameliorated in 1533/4, went from strength to strength. Already during the Sinxen mart of 1533 the new trading environment had become clear as interest rates once again edged upwards at Antwerp. Mindful of their successes at the fairs during the early part of the year and perhaps enticed by Chapuys' "friendly words" the Adventurers sent at the opening of the fair in June "more merchandise than they have done for a long time."[45] After its close in August, however, Vaughan reported to Cromwell that the merchants had not had "so good a

---

42   On Van Bombergen's analysis of the situation prevailing at the Bamus and Cold marts see ch. 7 above.

43   Ibid.

44   The recovery at the winter fair described by Van Bombergen and the more robust one at Easter referred to by Chapuys in a letter to Charles V (L&P, Henry VIII, VI, Nr. 351), occasioned by the fall in interest rates at that time, collapsed at the Sinxen mart of 1533 (ibid., VI, Nr. 934), as interest rates once again edged upwards, bringing what had been a very chequered year at Antwerp to a close. On the overall volume of trade in 1532/3 see ch. 8, Figure 8.1.

45   L&P, Henry VIII, VI, Nr. 653.

sale as expected."[46] Crisis conditions were returning to the Antwerp market and as interest rates, at first slowly and then rapidly, rose on the exchange there, during the course of 1533/4[47], trade through that city declined. As early as the winter fair, where the Adventurers were late in arriving, the market proved "not so quick in sale as it had been."[48] At the Easter fair there was hardly any mart at all and so it remained through the rest of the year.[49] Throughout the year crisis conditions prevailed on the Antwerp market and as the Italians ceased to buy commodities either at the fairs or more significantly through their agents in London the latter put out their funds on the exchanges. Interest rates at London, accordingly, fell and as English merchants utilised this cheap money to pursue their "direct commerce" the English export trade, now unimpeded by rising prices, again expanded, rising to previously unheard-of heights.

The commercial patterns and trends first established in 1528/9 had finally, with the resolution of the problems caused by inflationary pressures, been realised. The English export trade, deriving its impetus from the development of the nation's "direct" commerce, was set on a path of rapid growth. Antwerp's trade, on the other hand, stagnated. Trade thus evolved very differently in two quite separate and distinct trading systems, divided from each other by a barrier of bi-metallic premiums. That barrier, however, was not a permanent one.

As Netherlands gold prices rose from 1535–9 inter-bloc premiums were eliminated and the barriers came down, exposing the Italian merchant finance houses, who dominated Antwerp's trade towards Italy and Spain, to competition. New opportunities were thus opened up for the emancipated English merchants. These they exploited vigorously. During each subsequent period of financial dislocation at Antwerp (in 1535/6 and 1538–40) they made new inroads into that city's preserves.[50] Each crisis on the Antwerp Bourse witnessed an advance in England's exports and recessions in Antwerp's trade and in the output of those industries servicing that trade. Each return to normality at Antwerp (1534/5 and 1536–8) reversed the pattern. Each retreat, however, now left the English level of exports higher than before, as her merchants gradually took over an increasing share of the southern trades, forcing the Italian merchant-banking houses to abandon their commercial activities for purely financial ones.[51]

---

46 Ibid., VI, Nr. 934.

47 The rapid enhancement at the end of 1534, whilst related to Habsburg borrowing, was primarily the result of a new ordinance enacted at Antwerp. The effects of this ordinance on financial dealings at the fairs during 1534 are graphically described by Stephen Vaughan in a letter sent on the 13 December to Cromwell (BL, Galba B X, fo. 49).

48 On the 6 December it was said that "the merchant fleet going to Flanders is ladened and ready to make sail" (L&P, Henry VIII, VI, Nr. 1501) but from the 9th to the 15th of that month continuing negotiations in England and the Netherlands delayed its departure (ibid., VI, Nrs. 1510 and 1524) and then in January it failed to sail because of the weather (ibid., VII, Nr. 83). Nor when it finally arrived at Bergen late that month did the Adventurers find anything but a slack market (ibid., VII, No. 203).

49 Ibid., VII, Nr. 1536.

50 At these times the recurrent phrase used in correspondence relating to the state of trade at the Low Country fairs was that "the sale of cloth at the mart here is very evil." See for example L&P, Henry VIII, VIII, Nr. 1071/2 or X, Nr. 254.

51 See for instance the attitudes of the Italian merchant-bankers who tried to draw the van der Molen into such activities, F. EDLER, The Van der Molen, Commission Merchants of Antwerp: Trade

Up until 1535/6 the main spearhead of the English advance had lain with those who, whenever Antwerp was plagued by financial crises (in 1532 and 1533/4), fostered a direct sea link to Italy and Spain. In that year London merchants, like Thomas Pery, Philip Kerver, Richard Abbis and Richard Field, who were subsequently to play an important role in the growing and increasingly regular Anglo-Spanish trade, may be discerned lading ships like the *Erasmus* with wares destined for San Lucar.[52] At Southampton in the same year both London and Southampton burgesses freighted two London ships, a Southampton vessel and the Spanish *Casa Nova* to carry over a thousand "cloths" to Italy.[53] Their trade was, however, an expensive one due to the high cost of sea transport and when new opportunities for cheap land transport to Italy were opened up during the late thirties the seaborne trade to Italy was abandoned.[54] Thus in 1538–40, when the English next launched a concerted assault on Antwerp's remaining preserves, only the Spanish market was significantly catered for by these "direct" sea trades. Both London merchants, like Pery, and Bristol traders, like John Smith, who traded only as far as Spain, carried cargoes of cloth thence[55], whilst the Levant merchants increasingly organised their Mediterranean ventures from San Lucar de Barrameda, the Andalusia Company becoming dominated by such "Levant merchants" as William Ostrige, William Wilford and Thomas Starkey.[56]

During the years 1538–40, however, the Italian trade passed elsewhere. Parts of it were diverted to France, as the transit trade via Rouen and Lyon was revived.[57] More important, however, as the bi-metallic barriers came down, was the fusion of the pre-existing Germanic and Netherlands routes to Italy (Map 10.1). Throughout these years it was the German *Wantsinder* who led the onslaught on Antwerp's preserves carrying English wares, brought by Hanseatic and English shippers to Hamburg, southwards, either by way of Basle[58] and the St Gotthard Pass or via Erfurt and Nuremberg to ei-

---

with Italy, 1538–44, in: Medieval and Historiographical Essays in Honour of James Westfall Thompson, Chicago 1938, pp. 81–2 and note 39 on page 82 (ibid.).

52 CONNELL-SMITH, Forerunners of Drake, pp. 12–14.

53 A. RUDDOCK, London Capitalists and the Decline of Southampton in the Early Tudor Period, in: Economic History Review, Second Series, II, 2 (1949), pp. 142–3 and ID., Italian Merchants and Shipping in Southampton, 1270–1600, Southampton 1951, p. 247, n. 41 for the activities of Francesco di Marini as a factor of Southampton merchants in the "Italian trades" of 1532 and 1535/6. Ibid., p. 266 on Huttoft's venture in 1535/6.

54 EDLER, Van der Molen, p. 141 on the cheapness of land relative to sea transport from Antwerp to Italy, a point taken up more fully in ch. 11 below. W. BRULEZ, Les routes commerciales d' Angleterre en Italie au XVI siècle, in: Studi in onore di Amintore Fanfani IV, Milan 1962, pp. 81–2 on the relative cheapness of the Hamburg land route in comparison with that of Antwerp.

55 Bristol Record Office, Ashton Court MSS., AC/B.63; CONNELL-SMITH, Forerunners of Drake, p. 112.

56 HAKLUYT, Principal Navigations (London 1599–1600), II, pp. 96–99; RUDDOCK, Italian Merchants, pp. 247s., 266; CONNELL-SMITH, Forerunners of Drake, p. 94s.

57 J. KAULAK (ed.), Correspondance politique de MM de Castillon et de Marillac, ambassadeurs de France en Angleterre, 1537–42, Paris 1882, p. 227; R. GASCON, Grand commerce et vie urbaine au XVIe siècle. Lyon et ses marchands, Paris 1971, II, p. 597.

58 They were joined, moreover, by English merchants who established factors in centres along this route. The papers of one such factor have been preserved and published by H. ROBINSON (ed.), Zurich Letters, London 1842–5 and 1846–7.

ther Augsburg or Salzburg, for trans-shipment to Italy.[59] Perhaps no better testimony to the efficiency of Antwerp's new competitors can be provided than a letter written by Mary of Hungary to Charles V in 1546 in which she declared that FOR SOME TIME PAST trade had flowed to Rouen and to Hamburg which "is highly propitious for exit and entry of merchandise for Germany and by consequence for the transit towards Italy." Indeed, it "has proven better than Antwerp", which in consequence has lost much of its trade.[60] During each crisis which had beset the Antwerp money market during the last half of the 1530s (namely in 1535/6 and 1538–40) Anglo-French and Anglo-German alliances of merchants made new gains at Antwerp's expense. During each return to normality in that city (in 1534/5 and 1536–8) some of the lost ground was regained, but steadily over these years the effectiveness of Antwerp's resistance to the assault diminished until, as the new decade dawned, it virtually disappeared.

In 1540/1 the recovery in the Antwerp money market, which left the bill rate there a fraction ABOVE that prevailing in London, induced no major return of trade to the Scheldt or recovery at the fairs. The depressed cloth market rallied slightly but never regained its former prosperity whilst in England the boom in cloth sales continued unabated.[61] With no advantage in the finance market and with the impact of bi-metallic premiums (re-established as a result of the Netherlands monetary reform of 1539) on the English and German exchanges offset by lower transport costs, Antwerp merchants were forced to cede a share of the Italian trade to those competitors who shipped their wares via Hamburg or Rouen, just as they also had to concede a share of the trade to Spain to those Englishmen who now regularly ventured to Seville and San Lucar. 1541 thus finally confirmed a trend which may be traced back to the events of the 1520s whereby Antwerp steadily lost her grasp over English trade. With the recurrence of financial disorders on the Antwerp Bourse from September 1541 to the Peace of Crèpy three years later, and following the acute international financial crisis which broke on both the London and Antwerp Exchanges in 1541/2, the combined effects of short-term fluctuation and long-term trend reduced her share of that trade still further.[62] During the years 1543–5 it seems probable that no more than A THIRD[63], at

---

59   See EDLER, Van der Molen, p. 116 on the competition of the Germans on the Venetian market.

60   R. HAEPKE, Niederländische Akten und Urkunden zur Geschichte der Hanse und zur deutschen Seegeschichte, Munich / Leipzig / Lübeck 1913–1923, I, p. 445 as quoted in: BRULEZ, Routes commerciales, p. 179, notes 158–9.

61   EDLER, Van der Molen, p. 122s. and n. 159 on p. 112.

62   Ibid., p. 124s.

63   On average the annual English cloth export from Antwerp to Italy amounted to ca. 45,828 kerseys and 6,504 broadcloths. W. BRULEZ, L' exportation des Pays-Bas vers Italie par voie de terre au milieu du XVIe siècle, in: Annales, XIV (1959), pp. 461–491, and the same author's estimate derived therefrom in: ID., Routes commerciales, p. 129, n. 21. No indication is given of how the estimate for the Hamburg trade was arrived at and it seems incredibly low in relation to Ehrenberg's figures (R. EHRENBERG, Hamburg und England im Zeitalter der Königin Elisabeth, Jena 1896, p. 331), which relate only to cloths dyed there. In terms of English short cloths, this trade from Antwerp to Italy thus amounted to 21,780 "cloths" (i.e. [45,828 divided by 3]+6504), whilst total English exports amounted to 121,145 cloths per annum over the same period. J. D. GOULD, The Great Debasement. Currency and the Economy in Mid-Tudor England, London 1970, pp. 120, 173. Thus the English trade via Antwerp to Italy amounted to 18 per cent of the total. Unless the trade via Antwerp to Spain was considerably larger than that to Italy, which in the light of the preceding

very most, of English trade passed through Antwerp. Since the 1520 s a new era had dawned in European commercial history. For Antwerp it meant the beginning of the end. Increasingly dependent during the following years on commerce with the South and on control of the expanding English export trade, she gradually lost her grip on both of these last remaining remnants of her former commercial empire. For London, however, it marked a new beginning. Having freed her mercantile and financial communities from Antwerp's hegemony, they now established themselves on the path of independent prosperity. As this study closes, in 1544, the pattern for the future was already set. There might be subsequent periods (in 1544–49 and 1556–63) when the beneficent effects of cheap money allowed Antwerp's merchants to retrench their position, but each successive crisis in the city (during 1550–1555 and 1565–76) reaffirmed and accentuated the pattern formed out of the turmoil of the 1520s.

---

discussion seems improbable, then a "guesstimate" of a third seems not implausible. Certainly it seems compatible with the only other figure available of England's trade through Antwerp. In 1550, after a period of retrenchment and in a much more favourable situation for Antwerp's merchants, English "cloth" exports to Antwerp amounted to 66,812 (i.e. [49,964 kerseys divided by 3]+50,158 cloths) or 45 per cent of total exports. O. DE SMEDT, op. cit., II, pp. 434–5 as quoted in H. VAN DER WEE, The Growth of the Antwerp Market and the European Economy, Fourteenth–Sixteenth Centuries, 3 Vols., The Hague 1963, II, p. 186.

CHAPTER ELEVEN

BUSINESS STRATEGIES AND COMMERCIAL DEVELOPMENT, 1505–44

The decade 1519–28 witnessed dramatic changes in Antwerp's position within European financial and commercial systems. Prior to that time, when untroubled by financial or monetary disorders – in 1505–9, 1514–5, 1518–9 – the city, by the availability of cheap money on its Bourse, continued to draw to itself, by land and sea, merchants whose wares were subsequently redistributed throughout a commercial system which was of European-wide dimensions. As a result of steadily falling interest rates on the Antwerp Exchange, moreover, trade through the city had expanded to a high point at the latter date and English exports, still at that time overwhelmingly destined for the Brabant fairs, followed a similar course. Only occasionally was its position threatened when Habsburg intervention on the money market – in 1509–13, 1516–7 and 1520–2 – caused merchants to divert their commerce away from the city towards the paths of an "alternative commerce". Drawing on the resources of new financial centres – Lyon, London and Frankfurt – they created an alternative commercial system although as far as London was concerned this process was a lengthy one. Only gradually were the bimetallic impediments to the operation of its money market removed, as first (in 1509–13) France and the Levantine ports and then (between 1516/7 and 1520–2) Venice were drawn into its high-cost, alternative financial network. Yet this new commercial system had proven a poor substitute for trade through Antwerp and whilst on these occasions "direct" English commerce to new markets had expanded, aggregate English trade had markedly declined. At the close of the second decade of the sixteenth century Antwerp thus still reigned supreme and the development of England's export trade remained inextricably linked to its fortunes.

Then from 1519–28, as Antwerp was subject to the impact of successive, fiscal (1521 and 1522–3 as well as 1527–9), monetary (1525–6) and mining (1527/8) crises, her whole position within the European economy began to alter. Commercial trends were reversed as even when markets were untroubled by financial or monetary disorders – in 1523–4 and 1527 – a general enhancement of interest rates on the Antwerp bill market increased the finance costs of merchants visiting that city and a bi-metallic realignment of the Netherlands currencies created an endemic condition of premiums on its exchanges, deflecting merchants from visiting the towns on the Scheldt. Thus in 1523–4, as the English trade recovered from the previous years crisis, dear money and the withdrawal of the Spaniards, Hansards and French, which undermined commercial activity at the Bergen fairs, aborted the export boom, causing trade to stabilize at a lower level than before (viz. in 1518–9). Nor was the situation different in 1527. In

spite of the competitive advantage enjoyed by English producers over their Netherlands counterparts at this time, English trade, still tied to the Brabantine fairs failed to
recover beyond the level previously attained in 1523–4. The trade boom which had
characterised English commerce, both at Antwerp and in general, during the first two
decades of the sixteenth century, was over. During the 'twenties, whenever the English were active at the Low Counties fairs (in 1523–4 and during the summer of 1527),
due to high finance costs and an absence of many of their customers, trade stagnated
at a new low-level equilibrium, slightly below the peak of 1518–9. No less significant
for the future fate of the western metropolis were the changes taking place at this time
in that "alternative commerce" which emerged whenever crisis – in 1525–early 1527
and late 1527–1528 – beset the Antwerp market. During the previous crisis years this
trade had proven a poor substitute for trade through Antwerp but now during the
'twenties this situation began to change, on this occasion the crisis of 1525–early 1527
marking the turning point in the trend. Few, however, could have anticipated this
when the crisis first broke and the acute bi-metallic disequilibrium between England
and the Netherlands crippled commerce with that country whilst the dislocation of
sales-credit systems and Henrican depredations, in enhancing domestic interest rates,
prevented a revival of England's "alternative commerce". Yet when in late-1526 the
domestic situation eased for a moment and the "alternative" commerce again revived,
the strength of the "direct" trade boom was such as to significantly support the aggregate volume of English commerce in that year. Certainly the strength of this boom is
not explicable in terms of low interest rates on the London exchange. Indeed these
remained inordinately high at this time. Yet that rate now prevailed within a financial
network which thanks to the bi-metallic realignment of European currencies between
1515 and 1526 was of truly international dimensions. Over the winter of 1526/7,
therefore, there was a widening if not a deepening of commercial activity within the
network of England's "direct" trades. Moreover, when those trades were resumed after Michaelmas 1527 it looked as though this pattern would repeat itself. After the
Antwerp boom of the summer, it seemed probable that the direct trades would again
grow and aggregate English trade decline but that the downswing would now be only
of modest proportions (in comparison with 1509–13, 1516–7 and 1520–2). The London bill market, servicing an extended financial system, was still, like Lyon, not a
cheap source of funds. Then in 1528 when the Italians, because of the interruption of
their southern trades, failed "to buy the commodities of this realm" and instead "delivered their money to other merchants by exchange", interest rates fell, the "direct
commerce" expanded rapidly and aggregate English trade, instead of falling, actually
increased – to its highest point yet in the sixteenth century.

Out of the turmoil of the previous decade, by 1528, a whole new structure of
European commerce had been forged. From that date Antwerp's European business
supremacy had become a thing of the past. Her merchants and financiers now performed a more limited function within European trade. Behind a barrier of bi-metallic
premiums they serviced, when unimpeded by financial crises, the needs of the buoyant
trades to Spain and Italy. The corollary of these changes was the emergence of a
sphere of commercial activity independent of Antwerp, engrossing markets in northern and central Europe, France and the Levant, within which London acted as one of
the principal nodes. Within those networks, moreover, trade now from 1528 followed
a completely new course. Henceforth, for more than a decade, it was to be by the en-

deavours of English merchants in fostering their "direct" trades that English trade expansion took place. From 1528 each downswing in interest rates on the English exchanges (in 1528, 1532 and 1533/4, 1535/6 and 1538–1540), which occurred when the southern trades handled by the Netherland-Italian houses at Antwerp were in abeyance, carried English trade to ever higher levels as denizens utilised the money released by the Italians to expand their "direct" trades. At first this rapid expansion in England's export trades took place within its own independent trading system but then, from ca 1535, as the inter-bloc bi-metallic barrier crumbled, their onslaught was extended into the very heart of Antwerp's previously sacrosanct preserves. Only when there was an increase in London interest rates (in 1529–31, 1534/5 and 1536–8), which occurred when the trade via Antwerp was resumed, was there a retreat in English commercial activity, as the "direct" trades, starved of funds, declined and trade through Antwerp at first stabilized at, and then fell from the low equilibrium levels of the 1520s. Yet each subsequent fluctuation left interest rates on the London exchanges at a lower, and English trade at a higher level than before, as the long-term rate of growth in the "direct" trades contrasted with the declining English commerce through Antwerp. Thus paradoxically whilst English trade, during the decade from 1528, still drew benefit from its involvement in the southern European trades, handled by the Netherland-Italian houses at Antwerp, it was only when those trades were in decline that that the most rapid growth of English exports could occur. Only on such occasions, when crises beset the Antwerp market and impeded trade through that city to the South, was the necessary transfer of funds effected from the Italians, who seemingly used their resources inefficiently in the "easy" Ibero-Mediterranean trades, to the English, who deployed them with seemingly greater effect in their "difficult" direct commerce.

Whilst the paradox may be discerned, however, the explanation for the relatively efficient use of funding by the English merchants in difficult markets remains elusive. In part the answer may lie in the new forms of commercial organisation adopted by the English merchants at this time. During the years 1527–9 the organisation of commercial activity within the English "direct" trade underwent a major change as the temporary factorage system which had characterised it during the first quarter of the sixteenth century was replaced by a system of permanent factors not only in the French and Levantine trades, already referred to, but also in the commerce to Hamburg and Danzig, thereby reducing transactions costs.[1] The deficiencies of information and both temporal and spatial market imperfections imposed upon the supercargo, in the earlier intermittent trades, as a result of his restricted stay in a foreign port were seemingly removed. The factor permanently located abroad was in a position, at least theoretically, to explore market opportunities and accordingly through better information evolve more effective business strategies. He could discover where and at what time of the year goods were best bought or sold thereby diminishing price fluctuations

---

1   On the establishment of permanent factors at Chios see chapter 10, where references to similar practices at Bordeaux and Hamburg may be found as well. In 1528 merchants, like Howell, were also establishing permanent factors at Danzig (Ledger, fo. 74). On the impact of a permanent factorage system upon transactions costs see D. C. NORTH / R. P. THOMAS, An Economic Theory of the Growth of the Western World, in: Economic History Review, Second Series, XXIII, 1 (1970), p. 12s.

in commodity markets and allowing price maximization on the goods despatched to him and cost minimization in the acquisition of the commodities he wished to obtain for shipment home. He could explore the merits of local money markets and credit systems as a source of loans or as an outlet for the balances he often held on an intra-annual basis, again widening his options and affecting his finance costs. Overall, in theory, permanent factorage resulted in an improvement in the market situation confronting the merchant abroad. Yet in reality such gains were not so instantaneously achieved for with the establishment of such permanent factors in an alien environment the host merchants consistently tried to maintain market imperfections, restricting the incomer s movements and limiting his access to information. The location of a permanent factor abroad thus normally signalled the beginnings of a long and protracted process of negotiations from which he only at best slowly, and sometimes never, achieved the reductions in transactions costs inherent in his position.[2]

More immediate gains were achieved from the permanent factorage system through its impact on shipping costs. Vessels venturing on an ad hoc basis to foreign ports experienced a slow turn-around as their cargoes were sold and commodities were gathered for reshipment home. Indeed in this situation, which prevailed in England's "direct" commerce during the first quarter of the century, supercargo and purser had conflicting interests. The former, in order to make the best of a bad job in the temporally restricted access he had to markets, required as much time as possible to secure the most advantageous terms he could for the sales of his wares and the purchase of a return cargo. The purser, on the other hand, wanted a quick turn-around so that the ship on returning home could be redeployed, more voyages fitted into the season and fixed costs and freights reduced. The permanent factorage system resolved this conflict. On arrival in the foreign port the captain of the ship could immediately unload its cargo and on its transfer to the merchant's factor the latter assumed responsibility (in a markedly improved market situation) for obtaining the best prices for the goods. He had also, prior to the arrival of the ship, secured its return cargo which could be immediately put aboard. The merchant, through his factor, thus obtained the benefits of reduced transactions costs arising from the improved market situation. The purser could turn around the ship more rapidly and by spreading his fixed costs over more voyages reduce freight rates. Here then was a situation where the establishment of a permanent factorage system could bring about immediate gains through a reduction in shipping freight rates and between 1527/8–1541 there was just such a reduction in the English direct trades.[3] In the Anglo-Spanish trade, for instance, freight costs per ton-mile fell over this period from 0.26–0.3 to 0.15–0.23 pence[4] until at the latter date

---

2   It is hoped to undertake an analysis of the effects of such organisational changes in a future study.

3   For an investigation of such gains in a somewhat later context see for instance D. C. NORTH, Ocean Freight Rates and Economic Development, 1750–1913, in: Journal of Economic History, XVIII (1958), and ID., Sources of Productivity Change in Ocean Shipping, 1600–1850, in: Journal of Political Economy, LXXVI (1968); G. WALTON / J. F. SHEPHERD, Shipping, Maritime Trade, and the Development of Colonial North America (Cambridge, 1972), and C. K. HARLEY, Ocean Freight Rates and Productivity, 1740–1913: The Primacy of Mechanical Invention Reaffirmed, in: Journal of Economic History, XLVIII (1988).

4   The following calculations for the Anglo-Spanish trade have been made from data contained in Howell's Ledger, *passim* and J. VANES (ed.), The Ledger of John Smyth, 1538–50 (=Royal Commission in Historical Manuscripts, JP 19), London 1974, *passim* whilst those relating to Nether-

such rates compared very favourably with those charged in the Netherlands-Italian overland (6.75 pence per ton/mile) and sea (1.5 pence per ton/mile) trades. Even measured in terms of cost per completed journey (i.e. total freight, by whatever means of transport, divided by the shortest route to its destination) and allowing for differences in time taken (by including an interest charge per month of journey on each ton [560 kerseys] carried) the English merchant by 1541 enjoyed cheap freights (9.0 pence per ton/mile) in comparison with merchants engaged in the Netherlands trades, although amongst this latter group those who shipped by sea paid rather more (60.6 pence per ton/mile) than those who freighted by land (22.6 pence per ton mile). In part the explanation for this fall in freights may reside in the changing nature of the trade itself, for whilst English exports had passed via Antwerp to Spain ships trafficking between England and Spain had sailed outward-bound in ballast to return laden with Spanish wares. With the establishment of the "direct" export trade to Spain they secured freights in both directions and were accordingly able to reduce rates. This reduction in freight-rates, occasioned by changes in the trade, however, merely moved the English rate from a position (0.3 pence per ton/mile) above that prevailing at Antwerp (0.15 pence per ton/mile), where in its hey-day goods had been shipped to Spain as return cargo in the Biscayan or Andalusian fleets, to one (0.15–0.23 pence per ton/mile) at or near parity with the Antwerp freight rate (0.15 pence per ton/mile) and as such cannot explain the relative advantage enjoyed by the English in the 1540s. That must be sought in quicker voyages (achieved by the means described above[5]) – and lower monthly interest charges. By adopting better forms of commercial organisation, the merchants engaged in the new English direct trades thus gradually between 1527/8–41 improved their position as they created a trading environment within which they could operate as efficiently as had the Antwerp merchants in their hey-day.

Yet even as the position of the English merchants converged between 1527/8–41 on that enjoyed by the Italo-Netherlanders during their hey-day, there were signs that at Antwerp organisational change was also taking place – and not to the advantage of the Italo-Netherlanders. In that city a similar system to that being created by the English already existed amongst the German and Italian houses as the 'thirties began. During that decade, however, as an examination of the van Bombergen (1532–3) and Van der Molen (1538–44) papers reveals, amongst these houses, who continued to dominate the overland trade to Italy, there was an increasing tendency towards bureaucratization. Both of these firms acted at Antwerp on commission for Venetian merchant houses, buying and selling commodities for their clients and organizing the transportation of these wares, arranging the transmission of funds on the exchange and gathering relevant mercantile intelligence. Yet, separated in time by an interval of little more than five years, the manner of operation of the two houses was quite different. Antoine van Bombergen in 1532–3 undertook most of these operations

---

lands-Italian commerce are based on information contained in F. EDLER, The Van der Molen, Commission Merchants of Antwerp: Trade with Italy, 1538–44, in: Medieval and Historiographical Essays in Honour of James Westfall Thompson, Chicago 1938, pp. 130–43.

5 The Van der Molen correspondence (see chapter 7 above, n. 5) also suggests that in terms of the time taken between the embarkation of goods and their arrival at their destination changes were also taking place at Antwerp where, when on the odd occasion goods were despatched to Italy by sea, they were consigned to tramp-shipping and thus took a spatially extended and temporally protracted voyage to their destination.

van Bombergen in 1532–3 undertook most of these operations himself, personally selling his client's wares at the Brabant fairs and buying there the English kerseys and long cloths which he would ultimately dispatch to Italy. He also visited the Bourse in person, some times to put out money on the exchange for transmission to Italy but more often simply to gather commercial and financial market intelligence. At every turn he used free market institutions to undertake his transactions and when such local facilities at Antwerp proved inadequate he had recourse to a series of occasional correspondents to extend the markets within which he could operate. His operations, even more than those of his contemporary English counterparts engaged in that nation's "direct" trades, were conducted on the basis of excellent market intelligence in conditions of near-perfect competition. Van der Molen on the other hand in 1538–44 operated at Antwerp within a much more bureaucratically organized trading system. He spent most of his days in his office where his perception of market conditions was formed from a constant and voluminous stream of correspondence delivered by rapid postal service from his customers and agents. On the basis of this information he formulated purchase and sales strategies which were implemented through a commercial system which encompassed all aspects of the cloth trade from producer to customer. The house maintained factors in each of the main cloth producing areas. Adam van Riebecke was situated at Bruges to buy Flemish cloths. Jacob van der Tombe bought at Hondschoot the says woven in the small town and the adjacent countryside, as well as the finer products of the Bergues – Saint Winoc sayetterie. In London they dealt with Italian cloth agents like Martino de Frederico or Maurizio de Marini, a Genoese whose activities at the English capital span almost the whole ambit of this study.[6] In Lille and Valencienne they had agents through whom they could order worsteds. Whilst, therefore, they enjoyed some flexibility in purchasing by being able to shift orders between their agents, their overall pattern of cloth acquisition had become rigid and divorced from the free-play of the market which had itself been marginalized. A similar rigidity may be observed, moreover, in their provision of transport services. At Arnemuiden they maintained a forwarding and shipping agent, one Piero di Negrino, but his major duties were confined to the trans-shipment of incoming cloths into *shouts* for passage to Antwerp where they were stored and subsequently transported, in the care of professional carriers, to Italy. Once again a fixed pattern, this time of transportation, had imposed itself on their trade. Cloth (without passing through a market) was despatched to Italy by land and in the absence of any demand alternative modes of transport withered and died. Thus when the land route was cut and the van der Molen sought other ways of getting their goods to market they found no satisfactory alternative and were forced to embark their wares on "tramps" which would wend a long and circuitous route to Italy. Under the guidance of houses like the van der Molen the free-market institutions, from which van Bombergen had gained such strength, were disappearing or becoming buried under a welter of bureaucratic organizations.

Thus whilst transactions costs, particularly with regards to the provision of transport services, may have fallen in the English direct trades during the years 1527/8–41, such a fall can only provide a partial explanation for the RELATIVE greater effi-

---

6   A. RUDDOCK, Italian Merchants and Shipping in Southampton, 1270–1600, Southampton 1951, pp. 233–54.

ciency of the English merchants in comparison with their Italo-Netherlands counter-parts. The English merchants' greater efficiency owed as much to their rival's self-infliction of wounds. Just as Charles V had enhanced the Netherlanders' finance costs, relative to those of the English, by his constant intervention in the affairs of the Antwerp money market, so the Italo-Netherland merchant houses also had enhanced their own transactions costs above those of the English by their abandonment of free market institutions for intensely bureaucratic forms of organization.

PART IV

COMMODITY FLOWS: THE ENGLISH WOOL, CLOTH
AND METAL TRADES

CHAPTER TWELVE

THE CLOTH AND WOOL TRADES. THE HEAVY DRAPERIES,
1505–23[1]

The Anglo-Netherlands Cloth Trade. During the opening decade of the sixteenth century and particularly during the years from 1505–9, when its markets were untroubled by financial, monetary or commercial disorders, Antwerp, by the availability of cheap money on its Bourse, drew to itself, by land and sea, merchants whose produce was subsequently redistributed to markets within a commercial system which was of European-wide dimensions. For the English textile merchant, like his Netherlands counterpart, all paths led to Antwerp, where he could dispose of the cloths, kerseys, cottons and friezes, which were the staples of his trade, to others who would then distribute these wares to markets scattered the length and breadth of Europe. The most important of these markets lay, as in the fifteenth century, in central Europe where for almost half a century the trade in English textiles had expanded on the ruins of the old Rhenish industry.[2] Intermediaries in this trade were the merchants of Cologne and Frankfurt who each year either ordered from their London factors or bought at the Brabant fairs the short cloths of Suffolk or the West of England which were main items in their trade.[3] These wares, together with small quantities of Bruges and Amsterdam cloth, English cottons, Mechelin satins and Hondschoote says then passed from Cologne and Frankfurt eastward by cart along the great central European highway for final distribution, through Leipzig to Saxony and Bohemia-Moravia, through Augsburg to southern Germany and the Alpenlands or through Vienna to the lands of the Hungarian crown. Along the way they shared passage with the wares of those merchants who traded to Italy, merchants whose trade was in the years 1505–9 recovering from the effects of the Venetian financial crisis of 1503–5. Yet these merchants

---

1   In this and the following two chapters a completely new terminology has been employed for the various products of the Anglo-Netherlands textile industries. Because of highly confusing international differences in their usage, terms like "old" or "new drapery" have been abandoned in this text and a new classification of the products of the Anglo-Netherlands textile industry utilising a new nomenclature adopted. It is recommended that before commencing on Part IV of this study the reader thus familiarises himself with the contents of THE GLOSSARY OF ANGLO-NETHERLANDS TEXTILE TYPES in the appendix to this study.

2   A. DIETZ, Frankfurter Handelsgeschichte, Frankfurt-on-the-Main 1910–25, II, pp. 262–77.

3   H. POHL, Köln und Antwerpen um 1500, in: Mitteilungen aus dem Stadtarchiv von Köln, LX (1971), pp. 477–82 for a description of the Cologne merchants' cloth trade at Antwerp, whilst J. D. FUDGE, The German Hanse and England: Commercial and Political Interaction at the Close of the Middle Ages, Unpubl. University of Edinburgh Ph.D thesis, Edinburgh 1988, pp. 242–3, which has subsequently been published as ID., Cargoes, Embargoes and Emissaries. The Commercial and Political Interaction of England and the German Hanse, 1450–1510, Toronto 1995, provides information on the activities of the same group of merchants in England at this time.

shared not only a common route, but also common wares, for in their carts the Italian traders also predominantly carried the products of the Anglo-Netherlands heavy cloth industry. The crisis of 1503–5 had dealt a death blow to the manufacturers of Courtrai and Werwicq, traditional suppliers of the Italian market, but in their place, during the years 1505–9 arose the draperies of Menin and Armentières.[4] Produced with the same fine English wools and finished to perfection, these heavy, high quality cloths enjoyed a considerable vogue in Italian markets.[5] Indeed so successful had they become by 1507 that English exporters of long cloths, like Thomas Gerny, had their wares worked up and made in the manner of Menin by the craftsmen of Bergen-op-Zoom in order to pass them off on Italian buyers.[6] Thus both Italian and Central European trades passed along the same routes from Antwerp and were based on the same products of the heavy drapery, lighter cloths as yet playing only a minor role in these trades.

If the Italian and central European trades shared a common route and a common product so too did Antwerp's Baltic commerce. The ships which carried the cloths of Cologne merchants from London to the Netherlands, after disembarking these wares for transmission overland to the east, then sailed on to the northern sea, carrying the same English long and short cloths, together with small quantities of the cheap East Anglian doucken to customers in the lands bordering the Baltic.[7] There, however, they had to compete with the products of Low Countries manufacture. Paramount amongst these competitors, in the dominant heavy drapery trade, were the clothiers of Leiden, who in the years 1505–9 produced a colossal annual output of about 25,000 cloths, much of which was destined for shipment, via Amsterdam, to the Baltic where these cloths had for more than half a century enjoyed a secure share of the market.[8] Simi-

---

4   On the effects of the crisis on the industry of Courtrai see R. VAN UYTVEN, La Flandre et le Brabant, Terres de Promission sous les Ducs de Bourgogne?, in: Revue du Nord, XLIII (1961), p. 293s; O. MUS, De verhouding van der waard tot de drapier in de Kortrijkse draperie op het einde van 15e eeuwe, in: Annales de la Société d Emulation de Bruges, XCVIII (1961), p. 162s., and on its impact on the industry of Werwicq, H. E. DE SAGHER / J.-H. DE SAGHER / H. VAN WERVEKE / C. WYFFELS, Receuil de documents relatifs à l histoire de l industrie drapière en Flandre, 2e partie, Le sud-oeust de la Flandre depuis l époque Bourguignonne, Bruxelles 1951–66, III, p. 439s. (hereafter referred to as DE SAGHER, Documents); E. COORNAERT, Un centre industriel d autrefois. Le draperie-sayetterie d' Hondschoote, XIVe–XVIIIe siècles, Paris 1930, pp. 487–9.

5   DE SAGHER, Documents, I, pp. 99, 102–125; III, pp. 5–6, 71–2.

6   Ibid., III, Nr. 393 and p. 6, n. 1.

7   In the same ships, as carried Cologne merchants' cloths to Antwerp for trans-shipment eastward, cloths (predominantly Suffolk and Wiltshire shorts and the fine Coventry longs) of Danzig merchants were carried (TNA, E122/80/2: 1502/3) which subsequently passed through the Sound. Rigsarkivet, København, Sundtoldregudkab 1503 fos. 7, 12–4, 21.

8   N. W. POSTHUMUS, Geschiedenis van de Leidsche Lakenindustrie, 's Gravenhage 1908–39, I, p. 370; Hansisches Urkundenbuch (henceforth HUB 1–11), ed. by K. HÖHLBAUM (Vols. 1–3), J. KUNZE (vols. 4–6), H.-G. VON RUNDSTEDT (Vol. 7) and W. Stein (Vols. 8–11) and published at Halle 1876–96, Leipzig 1899–1907, Munich 1916 and Weimar 1939: HUB 9, No. 558; HUB 10, Nos. 72, 704–5. Akten und Recesse der Livländischen Standtage (henceforth A&R 1–3), ed. by O. STAVENHAGEN / L. ARBUSOW Sr. and Jr. / A. BAUER and published at Riga 1907–38: A&R 3, Nr. 52/13. Liv-, Est- und Curländisches Urkundenbuch (henceforth Livl. UB, I, [1–12], II, [1–3]), ed. by F. G. VON BUNGE (series. I, vols. 1–6), H. HILDEBRAND (Series I, Vols. 7–9), P. SCHWATZ (Series I, Vols. 10–12), L. ARBUSOW (Series II, Vols. 1–3) and published at Reval 1853–9, Riga 1867–73,

larly with regard to the *slechte draperie*, whose smaller market could not support such massive production centres, the East Anglian doucken manufacturers again found stiff competition in Baltic markets from clothiers of Naarden (estimated production ca. 1509, 9,000 cloths) and above all from the drapers of the Flemish towns of Dixmude, Tourcoing (production 4,000 cloths) and Poperinge (production 5,000 cloths).[9] Thus again the pattern repeats itself with trade, predominantly in heavy cloths, centring on Antwerp.

Finally turning to the French and Spanish trades, one may again see the same centripetal forces at work irresistibly drawing shipping to the Scheldt from which the merchants returned again carrying English and Low Countries cloth south to Rouen, Rochelle, Bordeaux and the Iberian ports. The cloths they carried, moreover, were again the products of the Anglo-Netherlands heavy drapery – English short cloths of diverse colours, the *ultrafini* of Armentières, the *luxus* of Menin.[10] Light cloths – English kerseys and dozens, Flemish says and the cheap grey rolls of Bruges – played, as elsewhere, a decidedly minor role in this trade.[11] Thus in the year that the young Henry ascended the English throne to become the eighth king of that name the Anglo-Netherlands textile trade was concentrated almost exclusively on Antwerp and the towns of the Scheldt estuary. It was a trade, moreover, dominated by the products of the heavy drapery.

Whenever, during the troubled years that followed, the Antwerp market operated under similar conditions to those prevailing in 1505–9 this commercial pattern, with

Riga / Moscow 1881, Riga / Moscow / Leipzig 1884–1914: Livl. UB, I [8], Nr. 851; I [9], Nr. 640; I [11], Nrs. 743, 753 and II [1], Nr. 31.

9   On Naarden and the industry of the northern Netherlands see A. C. J. DE VRANKRIJKER, De textielindustrie van Naarden, in: Tijdschrift voor Geschiedenis, LI (1936), p. 154; T. S. JANSMA, L' industrie lainière des Pays Bas du Nord et spécialement celle de Hollande (XIVe–XVIIe siècles): production, organisation, exportation, in: M. SPALLANZI (ed.), Produzione, commercio e consumo die panni di lana (nei secoli XII–XVII), Florence: Instituto internazionale di storia economica F. Datini Prato. Pubblicazioni, serie II, Atti della Prima settimana di studi 1976, and its markets in the Baltic HUB [10], No. 158; HUB [11], No. 1211; Livl. UB, I [11], Nr. 753 and II [2], Nr. 627. Information concerning the English East Anglian industry will be found in note 18 below, whilst on the sales of its products in the Baltic see e.g. Livl. UB, II [3], Nr. 453. The Flemish industry and its relations with the Hanse is the subject of a number of studies: M. BRAURE, Etudes économiques sur les Châtellenies de Lille, Douai et Orchies, in: Revue du Nord, XV (1928), p. 188; H. E. DE SAGHER, Une enquête sur la situation de l industrie drapière en Flandre à la fin de XVIe siècle, Etudes d histoire dédiées à la memoire de Henri Pirenne par ses anciens éleves, Bruxelles 1937, p. 11; A. LOTTIN, Histoire de Tourcoing, Dunkirk 1986; H. VAN WERVEKE, Die Stellung des hansischen Kaufmanns dem flandrischen Tuchproduzenten gegenüber, in: H. AUBIN et al., Beiträge zur Wirtschafts- und Stadtgeschichte. Festschrift für Hektor Ammann, Wiesbaden 1965, p. 298s., whilst on these relationships and market conditions in the Baltic see HUB [9], Nrs. 558, 744; HUB [10], Nrs. 49, 704. Die Recesse und andere Akten der Hansetage (hereafter HR, I[1-8], II[1-7], III[1-9] and IV[1]), series I, edited by W. JUNGHANS (Vol.1) and K. KOPPMANN (Vols. 2–8) and published at Leipzig 1870–97; series II, Vols. 1–7 edited by G. Freiherr von ROPPE and published at Leipzig 1876–92; series III, edited by D. SCHÄFER (Vols. 1–7) and D. SCHÄFER and F. TESCHEN (Vols. 8–9) which were published at Leipzig 1881–1913; Series IV, Vol. 1 edited by G. WENTZ and published at Weimar 1941: HR, III[2], Nrs. 162, 164; HR, III[3], Nr. 10; Livl. UB, II[2], Nr. 113.

10 DE SAGHER, Documents, III, Nr. 392; MUS, Kortrijk draperie, p. 169.

11 Z. W. SNELLER / W. G. UNGER, Bronnen tot de Geschiedenis van den Handel met Frankrijk, 's Gravenhage: Rijk Geschiedkundige Publicatien, G. Ser. LXX, 1930–42, I, Nr. 501.

one notable exception, repeated itself. As interest rates on the Antwerp exchanges fell through 1515 and 1518–9, moreover, the Anglo-Netherlands textile trade passing through Antwerp expanded, at first slowly and then in 1518–9 rapidly. The initial cause of retardation in the English trade during 1515 lay in a rise in cloth/wool prices, as a long-established, demographically-induced pattern of demand fluctuations imposed itself on domestic markets.[12] But even this rise in prices was, on this occasion, insufficient to totally eliminate the impact of cheap money. As domestic prices thus increased, foreign currency prices for the products of the English industry fell, if slightly, and trade increased. The trade of English exporters, who like Thomas Kitson or William Mucklow still dispatched predominantly the products of the heavy drapery to Antwerp, expanded if somewhat slowly.[13] In the Netherlands, on the other hand, stable domestic prices and falling finance costs led to a veritable commercial and industrial boom.[14] There trade and production, in centres like Menin and Armentières, increased markedly. With the removal of this impediment to growth in England, due to a fall in domestic cloth prices, trade expanded rapidly through 1518–9, as it did also in the Netherlands due to a fall in the export price of cloths caused by the debasement of the *livre de gros*. By the latter date, the Anglo-Netherlands textile trade was larger than a decade earlier but still retained, with one exception, the characteristic features of the earlier period. It was still channelled almost exclusively through Antwerp and it was still dominated by the products of the heavy drapery.

---

12 For an analysis of these fluctuations, see below, and particularly note 45.

13 Cambridge University Library (hereafter CUL), Hengrave Hall MSS., 78/1; Birmingham Public Library, William Mucklow's Ledger.

14 Sources for figures 12.1–2 and 14.1: Netherlands and France: DE SAGHER, Documents, II, Nrs. 257, 263–4, 274, 284 and 630–1; III, Nrs. 409, 415, 459, 475. VAN UYTVEN, La Flandre et le Brabant, p. 294. COORNAERT, Centre industriel, p. 486s. MUS, Kortrijk draperie, p. 163. POSTHUMUS, Leidsche Lakenindustrie, as quoted in H. VAN DER WEE, The Growth of the Antwerp Market and the European Economy. Fourteenth–Sixteenth Centuries, The Hague 1963, III, graph 24, p. 60; I, Appendix 46/1, pp. 530–1. R. SPRANDEL, Zur Tuchproduktion in der Gegend von Ypern, in: Vierteljahrschrift für Sozial- und Wirtschaftsgeschichte, LIV (1967), derived from DE SAGHER, Documents, II. P. DEYON / A. LOTTIN, Évolution de la production textile à Lille aux XVIe et XVIIe siècles, in: Revue du Nord, XLIX (1967), pp. 23–33; P. DEYON Variations de la production textile au XVIe et XVIIe siècles, in: Annales, XVIII (1963), p. 948s., and ID., Amiens, capitale provinciale:étude sur la société urbaine au XVIIe siècle, Paris 1967. Italy: D. SELLA, The Rise and Fall of the Venetian Woollen Industry, in: B. PULLEN (ed.), Crisis and Change in the Venetian Economy of the Sixteenth and Seventeenth Centuries, London 1968, p. 109 and ID., Commerci e industrie a Venezia nel secolo XVII, Venice 1961, p. 117s.

Figure 12.1: Flemish Heavy Drapery, 1493–1593

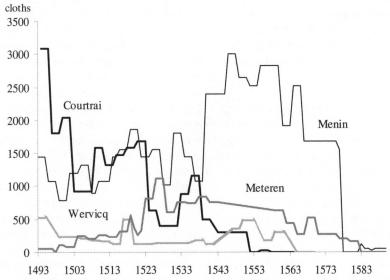

The exception was the cloth trade to the eastern Baltic. Here, as has been suggested, the rapid devaluation of the indigenous currencies after 1515 led to an appreciation of both the Flemish pound and the pound sterling in terms of these moneys.[15] Foreign currency prices of Anglo-Netherlands textiles, falling elsewhere from 1515 through 1518–9, actually increased on Baltic markets, rising at Riga by as much as an eighth. This posed major problems for exporters whose traditional wares were over-priced. In order, therefore, to make themselves more competitive they re-orientated their purchasing strategies towards the acquisition of supplies of lighter, and cheaper, cloths. Accordingly the producers of heavy draperies for the Baltic market, like Leiden or Coventry, found their markets contracting and output fell.[16]

Their loss, however, was the *slechte draperie* producers' gain and the one who could respond to the challenge of rising demand would take the prize. The worsted and doucken manufacturer of East Anglia, in spite of experimentation with the labour saving étamette, failed.[17] Increasing demand forced up cloth prices in spite of that

---

15   See ch. 8 above.

16   POSTHUMUS, Leidsche Lakenindustrie, as quoted in VAN DER WEE, Antwerp, III, graph 24, p. 60; H. BRAND, A Medieval Industry in Decline: the Leiden Drapery in the Early Sixteenth Century, in: M. BOONE / W. PREVENIER (eds.), La draperie ancienne des Pays Bas: débouchés et stratégies de survie (14e–16e siècles), Leuven / Appeldorn: Studies in Urban Social, Economic and Political History of the Medieval and Modern Low Countries, 1993, pp. 121–149 and the excellent study of the final death throws of the Coventry industry by C. PHYTHIAN-ADAMS, Desolation of a City. Coventry and the Urban Crisis of the Late Middle Ages, Cambridge 1979.

17   On the nature of the doucken and étamette, see the appendix to this study. The latter cloth, a worsted utilising the same low quality wools as other products of this genre, was introduced under the tight labour market conditions of the early and mid-1510s because, being woven on a narrower loom, less labour was required than in the production of the normal worsted. On labour market conditions at this time see I. BLANCHARD, Population Change, Enclosure and the Early Tudor Economy, in: Economic History Review, Second Series, XXIII, 3 (1970), p. 431 and for a careful

general fall in English wool prices, which gave the heavy cloth producer his advantage in the market during these years.[18] No more successful were the drapers of Naarden whose raw materials – Westphalian wool and Hessian dyes – were enhanced in price by the increase in the value of the Rhenish gulden in terms of the Low Countries' money of account.[19] Ultimately the prize fell to the Flemish doucken manufactures who increasingly relied upon "Ostland" wool, a product singularly cheap in 1515–9 due to the debasement of the Baltic currencies.[20] The years 1515–9 which thus witnessed the decline of the Leiden and Coventry heavy draperies also saw a rapid increase in production at Poperinge and Tourcoing, raising the latter centres to a dominant position in Baltic markets and establishing for the first time a product of the light drapery amongst the heavy cloths which continued to dominate the Anglo-Netherlands textile trades under conditions of commercial stability at Antwerp.[21]

Yet if the conditions giving rise to the emergence of the light drapery were exceptional during the years of Antwerp's supremacy, they were not unfamiliar to the merchants who plied the trade routes of Europe during the second and third decades of the sixteenth century. Over and over again during these years Habsburg intervention in the Antwerp money (in 1509–13, 1516–7 and 1520–3) threatened the very foundations of the city's commercial supremacy. On these occasions interest rates rose and for those merchants who, like Thomas Kitson maintained their commitment to the Brabant fairs costs, and the foreign exchange price of their wares, increased. In an attempt to soften the impact of rising export prices they, like the merchants engaged in the Baltic trade, therefore eschewed the purchase of their traditional wares – the heavy draperies – and embraced the products of the light. Amongst Kitson's shipments during these years the products of the Cheshire, Lancashire and Welsh coarse woollen

---

analysis of the tangled evidence concerning the nature of the étamette, D. C. COLEMAN, An Innovation and its Diffusion: the New Draperies, in: Economic History Review, Second Series, XXII, 3 (1969), p. 420.

18   On the production of the étamette in the Norfolk worsted industry, see Norfolk and Norwich Record Office (henceforth referred to as NNRO), City Records. Press B. Case 10b, and on the increasing use of the narrow "stamyn" loom in the mid-1510s, Case 17 Press E: Second Worsted Weavers Book, fo. 28. Both the doucken and the various types of worsted utilised "mentill" warp, small "ouffe" and "hevyll" yarn spun from the wool of butcher's fells (see NNRO, Press D, Case 16d 2, fo. 169^v). Accordingly with the decline in the demand for butchers' meat in the late 1510s and early 1520s (H. P. R. FINBERG [ed.], Agrarian History of England and Wales [Cambridge, 1967], IV, p. 824) supplies of raw materials contracted under conditions of rising demand. Worsted prices thus rose (NNRO, Case 17 Press E, fos. 4, 8^v and 30^v). The same conditions, in the demand for income elastic products, as affected the meat market, were also felt in the high-grade cloth market causing a fall the demand for high-quality wether wool (BLANCHARD, Population Change, p. 442 and ID., Commercial Crisis and Change: Trade and the Industrial Economy of the North-East, 1509–1532, in: Northern History, VIII (1973), p. 73).

19   DE VANKRIJKER, De textielindustrie van Naarden, p. 155.

20   See below.

21   By ca. 1520, when there were some 300 workshops in the town, production at Poperinge (at 7–8,000 cloths) had almost doubled since the beginning of the century. M. BRAURE, Etudes économiques sur les Châtellenies de Lille, Douai et Orchies, in: Revue du Nord, XV (1928), p. 188; DE SAGHER, Une enquête, p. 11; A. LOTTIN, Histoire de Tourcoing, Dunkirk 1986. On the position of the town and Tourcoing in Baltic markets at this time, see A&R 3, Nr. 230/10.

manufactory – cottons and friezes – took pride of place.[22] Yet their efforts at product diversification seem to have been largely in vain for their trade, both individually and collectively, declined.

Figure 12.2. Northern Netherlands Heavy Drapery Production, 1493–1593

Nor was the fate of those who, on these occasions, diverted their trade towards the channels of the "alternative commerce" very different, for they now entered into a system where finance costs, though lower than on the Bourse of crisis-stricken Antwerp, were still, in comparison with more "normal" times, inordinately high. Their costs were thus enhanced and their traditional wares overpriced. Accordingly, like those merchants who remained wedded to the Brabant fairs, they followed down the path of product diversification. Thus as, at this time, South German merchants forged "new" links with the Baltic and central-eastern Europe they sought new and cheaper wares in order to successfully pursue their trade. In central Europe it was the products of the Netherlands light drapery – the doucken of Poperinge and the newly introduced étamettes of Leiden[23] – which were predominant in German long-distance commerce, a minor place only being yielded to the indigenous wares of Hesse-Nassau and Lotharingia.[24] But in the Baltic, where the effect of increased costs was exacerbated by

---

22   CUL, Hengrave Hall MSS, 78/1.

23   This "stammet", a twill made of dyed wool, like the Rattinen, a finer stronger small fulled stuff made of Spanish wool, which enjoyed a popularity in Leipzig's trade and were handled in large quantities on these occasions by such merchants as Simon Sander, Lukas Grimm and George Visher, were finished, rather than made in Leiden. G. FISCHER, Aus zwei Jahrhunderten Leipziger Handelsgeschichte, 1470–1650, Leipzig 1929, pp. 79, 282.

24   The major intermediary in this minor trade was Frankfurt. To the city were brought both the new light Lotharingian draperies – the red Spinal, white-grey Niklasport and Metz cloth – and the coarse, old-fashioned local cloths of Hesse-Nassau which were dispatched, on these occasions, eastward to Breslau or south-east to Augsburg. In the latter instance the initially intermittent trade in coarse textiles grew into a large scale commerce which encompassed in 1543 two-thirds of Augsburg's cloth trade going to Poland, Italy and the Levant. DIETZ, Frankfurter Handelsgeschichte, I, pp. 264–6.

the long-term decline in the international value of the groschen and mark, even these wares were too expensive and for the first time the cheap cloths of Ulm and Mulhausen made real inroads into the market along side the coarse textiles of Lübeck and the Wendish towns.[25]

The story is not dissimilar in the case of France. Here, when crisis conditions prevailed at Antwerp, an independent trading system emerged, providing new links between the Anglo-Netherlands cloth producers and their French customers. On these occasions, moreover, that route system merged with a new trans-continental one, as increasing costs and rising prices in the Antwerp/London trades to Spain, Italy and the Levant provided openings for merchants to establish lower cost links via Lyon between these producers and markets to the South. Compared to the trade through Antwerp in the hey-day of its commercial prosperity, however, this long-distance trade was expensive. Like their German counterparts, therefore, the French and Italian merchants attempted to soften the impact of increased costs by abandoning dealings in heavy draperies and taking up the trade in lighter stuffs. The heavy cloth market was thus ceded to the indigenous producer, like the Florentine *garbo*[26] manufacturer or the Languedocian drapers of Perpignon and Carcassonne, who in "normal" circumstances could not compete with the northern heavy draperies but who now briefly flourished during these years. The market for cheaper wares came to be increasingly dominated by the products of the Anglo-Netherlands light drapery – the English kersey and the Hondschoote say.[27]

Finally there is the English "alternative commerce", centred on London, which gradually evolved during the Antwerp crises of 1509–13 and 1516–7 and only assumed truly international dimensions in 1520–3. During these latter years, whilst Antwerp's trade was paralysed, English ships ventured far and wide carrying cargoes

---

25 Such cloths normally unrepresented in the Hanseatic records of the early sixteenth century are referred to therein ONLY during the crisis years of the late 1510s and then only in relation to the eastern Baltic. Livl. UB., II^2, Nrs. 656 and 672, A&R^3, Nrs. 52/13 and 110/7.

26 These cloths were made from wool coming from the northern coast of Africa – *Stati Barbareschi* – and in particular Gerba island as well as from the French Mediterranean coast. H. HOSHINO, L' arte della lana a Firenze nel Basso Medioevo, Firenze 1980, pp. 123–4 and P. MALANIMA, La decadenza di un economia cittadina – l industria di Firenze nei secolo XVI–XVII, Bologna 1982. Such wool was widely used in the production of low and middle grade cloths which had enjoyed a certain vogue in the mid- to late fifteenth century. A. MOZZATO, Circulation, production, quality and retail of raw wool and woollen cloth in Venice, unpublished paper presented at Ester Seminar, held at Jyvaskyla, October 1998.

27 This conclusion is based upon the purchases of cloth at Ancona recorded in the registers of Antonio Stracca (Archivio di Stato, Ancona, II ASA, 13–6), details of which were kindly provided me by Dr Peter Earle, and on the trade through Lyon. R. GASCON, Grand commerce et vie urbaine au XVIe siècle. Lyon et ses marchands, Paris 1971, I, p. 69. On the Italian industry see ch. 13 below, whilst on the Languedoc industry the rather dated study of P. BOISSONNADE, L' industrie languedocienne pendant les soixante, premières années du XVIIe siècle, in: Annales du Midi (1909), is still of use, and the question of competition between northern and domestic cloth production on southern French markets is dealt with by E. LE ROY LADURIE, Les Paysans de Langudoc, Paris 1966, I, pp. 124–6. Both of these studies, however, have now been largely superseded by the study of P. WOLFF, Esquisse d' une histoire de la draperie en Languedoc du XIIe siècle au XVIIIe siècle, in: Produzione, commercio e consumo dei panni di lana, secc. XII–XVIII (=Pubblicazioni dell'Istituto Internazionale di Storia Economica Francesco Datini, Serie II, Atti delle Settimana di Studi, Vol. 2), Prato 1970.

for merchants who, because of the high cost of finance raised on the London market, were once again forced along the path of product diversification, substituting light for heavy draperies. Levant merchants shipped "fine kerseys of diverse colours, coarse kerseys, white western dozens, cottons, certain cloths called 'scatutes' and others called cardinal whites."[28] Bordeaux traders carried Cheshire and northern cottons together with small quantities of Coggeshal cloth.[29] Their counterparts venturing to Spain freighted such cheap cloths as kerseys, "vesys", blankets and medleys as well as small amounts of the dearer Suffolk and Wiltshire short cloths.[30] Other examples could be given but these will perhaps suffice to show the importance of the light draperies amongst the cargoes of vessels engaged in England's "alternative commerce" during the crisis years of the second and third decades of the sixteenth century. Again the now familiar pattern repeated itself. As Antwerp's trade declined the independent trades of centres like London grew. As merchants diversified their trading activities they also diversified their export mix. But neither the development of the "direct" trades nor the increasing export of light draperies compensated for the decline in the heavy drapery trade through Antwerp and in aggregate the cloth trade declined.

Thus as long as tranquillity pervaded Antwerp's finance and commodity markets (in 1492–7[31], 1505–9, 1514–5 and 1518–9), trade in and the output of the products of the Anglo-Netherlands heavy drapery expanded, although after ca.1515 the industry underwent a process of structural displacement as changes in Baltic markets undermined the position of heavy drapery producers at Leiden and Coventry and resulted in the emergence of "new" light drapery centres catering for that market in Flemish Flanders. Yet in "normal" trading conditions the position thus acquired by the doucken producers of Dixmude, Poperinge and Tourcoing was still an exceptional one. When, however, Antwerp's money market was subject to the depredations of the Habsburgs (in 1509–13, 1516–7 and 1520–3) it was not. On these occasions trade passed elsewhere, to Lyon, Frankfurt and London, bringing into existence an "alternative" system of commerce. The new network was a poor substitute for the old, however, and with rising costs a rationalisation of the European cloth market took place. As overall prices rose during each of these crises the products of the heavy drapery became less attractive to consumers and the Anglo-Netherlands producer ceded part of this, probably declining, market to indigenous suppliers in France and Italy whose industries, flattened by the competition of "northern" cloths in more normal circumstances, enjoyed a brief revival at these times. English and Low Countries manufacturers output of heavy draperies thus contracted and international trade in that product declined. Merchants accordingly turned their attention to the growing market for

---

28 R. HAKLUYT, The Principal Navigations, Voyages, Traffiques and Discoveries of the English Nation, 3 Vols. in 2, London 1599–1600, I, p. 46.

29 Ipswich and East Suffolk Record Office, C 13/15/1; CUL, Hengrave Hall MSS, 78/1.

30 Ipswich and East Suffolk Record Office, C 13/15/1 voyage of the *Santa Marya* and other vessels (unfoliated); Draper's Company, Howell's Ledger, fos. 18, 26.

31 This phase of Antwerp's evolution, as interest rates fell in the aftermath of the 1486–92 crisis, lies outside of the ambit of this study and the reader is referred to R. DAVIS, The Rise of Antwerp and its English Connection, 1406–1510, in D. C. COLEMAN / A. H. JOHN (eds.), Trade, Government and Economy in Pre-Industrial England. Essays Presented to F. J. Fisher, London 1976, pp. 2–16, for a brief précis of the literature concerning the events of these years.

cheap wares which they supplied with the products of the Anglo-Netherlands light drapery. During the crisis years these cloths swept all before them, only ceding ground in the Baltic and eastern Europe where the combination of structural and conjunctural change made even these wares expensive and opened up opportunities for the producers of the Nether Rhine, whose old-fashioned coarse cloths sold at a quarter to half the price of Anglo-Netherlands' wares, and their Wendish counterparts. For brief instances during the first quarter of the sixteenth century, therefore, as Anglo-Netherlands textile manufacturers in general lost ground on third-party markets to indigenous producers, an "alternative commerce" and an "alternative manufacture" challenged the hegemony of the heavy drapery in the trade that remained.

Anglo-Netherlands Textile Production and Markets. Even in the relatively peaceful conditions prevailing in European commerce during the first quarter of the sixteenth century, therefore, merchants had to make constant adjustments to their sales and purchasing strategies, seeking out new supplies of traditional wares when trade through Antwerp expanded (in 1492–7, 1505–9, 1514–5 and 1518–9) and obtaining a completely new range of cloths whenever that trade boom was interrupted (in 1509–13[32], 1516–7 and 1520–3) and difficult conditions at the Brabant fairs deflected trade along the paths of the "alternative" commerce. Yet surviving examples of their account books reveal that on these occasions, as in the management of their financial affairs or the organisation of their shipping requirements, they accomplished these adjustments, in the short-term at least, with relatively little difficulty.[33] Indeed at this time in England both merchants and manufacturers existed in a state of mutual harmony and there was an almost complete absence of those public disorders which from ca.1525 were associated with fluctuations in overseas trade.[34] Only as the period surveyed in this chapter drew to its close in 1522–3 were there any indications that all was not well, and even then it required the combined effects of an acute short-term trade downswing and a protracted process of sectoral decline, associated with changes in Baltic markets which affected Midlands and West Country heavy cloth producers, to bring even the hint of discontent to the surface. At Salisbury in 1522 the town council took alarm at the POSSIBILITY of "assemblies and riots."[35] At Coventry in December 1523 a conspiracy was unearthed, although this may have had more to do with the presence of the King's tax moneys in the city than with the effects of the short-term trade downswing which anyway was passing into recovery as the conspiracy was hatched.[36] Neither incident was of any real significance and they in no way seriously disturb that picture of a trade system, comprising interlocking commercial

---

32 There seems to have been a brief recovery in 1511 in what was otherwise a very protracted crisis.

33 For details of the merchants' account books and correspondence utilised in this study and the methodology employed in the extraction of data from them, see the references contained in the bibliography to this study.

34 On such social disturbances and their relationship to trade fluctuations in the years 1525–1545 see chapter 13 below, and for the years 1545–65 there is, of course, the classic study of F. J. FISHER, Commercial Trends and Policies in Sixteenth Century England, Economic History Review, First Series, X, 2 (1940), reprinted in: E. M. CARUS-WILSON (ed.), Essays in Economic History, London 1954, pp. 152–172.

35 Salisbury City Muniments, General Entry Book B, fos. 247 and 248[v].

36 PHYTHIAN-ADAMS, Desolation, pp. 61s., 253s.

and industrial elements, which could accommodate major trade fluctuations with the absolute minimum of disturbance.

The effectiveness of this system resided in its structure, within which the merchants comprised only one element. As has already been shown, the financial resources utilised by them were derived from a network which engrossed not only the mercantile balances of the London community but also, and predominantly, the funds made available to them, through an elaborate sales-credit network, by a multitude of petty merchants, manufacturers, yeomen and graziers. In "normal" circumstances exporters of wool, cloth or metals were able to finance their trade on the basis of the credit extended to them by their suppliers, only finally settling their outstanding debts after they had disposed of their wares and remitted the proceeds on the exchange to England. Their use of the facilities, available to them from Italian merchant-finance houses operating in Lombard Street, was confined to emergencies which created delays in their normal pattern of operations.[37] The realities of their financial situation lay not with these Italians but elsewhere, amongst the English peasantry – those men incomparable "in riches, freedom, liberty, welfare and all prosperity"[38] – who provided the merchants' finance and, in adjusting their credit-terms, tended to soften, by way of alterations in the merchants' cash-flow position, the impact of trade fluctuations. During the first quarter of the sixteenth century, therefore, the English merchants existed in a symbiotic, but subordinate credit-relationship with their suppliers which in the short-term afforded them considerable flexibility in the acquisition of financial resources but which in the long-term afforded them little freedom of action in the determination of their total funding. In the English finance market the merchants were merely passive price-takers accepting terms set by their peasant suppliers.

Their position with regard to the implementation of their cloth procurement strategies was broadly analogous. The flexibility they enjoyed in acquiring over time a constantly changing variety of dyed and undyed, heavy and light, cloths resulted from the peripheral position they occupied in relation to the English cloth market and from the non-specialised activities of peasant cloth manufacturers. Textiles were produced ubiquitously in England by a peasantry who eschewed functional specialisation and who were prepared constantly to shift the focus of their cash-earning activities in order to obtain a desired level of income – with the minimum amount of work.[39] Even in specifically "urban" environments, like Norwich, the workers, who enjoyed special legal privileges with regard to their cloth making activities, retained their agrarian roots and were required "yearly" to "leave weaving of worsteds, says and 'stamyns' for a whole month – from the Assumption of Our Lady 'til a month later for the re-

---

37 See chapter 6 above.

38 Extract from the state paper, quoted in R. H. TAWNEY, The Agrarian Problem in the Sixteenth Century, London 1912, p. 133.

39 On the nature of the peasants' cash-earning activities in one industry – mining – see I. BLANCHARD, The Miner and the Agricultural Community in Late Medieval England, in: Agricultural History Review, XX, 2 (1972), pp. 93–106 and ID., "Stannator Fabulosus", in: Agricultural History Review, XXII, 1 (1974), pp. 62–74; ID., Labour Productivity and Work Psychology in the English Mining Industry 1400–1600, in: Economic History Review, Second Series, XXXI, 1 (1978), pp. 1–15. Relevant evidence concerning the applicability of this analysis to those working in the textile industry is presented in chapter 13 below.

lease and help of husbandry in the time of harvest."[40] In such circumstances the merchant's skill was rooted in his knowledge of the cloth markets where the ubiquitous
peasant-producer sold his wares and within which the merchant was only a marginal
participant. On the basis of that knowledge he could select the items he required at
will, utilising the services, primarily available to satisfy the requirements of the domestic consumer, to ensure deliveries to the ports. In England the flexibility enjoyed
by merchants in obtaining varying quantities and types of cloths thus rested upon their
ability to tap, through the medium of the domestic market, an enormous number of
different sources of supply. When they required more cloth they extended their range
of suppliers within existing production regions. When they required different types of
cloth they drew on new supply networks spatially distant from those which had supplied their traditional wares. It was thus through their knowledge of, and access to a
cloth market which was of truly nation-wide dimensions that English merchants were
able to respond to every changing whim of the foreign consumer.[41]

Nor were their constantly changing patterns of acquisition within that extensive
market likely to pose major problems for manufacturers. These peasant clothier-
graziers, whose commercial activities were complementary to the requirements of satisfying the needs of self-consumption, could in part accommodate the merchants' requirements by a reallocation of output.[42] Where this was not possible, because of the
magnitude of demand changes, they had the means, moreover, to expand production.
Able to draw on a near perfect labour market within which price increases, although
affording the peasant-worker the opportunity for greater individual ease, caused an
inflow of labour to their enterprises, they were able to increase production easily in
conditions of rising demand. With a downswing in demand their workforce[43] simply
dispersed, taking up employment in a myriad of other activities. By increasing or de-
creasing stocking ratios on their land[44] they could similarly in the short-term adjust
their wool supply. That flexibility enjoyed by the English merchants in acquiring over
time a constantly changing variety of cloths thus resulted from the peripheral position
they occupied in relation to the English cloth market within which peasant cloth pro-

---

40   NNRO, Ordinances of the Worsted Weavers 1511, item 3.

41   Such a market had a long history and was already in existence at the very beginning of the period
     covered by this study when it was utilised, in the manner described above, not only by English
     merchants but also by aliens resident here, like the Hansards, whose activities, completely analo-
     gous in form to those later revealed by English merchants account books, are described by FUDGE,
     The German Hanse and England, p. 243.

42   The nature of the activities of the peasant clothier-grazier and the important role of self-
     consumption in the disposal of his output is revealed in series of account books from the 1470s of
     one such man, which have uniquely survived in the collection Bodleian Library, MSS. DD Weld,
     C19/4/1/1–3. It is hoped to publish shortly a study based on these documents.

43   The backward sloping *individual* labour-supply curve was thus compatible with the conventional
     industrial labour-supply curve. See BLANCHARD, Labour Productivity, pp. 2–7.

44   Each short-term upswing in rents and pastoral activity superimposed upon the long-term upward
     trend which culminated in ca. 1520 brought forth a flood of complaints about overstocking. A par-
     ticularly good example of the process will be found in TNA, DL3/16 R 13a, describing the situa-
     tion on one pasture at the height of the pastoral boom. These fluctuations formed an integral part
     of the process described in note 45 below.

ducers pursued their non-specialised activities largely to meet (either through the market or self-consumption) the requirements of domestic consumers.

Map 12.1: Anglo-Netherlands Textile Industry, c. 1500

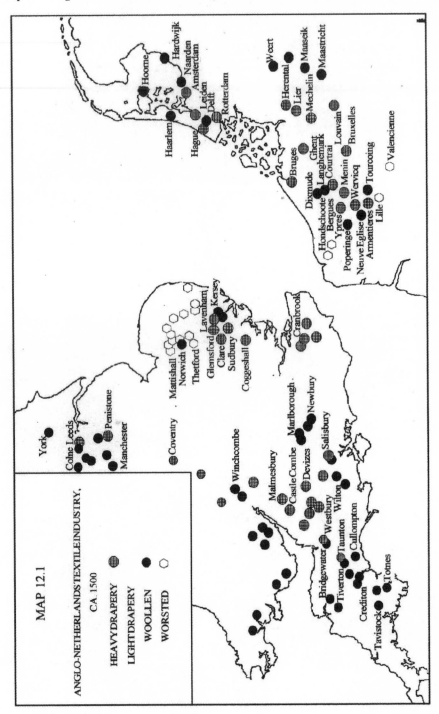

Yet those domestic consumers also, in large measure, determined the collective response of the merchants to long-term changes in foreign demand for their wares. In formulating cloth procurement strategies relating to such changes, the English merchants, during the first quarter of the sixteenth century, were constrained rather than assured more flexibility by the prevailing market situation.[45] In the acquisition of the cloths they required to trade abroad, as in the determination of their financial requirements, they enjoyed very little freedom of action, being unable to the determine the amount of cloth which would be made available to them at a competitive price, as a long established, demographically-induced pattern of demand fluctuations imposed itself on the markets wherein they acquired their cloth. The merchants were thus merely passive price-takers in a market dominated by the domestic consumer. At best, as in 1515 for instance when they were afforded new opportunities to modify their bids for the cloth they required by the availability of cheap money at Antwerp, they were able to make only marginal adjustments to their purchasing patterns.[46] During the first quarter of the sixteenth century, therefore, the English merchants existed in a symbiotic, but subordinate, relationship with their suppliers which, whilst affording them considerable flexibility in the acquisition of varying product-mixes and minimizing social tensions in their dealings, imposed strong constraints on the implementation of procurement strategies. The course of English overseas trade at this time moved (inversely) in the medium-term to the rhythms of the domestic market and in the short-term to the tempo of commercial activity at Antwerp, the merchant responding to these changes but not determining them.

In the Netherlands the situation was very different. Changes in the requirements of domestic consumers played a much lesser role in determining the overall evolution of the cloth market at this time. Their demands were largely satisfied by what historians have come to call, utilising yet another historiographical typology, the "petite draperie", whose manufacturers produced either inexpensive worsteds or a rather old-fashioned small coarse cloth.[47] This manufactory, concentrated in Holland and

---

45 For an analysis of these fluctuations, rooted in an inverse relationship between population movements and changes in incomes/demand in the dominant domestic market for cloth, which, again, through an inverse relationship between domestic demand/prices and the competitive position of English goods abroad, affected the minor export trades of the later Middle Ages, see I. BLANCH-ARD (ed.), The Duchy of Lancaster Estates in Derbyshire 1485–1540, Derbyshire Archaeological Society, Record Series, Vol. 3 for 1967, Kendal 1971, introduction, section 3, pp. 15–6 and n. 28. Through the mechanisms of the contemporary sales-credit system (see chapter 6) changes in the availability of mercantile finance tended to soften the impact of these fluctuations by way of alterations in the merchants cash flow position.

46 Such changes, described above, allowed them to raise their bids for cloths in line with and even marginally in excess of those of domestic consumers secure in the knowledge that the marginal addition to the domestic price of their wares could be born by foreign merchants, who, enjoying a reduction in their finance costs, would still be able to reduce the foreign exchange value of the goods at their final point of sale. The amount they could raise their domestic bid was, however, a matter of very fine judgement.

47 The production and marketing patterns of the small manufacturers of the "petite draperie" are poorly dealt with in the literature and normally only appear to view on those rare occasions when their wares entered into international trade (present chapter, notes 23–7). The only exception to this general rule relates to the "petite draperie" of the region of Brabant to the north-east of Brussels, where the manufacturers of Weert and other centres, like their English counterparts, worked up local wools. These producers have been in relation to the sixteenth century carefully analysed

Friesland, in the region of Brabant to the north-east of Brussels, in the lands of Flanders west of Ypres and in Lotharingia-Ardenne, like the English industry, depended on local wool supplies and catered predominantly for domestic demand, but, unlike in England, its product in "normal" trading circumstances found no place in international trade (Map 12.2) In this period it was only when crisis conditions beset the Antwerp market and merchants required a cheaper product that these wares, like the coarse English woollens, transcended national frontiers. During the first two decades of the sixteenth century, however, such circumstances provided but passing interludes in an industry which formed a separate and distinct sector largely divorced from the international market and within which the tempo of industrial activity moved in much the same manner as in England, at least until productivity changes in Netherlands agriculture began to make themselves felt during the 1520s and the two industries experienced a divergent development path. Output in the Low Countries was thus divided into two separate and largely distinct sectors: there was the "petite draperie", predominantly orientated towards the satisfaction of domestic demand, but on occasion, when commercial crises ephemerally beset the Antwerp market, providing a product which could be drawn briefly into the supply channels of international trade, and there was the "grande draperie", which is of primary concern in this study, catering at all times for the requirements of the international market and evolving to a tempo set by the rhythms of that market.

In the case of this latter "grande draperie" the export market thus exercised a much more direct influence on the fortunes of the cloth producers than it did on either the Netherlands small-cloth manufacturers or indeed on contemporary English cloth makers. For these producers the course of trade moved in accord with the rhythms of the Antwerp Bourse and where the merchants, who frequented that institution for their finance, led, the manufacturers followed. Daily both merchants and manufacturers carefully noted the quotations on the Exchange and diligently gathered any news of wars, bankruptcy or monetary disorder which might upset the delicate balance of rates at that institution. The singular importance attached to this intelligence by the business community is not hard to understand, for, in large measure, upon the movement of the Antwerp exchange depended the fortunes of trade through that city and accordingly manufacturers' sales of their produce. Dear money augured badly for commerce. Those merchants who borrowed money to buy wares would find their costs enhanced, and, fearing lest their goods be overpriced on distant markets, would cut back on their purchases. In such circumstances the mart was likely to be slack and those bringing their wares thence would not easily vent them. Cheap money, on the other hand, opened up the prospect of buoyant business. By reducing the foreign exchange price

by VAN DER WEE, Antwerp, II, pp. 134, 137, 162 and 194; III, graphs 17–8 pp. 47–8 and J. P. PEETERS, Het verval van de lakennijverheid te Mechelen in de 16de eeuw en het experiment met de volmolen (1520–1580), in: Handelingen van de koninklijke Kring voor Oudheidkunde, Letteren en Kunst van Mechelen, LXXXIX (1985); ID., Bouwstoffen voor de geschiedenis der laatmiddeleeuwse stadsdraperie in een klein Brabants produktiecentrum: Vilvoorde (1357–1578), in: Bulletin de la commission royale de l'histoire, CLI (1985), and ID., Sterkte en zwakte van Mechelse draperie in der overgang van middeleeuwen naar nieuwe tijd (1470–1520), in: Handelingen van de koninklijke Kring voor Oudheidkunde, Letteren en Kunst van Mechelen, CX (1986); R. VAN UYTVEN, La draperie brabançonne et malinoise du XIIe au XVIIe siècle: grandeur éphémère et décadence, in: SPALLANZI (ed.), Produzione, pp. 85–97.

of commodities at their final point of sale, it increased their competitiveness and sales potential. Merchants thus flocked to buy such wares at the mart where sellers found plentiful takers for their produce. The fortunes of these manufacturers were intimately interlinked with those of the merchants for upon the latter's purchases the formers' volume of business depended. The Netherlands cloth makers producing the heavy fabrics of the "grande draperie" thus, because of this dependence on their nation's export trades, faced a completely different product market situation to that confronting either their fellow small cloth producers in the Netherlands or the English textile makers.[48] Output in these centres (Figure 12.1/2 and Map 12.2) moved in accord with changes in the international not the domestic market.

The merchant in the Netherlands, accordingly, enjoyed much more room to manoeuvre than his English counterpart. When crisis conditions prevailed on the Antwerp market (in 1509–13, 1516–7 and 1520–3) he could, like the English merchant, totally alter his product-mix. In both cases this meant acquiring cheap coarse (woollen and worsted) textiles which were primarily designed to satisfy the demands of domestic consumers and in each instance they seemed to have experienced no difficulty in purchasing such wares which were very different from their traditional trade goods. In boom conditions at Antwerp (in 1505–9, 1514–5 and 1518–9), when the products of the heavy drapery reasserted their position in an expanding trade, however, the two groups of merchants experienced quite different situations. The English merchants in acquiring increasing supplies of these wares were constrained, in the formulation of their procurement strategies, by conditions prevailing in the domestic market, which on occasion (in 1515 for instance) could limit their ability to purchase the required quantities of the heavy draperies at a competitive price. The Netherlands merchants, able to draw their supplies from the heavy cloth manufacturers of the "grande draperie", were under no such constraint. Within the Netherlands industry these producers constituted a totally separate and distinct entity, divorced from meeting the demands of consumers in the domestic market, and able to respond quickly and effectively to satisfy the requirements of the international merchant group. The Netherlands merchant thus, thanks to the responsiveness of his suppliers, enjoyed a slight advantage over his English counterpart during the boom years of the 1510s.

Anglo-Netherlands Wool Trades. In part these differences in the Netherlands and English "grande draperie", which gave the former nation's merchants their edge, resided in their respective industrial raw material supply systems. The English, as an Italian visitor to the kingdom at the end of the fifteenth century noted, had "an enormous number of sheep, which yield(ed) them quantities of wool of the best quality."[49] Everywhere the peasantry reared sheep. Everywhere the peasantry made up the wool from those sheep into yarn and, more often than not, then had the yarn woven into

---

48   A comparison of production trends in the Netherlands cloth production centres of the "grande draperie", illustrated in Figure 12.1, with changes in the volume of commercial activity there, illustrated in Figure 8.1, reveals a strong positive correlation quite unlike the negative correlation existing between trends in English pastoral activity (and therefore industrial activity based on pastoral products like wool) and the course of English overseas trade, on which see BLANCHARD (ed.), Duchy of Lancaster Estates, introduction, section 3, pp.15–6 and n. 28, and the discussion in note 45 above.

49   C. A. SNEYD (ed.), A Relation, or Rather a True Account of the Island of England about 1500, in: Camden Society, Old Series, XXXVII (1847).

cloth. In the case of lesser men who kept a few sheep, primarily to provide "mylke for their sustenance" without which they would have had "nethur mete ne drynke to putte in ther hedes[50]", this meant the spinning of a few pounds of wool into yarn which was subsequently delivered on contract to the local weaver who, by working up the materials into such items as a blanket or coverlet, created a product which would then be returned to the family for their own use. For their richer neighbours, with as many as 200–400 sheep, the family enterprise involving the spinning of yarn and its fabrication into cloth for self consumption often merged into a commercial business involving contract labour on a far larger scale and engaging the head of the household – the clothier/grazier of the later Middle Ages – in market dealings in order to realise cash from his surplus output. In these circumstances each individual cloth producer worked up the wool from his own flocks and the industrial wool market was virtually non-existent.[51] The flexibility enjoyed by merchants in obtaining varying quantities and types of cloths accordingly rested upon their ability to tap, through the medium of the domestic market, the cloth supplies manufactured by these individual cloth producers each working up his own wools. As has been suggested, when they required more cloth they extended their range of suppliers within existing production regions. When they required different types of cloth they drew on new regional supply networks spatially distant from those which had supplied their traditional wares. In the short-term it was thus through their knowledge of, and access to a cloth market of truly nation-wide dimensions which embraced a myriad of small producers each working-up his own wools that English merchants were able to respond to the changing whims of the foreign consumer. Yet in the medium- and long-term their dependence on that market, wherein activity responded to a long-established, demographically-induced pattern of demand fluctuations, also constrained their scope for independent action. As the peasantry adjusted their demand patterns, causing English overseas trade at this time to move (inversely) in the medium-term to the rhythms of the domestic market, the merchants could merely respond to the course of events thereby, in the absence of alternative sources of supply, adversely affecting their ability to adjust to the prevailing international market situation.

In the Netherlands the situation was somewhat different, paradoxically, because that country did not possess that "enormous number of sheep, which yield(ed) in England vast quantities of wool of the best quality." Wool production in the Low Countries was neither quantitatively nor qualitatively comparable with England. Yet its role in supplying the domestic industry should not be underestimated on that account. In Veluwe, North Holland and Friesland, Flanders and Artois, the region about Brussels and Lotharingia-Ardenne, lord and peasant alike kept not insignificant numbers of sheep whose fleeces provided the raw materials for the "petite draperie", an industry which, like the English manufactory, depended on local wool supplies and catered predominantly for domestic demand (Map 12.2). Unlike in England, however, its product in "normal" trading circumstances found no place in international commerce.

---

50 BLANCHARD (ed.), Duchy of Lancaster Estates, p. 14.

51 In the case of woollens it may just have survived into the later Middle Ages to satisfy the requirements of the diminutive urban luxury cloth manufactory. In the production of fine worsted even this trade did not exist. In Norwich for instance, the main source of wool was from the fells of animals butchered for meat. See NNRO, Press D, Case 16d 2, fo. 169[v].

During the first quarter of the sixteenth century it was only occasionally, when crisis conditions beset the Antwerp market and merchants required a cheaper product, that production of these wares increased and the product transcended national frontiers. In these instances, when the light cloths of the "petite draperie" were ephemerally elevated into the ranks of the "grande draperie", however, the inadequacies of local wool supplies[52] became only too apparent. Manufacturers accordingly at these times remedied the deficiencies of local supplies by importing wools from elsewhere, bringing into existence a temporally intermittent and organizationally informal commercial network which afforded them considerable flexibility in adjusting wool supplies to their changing production patterns. The quantitative inadequacies in native wool supplies thus occasionally, during the first quarter of the sixteenth century, led Netherlands manufacturers of the light draperies to have recourse to international raw material supply systems.

Such a dependence on international raw material supply systems had for a long time past been an endemic aspect of the everyday industrial life of Netherlands manufacturers producing the fine heavy cloths of the "grande draperie". In this instance, however, it was the qualitative as well as the quantitative inadequacies of native wool supplies, the lack of those vast "quantities of wool of the best quality" that the English enjoyed, which was of paramount importance in forcing producers over onto international supply networks. Native wools had always been totally unsuitable for the fine fabrics which were the hall mark of producers in this sector of the Netherlands industry and as such their use was specifically prohibited in the regulations surrounding the production of the heavy drapery. Manufacturers of these fabrics thus used only high quality imported wools which in ca. 1500 were supplied from England, Spain and on occasion Scotland (although in this instance only the very best grades of Scots wool met the qualitative requirements of Netherlands producers). For many years prior to this date such wools had been imported into the Low Countries and as the sixteenth century began there was already in existence a well developed and organizationally stable industrial wool market, within which manufacturers were able to continually alter both the quantities and types of wool they purchased, thereby allowing them to vary their production patterns and satisfy the merchants' changing requirements. The export sector of the Netherlands cloth manufactory – the "grande draperie" – encompassing both light and heavy cloth producers, thus, unlike in England, formed a separate and distinct entity divorced from both domestic markets and native wool supplies. Producers therein, unlike their English counterparts, could accordingly respond directly to the requirements of the export merchants, flexibility being assured in this instance by the manufacturers of the "grande draperie" who, in utilising the facilities

---

52 Again in the current state of the historiography of the Low Countries industry it is very difficult to assess either the role or importance of domestic wool supplies to the Netherlands textile industries, but the matter is briefly discussed in: A. VERHULST, De inlandse wol in de textielnijverheid van de Nederlanden van de 12e tot de 17e: produktie, handel en verwerking, Bijdragen en Mededelingen betreffende de Geschiedenis de Nederlanden, LXXXV, 1 (1970), pp. 6–18, a study originally presented as a paper, in: ID., La laine indigène dans les anciens Pays-Bas entre le XIIe et le XVIIe siècle. Mise en oeuvre industrielle, production et commerce at the Prima settimana di studio del Centro Internazionale di Storia Economica Francesco Datini, held at Prato, 18–24 April 1969, which subsequently appeared in the publications of the Institute, Serie II – Atti delle Settimane di Studi, Vol. 1.

of a well developed and organizationally stable industrial wool market, were able to continually alter both the quantities and types of wool they purchased, vary their production patterns and satisfy the merchants changing requirements.

In part therefore the effectiveness of the Netherlands merchants in promoting their trade in Low Countries textiles during the first quarter of the sixteenth century rested on their relationship with their suppliers – the light and heavy cloth producers of the "grande draperie" – manufacturers who, by utilising the facilities of a well developed industrial wool market, were in a position to respond quickly and effectively in satisfying the merchants' constantly changing requirements. With regard to the heavy cloth manufacturers this meant using the facilities of a long-established industrial wool market, which was centred on Bruges rather than Antwerp, and which, throughout the period of this study (1505–1544), maintained a basically stable organizational form.[53] For the light cloth producer it meant availing themselves of the facilities provided by a much more informally organized commercial network, with strong regional characteristics, which, in as far as it was centred on the marts of the Scheldt estuary, evolved under the umbrella provided by the older organization. In either case, however, producers enjoyed much greater freedom of action than their English counterparts, being able to draw their supplies of wool through an international commercial system which operated on the basis of a multi-national resource base and which was unaffected by changes in the Netherlands domestic situation.

The older element in this commercial system already in ca. 1500 had a long history behind it and throughout the period of this study (1505–1544), maintained a basically stable organizational form. During these years the English continued their long-established trade in fine wools at Calais. Year after year, when unimpeded by political restraint or embargo, the English wool fleet sailed for the Staple.[54] There successive

---

53 The organization of the English trade revealed in the Cely papers (1472–1488) is described in the classic studies: E. POWER, The English Wool Trade in the Reign of Edward IV, in: Cambridge Historical Journal, II (1926–8); EAD., The Wool Trade in the Fifteenth Century, in: EAD. / M. M. POSTAN (eds.), Studies in English Trade in the Fifteenth Century, London 1933, and EAD., The Wool Trade in English Medieval History, Oxford 1941; A. HANHAM, Foreign Exchange and the English Wool Merchant in the Late Fifteenth Century, in: Bulletin of the Institute of Historical Research, XLVI (1973); EAD., Profits on English Wool Exports, 1472–1544, in: ibidem, LV (1982), and her excellent study: EAD., The Celys and their World. An English merchant family of the fifteenth century, Cambridge 1985; T. H. LLOYD, The English Wool Trade in the Middle Ages, Cambridge 1977. Many of the original letters have also been published in H. HALL, The English Staple, Gentleman's Magazine, CCLV (1883); H. E. MALDEN (ed.), The Cely Papers: Selections from the Correspondence and Memoranda of the Cely Family, Merchants of the Staple, AD 1475–1488, in: Camden Society, Third Series, I (1900) and A. HANHAM (ed.), The Cely Letters, 1472–1488, Early English Text Society, CCLXXIII (1975). Subsequent descriptions of the organization of the trade will be found in Richard Hill's Commonplace Book of 1506 (Balliol MS. 354); the enormous collection of Johnson Papers (1534–1552), of which only the letters have been edited by B. WINCHESTER (ed.), The Johnson Letters, 1542–1552, Unpublished London PhD Thesis 1953, whilst the accounts (TNA, SP1/185, 196 and 244; SP 46/5–7, copies of which are in the author's possession) remain amongst the MS collections of State Papers, and E. E. RICH (ed.), The Ordinance Book of the Merchants of the Staple, Cambridge 1937, relating to conditions in 1565. A comparison of these studies reveals a basic stability of organizational form in the trade throughout the period of this study (1505–1544) and, in spite of the loss of Calais, beyond.

54 The remarkably fine series of London wool customs records which link the periods covered by the Cely (1472–1488) and Johnson (1534–52) papers (viz. TNA, E 122/73/4; 78/5, 8, 10; 79/9, 17–8;

generations of Staplers conducted their business in much the same way as had the Celys: they unloaded the ships and registered their consignments with the collectors or wool-packers; sorted their wares into "old" and "new" wools, transported the product to the Calais mart and there, usually extending credit, sold it.[55] Their principal customers throughout the period remained the Flemish and Burgalese wool merchants of Bruges who on acquiring the prized high-quality English wools arranged for their transport by land or sea to that city from whence they were sold on to customers in the heavy drapery districts of the Low Countries.[56] These Bruges merchants[57] also handled the large cargoes of fine Spanish wool which arrived with Basque iron aboard the Biscayan fleet that anchored in the Ecluse during June each year, as well as the lesser cargoes shipped from the south-western Spanish ports. By far the largest part of the trade in fine English and Spanish wools thus passed through Bruges whose merchants distributed the product to the manufacturers of the Netherlands heavy drapery. Not surprisingly in these circumstances therefore Scots merchants, trading out of Middleburg, also reserved their better quality wools for this trade with the Bruges merchants.[58] Annually when the Edinburgh wool fleet arrived at Middleburg and its Aberdeen counterpart anchored at Veere one of the first tasks of the Scots merchants and factors was to sort and grade the incoming cargoes. Thereafter, whilst the greater part of their wools was distributed through the informal channels of the light drapery sup-

---

81/11, 13 82/1, 5–6; 83/3, 8, 16; 85/10; 166/12; 195/27; 203/6; 204/1–9) reveal both the changing personnel involved in the trade, as well as the long-term stability in its organization.

55 Credit terms were used to maintain price stability over time. On a depressed market prices were maintained and abatements were made by lengthening credit-terms. On a rising market prices were not enhanced but credit was shortened.

56 Small consignments of high-quality wool were also sold direct to clothiers but most Staplers probably followed the practice of the Celys and Johnsons selling large consignments (30–60 Calais sacks) to the Bruges merchants.

57 Burgos in Northern Castile and its merchant community dominated the northern Spanish wool trade, controlling the internal supply network and both ends of the external trade between the Cantabrian coast and Flanders or France, see C. R. PHILLIPS, The Spanish Wool Trade, 1500–1780, in: Journal of Economic History, XLII, 4 (1982), pp. 789–91; J. MARECHALL, La colonie espagnole de Bruges du XIVe au XVIe siècle, in: Revue du Nord, XXXV (1953), pp. 5–40; W. R. CHILDS, Anglo-Castilian Trade in the later Middle Ages, Manchester 1978, pp. 215–6, and C. VERLINDEN, A propos de la politique économique des ducs de Bourgogne à l' égard de l' Espagne, in: Hispania, X (1950), pp. 681–715. J. H. EDWARD, El comercio lanero en Córdoba bajo los Reyes Católicos, paper presented at the I Congreso de Historia de Andalusía in December 1976 (subsequently published in the Acta of the Congress, Madrid 1978, I, pp. 423–8) shows that they also dominated the Cordoban market from 1471–1514, although here they met with competition from the Sevillian-Genoese, PIKE, Aristocrats and Traders, pp. 61, 123–6. Finally on the arrival of these fleets in the Ecluse during the years 1486–1500, see L. GILLIODTS-VAN SEVEREN (ed.), Inventaire des Archives de Bruges: Série 1 Treizième au seizième siècle, 6 Vols., introduction and 2 indices, Bruges 1878–1885, IV, p. 450 and VI, pp. 275–6.

58 A vivid picture of the Scots wool trade during the years 1492–1503 can be constructed from C. INNES (ed.), The Ledger of Andrew Halyburton, Conservator of the Privileges of the Scotch Nation in the Netherlands, 1492–1503, Edinburgh 1867, henceforth referred to as "Halyburton's Ledger"; W. S. UNGER, De Tol van Iersekerood, 1321–1572, Rijks Geschiedkundige Publicatien, Kl. Ser. XXIX, s' Gravenhage 1939, and National Archives of Scotland, Register House, Edinburgh (hereafter referred to as NAS), E71/1/1, which may be set in a longer time perspective by reference to J. DAVIDSON / A. GRAY, The Scottish Staple at Veere, London 1909 and M. P. ROOSEBOOM, The Scottish Staple in the Netherlands, The Hague 1910.

ply system, the best was sold to these same Bruges merchants and trans-shipped by *schout* to the Dam. The fine wool trade was thus already at the beginning of the sixteenth century handled by merchants who could avail themselves of the facilities of a well developed and organizationally stable industrial wool market which at that time and subsequently operated to isolate consumers from the effects of supply-source price fluctuations.[59]

The coarse wool and fell trade, which provided raw materials for those producers of light draperies engaged in the export trade, was, as the sixteenth century opened, a much more temporally intermittent business which was organized through a rather informal and regionally fragmented commercial network. Even as the new century began, amidst the turmoil of crisis conditions at Antwerp, which during the years 1497–1503 afforded these producers new opportunities to promote their trade to central and eastern Europe, however, the main features of their supply systems may be discerned. In the western Netherlands the marts of the Scheldt estuary provided the major focus for this supply system. In part, it catered for the requirements of manufacturers in the cloth-making districts of Flanders located to the west of Ypres, supplementing on this occasion the producers' normal native wool supplies drawn from Flanders and particularly les Quartre-Métiers, Artois and Boulonnais, and Hainault. In this instance manufacturers obtained some of the incremental supplies of wool through contracts with one of their major customers, the Easterlings who at this time, as during previous crisis years (1486–92 for instance), may be discerned importing "Ostland" wool from Pomerania, Poland and Silesia.[60] Equally important at this time, however, were the supplies they obtained from merchants operating under the umbrella provided by the older wool trading system. For the doucken makers of Dixmude, Poperinge and Tourcoing this meant having recourse to the Scots.[61] For these Scots merchants, however, this trade with the Flemings was only one aspect of a multi-layered commercial system which encompassed many other elements in the

59 On domestic English wool prices see P. BOWDEN, Statistical Appendix, in: J. THIRSK (ed.), The Agrarian History of England and Wales, Cambridge 1967, IV, pp. 840–4 and T. H. LLOYD, The Movement of Wool Prices in Medieval England, Cambridge: Economic History Review Supplement, VI (1973). The figures derived from this latter work have, however, been recalculated to overcome the statistical deficiencies of their original presentation, on which see History, LX, 198 (1975), p. 110s. On sales prices in the Low Countries in the years to 1532, see J. H. MUNRO, Wool Price Schedules and the Qualities of English Wools in the Later Middle Ages, c.1270–1499, in: Textile History, IX (1978); HANHAM, The Celys, pp. 145–7; L&P, Henry VIII, VIII, Appendix 20/1–5. The subsequent break up of this system and collapse of the English wool trade under the impact of English government policies from 1527 and inflationary pressures during the years after 1532 is considered in chapter 13 below.

60 See UNGER, Tol van Iersekerood; H. VAN WERVEKE, Die Stellung des hansischen Kaufmanns dem flandrischen Tuchproduzenten gegenüber, in: AUBIN et al. (eds.), Beiträge, and I. BLANCHARD, Northern Wools and Netherlands Markets at the Close of the Middle Ages, in: G. G. SIMPSON (ed.), Scotland and the Low Countries 1124–1994, Phantassie 1996, pp. 76–88.

61 See Halyburton's Ledger, pp. 14, 17, 24, 29, 42, 44, 46, 66, 68, 77, 79, 82, 111, 113, 115, 118, 126, 131, 136, 143, 177, 188, 193, 195, 199, 207, 219, 221–2, 228–9, 231, 241, 244. An analysis of this branch of the trade reveals a marked increase in activity during the years 1497–1503. It is perhaps worth noting that at this time the say manufacturers of Hondschoote continued to operate solely on the basis of native wools, the drapers buying "fleeces, packets of a few pounds at the local centres of Bergues, Loo, Dixmude [...]", COORNAERT, Un centre industriel, p. 192.

western Netherlands wool trade. As has already been indicated they were also involved in the fine wool trade at Bruges.[62] Further they sold fells to the manufacturers
of Ghent and Mechelin[63] and, far more importantly, to the Hollanders (of the Hague,
Hoorne and Delft[64]) who were also major purchasers of such wares at Calais. The
principal West Netherlands producers of light draperies for the export market – in
Holland and the cloth-making districts of Flanders located to the west of Ypres – thus
had access to a well organised industrial wool market wherein Scots and Newcastle
merchants, Easterlings and Staplers, operating under the umbrella provided by the
older wool trading system, were able to supply coarse wools and fells wherever and
whenever they were required, the pattern of commercial activity first revealed in
1497–1503 repeating itself thereafter during the next quarter of a century as occasion
dictated.

These light cloth producers counterparts in the eastern provinces of the Netherlands also enjoyed access to a similar well-organised, regional industrial wool market,
in this instance centred on Frankfurt.[65] Through the fair town passed Rhenish wools
which, since the decline of the local cloth industry in the late fifteenth century, were
distributed north to Utrecht, Naarden and Amersfoort[66] or west to Lotharingia and
Aachen. From Hesse and the lands of Hesse-Kassel wools and dyestuffs, collected at
Fritzlar, Frankenberg and Sprangenberg, also were brought to Frankfurt for redistribu-
tion to Nuremberg and Ulm; Epinal and St Nikolasport in Lotharingia; Sedan, Arras,
Tournai and Mons, and Maastricht and Aachen.[67] Finally, these local, middle-German
wool supplies were on occasion supplemented at Frankfurt by more exotic produce as
merchants out of Leipzig brought Lausitz, Bohemian, Silesian and Polish wools and
others from Naumburg and transported Thuringian wools to the fair, where they were
bought by manufacturers from Maastricht, Aachen, Malmedy and Trier. The principal
East Netherlands producers of light draperies for the export market – in the cloth-
making districts of eastern Holland and Gelderland, and, Ardenne-Lotharingia – thus,
like the equivalent producers in the west of the country, had access to a well organised

---

62   See present chapter, above.

63   M. BOONE, Nieuwe teksten over de Gentse draperie: Woolaanvoier, productiewijze en contro-
     lepraktijken (c. 1456–1468), in: Bulletin de la commission royale d' histoire, XIV (1988), pp. 1–
     62; J. P. PEETERS, Sterkte en zwakte van Mechelse draperie in der overgang van middeleeuwen
     naar nieuwe tijd (1470–1520), in: Handelingen van de koninklijke Kring voor Oudheidkunde, Let-
     teren en Kunst van Mechelen, CX (1986).

64   T. S. JANSMA, L' industrie lainière des Pays Bas du Nord et spécialement celle de Hollande
     (XIVe–XVIIe siècles): production, organisation, exportation, in: SPALLANZI (ed.), Produzione; H.
     E. VAN GELDER, De Draperye van den Haage, in: Die Haghe (1907). On Scots sales of fells and
     low quality wools to the Hollanders see Halyburton's Ledger, pp. 19, 21, 23, 40, 42, 44, 46, 53,
     64, 68, 71, 76, 90, 112, 209 and 211. On the purchases of these wares at Calais, HANHAM, The
     Celys, pp. 159–163 and POWER, English Wool Trade, pp. 60–1.

65   DIETZ, Frankfurter Handelsgeschichte, pp. 254–262.

66   DE VRANKRIJKER, Naarden, p. 155; L. NOORDEGRAAF, Textielnijver in Alkmaar, 1500–1850, in:
     Alkmaarse Historische Reeks, V (1982), pp. 39–64, whilst DIETZ, Frankfurter Handelsgeschichte,
     p. 260 provides evidence that these wools were also via Hamburg drawn into the "Ostland" wool
     trade.

67   H. AMMANN, Der Hessische Raum in der mittelalterlichen Wirtschaft, in: Hessisches Jahrbuch für
     Landesgeschichte, VIII (1958).

industrial wool market wherein German merchants were able, for the next quarter of a century, to supply coarse wools and fells as they were required.

In part therefore the effectiveness of the Netherlands merchants in promoting their trade in Low Countries textiles during the first quarter of the sixteenth century rested on their relationship with their suppliers – the light and heavy cloth producers of the "grande draperie" – manufacturers who, by utilising the facilities of a series of well developed industrial wool markets, were able to continually alter both the quantities and types of wool they purchased, vary their production patterns and satisfy the merchants' changing requirements. Within the basically stable organizational structure of Netherlands wool markets, the constituent trades were thus in a perpetual state of flux as merchants constantly adjusted supplies to the changing requirements of manufacturer and cloth merchant, providing them with the raw materials they wanted at a price they could afford.

In their operations these wool merchants, moreover, proved remarkably effective. During the first great cycle in the Anglo-Netherlands cloth trade (1492–1523), which was dominated by the products of the heavy drapery, they were able to supply Netherlands manufacturers with an ever increasing quantity of fine wools at stable prices[68], thereby isolating them from the effects of those wool price fluctuations which on occasion (in 1515 for instance) constrained the activities of their English rivals. As trade in the Anglo-Netherlands heavy draperies increased (Figure 8.1), the Netherlands production of these cloths also increased (Figure 12.1/2) drawing on a steadily growing supply of imported fine wools (Figure 12.3).

---

68   On the English wool trade see E. M. CARUS-WILSON / O. COLEMAN, England's Export Trade 1275–1547, Oxford 1963, pp. 69–74, 122–139, and J. D. GOULD, The Great Debasement. Currency and the Economy in Mid-Tudor England, Oxford 1970, Appendix C, p. 182. Statistical materials for the Spanish wool trade pose greater problems. Consistent and continuous data is only available from the reign of Philip II and has been presented in the studies of H. LEPEYRE, Le commerce des laines en Espagne sous Philippe II, in: Bulletin de la société d histoire moderne, sèrie II, XIV (1955); Les exportations de laine de Castille sous le regne de Philippe II, in: M Spallanzi (ed.), La lana come materia prima. I fenomeni della sua produzione e circulazione nei secoli XIII–XVII (=Instituto internazionale di storia economica F Datini Prato. Pubblicazioni, serie II, 1, Atti della Prima settimana di studi [18–24 aprile 1969]), Florence 1974, pp. 221–239, subsequently expanded in chapter 4 of ID., El comercio exterior de Castillo a través de la aduanas de Felipe II, Valladolid 1981. J. ISRAEL, Spanish Wool Exports and the European Economy, 1610–1640, in: Economic History Review, Second Series, XXXIII, 2 (1980) and PHILLIPS, Spanish Wool Trade. This latter excellent study, however, also draws together the scattered statistical materials available for the years to 1564, which may be further supplemented for the closing years of the fifteenth century from GILLIODTS VAN SEVEREN (ed.), Inventaire, Vol. 4, p. 450 and Vol. 6, p. 275s., and J. FINOT, Etude historique sur les relations commerciales entre la Flandre et l Espagne au moyen age, Paris 1899, p. 223.

Figure 12.3: English and Spanish Wool Trade, 1492–1542

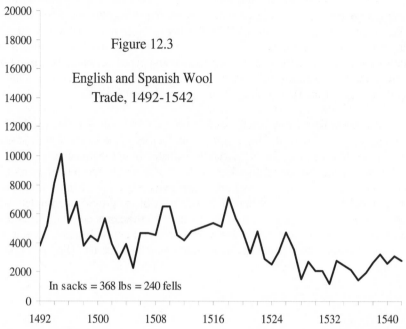

Figure 12.3

English and Spanish Wool
Trade, 1492-1542

In sacks = 368 lbs = 240 fells

Initially, in the aftermath of the crisis of 1486–92, the main source of such wools was England but as the first trade upswing of the new cycle approached its peak in 1495–6 the price of English wool at Calais began to edge upwards.[69] At this point therefore the Bruges merchants shifted to a "new" supply source. By 1499–1500 Spanish wool (ca. 4,000 English sacks annually) once more found a place on the Bruges market, re-establishing its pre-crisis position in the trade and creating a new market equilibrium between the two products.[70] Henceforth, from 1497–1523 the English wool trade continued, but during each successive boom (in 1505–9, 1514–5 and 1518–9) sales, at ca. 9,000–10,000 sacks a year, never again achieved the levels of 1495–6 and when crises beset the heavy cloth trade (in 1497–1503, 1509–13, 1516–7 and 1520–3) they amounted to no more than 5,000–7,000 sacks a year. The English now had to share the market with Spanish wool which over the same period 1497–1523 was imported in quantities of between ca. 4,000 and 6,000 English sacks a year.[71] In aggregate, how-

---

69   HANHAM, The Celys, Table 2, p. 146.

70   GILLIODTS VAN SEVEREN (ed.), Inventaire, Vol. 4, p. 450 and Vol. 6, p. 275s. In 1486–7, as the previous trade boom gave way to crisis conditions on Low Country markets, on average six Anda-lusian and Biscayan ships a year put into the Ecluse. In 1499–1500 they numbered on average 4–5 a year. Assuming that, as later, these ships carried about 750–800 sacks of wool each (see T. MAZO, Solano, El comercio de lanas por el puerto de Santander con Flandes y Francia en los años 1545–1551, in: Aportación al estudio de la historia económica de la Montaña, Santander 1957, pp. 316–48, then the trade at this time amounted to ca. 4,000 sacks a year.

71   When crisis conditions prevailed in the heavy drapery trades (e.g. in 1499–1500) Spanish wool exports, as has been suggested (in n. 70 above), amounted to ca. 4,000 sacks a year. In boom con-

ever, the shift in sources of supply allowed the wool boom to continue, imports rising
to 14,000 sacks a year in 1499–1500 and almost 15,000 sacks in 1508/9. It also allowed the market price of fine wools to once again fall in 1499 to pre-1496 levels and
thereafter to remain at that price to 1523.[72] The heavy-cloth manufacturers of the Low
countries, by utilising the facilities of a well developed industrial wool market, thus
were able to alter continually both the quantities and types of wool they purchased,
vary their production patterns and satisfy the merchants' changing requirements during the boom years of the first great cycle in the Anglo-Netherlands cloth trade (1492–
1523).

When that trade boom was briefly stayed (in 1486–92, 1497–1503, 1509–13 and
1516–7) and the products of the light-cloth manufactory came to the fore, moreover,
cloth makers in this sector of the Netherlands industry found themselves equally well
provided with facilities to secure supplies of the coarse wools and fells they required.
Unfortunately because of the informal and fragmented structure of these markets and
the temporal instability of activity therein it is impossible to provide a complete statistical overview of this trade. Only within the western Netherlands commercial network,
centred on the Scheldt, is such an overview possible and here a broadly similar long-
term trend in imports to that in the fine wool trade may be discerned (Figure 12.4).[73]

---

ditions (such as characterised the years 1505–9) they amounted to ca. 6,000 sacks a year, PHILLIPS,
Spanish Wool Trade, p. 778s.

72   It is surely significant in this context that the 1499 Netherlands wool price schedule was published
for current use in 1523. MUNRO, Wool-price Schedules, pp. 154–5.

73   Sources for Figure 12.4 are as follows: English fells, traded through the Calais Staple: P. RAMSEY,
Overseas Trade in the Reign of Henry VII: The Evidence of Customs Accounts, in: Economic His-
tory Review, Second Series, VI, 2 (1953), p. 181 and G. SCHANZ, Englische Handelspolitik gegen
Ende des Mittelalters mit besonderer Berücksichtigung des Zeitalters der beiden ersten Tudors
Heinrich VII und Heinrich VIII, 2 Vols. Leipzig 1881, II, pp. 76–85, which distinguish the trade in
fells and wool. Newcastle wool and fells: CARUS-WILSON / COLEMAN, England's Export Trade,
pp. 69–74, 122–139. Scots wool: Rotuli Scaccarii Regum Scotorum (Edinburgh, 1889–1897),
Vols. XII–XVIII. I should like to thank Dr Martin Rorke for affording me access to his critical
data set of the Scottish customs records. For a description of the Scots customs system A.
MURRAY, The Exchequer and the Crown Revenue of Scotland, 1437–1542, Unpubl. University of
Edinburgh PhD Thesis, Edinburgh 1961, pp. 142–146. "Ostland" wool: Wojéwodzkie Archiwum
Panstwowe w Gdansk, Komora Palowa, Pfahlkammerechnung 300, 19/7–11, encompassing Polish
exports through the Sound and thus a minimum figure excluding exports from Pomerania and central Europe via Hamburg.

Figure 12.4: The Northern Wool Trade, 1490–1540

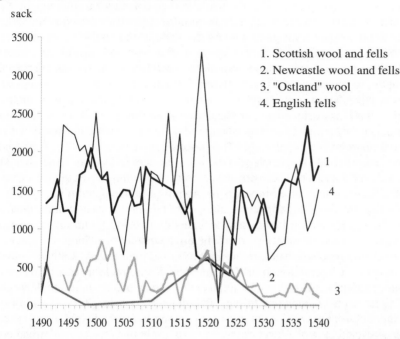

sack

1. Scottish wool and fells
2. Newcastle wool and fells
3. "Ostland" wool
4. English fells

The picture of the trade revealed is a complex one. During the years 1497–1515 northern British – Scots and Newcastle – coarse wool and fells dominated the markets of the Scheldt supplying annually 2,000–2,250 sacks during booms (in 1497–1503 and 1509–1513) and 1,600–1,750 sacks during intervening slumps (in 1504–1508 and 1514–1515) in the trade. These supplies were further augmented, moreover, by the trade in English fells, through the Calais Staple, which amounted annually in boom years to about 1,800 sacks and in slumps to 1,250 sacks – at least until 1514/5. Throughout the period 1497–1515 therefore British produce dominated Netherlands markets for coarse wools and fells, the trade rising to some 4,000 sacks a year in boom conditions and stabilizing at 3,000–3,500 sacks during the intervening slumps.

Progressive debasements of the Baltic currencies during the years 1486–1497 and 1515–1527, however, served to alter significantly trade patterns at these times. By undermining the position of the Leiden "heavy" draperies on northern markets and causing merchants to acquire, in "normal" circumstances (during 1493–1496, 1514–1515 and 1518–1520) at Antwerp, the "light" cloths of the Hague, Hoorne and Delft to sell there, they caused an augmentation in the demand for fells, particularly English, at a time when the market for this produce was normally depressed. Debasement, in lowering the foreign exchange price of Baltic produce on Low Countries markets, also introduced a new competitor into the trade – "Ostland" wool. As a result the market was transformed. The English trade, via the Calais Staple, increased to some 2,000–2,750 sacks a year. The northern British trade, on the other hand, declined to 600–1,500 sacks as its position on Netherlands markets was usurped by "Ostland" wool, some 500–600 sacks of which were imported at these times.

   Patterns of commercial development in the northern coarse-wool and fell trade
were thus far more complex than in the better known commerce in fine wools. Yet it
was no less efficient in meeting the raw material requirements of those Netherlands
producers of the *schlechte draperie* who by the close of the 1492–1523/6 trade cycle
had established themselves in a position of parity with the previously important
heavy-cloth producers. In the coarse wool and fell markets of the western Netherlands
alone supplies which between 1493–1515 had fluctuated between ca. 3,500 and 4,000
sacks a year thereafter increased to 5,000 sacks in 1518–1520. If analogous conditions
prevailed on the Frankfurt market then the coarse wool and fell trade had finally come
of age and had for the first time also established itself on a position of parity with the
previously important and better known fine wool trade. In the case of the Netherlands
schlechte draperie and its associated raw material supply system, therefore, 1520
marked the beginnings of a new era. Henceforth following the exchange crises of
1521 and 1522–3, whilst production of the Anglo-Netherlands "heavy" drapery underwent a process of terminal decline, the "light" draperies went from strength to
strength. Those crises and the monetary disorders of 1531–1532, however, ensured a
transformation of its wool supply system. The establishment of a "hard" currency system, based on the Joachimsthaler, in the Baltic caused the trade in "Ostland" wool to
collapse and the northern British, and particularly Scots, trade to re-establish itself.
Inflationary pressures undermined the English wool trade and again ensured its subor-
dination to its Scots counterpart. In part, therefore, pre-existing trading patterns re-
asserted themselves, but with a total commerce in 1540/1, at the height of the contemporary trade-cycle below the level of the previous cycle this "traditional" trade could
no longer satisfy the requirements of "light" cloth producers and was eclipsed – by
those innovating farmers who were contemporaneously transforming Netherlands agriculture and its associated wool supply system.

CHAPTER THIRTEEN

THE CLOTH AND WOOL TRADES. CRISIS AND
TRANSFORMATION, 1523–32

The Anglo-Netherlands Cloth Trade. The 1520s saw the Anglo-Netherlands textile merchants' world turned upside down. What previously had been exceptional in their experience now became normal whilst circumstances which once had been regarded as normal became exceptional. The English merchants visiting the Brabant fairs experienced successive crises on the Antwerp exchanges, in 1520–3, 1525–early 1527 and late 1527–1529, which disrupted their trade. For their Netherlands counterparts the crisis which had begun in 1520 continued until late 1525 creating a bleak situation which was relieved only by the return of the English to the fairs during 1523–4. Thereafter over the winter of 1525/6 and the spring of 1526 there was a brief recovery in commercial and industrial activity in the Low Countries but it was not to last and through the remainder of that year into early 1527 crisis conditions once more prevailed. The central European mining disorders of late 1527, moreover, ushered in a new phase of crises there which continued until 1529. For seven or eight years of this decade crisis conditions prevailed at Antwerp deflecting trade from that city along the paths of western Europe's "alternative commerce" and bringing the light cloths of the "alternative manufacture" to the fore in a trade which now settled at a lower level than before. In these circumstances conditions propitious for the pursuance of the traditional trade through Antwerp in the traditional heavy draperies were rare. For the English they existed for some eighteenth months in 1523–4 and for barely six months each year in 1527 and 1529. For the Netherlanders the situation was not very different. So-called "normal" conditions prevailed only briefly for six months in each of the years 1525/6, 1527 and 1529. Crisis conditions which had been an intermittent and ephemeral phenomenon during the previous two decades thus now became the normative experience of Anglo-Netherlands textile merchants during the 1520s.

As the decade began, however, few merchants could have anticipated the trials and tribulations to come. With the ending of the 1520–3 crisis for many the time must have seemed ripe for the resumption of old habits and the reestablishment of old trading patterns. Nor were their expectations to remain entirely unrealized at that time. Through 1523–4 trade once more began to assume at least some of the features which had characterised Antwerp's commerce during its hey day. Of paramount importance in the new situation was the revival of Anglo-Netherlands trade. London merchants, who had withdrawn from the Brabant fairs in large numbers during the previous crisis, once more in 1523 flocked to the towns of the Scheldt estuary. English exports, in general and those destined for the Netherlands in particular, increased as the traditional trade reasserted itself, almost re-attaining in 1524 the previous high levels achieved before the crisis of 1520–3 (Figure 8.1).The products of the English heavy drapery – West Country "whites", Suffolk short cloths and Kentish "longs" – sold readily at the Bergen and Antwerp fairs[1] to the Cologne merchants who once again traversed the great central European highway to Frankfurt from whence their wares passed via Leipzig to Saxony and the Czech lands, or to Augsburg supplying the Alpenlands and South Germany or finally to Vienna, the main market for the lands of the Hungarian crown. Along the way they shared passage with the other merchants who carried the same types of cloth, via the Brenner or Rescheneideck passes, to Verona and Venice (Map 8.1). 1523–4 thus witnessed the re-establishment of one major element in Antwerp's traditional commercial network – the trans-continental trade to Central Europe and Italy. It also witnessed the return of the English to the Brabant fairs where, operating in the context of "low" finance costs on the London-Antwerp-Central Europe-Italian exchanges[2], they experienced a series of extremely active marts as Hansards, Italians and their Netherlands agents flocked to buy their wares. The foreigners' avid desire to obtain the English heavy draperies brought by the Merchant Adventurers was compounded on this occasion, moreover, by the incredible cheapness of these cloths. As the English cloth market equilibrated downwards to a new low price level in 1523, English merchants were able to acquire their export wares at prices which had been unknown for more than fifteen years (Figure 7.1). Able, accordingly, to undersell their Netherlands competitors, whose cloths were subject to inflationary pressures which edged their price upwards at this time, the English swept all before them at the marts denying the drapers of Menin and Armentières a place at the feast.[3]

Nor were these producers alone amongst Netherlands manufacturers of heavy draperies in experiencing difficulties during 1523–4 for amidst all the bustle occasioned by the return of the English there were signs, for those who looked carefully, that times were changing as at the Cold mart of 1523/4 war and rising bi-metallic premiums deflected the French from returning to the Bergen fair. Far more ominous than the French episode, however, was the effect of the emergence of sizeable premiums on the exchanges with the Baltic and Spain which undermined that other major element in Antwerp's commercial economy – the maritime trades. Spanish and Portuguese ships, which had vacated the Scheldt anchorages in 1521–2, at no time during 1523–4 returned because of the rise in premiums on the Antwerp–Medina del Campo exchange. Then at the Cold mart of 1523/4 the Baltic grain fleet again failed to arrive, as in 1521 precipitating famine conditions in the Netherlands. Antwerp's maritime commerce was in total disarray. Business at the Bergen fairs declined and the revenues of the Zeeland water toll, already declining through 1520–2, continued to fall (Figure 8.1). The continuing rise in Netherlands gold prices through 1523–4, by deflecting Spanish, French and Eastland merchants from the Brabant fairs, thus not only

---

1   During 1523–4 merchants, like Thomas Kitson, increasingly came to export to the Netherlands the products of the heavy drapery, the trade reaching its height at the Sinxen mart of 1524 (Cambridge University Library, Hengrave Hall MSS, 78/1).

2   See chapter 9.

3   For a fuller discussion of the commercial trends outlined in this and the next paragraph see chapter 2, chapter 7 and chapter 9.

tempered the full impact of the Anglo-Netherlands trade boom causing it to peak at a lower level than in 1518/9 but also precipitated a severe sectoral crisis in Antwerp's trade which fundamentally weakened the position of heavy cloth producers in the Netherlands. Subject to intense English competition in the transcontinental trade to central Europe and Italy and a collapse in their commerce to France and Spain the drapers of Menin and Armentières succumbed, production falling heavily in these centres.[4] At Leiden, where producers were dependent on Baltic markets to vend their cloths, output similarly declined.[5] Everywhere in the Netherlands the heavy draperies were in retreat (Figure 12.1/2). In their place merchants, faced with crisis conditions, bought the produce of the light drapery (Figure 13.1). Low Country cloth markets were in fact in 1523–4 undergoing a severe crisis which as before undermined the position of local producers of heavy cloth and brought the products of the light drapery to the fore. Only the buoyancy of the Anglo-Netherlands trade in the products of the English heavy drapery obscured the overall picture so that merchants, who clung tenaciously to past concepts of "normality", were afforded a false sense of security.

When, however, from the Cold mart of 1524/5 Netherlands gold prices began to rise rapidly and the sectoral crisis turned into a general one their illusions were stripped away. During that winter, even in the previously buoyant English trade, the first ominous signs of recession began to appear as merchants, like Kitson, began to react to the re-emergence of premiums on all exchange dealings between London-Antwerp and the rest of Europe. His shipments which had reached their highest level in 1524 and which had been made up predominantly of Wiltshire "whites", began to decline during 1525 and the proportion of cheap light stuffs, overwhelmingly cottons but with an increasing quantity of kersey, grew.[6] Monetary instability and tight money on the London money market thus combined, from Christmas 1524, to cause the beginnings of a severe crisis in English overseas trade. Not even the heavy deflation in English raw material and cloth prices, induced by monetary disorders across the Channel, could save the day.[7] In 1525 England was dragged into that crisis which since 1520 had plagued Netherlands merchants and manufacturers. If conditions in England were bad, however, in the Netherlands they were nothing short of disastrous as monetary disorders crippled the exchanges and inflationary pressures shifted the whole price level upwards. Inevitably in these circumstances things went from bad to worse for Netherlands producers of heavy draperies and output plummeted but much more ominous was the weak response to the new situation in centres of light cloth production (Figures 12.1/2, 13.1). The whole market for Anglo-Netherlands textiles was contracting as both England and the Low Countries were drawn into a European-wide situation where trade in goods was displaced by commerce in bullion.

4   H. E. SAGHER / J.-H. DE SAGHER / H. VAN WERVEKE / C. WYFFELS (eds.), Receuil de documents relatifs à l' histoire de l' industrie drapière en Flandre. 2e partie, Le sud-oeust de la Flandre depuis l' époque Bourguignonne, Bruxelles 1951–66, I , pp. 453–7 and III, pp. 70–3

5   N. W. POSTHUMUS, Geschiedenis van de Leidsche Lakenindustrie, 's Gravenhage 1908–39, I, p. 370.

6   CUL, Hengrave Hall MSS, 78/1.

7   See chapter 7 and Figure 7.1.

Figure 13.1: Netherlands Textile Production, 1493–1593

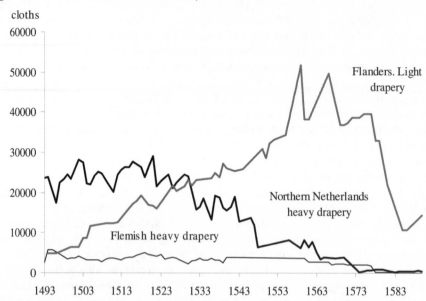

The attempts of the Netherlands authorities during November 1525 to resolve this problem by halting the rapid rise in gold prices and restoring the bi-metallic equilibrium of an earlier age (by raising silver prices) were moreover a very mixed blessing. For the English these measures served merely to ossify the "crisis situation" on the London "exchange". High interest rates on the London market, by preventing any further outflow of gold, might ensure monetary order and the stabilization of wool-cloth prices at the low levels of 1525, but continuing high potential profits on specie dealings meant a prolongation of high finance costs. Thus trapped within a bi-metallic prison and burdened with the high cost of commercial credit the English merchant found no relief from the continuing crisis.[8] Many merchants accordingly succumbed. English trade continued to decline and in the period down to the suspension of shipments at the Bamus mart of 1526 the products of the light drapery assumed an increasingly important position in the dwindling volume of cloth exports.[9] The export market for the products of the English heavy drapery was thus doubly diminished and manufacturers, for the first time unable to significantly diversify output into domestic trade, experienced major difficulties which were exacerbated by the exigencies of royal finance.[10] Output declined and unemployment rose. In Suffolk clothiers laid off their workman causing "women to weep and young folks to cry, and men who had no work to rage and assemble themselves in companies."[11] At Laneham, Sudbury and Hadley

---

8   See chapter 6.

9   See figure 8.1 and CUL, Hengrave Hall MSS, 78/1.

10   I. BLANCHARD, Population Change, Enclosure and the Early Tudor Economy, in: Economic History Review, Second Series, XXIII, 3 (1970), p. 442 and ch. 7 above.

11   E. HALL, Chronicle, London 1809, p. 699s.

and the cloth towns thereabout a reputed 4,000 men came out in open revolt.[12] Throughout the clothing districts

> [t]he clothiers all, not able to maintain
> The many of them 'longing, have put off
> The spinsters, carders, fullers, weavers who,
> Unfit for other life, compelled by hunger
> And lack of other means, in desperate manner
> Daring th' events to the teeth, are all in uproar
> And danger serves among them.[13]

Industrial stagnation and labour unrest thus for the first time in England followed in the wake of the commercial crisis.

Yet whilst the Netherlands monetary reform of November 1525 exacerbated the already developing crisis in English trade, contributing to the state of commercial and industrial decay which prevailed throughout 1525 and 1526, at Antwerp it paved the way for the return of the Germans and Spaniards.[14] Business at the Bergen fairs, declining since 1521/2, recovered at the Cold mart of 1525/6 and when in the spring of 1526 a Spanish fleet of no less than fifty ships entered the Scheldt estuary the gains of the previous winter were consolidated.[15] From November 1525 through to the spring of 1526 the Netherlands economy enjoyed a high, if ephemeral, level of commercial and industrial prosperity (Figures 8.1, 12.1/2 and 13.1).[16] As de Lucy noted, however, this situation was not to last. As early as December 1525 it was clear to him that the monetary ordinance of the previous month had failed to stay the rise in Netherlands gold prices.[17] When, therefore, at the Easter and Whitsun fairs of 1526 the situation of monetary instability and bimetallic imbalance existing before the reform was re-established, the trade depression which had continued in England throughout 1525–6, accordingly became more general and deepened, whilst unemployment and bankruptcy amongst manufacturers spread from Suffolk to Leiden.[18] From April to December 1526 continental European commerce suffered a prolonged malaise, as the trade in goods was again displaced by a trade in specie, and English trade thence ground to a halt from the Bamus mart of 1526.[19] Nor, at least until the ephemeral stabilization of the London money market in October–November, were English mer-

---

12   Ibid., p. 699.

13   The speech is that put by Shakespeare into Norfolk's mouth in *Henry VIII*, Act 1, scene 2, ll. 29–37.

14   H. VAN DER WEE, The Growth of the Antwerp Market and the European Economy. Fourteenth–Sixteenth Centuries, 3 Vols., The Hague 1963, II, p. 177.

15   K. SLOOTSMAN, Brabantse kooplieden op de Bergse jaarmarkten, in: Oudheidkundige Kring. De Ghulden Roos Roosendaal, Jaarboek, XXIII (1963), p. 48.

16   See chapter 9 above and on the industrial prosperity of those centres servicing the requirements of the Baltic (*A&R* 3, Nr. 230/10), Spanish and Central European trades (DE SAGHER et al., Documents, I, pp. 453–7; III, pp. 72, 90.

17   A. LOUANT (ed.), Le Journal d' un Bourgeoisie de Mons, 1505–1536, Brussels 1969, Nr. 631, p. 257.

18   VAN DER WEE, Antwerp, II, p. 146.

19   Chapter 9.

chants, because of high interest rates, able to diversify their trade. Commercial activity thus relentlessly declined and, as Netherlands gold prices continued their dizzy flight, there seemed no hope of relief. It was thus an act of desperation, the resort of drowning men grasping at straws, when, with the brief stabilization of conditions at London in October-November 1526, merchants of that city began to draw on supplies of incredibly low-priced cloths in an attempt to revive the "alternative commerce".[20] During the last quarter of the year, as the Antwerp bill rate at usance rose from 13 to 22 per cent whilst London rates briefly stabilized at the former level, the products of the English light drapery were once more despatched to Spain, Italy (via Lyon) and to the Levant, but it was a passing interlude and with the collapse of the London market in December few would, for the moment, venture their capital in such a manner.[21] Only monetary stabilization in the Netherlands could seemingly save the day.

This occurred during the Cold mart of 1526/7 with the Netherlands monetary ordinance of the 10th December. From that date until the completion of the reform on the first of March 1527 interest rates fell on both the London and Antwerp money markets and "premiums" disappeared on their respective exchanges.[22] By March 1527 the problems which beset the Anglo-Netherlands monetary and financial systems seemed well on the way to being resolved, although interest rates remained considerably higher than during preceding periods of Antwerp's prosperity, and all augured well for a return to "normality". But it was not to be. The European cloth market in 1527 was a very different one from that which had existed a decade earlier. The Netherlands monetary reform of 1526/7 together with the Venetian one of 1527 established Antwerp's future pattern of financial and commercial influence, the bi-metallic equilibrium between the Spanish, Venetian and Netherlands currencies thereby created, facilitating inter-market monetary transfers in the southern trades. The old European-wide hegemony, already crumbling in 1523–4, was now replaced by a more limited financial function – the servicing of Ibero-Mediterranean commerce. The corollary of these changes, which concentrated the activities of the Antwerp financial and mercantile community on southern trade, was the emergence of another bimetallic system centred on London and encompassing the markets which were served by the maritime traffic traversing northern seas. Two distinct spheres of commercial activity had thus

---

20 See Figure 7.1, which reveals the incredibly low English wool-cloth prices caused by specie outflows (chapter 7) and the resultant acute deflationary pressures in the economy at this time.

21 See *Howell's Ledger*, fos. 39, 44–7, 51–2, 54–6 for cloth exports October 1526–March 1527. It seems probable that some of this cloth sent to Spain was subsequently re-shipped to Spanish America. See G. CONNELL-SMITH, The Ledger of Thomas Howell, in: Economic History Review, Second Series, III, 3 (1951), p. 368; ID. Forerunners of Drake: A Study of English Trade with Spain in the Early Tudor Period, London 1954, p. 74s., where, as the colony entered on a phase of expanding economic activity, English textiles enjoyed a certain popularity. R. PIKE, Enterprise and Adventure: The Genoese at Seville and the Opening of the New World, Ithaca / New York 1966, p. 210, n. 26. From March 1527, however the direct trade from England declined (see *Howell's Ledger,* fo. 47 which reveals no further shipments of cloth) and Spain and its colonies obtained supplies of the English product via Antwerp (chapter 9). On the Levant trade at this time see CUL, Hengrave Hall MSS, 78/1, whilst P. EARLE, The Commercial Development of Ancona, 1497–1551, in: Economic History Review, Second Series, XVII, 2 (1969) p. 35, n. 4 provides evidence of shipments via Lyon to Ancona.

22 At the close of the winter fair the downward movement in rates on the Antwerp exchanges was briefly reversed in an incident described in chapter 5.

come into existence during the years 1524–7: one orientated towards the south, buoyant and expansive, was serviced by the Antwerp merchant community; the other, fraught with difficulties from its inception, drew upon the financial and commercial resources of London.

In this new commercial environment the Netherlands merchant was well placed to pursue his business. The Netherlands manufacturer was not. Since 1523, with the equilibration of raw material costs, they enjoyed no particular advantage over their English rivals and indeed during 1525–6, as Netherlands wool prices rose and English fell as a result of the contemporary monetary disorders, they had been seriously disadvantaged. In the aftermath of the Netherlands monetary reforms this situation was rectified and from 1527–9 the two groups of cloth manufactures once again enjoyed broadly similar raw material costs. In England, however, from 1523 the fall in raw material costs had also been associated with a parallel fall in labour costs and accordingly over the years 1523–9 cloth and wool prices diverged – to the advantage of the English manufacturer. In 1527 the English cloth maker thus came into his own. In both spheres of commercial activity his product enjoyed a superior competitive position in relation to his Netherlands rival.[23]

The re-establishment of a "normal" trading environment at Antwerp over the winter of 1526/7 thus took place in circumstances very reminiscent of 1523. Falling interest rates again encouraged merchants to establish a connection, through that city, between suppliers of cheap English cloth and the expanding markets of southern Europe. Spanish ships, absent since the previous year, once more returned to the Scheldt and throughout the year January 1527/8 the Iberians were active buyers at the Low Country fairs.[24] Cologne and Italian merchants, similarly absent during the previous year, also returned in the spring of 1527 eager to buy English cloths for transmission along the central European highway to the south.[25] Trade which had been slack during 1526, began to recover and rose to such a frenzy during the spring of 1527 that indigenous production declined in the face of the commercial onslaught which at the time of the winter and Easter fairs, channelled almost 20,000 kerseys and an indeterminate number of English cloths to Venice.[26] The trade boom was halted in April with the financial crisis at Antwerp, occasioned by Habsburg intervention in the market,[27] but al-

---

23 Present chapter, below.

24 *L&P, Henry VIII,* IV (2), Nr. 4404.

25 M. UNGER, Die Leipziger Messe und die Niederlande im 16. und 17. Jahrhundert, in: Hansische Geschichtsblätter, LXXXI (1963), pp. 21, 25–6, 29 and chapter 9 above. It seems probable that the low interest rates at Frankfurt and Leipzig, occasioned by the silver boom of 1526/7 (Figure 1.1 and chapter 1, notes 1–2) offset the impact of premiums on the Antwerp exchanges in early 1527 and encouraged an indirect trade in English cloth, via Antwerp, to Central Europe rather than a direct trade such as emerged during 1528–30 (chapter 9).

26 On indigenous Netherlands production see DE SAGHER et al (eds.), Documents, II, Nrs. 257, 263–4, 274, 284, 630–1; III , Nrs. 409, 415, 459, 475; E. COORNAERT, Le draperie-sayetterie d' Hondschoote, Paris 1930, p. 486s.; R. SPRANDEL, Zur Tuchproduktion in der Gegend von Ypern, in: Vierteljahrschrift für Sozial- und Wirtschaftsgeschichte, LIV (1967), derived from DE SAGHER et al (eds.), Documents, II. On the transit trade in kerseys see the report of the Venetian Senate dated 30. 8. 1527 as quoted by W. BRULEZ, Les routes commerciales d Angleterre en Italie au XVI siècle, in: Studi in onore di Amintore Fanfani, Milan 1962, IV, p. 129, n. 21.

27 See chapter 5.

though this led to a collapse of the "second buying" at London during the first week of
the month it afforded no relief to the Netherlands producer.[28] Also the crisis was
short-lived and with the recovery of the market in time for the Sinxen mart all seemed
set for a renewal of the English onslaught. At this point in time, however, the Netherlands producer found an odd ally in Henry VIII who in July attempted to divert the
resurgent English trade from the Brabant fairs to Calais, during the prelude to open
Franco-Imperial hostilities.[29] The indignation of the Italians, Spaniards and Flemings
who had flocked to the fair to buy English cloths that summer is not hard to imagine.
Hacket reported their openly hostile behaviour.[30] Feelings were probably no less intense in London. Merchants who had flocked to the "first buying" for the Sinxen mart
in mid-May subsequently abandoned the halls during the period of the fair. The English manufacturer's loss, however, was his Netherlands counterpart's gain. Protected
by the ineptness of Henrican policy the light cloths of Flanders, and particularly those
of Neuve Eglise and the region south west of Ypres, found a ready vent at the Sinxen
mart occasioning an expansion of production and heavy imports of Spanish wool. If
the Netherlands prosperity of the summer of 1527 was based, however, on the ineptness of English government policy, the local Flemish magistrates were intent on ensuring that the favourable circumstances for local manufacturers created by those
policies would not be short-lived. When Henry's policy was reversed in time for a
resurgence of English exports at the Bamus mart, therefore, ordinances were passed,
operative from the second week of September, "that no one should admit any English
cloths."[31] The developing English boom, which had pushed up cloth prices at Blackwell Hall to enormous heights at the close of August, collapsed. Netherlands manufacturers continued to prosper. All seemed set for an expansion of the trade in Netherlands textiles to the south when the news from Leipzig, of the central European mining disorders, broke.

From Michaelmas 1527 the traditional trade route linking Antwerp via Frankfurt
to Venice was cut and through the autumn and winter of 1527/8 a financial crisis developed on the Antwerp money market of such severity as to deter merchants from
venturing to that city. Crisis conditions had yet again returned to Antwerp and it was
time once more to revive the "alternative commerce." Thus during the period from
late-1527 to early-1529, whilst Antwerp was subject to acute monetary and financial
dislocation, English cloths (predominantly kerseys) passed via Lyon to the Mediterranean whilst similar wares were shipped (when unimpeded by trade restraints) in English vessels to Spain. Yet as before, during previous crises, the "new" trade did not
compensate for the decline of the old. Nor, at least initially, did the growth of England's direct trades within its own commercial system alleviate the situation and during 1527/8 the nation's exports of cloth stagnated at their former levels. With the application of Italian funding to the London exchanges in 1528, however, the situation
was transformed. In 1528/9 whilst the trade to Spain and Italy continued to decline,
commercial activity encompassed within the bounds of England's direct trading sys-

28   See chapter 9.
29   *L&P, Henry VIII,* IV (2), Nr. 3262.
30   Ibid., Nr. 3313.
31   TNA, SP1/44 fo. 99[v].

tem increased prodigiously, pushing up the nation's total cloth trade to its highest point yet in the sixteenth century. As a result of the availability of cheap money and the existence of merchants who knew how to use it, English commerce had at last come into its own. In this process, moreover, English manufacturers played their own special role. Responding to the changes of the years 1527–9 they now produced cheap light cloths suitable for the "difficult" markets opened up by merchants engaged in the "direct" commerce, and in the process caused a complete re-structuring of the export sector of the English cloth industry.

Each summer from 1527 merchants engaged in the "direct" trade, who were bound for markets where because of the enhanced value of the Anglo-Netherlands currencies only cheap cloths would sell, sought out the products of the light drapery. They sought, moreover, English light draperies which, as a result of their relatively low export price, now displaced their Netherlands counterparts. In the Baltic the products of the East Anglian light drapery found favour amongst customers who had previously bought the products of Poperinge and Tourcoing.[32] Production, accordingly, in the years following 1527 grew. At Norwich it was reported to the municipal assembly that

> from the wool ('nyles') [...] have been made many and diverse pieces of blanket, as of flock, called draught flock and crop flock many and diverse 'douges' (*ie. Doucken, I. Blanchard*) have been made [...],

which was

> a great help and release to the poor citizens and inhabitants within the city, in that poor women, weavers, shearmen and other artificers were holden to work [...].[33]

Employment expanded, absorbing the local unemployed and causing the immigration of "foreigners", but the supply of wool did not.[34] At the height of the boom manufacturers, in attempts to economise on the increasingly inadequate supplies of wool, adulterated their product.[35] Similar demand induced pressures caused kersey manufacturers also to undertake such "deceits" but in this instance fraudulent practice combined with technological change to create a new cloth.[36] A transformation was afoot which remains shrouded in mystery if only because of the retention of an old nomenclature for a new product.[37] During the fifteenth century and the first quarter of the sixteenth

---

32 In 1526 the cloths of Poperinge and Tourcoing were still greatly demanded in Baltic markets (*A&R³*, Nr. 230/10), but rising prices between that date and 1530 made them totally uncompetitive (*HR*, III⁹, Nrs. 558/170, 589/57, 591/15, 598/14 and 652/9) and they were gradually displaced by English wares (*A&R³*, Nr. 301/2; *HR*, III9, Nr. 652/9).

33 NNRO, City Records, Press D, Case 16 d 2, fo.167ᵛ.

34 Ibid., fos. 152ᵛ–153, 155, 168.

35 NNRO, City Records, Press E, shelf 17d. Second book of worsted weavers, 1511–1638. See the abnormally high proportion of presentments for faulty workmanship during the years 1527–30.

36 *L&P. Henry VIII*, IV (2), Nr. 3915.

37 The kersey was a narrow cloth (1.25 yards) in comparison with either the short or long broadcloth (1.75 yards) and varied in length between the 12 yards of the Devon "dozen" and the normal 17–8 yards. On the length of the kersey see *Statutes of the Realm* (London, 1819), IV (1), pp. 136–7:

the kersey seems, apart from size, indistinguishable from such heavy drapery products as the long cloths of Kent, Worcester and Coventry weighing some 1.7 lbs. per square yard. It was certainly heavier and perhaps of better quality than the renowned short cloth (which weighed 1.3–1.6 lbs. per square yard). Yet in the second quarter of the sixteenth century, throughout England and without any deterioration in the quality of the wool utilised, it seems to have been transformed into a light cloth weighing only 0.9 lbs. per square yard.[38] How this metamorphosis took place is unclear but it may be associated with some change in the nature of the warp thread. Certainly kersey (or carsey) yarn[39] seems to have been sufficiently distinctive to be sold under that name and utilised in the production of various other materials. If the origins of the new cloth remain obscure, however, its impact on English commerce did not. The kersey and the East Anglian doucken stood in the vanguard of the "direct" commerce and as the commodity mixes in these trades shifted during the years 1527–9 towards the new products, reducing foreign currency export prices, they played their part in encouraging the growth of these trades and of England's cloth exports in general.[40]

Such was not the case, however, in the export trade via Antwerp to the south wherein merchants during the early part of 1527 had still clung tenaciously to the once ubiquitous heavy draperies.[41] Tied overwhelmingly to the export of one product the merchants engaged in these southern trades gained relatively little advantage from price movements in comparison with those who pursued the paths of the "direct" commerce.[42] Moreover, because of the slight margins upon which they operated, their

---

Statute 5/6 Edward VI c. 6. No width is given. On widths see for instance R. P. CHOPE, The Aulnager in Devon, in: Transactions of the Devon Association, XLIV (1912), p. 594. The weight of the fifteenth-century kersey may be derived from information in E. M. CARUS-WILSON, Trends in the Export of English Woollens in the Fourteenth Century, Economic History Review, Second Series, III, 2 (1950), p. 169, n. 4. It is noticeable that when conditions favoured the export of light draperies during the years down to 1520, singularly few kerseys will be found amongst exports. Under such circumstances the favoured light drapery seems to have been the Chester or northern cotton, together with some friezes (see e.g. CUL, Hengrave Hall MSS, 78/1). Only during the 'twenties were such wares gradually displaced by the kersey (see also sections below).

38   Statute 5/6 Edward VI c. 6.

39   On the use of kersey (carsey) yarn in worsted products see K. ALLISON, The Norfolk Worsted Industry in the Sixteenth and Seventeenth Centuries. I. The Traditional Industry, in: Yorkshire Bulletin of Economic and Social History, XII, 2 (1960), p. 76. The author's identification (ibid., p. 82, n. 19) of this yarn with Jarsey or Garnesey (Jersey or Guernsey?) yarn, however, seems improbable. Perhaps some light might be thrown on the nature of the yarn by an analysis of the kersey and broadcloth samples preserved in BL, Lansdowne C. IV, 24 fos. 92^v–93^r.

40   In the Levant trade kerseys and blankets predominated in the cloth export trade (see chapter 12, n. 28), in the French trade cottons, "vesys" and some broadcloths were shipped (ibid., n. 30). Central European markets were supplied until September 1527 with kerseys and blankets and thereafter kerseys and West Country "whites" (the cheapest heavy drapery utilising high quality wool) were shipped thence via Hamburg (ibid., notes 23–26). Finally in the Baltic East Anglian doucken came to the fore (chapter 12, note 18). On relative price movements see ibid., note 59.

41   See present chapter above.

42   Over the years 1526–31 the foreign currency price of cloth, even in the expensive Riga market (supplied via Danzig by the "direct" trade) declined relatively to the foreign currency price on such southern markets as Ancona or Venice (supplied via Antwerp) by some 10 per cent. On Riga prices see G. MICKWITZ, Aus Revaler Handelsbüchern. Zur Technik des Ostseehandels in der ersten Hälfte des 16. Jahrhunderts, Helsingfors 1938, p. 100s. I am greatly indebted to Dr Peter Earle for

trade was subject to marked fluctuations. Relatively small movements on the Antwerp Exchange precipitated acute crises during which the English product gave way on southern markets to the heavy cloths of Venice[43] and Languedoc: products against which even the kersey, which was substituted for the heavy English cloth under such circumstances, made little progress.[44] The heavy cloth producer, tied from 1527 to the trade to southern European markets via Antwerp and unable to diversify into other markets, was accordingly dangerously exposed.[45] Just how exposed he was is revealed by the crisis which began with the Netherlands embargo of September 1527.[46]

Initially the crisis precipitated a slow retreat over the winter of 1527/8. It deepened dramatically, however with the restraint of January 1528, because this coincided

---

providing me with information concerning cloth prices at Ancona, derived from his researches in the notarial records of that city. This data valuably supplements that contained in the van Bombergen correspondence (see chapter 7, n. 1).

43 On the poor performance of the kersey in the southern trades during the crisis of 1527–8 see ch. 9, a picture which is confirmed by the notarial records examined by Dr Earle at Ancona for whilst, in the transactions he examined for the period of the developing crisis of 1527, the kersey gained ground at the expense of such Anglo-Netherlands heavy draperies as the *ultrafini* of Armentières and the *panni de Londra,* both groups of products gave way to indigenous cloths, particularly the modestly priced *sopromani* of Florence. The major beneficiary, however, amongst the Italian heavy drapery producers was Venice which witnessed a considerable expansion of output in 1527/8, see D. SELLA, The Rise and Fall of the Venetian Woollen Industry, in: B. PULLEN (ed.), Crisis and Change in the Venetian Economy of the Sixteenth and Seventeenth Centuries, London 1968, pp. 106–115, and ID., Commerci e industrie a Venezia nel secolo XVII, Venice / Rome 1961, p. 117s. For Florence the events of 1527/8, when her workshops could muster an output of 14,000 *garbi,* merely provided a respite during an acute short-term crisis in the industry which culminated in 1529 when the Venetian ambassador declared that her production is practically at a standstill (*Relazione di Firenze del clarissimo Marco Foscari, 1527* as quoted by EARLE, Commercial Development, p. 34, n. 2; the report of the Venetian ambassador is quoted in SELLA, Rise and Fall, p. 106. These short-term changes may be set in a longer term context by reference to H. HOSHINO, L' arte della lana a Firenze nel Basso Medioevo, Florence 1980; M. CARMONA, Sull' economia toscana del 500 e del 600, in: Archivio storico italiano, CXX (1962), pp. 38, 44; P. MALANIMA, La decadenza di un economia cittadina – l' industria di Firenze nei secolo XVI–XVII, Bologna 1982, and R. ROMANO, A Florence au XVIIe siècle. Industries textiles et conjuncture, in: Annales, VII (1952), p. 511.

44 The Anconese notarial registers also highlight the rise of another south European competitor on Italian markets during 1527/8 – *panni limosiari.* On the cloths of the Puy de Dôme and Languedoc, traded via Lyon, see the rather dated study of P. BOISSONNADE, L' industrie languedocienne pendant les soixante, premières années du XVIIe siècle, in: Annales du Midi (1909), which is still of use, and the question of competition between northern and domestic cloth production on southern French markets is dealt with by E. LE ROY LADURIE, Les Paysans de Languedoc, Paris 1966, I, pp. 124–6. Both of these studies, however, have now been largely superseded by the study of P. WOLFF, Esquisse d une histoire de la draperie en Languedoc du XIIe siècle au XVIIIe siècle, in: Produzione, commercio e consumo dei panni di lana, secc. XII–XVIII, Pubblicazioni dell' Istituto Internazionale di Storia Economica "Francesco Datini", Serie II / Atti delle Settimana di Studi, Vol. 2. Prato 1970.

45 For the reasons given in chapter 7 heavy draperies could find little vent amongst merchants garnering cargoes for the direct trades. Moreover, from c.1515 consumers in the home market seem to have been turning towards the light draperies, a tendency accentuated during 1527–8 by the prevailing famine conditions.

46 On the place of the embargo of September 1527 in the developing crisis of that year see chapter 9.

with a weak recovery in the "alternative commerce"[47] and overlaid an intra-annual recession in the "direct" trades. From September 1527–March 1528 "broadcloths, kerseys and cottons" all remained unsold at Blackwell Hall.[48] Throughout England clothiers denied a vent for their wares experienced difficulties and laid off their work forces. In Norfolk and Suffolk a lack of work opportunities coupled with the prevailing famine conditions led to a growth of vagabondage, providing a field day for the surly Duke of Norfolk who seems to have relished the task of chastising the unfortunates.[49] In the Suffolk clothing village of Laneham there were rumours of seditious speeches and secret assemblies.[50] Unrest seethed below the surface in the heavy drapery districts. Nor during December and January were the light drapery districts immune. Brian Higden wrote to Wolsey from York that "cloth making is sore decayed as merchants [...] buy no cloth in this county."[51] Times were hard and in March 1528, as "few merchants or none bought any cloths at all", the number of unsold cloths rose ominously. The government panicked. Wolsey summoned the London merchants to him and harangued them.[52] Yet his speech, vituperous as it was, passed unheeded, for the merchants noted "we have so many cloths on our hands that we do not know how to utter them." No more cloths were bought but attitudes were significantly polarised within the merchant community as during March and April 1528 the general crisis merged into a sectoral one affecting only the most expensive products of the heavy drapery.[53]

As early as the 16th March a meeting of the court of aldermen displayed a somewhat more quiescent attitude. In response to the Cardinal's demand that

> they should see that such clothes as now be or hereafter shalbe brought to the selde of Blakwell hall to be solde may be bought to the intent that suche persones as be the makers of the seyd clothes in the cuntrey may be sett a werk [...]

---

47 On the slump in Anglo-Netherlands commerce and on the weak recovery of the "alternative" commerce see chapter 9. The rise of the "direct" trades imposed a new rhythm of activity in English cloth markets, superimposed on the pre-existing one dominated by the timing of the Bergen and Antwerp fairs (on which see Figure 6.1 in chapter 6). In the Baltic and North Sea trades vessels normally left from March-May in order to return in August, thereby avoiding the necessity of over-wintering in a foreign port. Ships tardy in sailing, delaying their departure until October (the last possible date) normally did not return until the following summer. In the French trades, buying in the market was conditional upon the arrival of French ships carrying woad and pastel in late February-March and the departure of the wine shippers in July-August. The Levantine voyages also departed in the summer. Buying for the "direct" trades accordingly began in March and rose to a peak in May-August. Thereafter the activities of the "direct" traders diminished, precipitating an intra-annual recession in demand from September through to February.

48 HALL, Chronicle, p. 745.

49 *L&P, Henry VIII*, IV (2), No. 3664.

50 Ibid., Nr. 3703.

51 TNA, SP1/46 fo. 160.

52 HALL, Chronicle, p. 745s.

53 Ibid., p. 746.

they agreed "that they wold do the best they can."[54] Yet this was a meeting where the richer merchants, who could diversify their activities into the "direct" trades, were highly represented. Elsewhere others were not so accommodating and as the sectoral crisis, which now affected only those who were dependent exclusively on the Antwerp trade for their livelihood, developed, rumours circulated of an assembly "at the whim and counsel of some merchants to make away with the Cardinal."[55] Certainly amongst the merchants who frequented the heavy drapery halls (e.g. Colchester Hall) there was much seditious talk in the months following March 1528.[56] Nor did such uttering fall on unreceptive ears, for clothiers, unable to sell on a depressed market and subject to government pressure to keep their workforces employed, were in danger of going bankrupt. In Suffolk, in May, various substantial clothiers declared to Norfolk that "unless remedy be found" for the lack of sales at London, "it shall not be in their power passing a fortnight or three weeks at most to set their workfolks on work."[57] In Essex, even earlier, clothiers, like Joseph Boswell, complained that they had "barely enough money to set the spinners awork."[58] The Kentish clothiers were in a like state being ready "to discharge any artificers so as to cause unlawful assemblies."[59] Thus throughout Suffolk, Essex and Kent, where the most expensive products of the heavy drapery were manufactured for the trade via Antwerp to the South, unemployment continued to increase from March 1528 and discontent seethed below the surface, becoming overt at Cranbrook and other Kentish clothing villages.[60] In Hampshire, Wiltshire and Berkshire, where clothiers found during the summer of 1528 a vent amongst the Hamburg merchants for their cheaper cloths, Berkeley could report that "the king's subjects are loyal and the clothiers are willing to set their men to work."[61] In the light drapery areas of the North, East Anglia and the West Country the "crisis" of March–December 1528 passed by unnoticed as production grew to meet the needs of the rapidly expanding "direct" trades.[62] The signs for the future were now clear. The more expensive branches of the heavy drapery, from 1527 entirely dependent upon remaining competitive in the southern trades, were dangerously exposed. In the short run the manufacturing crisis subsided in 1529 as the trade to the South was resumed, but henceforth, even under favourable trading conditions at Antwerp such as prevailed until 1531, the heavy cloth manufacturer had to content himself with playing a relatively minor role in the export sector of the English cloth industry. From 1527 industrial domination passed to the producer of the light drapery.

The decade 1523–1532 had thus witnessed a fundamental transformation of the Anglo-Netherlands textile trades. Successive financial crises in conditions of general rate enhancement on the Antwerp Bourse created circumstances which were singu-

---

54   Corporation of London Record Office, Guildhall. Repertory 7, fo. 246$^\mathrm{v}$.

55   LOUANT (ed.), Le Journal, Nr. 715, p. 288.

56   TNA, SP1/47 fos. 164–5, 176–8.

57   TNA, SP1/48 fos. 2–3.

58   TNA, SP1/47 fos. 176–8.

59   TNA, SP1/48 fos. 28, 34–5, 47–8, 51–3, 82–4.

60   *L&P, Henry VIII*, IV (2), Nrs. 4276, 4287, 4296, 4300–1, 4310 and 4331.

61   TNA, SP1/47 fos. 122–3.

62   See chapter 9.

larly unpropitious for the pursuance of the traditional trade through that city in the traditional "heavy draperies". For the English "normal" conditions existed for some eighteenth months in 1523–4 and for barely six months each year in 1527 and 1529 before "normality" seemingly returned in 1530–1. For the Netherlanders the situation was not very different. So-called "normal" conditions prevailed only briefly for six months in each of the years 1525/6, 1527 and 1529 before market stabilization once again occurred in 1530–1. Crisis conditions which had been an intermittent and ephemeral phenomenon during the previous two decades thus now became the normative experience of Anglo-Netherlands textile merchants who during the 1520s increasingly frequently trod the paths of the "alternative commerce", pursuing a trade which engendered a corresponding growth in the importance of the "light draperies".

The monetary crisis of 1525–6 and Netherlands monetary reform of the winter of 1526/7, moreover, ensured that the previously intermittent "alternative commerce" and associated trade in cheap, light cloths would assume a new permanent place in European trade. From that winter Antwerp's old European-wide hegemony, already crumbling in 1523–4, was replaced by a more limited function – the servicing of Ibero-Mediterranean commerce which, in "normal" trading conditions (1527 and 1529–1531/2), became the sole preserve of the trader in "heavy draperies". Elsewhere during these years Antwerp was displaced by London within a new bi-metallic and commercial system where, in either crisis or non-crisis years, only the products of the "light drapery" found a ready market. 1527/8 thus marked the beginnings of a new age in the Anglo-Netherlands textile trades. Whilst crisis conditions prevailed in that year at the Brabant fairs, merchants pursuing both the "alternative" and "direct" commerce pushed the cloth trade to previously unprecedented heights and within these trades the products of the "light drapery" reigned supreme. Subsequently, from 1529–1531/2, as the "alternative commerce" declined and commercial activity re-orientated towards Antwerp, the products of the "heavy drapery" once more re-established their position but now only in the Ibero-Mediterranean trades through that city. Elsewhere the trade in the cheap cloths of the "light drapery" was maintained, if at a lower level than before, as English merchants in association with their continental European counterparts continued to pursue their "direct commerce". The "light drapery" had thus for the first time secured a permanent place in the Anglo-Netherlands textile trades.

Anglo-Netherlands Textile Production and Markets. In response to these changes in the textile trades the Anglo-Netherlands cloth manufactory was transformed. Production of, and trade in the "heavy draperies", which had peaked in 1519, thereafter steadily declined. Each successive cyclical peak saw commercial-industrial activity (in 1523–4, 1527 and 1529–1531/2) settle at a lower level than before. Each downturn in activity (in 1525–6 and 1527–9) precipitated crisis conditions in this sector of the industry which were associated with increasingly intense phases of unemployment and civil disorder. In contrast producers of the "light draperies" experienced during these years a period of great prosperity. Relentlessly, through boom and slump, production and trade in these wares increased until during the years after 1528 these erstwhile products of "petite draperie" become a permanent, integral part of the "grande draperie". The export sector of the Anglo-Netherlands cloth manufactory thus, amidst the turmoil associated with the process of structural change, during the years 1523–32 both expanded and re-orientated towards the production of the "light draperies". On those occasions (in 1523–4, 1527 and 1529–1531/2) when trade in the products of this manufactory was directed towards Antwerp, moreover, it was the wares of the English producer which established their ascendancy. Through successive trade booms at the Brabant fairs English cloths displaced those of the Netherlands, causing Low Countries' producers to clamour in 1527 and 1532 for protection against the English onslaught. As output in the Anglo-Netherlands textile manufactory thus both expanded and re-orientated towards the production of the "light draperies", the English sector of that manufactory, previously eclipsed by its Netherlands' rival, also came to the fore.

This supremacy of the English product on the market places of Europe rested in part on a complete reorganisation during the 1520s of that nation's industry. As has been suggested, both the strengths and weaknesses of English cloth traders' position during the first quarter of the sixteenth century had been rooted in the existence of a symbiotic, but subordinate, relationship between the merchants and their suppliers – the non-specialist English peasant cloth manufacturers. This relationship had afforded them considerable flexibility in the acquisition of varying product-mixes for their trade and had minimized social tensions in their dealings. It had also imposed, however, strong constraints on the implementation of procurement strategies. The course of English overseas trade at this time had moved (inversely) in the medium-term to the rhythms of the domestic market and in the short-term to the tempo of commercial activity at Antwerp, the merchant responding to these changes but not determining them.[63] From ca. 1517/8, however, this situation had begun to undergo major changes. The long-established, demographically-induced pattern of demand fluctuations, which had previously determined the course of English domestic and, indirectly, overseas trade, continued to impose itself on the markets wherein the merchants acquired their cloths but now these fluctuations took place upon a rising rather than a falling population trend.[64] As a result, in the aftermath of the harvest failures of 1520–2[65], the old games were played out at a new equilibrium level and the English clothier found, within prevailing forms of industrial organisation, both his product and factor market situations transformed.

Mounting population pressure, by slackening the peasantry's control over agricultural resources, led to a slow process of immiseration. Successive runs of bad harvests (in 1520–2 and 1527–9) hastened that process and in reducing disposable income adversely affected the demand for cloth in the domestic market. Accordingly prices fell.[66] Initially, from ca. 1517/8–23 the process was a simple cyclical one, the demographic upswing of these years combining with deflationary pressures to re-establish cloth/wool prices at 1514-levels. Subsequently, as in the aftermath of the harvest failures of 1520–2 population growth was sustained, cloth/wool price re-equilibration occurred. The second cycle, which ran its course during the years 1523–32, took place

---

63 See chapter 12.

64 I. BLANCHARD, Population Change, Enclosure and the Early Tudor Economy, in: Economic History Review, Second Series, XXIII, 3 (1970), pp. 427–445 and L. R. POOS, The Rural Population of Essex in the Later Middle Ages, in: Economic History Review, Second Series, XXXVIII, 4 (1985), pp. 515–530.

65 W. G. Hoskins, Harvest Fluctuations and English Economic History 1480–1619, in: Agricultural History Review, XII, 1 (1964), p. 39 and C. J. HARRISON, Grain Price Analysis and Harvest Qualities, 1465–1634, in: Agricultural History Review, XIX, 2 (1964), p. 152.

66 See Figure 7.1.

at a lower level than before. Even at the cyclical peak in 1527 prices were well below those at the previous peak of 1517/8 and in the aftermath of the harvest failures of 1527–9 cloth/wool prices plummeted to a new all-time low. Thus during the years 1523–32 the clothier found the domestic market for his wares weakening. The exporter of English cloths, on the other hand, found his competitive position on foreign markets immensely strengthened and, in favourable conditions for the pursuit of his trade (in 1523–4 and 1527–9), became increasingly active at the cloth halls. The balance of activity between domestic and export markets for cloth was shifting and whilst during these years the long-established, demographically-induced pattern of domestic demand fluctuations continued to influence market conditions its impact was weakening as prices for the first time also began to respond to changes in England's cloth export trade. In these circumstances the overseas merchant, who down to 1523 had been a price-taker in a market dominated by the domestic consumer, became a price-giver. The process by which he achieved this position, however, was not to be soon accomplished. The impoverishment of the population at home and rising transactions costs abroad by causing a shift in purchasing patterns towards the products of the "light drapery" left the manufacturers of these cheap, slight cloths in much the same position as he had been before. In most circumstances during the years 1523–32 they remained able to reallocate sales of their wares between domestic and foreign markets as events dictated, maintaining production and employment in this sector of the industry. Only once, during the winter and spring of 1527/8, did they find their position threatened as famine conditions in England prevented increased sales at home during a period of recession in overseas trade.[67] Yet such a turn of events remained exceptional for producers of the "light drapery" at this time. For manufacturers of the "heavy draperies" it did not. As impoverished English consumers increasingly acquired the cheap, slight cloths of the "light drapery", manufacturers of the "heavy draperies" were marginalised in the domestic market and increasingly dependent on export sales which at least allowed them to maintain both production and employment during the years 1523–4, 1527 and 1529–1531/2. When crisis at Antwerp in 1525–6 and 1527–9 undermined this trade, however, they found themselves hopelessly exposed. Unemployment increased and civil disturbance became the order of the day.[68] As the English population thus underwent a gradual yet relentless process of impoverishment, falling cloth/wool prices and a reorientation of English textile production towards the products of the "light drapery" strengthened that nation's competitive position on international cloth markets. Overseas trade expanded and the merchant assumed the position of arbitrator in the fortunes of at least one section of the English cloth industry. Each year, during the decade 1523–32, English producers of the "heavy drapery" anxiously awaited news of the overseas merchants' dealings and of the course of trade on foreign markets, for upon that news now depended their very livelihood.

No less concerned with this news, which percolated down to them from their masters, were the workers in this sector of the English cloth industry whose position had also deteriorated during these years as a result of the process of demographic change.

---

67   On the trade stoppage and its effects see present chapter, above, whilst on the famine of 1527/8 see HOSKINS, Harvest Fluctuations, p. 34s., and D. DRUMMOND, The Famine of 1527 in Essex, in: Local Population Studies, XXVI (1981).

68   See present chapter, above.

In the period down to ca. 1523 this group had enjoyed a somewhat enviable position in an essentially rustic form of industrial organisation.[69] Pivotal to this system was the independent master weaver who provided a link between the self-consumption patterns of the English peasantry and the commercial activities of the clothier-grazier. In the case of lesser members of the peasantry who kept a few sheep, primarily to provide "mylke for their sustenance" without which they would have had "nethur mete ne drynke to putte in ther hedes", involvement in textile production had meant the domestic spinning of a few pounds of wool into yarn which was subsequently delivered on contract to the local weaver who, by working up the materials into such items as a blanket or coverlet, created a product which would then be returned to the family for their own use. The clothier-grazier was no less involved with the master weaver.[70] Having put out the wool from his flock of 200–400 sheep (i.e. 1–2 sacks a year) to his own and his neighbours wives for spinning, he also delivered this yarn to the same master weaver, who, working on the basis of a two-year contract for him, produced for ca. 13s 4d the cloths (200 yards or 8 "cloths" a year) with which the clothier would accoutre his family (ca. 128 yards) and obtain cash (ca. 95 yards = ca. £3 11s 3d[71]). Within those neighbour-kin networks of village society which bound together the organisational structure of the rural manufactory the master weaver enjoyed a rather favourable position which served as an bellwether for the fortunes of all those engaged in this rustic pursuit. His work for his neighbours allowed him to keep the clothier at arm's length and secured for him returns to capital and enterprise as well as to labour. Those returns, moreover, assured him, as it did his fellows in the manufactory, an ample and sufficient cash income which was commensurate with the sustenance they enjoyed from their holdings and their place in the hierarchical ordering of village society.[72]

Within some two decades, however, in the production of "heavy" draperies at least, as labour markets weakened in conditions of increasing population pressure, his position and that of his peer group had totally changed. A petition of the weavers of Ipswich, Hadleigh, Lavenham and Bergholt in 1539 reveals the new situation prevailing at that time only too clearly when they declared that

---

69 See chapter 12.

70 As indicated in chapter 12, note 42 above the nature of the activities of the peasant clothier-grazier and the important role of self consumption in the disposal of his output is revealed in a series of account books from the 1470s of one such man, which have uniquely survived in the collection Bodleian Library, MSS. DD Weld, C19/4/1/1–3, which provide the information below. 400 sheep with an average fleece weight of ca. 1.5 lbs per animal (J. P. BISCHOFF, Fleece Weights and Sheep Breeds in Late Thirteenth- and Early Fourteenth Century England, in: Agricultural History, LVII, 2 [1982] and K. J. ALLISON, Flock Management in the Sixteenth and Seventeenth Centuries, in: Economic History Review, Second Series, XI [1958], p. 105) would produce about 600 lbs wool which would be spun into 400 lbs of yarn (CARUS-WILSON, Trends, p. 169, n. 4) at ca. 6d per stone of yarn. A 15-yard (pre-1520) kersey would be made from just over 2 stones of yarn, the cost of weaving being 1 shilling.

71 At the price of ca. 9d a yard prevailing for kerseys between 1470 and 1520.

72 See I. BLANCHARD, Consumption and Hierarchy in English Peasant Society, 1400–1600, Chicago Economic History Workshop Papers, No. 20 (1980), pp. 1–12; ID., Konsumpcja ne wsi angielskiej, 1580–1680, in: Kwartalnik Historii Kultury Materialnij, XXX, 1 (1982), and ID., Les travailleurs industrielles au moyen âge: les industries textiles et minières, unpublished paper presented at seminars conducted in 1996 at the École des Hautes Études en Sciences Sociales, Paris 1996.

[c]lothiers have their own looms and weavers and fullers in their own houses so that master weavers are rendered destitute for the rich men, the clothiers, have concluded and agreed amongst themselves to pay only one price for weaving, which is too little to sustain the household even by working night and day, holiday and workday.[73]

Presented in an extreme and rather dramatic form the fate of the Suffolk weavers was representative of the lot of many English workers in manufactory during the fateful 1520s and 1530s. As their neighbours' command over landed resources weakened and they were forced to adopt a more farinaceous diet, supplies of wool delivered to the master weavers declined and customers were loathe to have it made up into the wool-intensive "heavy" draperies. The weavers' "private" business, which had allowed them to keep the clothier at arm's length and had secured for them returns to capital and enterprise as well as to labour, was thus eroded. Increasingly during these two decades they found themselves with only their labour to sell and the only groups who were in a position to hire them were those clothiers who found a market for their wares abroad. By 1540 the master weavers, at least in the "heavy" drapery trades, could no longer maintain an independent position. As the Suffolk weavers indicated they no longer possessed their own tools but rather were forced to labour at looms provided by their employers. They also now worked with raw materials provided by those employers and given the contemporary low wage rates and high price of wool, in order to prevent the workforce stealing and selling the wool to augment their mea-gre earnings clothiers concentrated "weavers and fullers in their own houses" where every aspect of their activity could be supervised. The erstwhile independent master weavers had been reduced to the position of highly supervised wage labourers. They had also, in conditions of resurgent population growth and falling real wages, been "rendered destitute". Continuing to adhere to the work-norms of village society, as the clothiers "agreed amongst themselves to pay only one price for weaving" in accord with prevailing low market wage rates, the weavers, like other members of peasant society, were constrained to increase their labour intensity in order to maintain their household consumption at the levels required of them by their peers in peasant soci-ety. As the Suffolk weavers declared in 1539 even "by working night and day, holiday and workday" at prevailing piece rates they had only a forlorn hope of earning the cash they required to pay their rents and buy those packages of consumer goods which were the material embodiment of their position in society. The lot of these Suffolk weavers, or others labouring in the production of "heavy" draperies, might well not be entirely representative of that of workers in the cloth industry as a whole and it is probable that those engaged in the manufacture of "light" draperies felt only the muted effects of these changes but certainly these textile workers' experience was shared by others employed in the export industries of this period.

During the 1520s and 1530s those engaged in the lead and tin industries felt the impact of exactly the same forces at work in their labour markets. Increasingly during these two decades as smelters bought into the resource base of their industries becom-ing, particularly after 1536, owners of the miners' "meers", the previously independ-

---

73 "The History of the Cloth Industry in Suffolk", in: R. H. TAWNEY (ed.), Studies in Economic His-tory: The Collected Papers of George Unwin, London 1927, reprinted from Victoria County His-tory, Suffolk, II, pp. 254–271.

ent miners who, like the master weavers, had received returns to capital and enterprise as well as to labour, were reduced to the position of wage labourers.[74] They were also, in the prevailing conditions of resurgent population growth and falling real wages, impoverished. Previously able to indulge their high leisure preference by spending only some 54 "man-days" each year on extractive work they were now forced to increase their levels of labour intensity to 84 "man-days" in order to maintain their household consumption at the levels required of them by their peers in peasant society.[75] Unfortunately in the case of these miners it is now impossible to determine whether this increase in labour intensity was achieved by changes in the numbers of hours worked per day or by alterations in the number of days worked per year but perhaps they adhered to the behavioural patterns, later recalled by Harrison in the 1570s as characteristic of the period of his youth forty years before, when he declared that

> [h]eretofore there has been much time spent in eating and drinking than commonly is in these days, for whereas of old we had breakfasts in the forenoon, beverages or nuncheons after dinner, and thereto reresuppers (i.e. second or late suppers) generally when it was time to go to rest [...] Now these odd repasts [...] are very well left and each one in manner [...] contenteth himself with dinner and supper only [...].[76]

Clearly already in the 1530s peasant-workers were established on that path which during the next forty years would force them to work harder in order to maintain their state of material prosperity and would make them secure the time for this extra work by abandoning breakfast and afternoon drinking. Whether engaged in the export industries or other sectors of the economy, peasant-workers seemingly were already, when first observed by the young Harrison in the second quarter of the sixteenth century, altering the ritual elements of their flexible time in order to increase overall labour intensity levels so that they could maintain status-related consumption and leisure time differentials within village society in difficult times. In the process they were also transforming England into a low-wage economy similar to that emerging contemporaneously in the Netherlands (Figure 13.2).[77]

---

74 I. BLANCHARD, La loi minière anglaise 1150–1850. Une etude de la loi et de son impact sur le developpement économique 2e partie. Mythe, 1550–1850, unpublished paper presented at the École des Hautes Études en Sciences Sociales, Paris 1985.

75 I. BLANCHARD, Labour Productivity and Work Psychology in the English Mining Industry 1400–1600, in: Economic History Review, Second Series, XXXI, 1 (1978), pp. 1–15.

76 Quoted and analysed in I. BLANCHARD, Introduction, in ID. (ed.), Labour and Leisure in Historical Perspective. Thirteenth to Twentieth Centuries, Stuttgart 1994, p. 22s.

77 H. P. R. FINBERG (ed.), The Agrarian History of England and Wales, Vol. IV: 1500–1640 (ed. J. THIRSK), Cambridge 1967, Statistical Appendix, Tables VI, pp. 847–848; XV, p. 864. VAN DER WEE, Antwerp, I, App. 1, p. 177 and 39, pp. 452–454, 473s..

Figure 13.2: Real Wages: (a) England and (b) the Netherlands, 1501–1542

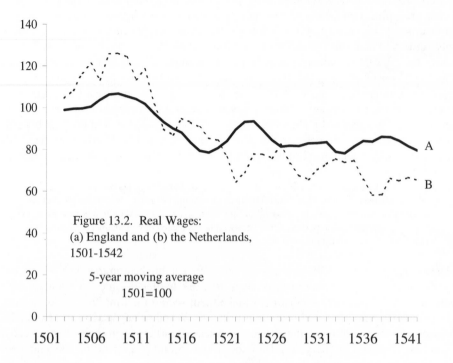

Figure 13.2. Real Wages:
(a) England and (b) the Netherlands,
1501-1542

5-year moving average
1501=100

Anglo-Netherlands Wool Trades. As far as Anglo-Netherlands textile producers were concerned these years saw no less significant changes take place with regard to their wool supplies. In England, as has been suggested, during the years to 1532 fundamental changes in the economy effected a major transformation in domestic wool markets. From ca. 1517/8, the long-established, demographically-induced pattern of demand fluctuations, which had previously determined the course of English domestic and, indirectly, overseas trade, continued to impose itself on the markets wherein the wool dealers acquired their wares but now these fluctuations took place upon a rising rather than a falling population trend. As a result, in the aftermath of the harvest failures of 1520–2, the old games were played out at a new low-price equilibrium level and the English wool dealers found the markets within which they acquired their wares transformed. Mounting population pressure, by slackening the peasantry's control over agricultural resources, led to a slow process of immiseration. Successive runs of bad harvests (in 1520–2 and 1527–9) hastened that process and in reducing disposable income adversely affected the demand for wool from clothiers supplying the dwindling domestic market. Accordingly prices fell.[78] Initially, from ca. 1517/8–23 the process was a simple cyclical one, the demographic upswing of these years combining with deflationary pressures to re-establish wool prices at 1514-levels. Subsequently, as in the aftermath of the harvest failures of 1520–2 population growth was sustained,

---

78   See Figure 7.1.

wool price re-equilibration occurred. The second cycle, which ran its course during the years 1523–32, took place at a lower level than before. Even at the cyclical peak in 1527 prices were well below those at the previous peak of 1517/8 and in the aftermath of the harvest failures of 1527–9 wool prices plummeted to a new all-time low. Thus during the years 1523–32 the wool dealer found the domestic market in which he acquired his wares weakening. The Stapler and northern English coarse wool and fell dealer on the other hand, found their competitive position on foreign markets immensely strengthened and, in favourable conditions for the pursuit of their trade, became increasingly active.

Even as the first great cycle in the Anglo-Netherlands cloth trade (1492–1523) drew to its close English wool merchants, able during the years ca. 1517/8–1523 to obtain their wares at progressively lower domestic prices and largely free of competition from their major international rivals, came to dominate Netherlands wool markets. The Staplers dealing in fine wools, whose products steadily displaced the Spanish wools of the Flemish and Burgalese merchants at Bruges during the years 1517/8–1520 thereafter, with the withdrawal in 1521–1523 of Spanish ships from the Scheldt anchorages because of the rise in premiums on the Antwerp-Medina del Campo exchange[79], came to completely dominate the market in fine wools. The progressive debasements of the Baltic currencies after ca. 1515 by undermining the position of the Leiden "heavy" draperies on northern markets, however, weakened the position of suppliers of such raw materials whilst enhanced transactions costs, as result of the Antwerp exchange crises of 1521 and 1522–1523, caused an overall reduction in demand for these products so that English dominance was achieved in a fine wool market which was becoming increasingly restricted. Far more important at this time was the growing market for coarse wools and fells and once again therein it was the English product which reigned supreme. The progressive debasements of the Baltic currencies in undermining the position of the Leiden "heavy" draperies and causing merchants to acquire, in "normal" circumstances (1518–1520) at Antwerp, the "light" cloths of the Hague, Hoorne and Delft to sell on Baltic markets, caused an augmentation in the demand for fells at a time when the market for this produce was normally depressed. Debasement, in lowering the foreign exchange price of Baltic produce on Low Countries markets, also introduced a new competitor into the trade – "Ostland" wool. As a result the market was transformed. The Scots trade declined to 600–1,500 sacks as its position on Netherlands markets was usurped by "Ostland" wool, some 500–600 sacks of which were imported at these times. The English product, shipped either directly from the Tyne or transported via the Calais Staple, however, increased to some 2,750–3,750 sacks a year. For the first time during these years (1518–1520) the coarse wool and fell market had come into its own and in the absence of Scots competition it was the English product which reigned supreme with exports running at about two-thirds the levels attained in the fine wool trade. When, as a result of the emergence of crisis conditions at Antwerp (in 1521 and 1522–1523), transactions cost

---

79   See chapter 3, note 11, and VAN DER WEE, Antwerp, II, p. 144. On the role of the Spanish at the Bergen fairs see F. EDLER, The Van der Molen, Commission Merchants of Antwerp: Trade with Italy, 1538–44, in: Medieval and Historiographical Essays in Honour of James Westfall Thompson, Chicago 1938, p. 116s., whose description of their trade is confirmed by the Welser letters quoted in VAN DER WEE, Antwerp, II, p. 177.

were enhanced and the cloth trade and in particular that in "heavy" draperies collapsed, moreover, the coarse wool and fell trade again increased its share of the dominant but declining English wool trade, exports of these wares running at about three-quarters of the level attained in the contemporary fine wool trade. At the increasingly low domestic price levels prevailing during the years 1517/8–1523 English wool dealers and particularly exporters of coarse wool and fells were able to dominate Netherlands markets for their wares. They did so, moreover, in extremely difficult circumstances for, as the first great cycle in the Anglo-Netherlands cloth trade drew to its close, the crisis conditions prevailing in 1522–1523 ensured that aggregate demand in those markets was much reduced.

When the crisis on the Antwerp bourse subsided and a second long-cycle in the Anglo-Netherlands cloth trade (1516/22–1542/7) imposed a new buoyant level of activity at the Brabant fairs the English wool dealers were thus in a strong position to take advantage of the new situation. Operating in a domestic market where in the aftermath of the harvest failures of 1520–1522 wool prices had re-equilibrated at a new low level and increasingly moved to the tempo of the export rather than the domestic trades they were ideally placed to increase the export of their wares – but not until 1525/6. Initially as, from the time of the 1523/4 Cold mart, the cloth trade once again expanded it was the English product which established its ascendancy at the Netherlands marts. Low Country producers, and particularly Flemish manufacturers of the "heavy" drapery, subject to English competition and enhanced raw material costs, experienced acute difficulties which caused them to reduce their purchases of fine wool. Thus in spite of the absence of Spanish competition, the English wool exporter, derived little benefit from the boom, only an increase in coarse wool and fell exports preventing a total collapse in their trade. When in 1524/5 the sectoral crisis gave way, in conditions of acute monetary disorder, to a general one affecting every aspect of the Anglo-Netherlands textile manufactory, even this prop was removed. Thereafter as long as gold prices continued their giddy flight on Netherlands specie markets, the wool trade, like that in cloth, remained depressed. Only when the Netherlands authorities were able to restore some order in the monetary chaos (over the winter-spring of 1525/6 and 1526/7) were the wool dealers, like other merchants, offered any relief. On the first of these occasions, in conditions of international price equilibration but continuing high finance costs at London, English wool exports increased and domestic prices rose. Netherlands prices, on the other hand, in acutely deflationary conditions occasioned by the monetary reform of November 1525, fell to pre-crisis levels and the English wool dealers ephemerally found a ready market for their wares amongst those Netherlands clothiers who now in the absence of English competition sold their wares to the Germans and Spaniards who briefly flocked to the Low Country fairs. When, over the summer and autumn of 1526, Netherlands gold price resumed their upward flight, however, the trade boom aborted. Prices in the Low Countries again increased and English wool prices again fell. Only a final and definitive monetary reform in the Netherlands could seemingly save the day. This occurred during the Cold mart of 1526/7 with the Netherlands monetary ordinance of the 10 December which ushered in what was to prove an extremely eventful year for English wool dealers. From December to the completion of the monetary reform on 1 March 1527 interest rates fell on both the London and Antwerp money markets and premiums disappeared on their respective exchanges. By March the problems which beset the Anglo-Netherlands monetary and financial systems seemed well on the way to being resolved, and at the prevailing low prices and with the availability of cheap commercial credit Staplers found themselves able readily to vend their wares. Thus through the winter-spring of 1525/6 and 1526/7 English fine wool exports rapidly increased. Bruges dealers flocked to the Calais market and the product once more establish a dominant position amongst Low Country consumers. At domestic price which even at their cyclical peak in 1527 were well below those at the previous peak of 1517/8, the English product reigned supreme on rapidly expanding Netherlands markets for fine wool.

Then, as a result of the brief Antwerp financial crisis of April 1527 and the ineptitude of Henrican commercial policy at the time of the subsequent Sinxen mart the trade boom collapsed. These short-term crises, however, broke on a market which in 1527 was itself undergoing a process of fundamental structural change which made it very different from that which had existed before the crisis of 1525–6. The Netherlands monetary reform of the winter of 1526/7 together with the Venetian one of 1527 established a new pattern of financial influence for Antwerp's bill brokers. The emergent bi-metallic equilibrium between the Spanish, Venetian and Netherlands currencies facilitated inter-market monetary transfers in the southern trades and in reducing their transactions costs allowed Burgalese merchants shipping Spanish wool to undercut their English rivals on the Bruges fine wool market. When therefore Netherlands producers, protected by the ineptness of Henrican policy, found a ready vent for their wares at the Sinxen mart and increased their output this occasioned heavy imports of Spanish rather than English wool[80] and henceforth during both booms (summer 1527) and slumps (winter 1527/8) in the "heavy" drapery trades, this pattern of behaviour continued to prevail. Only when, in the aftermath of the harvest failures of 1527–9, wool prices in England plummeted to a new all-time low equilibrium level could the domestic product in 1529–1530 mount a challenge to the Spanish hegemony. Both English fine and coarse wool-fell exports again increased but not for long.

In the next year 1531/2, as acute inflationary pressures pervaded the economy, wool prices rapidly increased causing great concern to the English government who immediately instituted a major enquiry into the state of the trade at what proved to be the point of its final demise. As in the "Age of the Celys" some half a century before, Cotswold wool continued to hold pride of place with West Country (Lemster and March) produce in the contemporary fine wool trade.[81] These wools which had been obtainable during the years 1529–1530 at between £5 4s to £8 13s 4d a sack, now, during the years 1532–1534, as inflationary pressures pervaded the economy, could not be bought for less than £6 6s 8d to £13 10s.[82] Views varied, however, with regard to the reasons for this price increase. Convinced of the indispensability of such wools

---

80 TNA, SP1/44 fo. 99ᵛ.

81 *L&P, Henry VIII*, IX, App. Nr. 20–1 (*The quantities of wool that go out of diverse places in England*), 2–3 (*Profits made by merchants selling their wools at Calais*), 4–5 (*The rate and prices of wool brought to the Staple*) and ibid., X, Nr. 247 (*The price that wool was bought for in years past and price at which they are sold this year*). These documents are undated but, on the basis of internal evidence, seem to relate to 1532/3.

82 It should be noted that this data, collected in the summer of 1533, relates to a short-term downswing in prices occasioned by Henry VIII's "closure of trade" at the Staple, between the inflationary peaks of 1532 and 1534.

to French and Netherlands clothiers, the Crown perceived of the price increase as arising from the Staplers exploitation of their monopolistic position and to reinforce their
action, perhaps in the hope of raising new loans from them, in the summer of 1533,
ordered a "closure of trade" at the Staple.[83] The results of this action are readily ob-
servable. English exports of fine wools declined and with them domestic prices of the
commodity. Netherlands prices of English wool after initially edging upwards fell
heavily. In part this was due to the acute contemporary conditions of monetary deflation in the Low Countries but it also owed much to "real" factors whose impact had,
moreover, been highly predictable. Even as the "closure of trade" at the Staple had in
the last week of August become operative both the Imperial ambassador, Chapuys,
and the Regent's plenipotentiary, de la Sauch, had warned the king that

> he was much mistaken if he thought that the Low Countries could not live without his wools,
> considering the abundance of them in Spain and the French who made more cloth than the
> Low Countries did not care for his wool or Staple, moreover they made very fine cloths
> though they had not such fine wool as that of Spain so that the Low Countries could all the
> more easily dispense with wool from here [...] already several merchants had made arrange-
> ments for getting their wool from Spain [...].[84]

Their perception of market conditions was shared, moreover, by the English wool
merchants if not by their king. They were only too aware that an enhancement in the
price of their wares would cause Netherlands clothiers to shift to the purchase of
Spanish wool and accordingly responded appropriately. Whilst the price of the wools
which were the staples of their trade – "Cotes", Lemster and March – increased by at
least a third during the years 1529–1530 to 1532–1534, by increasing their purchases
of lower-priced "Clift" wool[85] they were able to limit the average price increase of
their fine wool export mix to some 15 per cent and restrict the decline in their trade to
some 15–30 per cent. When free from the effects of royal intervention in their affairs
the Staplers found that, at the new high domestic price levels of the years 1532–1534,
they could sell some 2,000–2,800 sacks of their fine wool to Netherlands consumers.
Nor during the subsequent decade 1535–1544 did this situation significantly change.
Once again the English trade fluctuated between ca. 2,000–2,800 sacks a year in response to variations in the new high-level foreign exchange price for the English
product. As the Imperial envoys had warned would happen from 1532 England was
eclipsed as a source of fine wool supplies for Netherlands and French producers of
"heavy" draperies. From that time these clothiers increasingly bought Spanish wool
and as this trade rapidly grew to new and ever higher levels – amounting to some
20,000 sacks a year in the early 1540s[86] – they enjoyed those benefits deriving from a

83 *L&P, Henry VIII*, VI, Nrs. 1018, 1047.

84 BL, Additional MS, 28,173 fo. 272.

85 "Cotes", old and young, and wools from Leominster Soke ("Lemster") and the March of Shrop-
    shire ("March") which had dominated the fine wool export trade during the years 1529–1530,
    comprised 41 and 28 per cent respectively of the wool available for export in 1532/3, the residual
    31 per cent being made up of "Clift" wool which like East Anglian – Lindsey & Kesteven, Hol-
    land & Rutland and Norfolk – and Berkshire wools had found no place in the earlier trade.

86 C. R. PHILLIPS, The Spanish Wool Trade, 1500–1780, in: The Journal of Economic History, XLII,
    4 (1982), p. 779s.

regular and cheap supply of raw materials which were denied their English rivals. The English producers of "heavy" draperies, like that nation's fine wool dealers, were thus from ca. 1532 seriously disadvantaged in relation to their Netherlands counterparts with regard to the cost of their raw materials.

English traders in coarse wools and fells, however, fared somewhat better. Following the exchange crises of 1521 and 1522–3 pre-existing trading patterns re-asserted themselves in the commercial complex within which they operated. As increasing supplies of Joachimsthalers flooded Baltic specie markets, once more creating a "hard" monetary zone in the region and raising the foreign exchange price of "Ostland" wool on Netherlands markets, the trade in that commodity dwindled to a point of final extinction in the early 1530s. With the elimination of competition from this quarter the Scots trade to the Low Country marts was re-established and in "normal" trading conditions at the marts (1525–1526, 1529–1530, 1533–1534 and 1537–1538) expanded rapidly engendering a countervailing movement in Newcastle's trade. Very different to the position of the Newcastle merchants in the years to 1532, however, was that of the English Staplers, trading in fells, who, in conditions of enhanced transactions costs at Antwerp, seized each opportunity afforded by Scottish trade decline (1523–1524 and 1527–1528) to expand their commerce. On each of these occasions the English fine wool dealers, like their counterparts in the "heavy" drapery trades, attempted to offset the increase in foreign exchange prices for their wares by increasing their purchases of lower-priced produce in order to limit the average price increase of their export commodity mix. As a result of these actions, whilst the aggregate English wool trade to Calais declined, that in fells increased both absolutely and relative to the fine wool trade. For the moment, however, the impact of these changes was ephemeral and with the re-establishment of favourable conditions in the fine wool trade (in 1525–1526 and 1529–1530) the Staplers abandoned their flirtation with fells, ceding that market to the Scots. When, however, inflationary pressures pervaded the English economy during the years 1531/2–1533/4, the whole situation was transformed. In the short term, as a result of these monetarily induced price changes and Henry VIII's ill-advised "closure of trade" at the Staple, the English commerce in both wools and fells collapsed. With the lifting of the embargo and recovery of the English trade (ca. 1535–1539), however, the Staplers, cognizant of the prevailing high domestic and foreign currency prices of their wares, completely altered their business strategies. As before they attempted to offset the increase in foreign exchange prices for their wares by increasing their purchases of lower-priced produce in order to limit the average price increase of their export commodity mix thereby stabilizing their trade in fine wools at the levels (2,000–2,800 sacks a year) first established during the years 1532–1534. Far more important, however, was their shift to the purchase of low-price wool fells. From 1535 their trade in these wares, although subordinated to that of their Scots rivals, increased rapidly from about 1,000 to 2,000 sacks a year, on occasion (1535–1536) even surpassing in size the English fine wool trade. By altering the composition of their export trade the Staplers had thus survived by creating for themselves a niche within Netherlands markets for coarse wools and fells. The markets within which they now secured a place were not, however, particularly buoyant ones. With a total commerce in 1540/1, at the height of the contemporary trade-cycle, amounting to about 3,750 sacks activity at the Scheldt marts was still below previous peak levels (ca. 5,000 sacks in 1500 and 4,250 sacks in 1519).

Paradoxically, even as the rapid growth of Netherlands "light" drapery manufactory created an insatiable demand for coarse wool and fells, the overpriced products sold by Scots and English merchants were eclipsed as the focus of commercial activity shifted from the Scheldt marts to inland markets supplied by those innovating farmers[87] who were contemporaneously transforming Netherlands agriculture and its associated wool supply system. During the 1520s and 1530s, as a result of enhanced transactions costs in international supply networks and the re-emergence of a "hard" money zone in the Baltic, the foreign exchange price of Eastland grains had risen sharply in the towns of western Brabant. Initially in 1521 and 1523/4 the situation had been nothing short of catastrophic. Dislocations in French grain supplies coinciding with crisis conditions on the Antwerp Bourse which caused the withdrawal of Hanseatic grain ships from the Scheldt resulted in an acute famine. In Leuven, Malines and Vilvoorde women plundered the granaries of convents, burgesses and merchants causing the government to despatch 500 troops to contain the situation. In Ghent government officials were forced to buy grain to sell at lower prices to the poor. In Antwerp the Brabant grain market was attacked and farmers bringing grain thence were robbed of their wares. Throughout the towns of Brabant measures were taken to prevent fraud in the bakeries and stop speculation by grain merchants.[88] During these years, financial disorders on the Antwerp Bourse, in disrupting international trade and causing the dual ills of unemployment and famine had wrought havoc in the Netherlands economy. The legacy of enhanced transactions costs, moreover, boded ill for the future. Whilst, during the next two decades, these resulted in an overall rise in grain prices in the towns of western Brabant, however, when analogous crisis conditions to those prevailing in 1521 and 1523/4 reoccurred in 1527–1529, 1531/2, 1535/6 and 1538–40 the impact of the resultant interruptions in the Baltic grain trade became weaker and weaker. From ca. 1525 Brabantine grain dealers had begun to seek supplies from domestic producers who, particularly in the 'thirties, benefited from a series of dry summers and abundant harvests.[89] In the process they caused prices in the countryside, which had previously remained far below those of the Brabantine towns, to rapidly increase and converge on those in the towns.[90] They also by their actions imposed a new rhythm on the movement of Netherlands grain prices, the recurrence of famine conditions in 1530 resulting from domestic crop failure[91] rather than foreign trade stoppage. In an environment of increasing domestic market integration Netherlands farmers were confronted with a completely new and potentially profitable situation and rapidly seized the new opportunities opened up to them. In the vicinity of Antwerp there was a progressive extension of the town's polder and a similar process of land drainage may be discerned at this time in coastal Zeeland and Flanders. On both new and existing lands rents rose[92], moreover, as better techniques were applied

---

87   The following paragraph is, unless otherwise stated, based on materials presented in the discussion of the process of agrarian change in VAN DER WEE, Antwerp, II, ch. 6, section B § 1, pp. 157–168.

88   Ibid., ch. 6, section A § 3, pp. 150–153.

89   Ibid., I, Appendix 50, p. 557 and II, p. 167.

90   Ibid., III, Graph 19, p. 50s.

91   In that year North and South Beveland were almost entirely inundated by the sea. Polders in Flanders and around Antwerp were stricken: Ibid., II, p. 167.

92   Ibid., II, Tables XVIII/1–3, pp. 168–9; III, graphs 29–30, pp. 71–2.

causing a noticeable improvement in agricultural productivity. The use of external sources of fertilizer became common, creating a trade in manure and human excrement in the West Brabant urban zone. Farmers in the regions of friable, sandy and loam soils in Flanders and Zeeland ensured a similar high level of the manuring by the introduction of leguminous and root crop elements into their rotations and the use of these fodder crops to support the stall-feeding of animals which were bought-in to finish for metropolitan markets.

Increasing market integration and the associated process of regional specialization, as the peasantry were able to marginally abandon self-sufficiency in favour of commercial contacts, moreover, ensured them a regular supply of store-beasts. Large numbers of steers from northern pastures in Gelder, Friesland and the banks of the Rhine were driven to the markets of Lier and 's-Hertogenbosch each year where they were sold as store-beasts to be finished-off for urban consumption.[93] The *Pays de Herve*, located in the south-eastern part of the country beyond Maastricht, which at this time increasingly specialized in cattle rearing and dairy production, also played its part in this developing trade.[94] In the northern and south-eastern Netherlands increasing numbers of cattle were being reared to meet the demands of consumers in the western Brabant urban centres. To maintain maximum grassland productivity in these regions, however, cattle rearing was also usually associated with a sheep husbandry which not only provided the local peasantry with dairy produce and meat but also yielded the peasants an abundant supply of marketable fells.[95] In the conditions of high prices prevailing in the 1520s and 1530s, a new domestic producer had emerged who seemingly was able to marginally uncut foreign wares and satisfy the incremental demands of Netherlands producers of the "light" draperies.

As from 1527 Antwerp's old European-wide hegemony, already crumbling in 1523–4, was replaced by a more limited financial function – the servicing of Ibero-Mediterranean commerce – and a bi-partite structure was imposed upon European commercial networks the Anglo-Netherlands textile industry's raw material supply system assumed a more introspective character. English fine wools, overpriced on overseas markets from 1532 were thereafter exported only in diminutive quantities. Netherlands consumers of these wares increasingly bought Spanish wool and as the trade in this commodity rapidly increased to some 20,000 sacks a year, or some 50 percent more than at pre-1527 peaks, they benefited from a price stabilization which was denied their English rivals. In the Anglo-Scottish trade in coarse wools and fells a

---

93 I. BLANCHARD, The Continental European Cattle Trades, 1400–1600, in: Economic History Review, Second Series, XXXIX, 3 (1986), p. 428s., and H. VAN DER WEE / E. AERTS, The Lier Livestock Market and the Livestock Trade from the Fourteen to the Eighteenth Century, in: E. WESTERMANN (ed.), Internationaler Ochsenhandel, 1350–1750: Akten des 7th International History Congress (Edinburgh, 1978), Stuttgart 1987, p. 244s.

94 J. RUWET, L' agriculture et les classes rurales au Pays de Herve sous l' Ancien Régime (=Bibliothèque de la faculté de philosophie et lettres de 1 université de Liège, Fasc. C), Liège 1943, pp. 54–56 and VAN DER WEE, Antwerp, II, p. 170.

95 On the production and marketing of wool and fells in the Pays de Herve, see RUWET, Pays de Herve, p. 169s., whilst E. COORNAERT, Un centre industriel d' autrefois. La draperie-sayetterie de Hondschoote (XIVe–XVIIIe siècles), Rennes 1930, p. 190s., reveals the importance of the wools of Gelder, Friesland and the banks of the Rhine as well as those of Hainault to manufacturers of the "light" drapery.

similar overpricing from 1532 also led to a decline in exports and to the emergence of Netherlands producers of these materials who were able to marginally undercut foreign wares and satisfy the incremental demands of domestic producers of the "light" draperies. In the years after 1532, therefore, it was only Netherlands "heavy" drapery producers who were able to avail themselves of the services of an international raw material supply system capable of supplying increasing quantities of fine wool at stable prices. Netherlands manufacturers of "light" draperies increasingly assumed the introspective characteristics of their English counterparts, buying a greater and greater part of the coarse wools and fells they required from domestic sources.

Unlike Netherlands producers of the "heavy" drapery, therefore, BOTH English and Low Country manufacturers of "light" cloths, in turning to domestic sources of coarse wools and fells, experienced an enhancement in raw material costs. They, however, at the same time were also able to obtain labour at steadily falling wage rates. Factor market changes accordingly favoured the substitution of cheap labour for expensive raw materials and those who could achieve such a substitution would not only survive but would even prosper. In the manufacture of cheap woollens, the fabricators of coarse cloths or doucken – in England predominantly in Norfolk, in Holland in the textile towns about Naarden and in the southern Netherlands in the region south and south-west of Ypres – tied to traditional production techniques thus succumbed. Those who were able to assimilate the techniques involved in the production of the "new" kersey, however, fared far better. In mastering the labour-intensive techniques involved in fabricating the extra-strong warp thread, they were able to almost halve the amount of wool used in the production of the fabric and sell their cloths on the Antwerp mart at prices which were directly competitive with those of the Netherlands says which through a similar process of technological change had also during the course of the 1530s established themselves amongst the cheapest of the products available to Anglo-Netherlands cloth exporters.

CHAPTER FOURTEEN

THE CLOTH AND WOOL TRADES. THE SUPREMACY OF THE "LIGHT" DRAPERY, 1532–1542

By 1531 the products of the "light" drapery had already established themselves on a position of parity with the traditional "heavy" cloths in the Anglo-Netherlands textile trades. During the subsequent decade, 1532–1541, factor market changes, by raising the price of wool and lowering the cost of labour, had favoured a process of factor substitution which ensured that those amongst this group of manufacturers who could encompass this changing relationship in their production techniques would not only survive but could even prosper. In the manufacture of cheap woollens, the fabricators of coarse cloths or doucken – in England predominantly in Norfolk, in Holland in the textile towns about Naarden and in the southern Netherlands in the region south and south-west of Ypres – who remained tied to traditional techniques of manufactory thus succumbed. Those in England who were able to assimilate the techniques involved in the production of the "new" kersey, however, fared far better. By mastering the labour-intensive techniques involved in fabricating the extra-strong warp thread, they were able to almost halve the amount of wool used in the production of the fabric and to stabilize the price of their cloth when elsewhere prices were rising. An analogous process in the Netherlands, moreover, also resulted in the decline of the indigenous doucken and the spread of the multi-variant forms of the *sayetterie*. Again the key the success of the "new" product rested on the labour intensive techniques involved in the production of the extra-strong 2–3 double *fil sayette* which again allowed a marked reduction in the amount of wool used in these cloths which were only about half the weight of the standard worsted and could sell for as little as one Flemish stuiver per yard. Factor market changes, by favouring a process of input substitution, had encouraged an assimilation of techniques which embodied this relationship, allowing manufacturers to fabricate wares which by 1540 were amongst the cheapest available to consumers. Such a product, moreover, by that date was heavily in demand, particularly from Anglo-Netherlands textile exporters who from 1532 had seen their position on European markets seriously threatened by the potential overpricing of their traditional wares.

Monetary Disorder and Commercial Contraction, 1532–1534. The massive inflation in English cloth prices during the years 1531/2–1533/4 totally altered that nation's competitive position in the European cloth market. The more expensive products of the English "heavy" drapery, which even in 1529–1530 had only been sold in the cheaper southern markets, now found no vent at all, on account of their excessive price, amongst merchants like Antoine de Bombergen who traded thence.[1] A void was thus created in this market, which even the Netherlands producer, hampered from 1527 by the grotesque over-valuation of the *livre de gros*, by a markedly rigid price structure and by the financial crisis of 1532, made some attempt to fill. Production at Leiden, where drapers were in the process of re-orientation towards the southern trades, briefly recovered.[2] In the moribund centres of Wervicq and Courtrai a slight flurry of activity indicated that the flickerings of life still remained.[3] Amongst the newer centres, like Menin and Armentières, badly hit by English competition during the years 1529–1530, there was a brief revival.[4] In no case, however, was there a re-kindling of the flame of former glories: the Netherlands revaluation made sure of that.

The initiative now passed elsewhere. In the southern French and Italian markets the Languedocian and above all the Venetian producer came to the fore.[5] Each western crisis (1516–1517, 1520–1523 and 1526–1527) had afforded new opportunities to the manufacturers of the city on the lagoon and accordingly production had expanded.[6] Each resumption of normal commercial relations (1518–1519, 1524–1525 and 1528–1529) had witnessed a recession. Booms and slumps thus followed each other in rapid succession, but each time production stabilized at a higher level than before, as war, political turmoil and foreign occupation destroyed domestic competition. Como succumbed early, Brescia in 1512, Milan in the 1520s. In 1520–1523, only Florence remained to share with Venice the buoyant market conditions induced by the western crises of those years. Thereafter, even that city's industry, capable of supporting a production of 18,000–20,000 *garbi* and 4,000 cloths of San Martin at its height,

---

1   W. BRULEZ, Lettres commerciales de Daniel et Antoine de Bombergen à Antonio Grimani 1532–43, in: Bulletin de l' Institute Historique Belge de Rome, XXXI (1958), pp. 186–197.

2   N. W. POSTHUMUS, Geschiedenis van de Leidsche Lakenindustrie, 's Gravenhage 1908–39, as quoted in: H. VAN DER WEE, The Growth of the Antwerp Market and the European Economy. Fourteenth–Sixteenth Centuries, 3 Vols., The Hague 1963, III, Graph 24, p. 60; I, Appendix 46/1, p. 530s., and ID., De Uitvoer van Amsterdam 1543–5, Leiden 1971, p. 196s., 220.

3   E. COORNAERT, Un centre industriel d' autrefois. La draperie-sayetterie de Hondschoote (XIVe–XVIIIe siècles), Rennes 1930, p. 486 ss.

4   H. E. DE SAGHER / J.-H. DE SAGHER / H. VAN WERVEKE / C. WYFFELS, Receuil de documents relatifs à l' histoire de l' industrie drapière en Flandre, 2e partie, Le sud-oeust de la Flandre depuis l' époque Bourguignonne, Bruxelles 1951–66, III, p. 72.

5   On the Languedoc industry the rather dated study of P. BOISSONNADE, L' industrie languedocienne pendant les soixante, premières années du XVIIe siècle, in: Annales du Midi (1909) is still of use, and the question of competition between "northern" and domestic cloth production on southern French markets is dealt with by E. LE ROY LADURIE, Les Paysans de Langudoc, Paris 1966, Vol. I, pp. 124–6. Both of these studies, however, have now been largely superseded by the study of P. WOLFF, Esquisse d' une histoire de la draperie en Languedoc du XIIe siècle au XVIIIe siècle, in: Produzione, commercio e consumo dei panni di lana, secc. XII–XVIII (=Pubblicazioni dell' Istituto Internazionale di Storia Economica "Francesco Datini", Serie II Atti delle Settimana di Studi, Vol. 2), Prato 1970. The following description of the Venetian industry is based upon D. SELLA, The Rise and Fall of the Venetian Woollen Industry, in: B. PULLEN (ed.), Crisis and Change in the Venetian Economy of the Sixteenth and Seventeenth Centuries, London 1968, pp. 106–115.

6   It is unfortunately impossible to test the impact of the first (1509–1513) crisis upon the industry as the available production statistics only begin in 1516.

declined. In 1527 production had fallen to 14,000 *garbi*.[7] In 1529 the Venetian ambassador declared that "production is practically at a standstill." Thus when from 1531/2 a permanent "protection" was afforded the Italian producer, it was Venice who benefited, production there increasing by fifty per cent. The market ceded to the indigenous producer, however, was a declining one for, as overall prices of "heavy" cloths rose, consumers turned increasingly to cheaper and lighter stuffs.[8] In this expansive market the Netherlands producer came into his own. With falling export prices, induced by heavy domestic price deflation which offset the effects of the appreciation of the *livre de gros*, the products of the Netherlands "light" drapery – the says of Hondschoote and the half-cloths of Neuve Église – took an increasing share of an expanding market, displacing the English kersey which between 1528–1532 had increased in price on the Italian market by some 18.75 per cent.[9] Between 1530 and 1532, as the English economy was first subject to acute inflationary pressures, the domestic producer lost ground to his Netherlands counterpart in the expansive light cloth market of the south. But even within that market the Anglo-Netherlands producer was not secure for as the whole market equilibrated upwards in price and the cheaper, light cloths enjoyed a new vogue the very cheapest sector began to be penetrated by the "new draperies", the camlets and mohairs of the Ottoman Empire.[10]

The story is not dissimilar elsewhere. In the Baltic the "heavy" draperies disappeared entirely from the market. Light stuffs took their place and Netherlands *schlechte* draperies displaced English ones. The East Anglian industry, so buoyant during 1527–1529, collapsed. The same Norwich authorities, who had rhapsodised over the earlier prosperity of local *doucken* manufacture, in December 1532 lamented that it was now "most sore and grievously diminished; leaving the people for pure need to ask for their meat and drink."[11] In its place the manufacturers of Naarden and Arnhem expanded production. Utilising cheap imported raw materials to offset the impact of currency appreciation, the cloths of these towns displaced not only those of

7   "Relazione di Firenze del clarissimo Marco Foscari, 1527", as quoted in: P. EARLE, The Commercial Development of Ancona, 1497–1551, in: Economic History Review, Second Series, XVII, 2 (1969), p. 34, n. 2.

8   The rise in indigenous cloth prices through 1527–1528 which may be discerned from the Anconese notarial records of Antonio Stracca and Antonia Pavesi (Archivio di Stato, Ancona, II, ASA 17–8, 21 ASA 11 respectively) continued through to the 'forties, as is revealed in the notarial records of Girolama Giustiniani (31 ASA 13) and many others.

9   After rising from 8 ducats a kersey in January 1527 to 9.5 ducats in early 1532, prices fell to 9 ducats in late September. I am deeply indebted to Dr Peter Earle for providing me with this and other information concerning cloth prices at Ancona from his researches in the notarial records of that city. This data invaluably supplements that contained in the van der Molen correspondence, discussed in: F. EDLER, The Van der Molen, Commission Merchants of Antwerp: Trade with Italy, 1538–44, in: Medieval and Historiographical Essays in Honour of James Westfall Thompson, Chicago 1938, pp. 78–145; ID., Winchester Kerseys at Antwerp, 1538–1544, in: Economic History Review, First Series, VII (1936), pp. 57–62, and ID., Le commerce d'exportation des says d'Hondschoote vers l'Italie, d'après la correspondance d'une firme anversoise, entre 1538 et 1544, in: Revue du Nord, XXII (1936), pp. 249–266, and that of the van Bombergen: BRULEZ, Lettres commerciales, pp. 186–197.

10   Though camlets were not unknown on western European markets before the 1530s, they may be discerned arriving in increasing numbers at ports like Ancona during the years 1527–1542.

11   NNRO, City Records, Press D. Case 16d.2. fo. 169ᵛ.

England on Baltic market but also the products of Poperinge and Tourcoing whose manufacturers suffered from the effects of the Wendish embargo of 1532.[12] Even these products were expensive, however, and indigenous producers were afforded opportunities to squeeze in at the bottom of the market. How they responded is by no means clear, but it seems probable that during these years the Upper Lausitz manufacturers of centres like Görlitz and Thuringian producers of Zwickau took advantage of the dislocation of Westphalian and Harz production, occasioned by the central European financial crisis, to establish themselves in Baltic markets.[13]

In central Europe the English maintained their position in relation to Low Country competitors somewhat better, but at Augsburg and Nuremberg the more expensive English whites, dyed at Hamburg, began to loose ground in a declining market to the products of the Lotharingian industry – the red Spinal, the white and gray Niklasport and the cloths of Metz – an industry which began its period of greatest development in 1530.[14] Even in the expansive "light" drapery market the kersey began to face competition from such products as Augsburg fustians.[15]

Throughout Europe, as cloth prices rose, the "heavy" drapery gave way to the "light," a trend most pronounced in the Baltic and least marked in Spain.[16] The Anglo-Netherlands producers lost ground relative to other manufacturers, most significantly in the "heavy" cloth market where the Languedocian, Venetian and Lotharingian product triumphed and least noticeably in the "light" cloth market where competition from the coarse cloth manufactory of the Erzgebirge and from those who worked the exotic materials of Anatolia was as yet slight. The English mercantile and industrial communities ceded defeat at the hands of their Netherlands counterparts.

The Supremacy of the Anglo-Netherlands "Light" Drapery, 1534–1542. The years 1531/2–1533/4 had witnessed both a long-term restructuring of England's position in the European cloth market and a short-term crisis induced by Netherlands competition. The short-term crisis soon passed. The English, due to the closing of the domestic price differential, were able by 1534 to resume their dominant position within the Anglo-Netherlands commercial and industrial community. That commu-

12 R. HAEPKE, Niederländische Akten und Urkunden zur Geschichte der Hanse und zur deutschen Seegeschichte, Munich / Leipzig / Lübeck 1913–1923, I, pp. 118–122; L. GILLIODTS VAN SEVEREN, Cartulaire de l'ancienne Éstaple de Bruges, Bruges 1904–1905, II, p. 639, and DE SAGHER et al. (eds.), Receuil de documents, III, pp. 263, 416.

13 The story of the rise of the coarse drapery of central Europe during these years has yet to be told. Not uncommon in the Hanseatic records of the 1440s and 1450s it virtually disappears from them during the years 1460–1510, reappearing intermittently from 1510–1530. See e.g. G. VON BUNGE (ed.), Liv-, Est- und Curländisches Urkundenbuch, Reval 1853–1859, I 1, Nr. 19 and 337, n. 3. Thereafter it is difficult to trace until the 'fifties when it assumes a dominant position in the surviving records, eg. VALTIONARKISTO, Helsinki. Rakenskaper rorande tullen i Finland i 16 de och 17 de århundradena. Nr. 233a–c. Åbo 1549, 1556, 1559. G. MICKWITZ, Die Hansekaufleute in Wiborg, 1558–9, in: Historiallinen Arkisto, XLV (1939), p. 114s.

14 A. DIETZ, Frankfurter Handelsgeschichte, 5 Vols., Frankfurt-on-the-Main, 1910–25, Vol. II, p. 267.

15 On Augsburg fustian production see O. REUTHER, Die Entwicklung der Augsburger Textilindustrie, University of Munich Dissertation, Munich 1915, and C.-P. CLASEN, Die Augsburger Weber. Leistungen und Krisen des Textilgewerbes um 1600, Augsburg 1981, pp. 9–20.

16 G. MICKWITZ, Aus Revaler Handelsbüchern, Helsingfors 1938, p. 100s.; E. J. HAMILTON, American Treasure and the Price Revolution in Spain, 1501–1650, Cambridge, Mass. 1934, p. 320s.

nity, aided by both falling export prices and by its own efforts to re-orientate production and trade about the products of the "light drapery," was able by 1536 to re-establish itself at the centre of the European cloth market. By 1536, therefore, the crisis was a thing of the past and as production and trade continued to grow from 1536–1539 the products of the Low Countries and particularly the English cloth manufactory made new inroads into the European market. That market, however, was a very different one from that which had existed before the crisis. The new structure of commerce, forged in the years 1527–1529 and 1532–1534, remained intact throughout the 'thirties.

The products of the Anglo-Netherlands "light" cloth manufactory maintained their dominant position in the international textile trades. Only in one market – the Baltic – did they loose ground during the 'thirties. The enhanced value attached to the gold ducat on Baltic specie markets[17], in enhancing transactions costs through the creation of premiums on exchange dealings, offset the impact of falling domestic English prices from 1534 and made even the lightest cloths uncompetitive. Thus paradoxically whilst the volume of trade carried, either directly or indirectly, between England and the Baltic grew year by year from 1532–1539, the volume of cloth exports did not. An examination of the cargoes of vessels engaged in the trade reveals that most sailed in ballast. John Russel's ship, the *Christopher of Newcastle*, for instance, which left Lynn on the 13th May 1539 for the Baltic carried only nine cloths (five "set cloths" and four dozens) and was duly entered in the registers as entering the Sound in ballast.[18] Returning, however, it was loaded to the gun whales with sylvan products.[19] Or again, Thomas Melly's ship which left Woodbridge on the 10th February 1537 carried, apart from a bulk cargo of salt, only a small pack of northern straights and was again entered on the Sound Toll Registers as sailing in ballast.[20] Nor were Melly's or Russel's ventures atypical: vessel after vessel which may be identified as sailing from England for the Baltic, travelled in ballast. The days when the Hansards "hadd nede of more wollen clothe than England hadd nede of ther comodites [...]" and "they wer wont to bryng gold and silver uncoyned [...]" to England were past.[21] English cloths, even northern straights and dozens, were too expensive for Baltic customers and ac-

---

17   J. PELC, Ceny w Gdansku w XVI i XVII wieku, Lwów 1937, p. 2s.

18   N. E. BANG / K. KORST, (eds.), Tabeller over Skibsfart og Varetransport gennem Øresund 1661–1783 og gennem Storebælt 1701–1748, Vol. 1.1, Copenhagen / Leipzig 1939; pp. 2–6. The decline in the number of English ships passing through the Sound in 1538–9 does not conform to the trend in total shipping, which continued (after a brief pause in 1538) its path of growth, begun in 1532, to reach over a thousand ships in 1539. It may be that more of the English-carried trade in these years passed to Hamburg or Amsterdam. Certainly the number of English cloths dyed in the former city increased dramatically during 1538–1539 (R. EHRENBERG, Hamburg und England im Zeitalter der Königin Elisabeth [Jena, 1896], p. 331), but this may be accounted for by the diversion of the Italian trade there. Surer evidence perhaps of the English use of a continental entrepôt for Baltic wares is the increased number of ships entering English ports during 1538–1539, laded with Baltic wares, which cannot be traced passing through the Sound. TNA, E122/12/10, 99/23–4 and 210/4; Rigsarkivet København, Sundtoldreguskab, 1537–1539.

19   TNA, E122/99/24: left 13 May, Sundtoldregiskab, 1539 fos. 25 and 35, returned 10 August.

20   TNA, E122/210/4: left 10 February, Sundtoldregiskab, 1537 fos. 8 and 14, returned 7 June.

21   "A Treatise concerning the Staple and the Commodities of this Realm", in: R. H. TAWNEY / E. POWER (eds.), Tudor Economic Documents, London 1924, Vol. III, p. 108.

cordingly they carried thence gold to exchange for those "nedfull comodites for England: pitche, tarre, bowstavis, wex, flesh and such other."[22] Only the Hollanders now carried cheap west European textiles through the Sound, drawing heavily on the manufacturers of Naarden and its environs.[23] Yet even their products were relatively expensive and opportunities were opened up for indigenous producers. As has already been shown, during the opening years of the decade the coarse cloths of the Erzgebirge had begun their penetration of the market through Danzig. Now, with the adjustment of the south German houses to their new, more limited role in Central European trade, the Westphalian cloths of Münster and the Harz products of Göttingen and Mühlhausen also began to find their way via Frankfurt, Leipzig and Lübeck to the ports of the Baltic littoral. By 1540 they had already assumed an important position therein. The "light" cloth, and in this case the indigenous product, reigned supreme.[24]

Elsewhere the prospects for the English manufacturer and trader were somewhat rosier. In Central Europe as cheaper and lighter cloths came to the fore, the English fared far better. As the West of England white became increasingly expensive it gave way to the Lotharingian product. Yet whilst the latter industry grew at the expense of the former, both lost ground to lighter cloths and predominantly kerseys which were bought by south German merchants for distribution as far afield as Hungary.[25] The light cloth was again in the ascendant but now it was the English light cloth. In market after market the story repeats itself, even in the southern trades to Italy and Spain where the "heavy" draperies were able to regain some of the ground lost in 1532–4, the "light" cloth established its ascendancy. Here by 1539 many of the English and Netherlands products, ousted from the market because of their excessively high price at the beginning of the decade, may again be discerned amongst the purchases of Italian or Spanish merchants or their Netherlands agents. The van der Molen[26], for instance, bought for suppliers of the Italian courts *ultrafini* of Armentières, *nerelistes* of Menin, *nerelistes* and *rogelistes* of Ypres, cloths *della spada* of Haarlem and cloths *della chieve* of Leiden, as well as Suffolk and Kentish cloths. Similarly to Spain they shipped the cloths of Flanders and the cheaper English "heavy" draperies – the West of England whites and the even cheaper Penistone whites which dominated English "heavy" cloth exports to the Brabant Fairs.[27] The quantities, however, were small and both the van Bombergen and van der Molen correspondence reveals the overwhelming preponderance of "light" cloths – English kerseys; Hondschoote and Bergues says;

22   Ibid., see also A. ATTMAN, The Russian and Polish Markets in International Trade, 1500–1650, Gothenburg 1973, p. 100s.

23   N. W. POSTHUMUS, De Uitvoer van Amsterdam 1543–5, Leiden 1971, p. 187s.

24   See e.g. Stockholm Kammerarkivet, Tull och accis. Stockholms Tullrakenskaper, Vol. 291 for the year 1533–4.

25   G. SZÉKELY, Niederländische und englische Tucharten in Mitteleuropa des 13.–17. Jahrhunderts, Annales Universitas Scientiarum Budapestinensis de Rolando Eötvas nominatae. Sectio Historica, VIII (1966), pp. 33–35.

26   F. EDLER, The Van der Molen, Commission Merchants of Antwerp: Trade with Italy, 1538–44, Medieval and Historiographical Essays in Honour of James Westfall Thompson, Chicago 1938, pp. 98–100, and for a description of the types of cloth referred to, see n. 55, p. 96; n. 51, pp. 94–5; n. 63, p. 98 and n. 67, p. 99 in the same.

27   On the shift towards the cheaper Penistone whites in English exports during the 1530s, see CUL, Hengrave Hall MSS, 78/1.

ostades and *demi-ostades* of Amiens, Lille and Valenciennes and half-cloths of Neuve Église – in their trade to the south during the late 'thirties.

The day of the "light" cloth had arrived and industrially it swept all before it. Production in those towns where the most expensive forms of "heavy" drapery were manufactured declined. At Bruges, Ghent, St Omer, as well as Lille and other Walloon towns, centres of the *vielle draperie*, the industry, already in decay at the beginning of the century, finally collapsed.[28] Newer centres of manufacture, like Wervicq, Leiden, Commines, Halluin, Menin, Courtrai, Bailleul and La Bassée, as well as the Kentish and Suffolk cloth towns and the textile villages of the Lys valley, which had benefited from the expansion of the southern trades to 1530 (and in the case of the Netherlands industry to 1532), quickly followed suit. Everywhere the expensive "heavy" cloth industry was in retreat.[29] Decay or diversification were the only alternatives open to producers. Some followed the latter course of action, modifying their techniques in accord with the new cost structure of the 'thirties. In England a "newe collorred clothe called a 'meddley'" was developed in Kent and Suffolk.[30] At Bruges, continuing in a protracted tradition of (largely abortive) attempts at innovation, clothiers copied in 1532–1533 the techniques of the Armentières manufactory.[31] In neither case, however, was the surgery drastic enough. Production declined and as manufacturers attempted to economise by reducing labour costs disturbances[32] broke out in Kent in 1537 and Suffolk in 1539. For the manufacturers of the fine "heavy" draperies the choice was an unenviable one: either they could liquidate their enterprises immediately, or suffer a drawn-out, lingering decline associated with chronic unemployment and unrest. Even the position of the cheap heavy cloth producer was a precarious one. A market existed for their products in Spain and Italy, but only as long as costs were kept down. With Venetian and Languedocian competitors in the wings, avidly waiting to seize upon any sign of weakness, only the most enterprising Anglo-Netherlands producer could survive. In the Italian market it was the manufacturers of Armentières who prevailed. With access to cheap and plentiful supplies of Spanish wool and by a constant modification of their production techniques they proved capable of maintaining their competitive position.[33] Similarly in the trade to Spain the cheaper English broadcloths remained competitive with their Flemish counterparts and both made such successful inroads into the market that cries for protection arose

---

28 COORNAERT, Hondschoote, p. 23, n. 4.

29 Ibid., p. 24.

30 CUL, Hengrave Hall MSS, 78/2 fos. 15–16, 19.

31 On the continual (although usually abortive) attempts of Bruges manufacturers to adjust to new market situations see J. A. VAN HOUTTE, De Draperie van Leidse Lakens in Brugge, 1503–1516, in: Album Viaene (1970), pp. 331–339, as well as on the imitation of Leiden cloth; W. VAN WAESBERGHE, De Invoering van de nieuwe Textiel-nijverheden te Brugge en hun Reglementering (einde 15e–16 eeuw), Appeltjes van het Meetjesland (1969), pp. 218–238, and COORNAERT, Hondschoote, p. 26, n. 2 on the assimilation of the techniques employed at Armentières and the industry of the Lys valley.

32 L&P, Henry VIII, XII (2), Nr. 737; ibid., XIV (1), Nr. 874. The latter document, quoted above, is particularly interesting for the light it throws on the cloth workers' reactions to wage cuts.

33 DE SAGHER et al. (eds.), Documents, I, pp. 102–191 for eight cloth ordinances (document Nrs. 36–45) issued between 1510 and 1538.

from Spanish clothiers.[34] To achieve this success, however, English clothiers, seriously disadvantaged in relation to their Netherlands rivals by the high price of domestic wools, had been forced to experiment with cost reducing techniques. In the Yorkshire cheap broadcloth producing area, about Penistone, this took the form of "flocking" – utilising the cheapest grades of wool.[35] In the West of England manufacturers simply reduced the amount of wool in their cloths.[36] Even the most competitive sectors of the Anglo-Netherlands "heavy" drapery were thus by 1540 struggling for survival.

In the "light" cloth industry at this time, however, manufacturers found their order books bulging. Production within established centres of "light" cloth manufactory boomed. At Hondschoote and Bergues the output of says rose rapidly. At Naarden growing production created such pressure on Hessian wool supplies that prices rocketed and the German authorities, afraid of the ruin of the local industry, imposed an export ban in 1534.[37] In England the demand for kerseys was such that Italians were forced to buy the popular Winchcombes whilst still on the loom.[38] Success followed success and each advance caused others to emulate. During the 1530s manufacturers in many of the decayed centres of the "heavy" drapery took up the production of "light" stuffs. At St Omer the production of *petits draps de boure, de prenne ou de brequelin* was started in 1537.[39] In the Walloon towns of Arras, Béthune, Tournai, Valencienne, Mons and above all, Lille, the say and the ostade rapidly gained ground.[40] The day of the kersey and say had arrived and the Anglo-Netherlands manufacturer, by orientating his production about these "light" stuffs, had once more by 1541 re-established himself at the centre of the European cloth market.

The rapidity with which manufacturers had responded to the new conditions, which had emerged during the crisis of 1532–1534, had been stunning. When in 1542 analogous crisis conditions to those prevailing a decade earlier re-asserted themselves, moreover, they proved that their responses had not been a flash in the pan and that they were once more able to respond with similar rapidity to the new situation then emerging. In the short-term, the domestic inflation in English and Netherlands cloth prices again precipitated an acute commercial crisis in 1541–1542 during which England again lost ground to her Low Country competitors and both ceded markets to indigenous producers. The short-term crisis, however, soon passed. As prices fell from the crisis peak of 1542 to their new high level of 1543–1544 recovery began, whilst the closure of Anglo-Netherlands price differential again placed England in the vanguard of the advance. Yet the whole market, in which recovery took place, had equilibrated upwards in price.

---

34   L&P, Henry VIII, IV (2), Nr. 2987 and XIII (2), Nr. 383.

35   H. HEATON, The Yorkshire Woollen and Worsted Industries, 2nd ed., Oxford 1966, pp. 133–135.

36   CUL, Hengrave Hall MSS, 78/2 fo.15v ff. on the trend towards lighter cloths amongst the clothiers from whom Kitson bought his export wares.

37   A. DIETZ, Frankfurter Handelsgeschichte, 5 Vols. Frankfurt-on-the-Main 1910–25, II, p. 256.

38   F. EDLER, Winchester Kerseys at Antwerp, 1538–1544, in: Economic History Review, First Series, VII (1936), p. 60.

39   COORRNAERT, Hondschoote, p. 26, n. 2.

40   Ibid, p. 25.

The fate of the Anglo-Netherlands "heavy" drapery was sealed. In the Baltic the trade in these products no longer existed. Not one of the ships which may be discerned venturing thence during 1542–1544 from either England or Amsterdam carried "heavy" cloths.[41] In Central Europe, where the price rise was not so marked, the declining market passed to the Lotharingian producer.[42] Even in the southern trades via Antwerp to Italy "heavy" cloth exports amounted to no more than nine per cent of the total textile trade in 1543–1544.[43] What remained of the Italian "heavy" cloth market was ceded to the industries of Venice and Languedoc. Everywhere the "heavy" cloth industry was in retreat during these years and the Anglo-Netherlands manufacturer virtually abandoned the production of these wares.

The "light" cloth now dominated the European textile market and production of, and trade in this product expanded rapidly. But even these wares were now becoming expensive and during 1542–1544 the market for even cheaper cloths widened considerably. This trend was most pronounced in the Baltic where the products of the Anglo-Netherlands "light" drapery gave way to the coarse wares of central Europe. Producers of the light Holland cloths of Naarden, Arnhem, Amerforst, Deventner and Harderwijk, who had successfully from 1534 effected a transfer from the use of Hessian to domestic wools, still sold increasing quantities of their wares through Amsterdam, reaching ca. 11,000 cloths in 1544, but this was merely expansion on the ruins of the Anglo-Flemish *schlechte draprie*.[44] Most English ships venturing through the Sound sailed in ballast, carrying only very diminutive cargoes of the very cheapest cloths – *vesys* and northern kerseys. With its market gone, that sector of the English "light" cloth industry which was dependent on the Baltic trade – the East Anglian *doucken* manufactory – was now extinguished and in its place the capping trades arose.[45] Similarly in Flanders, *doucken* production at Poperinge and Tourcoing, which had amounted to about 15,000 cloths in 1532, collapsed in the face of northern competition, manufacturers turning to the production of other wares predominantly for southern markets. Thus whilst sectoral growth might occur within the Anglo-Netherlands *slechte draprie* overall it lost ground in Baltic markets, being displaced by the producers of the coarse wares of Westphalia, the Harz and the Erzgebirge whose cloths, during these years, continued on that ascent which before the decade was out would ensure to them total supremacy in the Baltic. Similarly in central Europe coarse cloth producers of indigenous origin increased their share of the textile trades. At Augsburg in 1543 such wares comprised two-thirds of the cloths sold.[46] Even in Italy, where the inflation in textile prices was relatively slight, the dominant

41   For Amsterdam: N. W. POSTHUMUS, De Uitvoer van Amsterdam 1543–5, Leiden 1971, Appendix D, p. 266s., and for the destination pp. 174ss. England (1542–1544) TNA, E122/99/27, 31; 64/15–16. Rigsarkivet København, Sundtoldreguskab 1542–1544.

42   DIETZ, Frankfurter Handelsgeschichte, II, p. 267.

43   W. BRULEZ, L' exportation des Pays-Bas vers Italie par voie de terre au milieu du XVIe siècle, in: Annales, 14 (1959), p. 479s.

44   POSTHUMUS, Uitvoer, p. 266s. (value of exports) and p. 242 (prices).

45   See the increased number of freemen entering these trades in W. RYE (ed.), Calendar of the Freemen of Norwich, 1317–1603, Norwich 1888, and W. HUDSON / J. C. TINGAY, Records of the City of Norwich, Norwich 1910.

46   DIETZ, Frankfurter Handelsgeschichte, II, p. 266.

position of the English kersey and Netherlands say was subject to a challenge from a somewhat exotic rival. The trickle of camlets and mohairs which had begun in the 1530s, from 1542 turned into a flood.

As the "light" drapery thus attained total supremacy in the European cloth market the "new" drapery began its challenge and once again Anglo-Netherlands clothiers were not slow to recognize the threat to their position. They responded as before by the creation of a new product – mixed cloths – serges and bays which, utilising a mixture of combed and carded wools, were able to attain approximately the limit of the prevailing technology to produce a light cloth (in this case weighing 0.58–0.64 lbs per square yard) purely from wool. Established in French Flanders and, in the case of bays, on both sides of the Channel in the late 1530s and early 1540s,[47] these were the vanguard of a new generation of "light" and "new" draperies which would ensure continuing Anglo-Netherlands textile supremacy during the new trade-cycle (1538/42–1568) which was now beginning.

The Anglo-Netherlands Wool and Cloth Trades, 1492–1542: An Overview. For some thirty years (ca. 1492–1522) when its markets were untroubled by financial, monetary or commercial disorders, Antwerp, by the availability of cheap money on its Bourse and the ability of dealers to effect low-cost inter-market monetary transfers within a stable bi-metallic system of European-wide dimensions, drew to itself, by land and sea, merchants whose produce was subsequently redistributed to markets across the continent. For the English textile merchants all paths led to Antwerp, where they could dispose of their wares to others who would then distribute them to markets scattered the length and breadth of Europe. Through their knowledge of, and access to a cloth market of truly nation-wide dimensions which embraced a myriad of small producers each working-up his own wools, moreover, these English merchants were able to respond to every changing whim of the foreign consumer. Yet the marginality of their position in relation to this market also had its disadvantages as in the medium- and long-term activity therein responded to a long-established, demographically-induced pattern of demand fluctuations. As the English peasantry adjusted their demand patterns, causing English overseas trade at this time to move (inversely) in the medium-term to the rhythms of the domestic market, the merchants could merely respond to the course of events benefiting from low domestic cloth price during the years ca. 1492–1508 but experiencing difficulties in obtaining supplies as prices rose from ca. 1509–1517/8 before a fall in prices to 1523 once more re-established their competitive position. Their Netherlands rivals at this time experienced no such difficulties. Changes in the requirements of domestic consumers in the Netherlands played a much lesser role in determining the overall evolution of the cloth market at this time. Their demands were largely satisfied by what historians have come to call the "petite draperie", whose manufacturers produced either inexpensive worsteds or a rather old-fashioned small coarse cloth. This manufactory, concentrated in Holland and

---

47   The following description of the bay is based upon J. E. PILGRIM, The Rise of the 'New Draperies' in Essex, in: University of Birmingham Historical Journal (subsequently re-named Midland History), VII (1959/60), p. 41. The weights have been transposed from the more accurate TNA, Fine Rolls, 394 as quoted in N. J. WILLIAMS, Two Documents Concerning the New Draperies, in: Economic History Review, Second Series, IV, 3 (1952), p. 354, rather than from the corrupt BL, Lansdowne MS, Vol. 27, Nr. 265 quoted by Pilgrim.

Friesland, in the region of Brabant to the north-east of Brussels, in the lands of Flanders west of Ypres and in Lotharingia-Ardenne, like the English industry, depended on local wool supplies and catered predominantly for domestic demand, but, unlike in England, its product in "normal" trading circumstances found no place in international trade. This was the preserve of Netherlands manufacturers producing the fine heavy cloths of the "grande draperie" who availed themselves of the services provided by a well developed and organizationally stable industrial wool market, within which manufacturers were able to continually alter both the quantities and types of wool they purchased, thereby allowing them to vary their production patterns and satisfy the merchants' changing requirements. The export sector of the Netherlands cloth manufactory – the "grande draperie" – thus, unlike in England, formed a separate and distinct entity divorced from both domestic markets and native wool supplies. Producers therein, unlike their English counterparts, could accordingly respond directly to the requirements of the export merchants, flexibility being assured in this instance by the manufacturers of the "grande draperie", who, in utilising the facilities of a well developed and organizationally stable industrial wool market, were able to continually alter both the quantities and types of wool they purchased, vary their production patterns and satisfy the merchants' changing requirements in conditions of stable prices. Whilst changing raw material supply prices during the years 1492–1522 thus went a long way to explaining changes in the relative fortunes of English and Netherlands suppliers of the Antwerp cloth market, however, the long-term decline in the cost of commercial credits on that city's Bourse ensured that in "normal" circumstances both prospered as the trade in the Anglo-Netherlands "heavy" draperies rapidly expanded.

Only occasionally was their position threatened when Habsburg intervention on Antwerp's Bourse (in 1509–13, 1516–7 and 1520–3), by raising the cost of commercial credit, deflected trade along the paths of an "alternative" commercial system and briefly brought the products of the "light" drapery to the fore. Such episodes were, however, of but ephemeral significance. Far more important were the effects of the rapid devaluation of eastern Baltic currencies after 1515 which led to an appreciation of both the Flemish pound and sterling in terms of these moneys. Foreign currency prices of Anglo-Netherlands products, falling from 1515 through 1518–9 in most other markets actually increased in the Baltic forcing exporters to reduce the average price of their commodity mix and in 1518–1519 creating a permanent niche for the products of the Anglo-Netherlands "light" drapery on European cloth markets.

When during the 'twenties such debasements became an endemic feature of everyday life, occasioning serious disturbances on the Antwerp exchanges in 1524–1526 and causing the subsequent disintegration of the previously unitary European monetary system which from the winter of 1526/7 split into "hard" and "soft" monetary zones, many may have considered that the world was changing in ways which were not for the better by far. If this was the case then they were soon to find that there was worse to come. Habsburg interventions during 1521 and 1522–1523 on the Antwerp Bourse may have seemed to many just another example of imperial financial mismanagement but the Regent's plundering of exchange reserves on this occasion left a long-term legacy of enhanced bill rates which if masked by the impact of other disorders during 1524–1526 thereafter from the winter of 1526/7 made itself felt on exchange dealings within the newly formed "hard" monetary zone with sufficient force to engender in 1528 a flight of capital from the city on the Scheldt. During the decade

1523–1532 the merchants' world had been turned upside down. Price movements, which had previously figured strongly in the formulation of their business strategies, now played a decidedly lesser role in their decision making. They now eagerly awaited every piece of news concerning exchange movements at Antwerp and the tidings were almost invariably bad. Crises (fiscal 1521, 1522/3 and 1527–1529; monetary 1525–1526 and mining 1527/8) followed each other in rapid succession and as their transactions costs were enhanced cloth traders experienced increasing difficulties in selling the "heavy" draperies which had been the staple of their trade. As before in crisis conditions, in order to reduce the average price of their export commodity mix, they turned to the acquisition of the products of the "light" drapery. In the Netherlands the transition was a difficult one. To expand output, producers of these wares, elevated from the ranks of the "petite draperie", needed to avail themselves of the services of dealers in that somewhat informally organized coarse wool-fell market which previously, like its fine wool counterpart, had always been able to satisfy their demands for increased supplies of raw material at stable prices. Yet as a result of successive crises during the 'twenties the operation of this market was seriously disturbed. Prices of coarse wools and fells rose, contributing from ca. 1525 to the beginnings of a process of technological change in Netherlands agriculture which in the long-term would yield abundant supplies of these raw materials but in the short-term could offer but little relief. In England the situation was very different. The English cloth traders' position during the 'twenties continued to be rooted in that symbiotic relationship between the merchants and their suppliers – the non-specialist English peasant cloth manufacturers – which previously had afforded them considerable flexibility in the acquisition of varying product-mixes for their trade and had minimized social tensions in their dealings. Now during the 1520s, however, mounting population pressure, by slackening the peasantry's control over agricultural resources, led to a slow process of immiseration. Successive runs of bad harvests (in 1520–2 and 1527–9) hastened that process and in reducing disposable income adversely affected the demand for cloth in the domestic market. Accordingly prices fell. Initially, from ca. 1517/8–23 the process was a simple cyclical one, the demographic upswing of these years combining with deflationary pressures to re-establish cloth/wool prices at 1514 levels. Subsequently, as in the aftermath of the harvest failures of 1520–2 population growth was sustained, cloth/wool price re-equilibration occurred. The second cycle, which ran its course during the years 1523–32, took place at a lower level than before. Even at the cyclical peak in 1527 prices were well below those at the previous peak of 1517/8 and in the aftermath of the harvest failures of 1527–9 cloth/wool prices plummeted to a new all-time low. Thus during the years 1523–32 the clothier found the domestic market for his wares weakening. The exporter of English cloths, on the other hand, found his competitive position on foreign markets immensely strengthened. Whilst the English merchant, shipping predominantly "light" draperies, gained a major competitive advantage over his Netherlands rival, however, both experienced the baleful effects of enhanced transactions costs which ensured that activity in the Anglo-Netherlands textile trade would remain at a level below its previous peak – at least until 1528 when the flight of Italian capital to the London market paved the way for a major "direct" trade boom within the "soft" monetary zone which carried English exports, predominantly of "light" draperies, to their highest point yet in the sixteenth century. Whether in boom conditions (1528) when the "light" draperies predominated in the "direct" trades, or recessions (1529–1531) when on returning to Antwerp the English trade declined and the products of the "heavy" drapery marginally improved their position, the English product, like its Netherlands counterpart, retained its "traditional" form, coarse woollens (like English cottons and straights or the Anglo-Netherlands *doucken*) predominating amongst the "light" draperies which had now established themselves on a parity with the traditional "heavy" draperies.

When during 1532–1534 monetary disorders, by enhancing the foreign currency prices of Anglo-Netherlands cloths, caused a major crisis in the trade in these wares the whole situation changed. At the new high price level prevailing through the subsequent decade before inflationary pressures in 1542–1544 caused prices again to rise, the most expensive products of the Anglo-Netherlands textile industry could not be sold and traders in these wares were forced to cede this market to indigenous producers of "heavy" draperies. Nor was it self-evident at this time that the "light" draperies, which merchants increasingly bought in order to reduce the average price of their export commodity mix, would fare much better in the new market situation. All of the major *doucken* manufacturers – in England predominantly in Norfolk, in Holland in the textile towns about Naarden and in the southern Netherlands in the region south and south-west of Ypres – experienced difficulties in obtaining adequate supplies of raw materials and, remaining tied to traditional techniques of manufactory, were forced to increase the price of their cloths which now, particularly on Baltic markets, also lost ground, this time to central European coarse woollens. Only where manufacturers were able to assimilate new production techniques appropriate to the prevailing factor market situation, of rising wool prices and falling labour costs, did they survive and indeed prosper. Thus in England it was those who were able to assimilate the techniques involved in the production of the "new" kersey who now came to the fore. By mastering the labour-intensive techniques involved in fabricating the extra-strong warp thread, they were able to almost halve the amount of wool used in the production of the fabric and were able to stabilize the price of their cloth when elsewhere they were rising. An analogous process in the Netherlands, moreover, also resulted in the spread of the multi-variant forms of the *sayetterie*. Again the key the success of the "new" product rested on the labour intensive techniques involved in the production of the extra-strong 2–3 double *fil sayette* which again allowed a marked reduction in the amount of wool used in these cloths which were only about half the weight of the standard worsted and could sell for as little as one Flemish stuiver per yard. The rapidity with which manufacturers responded to the new conditions, which emerged during the crisis of 1532–1534, was stunning. Production within established centres manufacturing these "light" cloths increased massively and as success followed success others emulated. During the late 1530s manufacturers in many of the decayed centres of the "heavy" drapery took up the production of these "light" stuffs. The day of the kersey and say had arrived and the Anglo-Netherlands manufacturer, by orientating his production about these "light" stuffs, had once more by 1541 provided the trader with a cheap product which allowed him to re-establish his position at the very centre of the European cloth market. When in 1542 analogous crisis conditions to those prevailing a decade earlier re-asserted themselves, moreover, they proved that their responses had not been a flash in the pan and that they were once more able to respond with similar rapidity to the new situation then emerging. As the whole market once more equilibrated upward in price and Anglo-Netherlands traders, dealing in "heavy" and even "light" draperies, experienced difficulties in selling their wares, manufacturers responded as before by the creation of a new product – mixed cloths – serges and bays which, utilising a mixture of combed and carded wools, were able to attain approximately the limit of the prevailing technology to produce a light cloth purely from wool. Established in French Flanders and, in the case of bays, on both sides of the Channel in the late 1530s and early 1540s, these products were now the vanguard of a new generation of "light" and "new" draperies which would ensure continuing Anglo-Netherlands textile supremacy during the new trade-cycle (1538/42–1568) which was now beginning.

From ca. 1527–8, in spite of the impoverishment of its consumers, the fragmentation of its markets and an enhancement in transactions costs, the Anglo-Netherlands cloth trade continued, after almost a decade of disorder, on its pre-existing growth path. As before this owed much to the enterprise and ingenuity of merchants and financiers, particularly at London, who sought the most efficient way of utilizing available financial, transport and commercial resources. From ca. 1532, however, the real growth initiatives had come from the textile manufacturer who in providing the merchants with cheap and readily saleable "light" and then "new" draperies laid the foundations of the new commercial expansion.

CHAPTER FIFTEEN

THE METAL TRADES. THE COMMERCE IN ENGLISH LEAD

In ca. 1500 the Venetian ambassador to England in his report to his masters concerning that nation's commercial prosperity singled out for special mention that the English "have an enormous number of sheep, which yield them quantities of wool of the best quality [...] and an infinity of lead and tin."[1] In focussing their attention on these commodities, however, he was being neither very original nor profound as for half a millennium (ca. 1100–1600) it was almost a commonplace that wool/cloth, lead and tin were the three jewels in England's commercial crown. In relation to their sale to European consumers, however, each of these commodities posed very different problems for the English merchants who traded in them. English cloth, as has been suggested, was sold to customers the length and breadth of the continent and beyond in what were very near perfect market conditions ensured by the existence of numerous competitors. The merchants' survival in such a constantly changing market situation, where transaction cost changes were superimposed on a long-term process of consumer immiseration, depended on the ability of both the English cloth manufacturer and the merchant who handled his wares to continually innovate. The former needed to produce an increasingly inexpensive cloth. The latter needed to get it to consumers as cheaply as possible. In the metal trades, the situation was quite different. The fortunes of both English mining-metallurgical entrepreneurs and merchants were intimately linked with those of European silver producers. These silver producers acted as both consumers and competitors in relation to their wares. In order to understand fully changes in the English metal – lead and tin – trades therefore it is necessary initially to consider briefly the development of the European silver industry in a temporally slightly longer time perspective.

The European Silver Industry (Figure 1.1/15.1). The great "silver famine" of the mid-fifteenth century had marked the end of an epoch in the history of the European mining and metallurgical industries.[2] The decline in the 1450s of silver exports from the mines of Serbia and Bosnia, which had provided the mainstay of European sup-

---

1   C. A. SNEYD (ed.), A Relation or Rather a True Account of the Island of England about 1500 (=Camden Society, Old Series, XXXVII), London 1847.

2   By far the most comprehensive study of the fifteenth-century "silver famine" is J. DAY, The Great Bullion Famine of the Fifteenth Century, in: Past and Present, 79 (1978), pp. 3–54, which may be supplemented by reference to I. BLANCHARD, Le marché égyptien des espèces et la crise d'or au quinzième siècle, unpublished paper presented at the École des Hautes Études en Sciences Sociales, Paris, April 1985.

plies for three-quarters of a century, occasioned more than short-term market supply crisis.[3] Producers, thrown back into a position of reliance upon traditional sources of supply found that the exploitative frontier of their industry, which obtained silver by the cupellation of argentiferous lead ores containing at least 20 ounces of silver per ton, was, if only temporarily, closed. The process of continual extension of the industrial resource-base, by the opening up of new reserves of argentiferous lead ores of progressively lower precious metal content, had finally ended. Across Europe, old abandoned mines were re-opened. Waste heaps, containing the discarded ores of past centuries, were sifted. The ores raised had only a meagre silver content, rarely containing more than 8–12.5 ounces of silver per ton, an amount which, because of the losses incurred in the extraction of the silver, rendered them barely worth refining. In relation to this new resource base, therefore, the existing technology was tested to its limits – and was found wanting. Production declined. Silver prices rose and an acute resource-induced crisis emerged which pervaded the whole European silver market.

The old medieval silver industry, whose technology complex encompassed elements whose history may be traced back to Antiquity, was now all but moribund. In its place, a new industry emerged. Within this new industry, producers exploited a new resource base of polymetallic ores – argentiferous copper, tin, cobalt, nickel and bismuth – by means of new technologies including, in the working of silver bearing copper, the *Saigerprozess*. The 1450s and 1460s thus witnessed the beginnings of a new central European industrial long-cycle.[4] Production, which had fallen to a few thousand marks of silver a year during the mid-fifteenth century crisis, thereafter steadily increased, rising rapidly to ca. 120,000 marks in 1477 and then more slowly to ca. 180,000 marks in 1540. Thereafter production declined, leading ultimately to the post-1561 collapse in output. For a century from ca. 1460–1560, European silver production was dominated by a new industry employing new techniques.

---

3   The literature on the mines of Serbia and Bosnia is now considerable but for a brief, if somewhat dated, survey, see D. KOVACEVIC, Dans la Serbie et la Bosnie médiéval: les mines d'or et d'argent, in: Annales E.S.C., 2 (1960), which may be updated by reference to S. CIRKOVIC, The Production of Gold, Silver and Copper in the Central Parts of the Balkans from the 13th to the 16th Century, in: H. KELLENBENZ (ed.), Precious Metal in the Age of Expansion, Stuttgart 1981, pp. 41–70.

4   The materials utilised in the construction of Figure 1.1/15.1 and employed in the following discussion of central European silver production will be fully discussed in a future study: I. BLANCHARD, Mining, Metallurgy and Minting in the Middle Ages, Vol. 4: From Europe and Africa to the Americas, 1460–1560, which is being prepared for publication. Preliminary findings derived from these materials are presented in H. VAN DER WEE / I. BLANCHARD, The Habsburgs and the Antwerp Money Market: the Exchange Crises of 1521 and 1522–3, in: I. BLANCHARD et al. (eds.), Industry and Finance in Early Modern History. Essays presented to George Hammersley on the occasion of his 74th birthday, Stuttgart 1992, pp. 28–30.

Figure 15.1 (as Figure 1.1): Central European Silver Production, 1470–1570

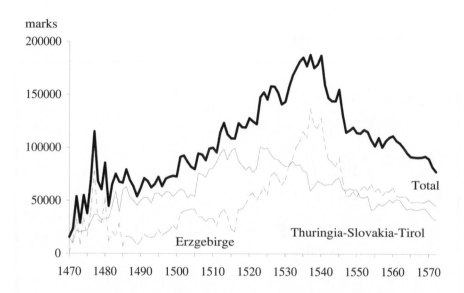

The earliest known use of the new technology dated back to the years ca. 1395–1415 when a favourable conjuncture in both copper and silver markets excited the interest of both Italians and Nurembergers in the silver bearing tetraedite copper ores of central Slovakia.[5] The gains were rich, as the new production centre at Neusohl became the focus of an industrial complex supplying raw materials to both Venice and Nuremberg. They were, however, also ephemeral being predicated on the contemporary crisis conditions prevailing in silver and copper markets. The abatement of silver price increases in the 1410s and the contemporary fall in copper prices relegated the Neusohl producer to the wings. From ca. 1415 the central Slovak argentiferous copper deposits were abandoned as Balkan production once more came to dominate international specie markets and the copper market was divided between Tyrolean-Balkan products in the south and the metal produced from the pyrites (chalkopyrites) of eastern Slovakia in the north-west. From ca. 1415–1450 production at Spis, whose wares had displaced those of Goslar on the markets of north-western Europe in the fourteenth century, was augmented by the output of new centres and non-argentiferous copper reigned supreme.[6] During the 1420s and 1430s it was the products of Gelnica,

---

5   J. VLACHOVIC, Slovenská Med v 16 a 17 storoci, Bratislava 1964, p. 23. W. VON STROMER, Nürnberger Unternehmer im Karpatenraum. Ein oberdeutsches Buntmetall-Oligopol 1396–1412, in: Kwartalnik historii kultury materialnej, XIV, 4 (1968), pp. 641–662 and ID., Das Zusammenspiel oberdeutscher und Florentiner Geldleute bei der Finanzierung von König Ruprechts Italienzug 1401–1402, in: Öffentliche Finanzen und privates Kapital im späten Mittelalter und in der ersten Hälfte des 16. Jahrhunderts, Forschungen zur Sozial- und Wirtschaftsgeschichte, Vol. 16, Stuttgart 1971.

6   A. FLECK, Beiträge zur Geschichte des Kupfers, Jena 1908, p. 34.

Lubietova and Smólnik mines, engrossed in the hands of Jan Falbrecht, the "Copper Baron", which began to enter the market. Output here steadily increased as that at Neusohl declined.[7]

Map 15.1: Lead and Silver Production

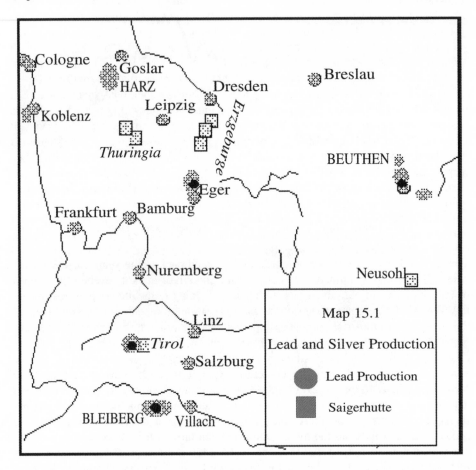

7   VLACHOVIC, Slovenská Med, p. 25.

Yet even as the products of the Serbian and Bosnian silver-lead mines once more after 1415 came to dominate European mint output and the non-argentiferous coppers of the Balkans, Tyrol and eastern Slovakia established their market hegemony there was no return to the status quo ante 1395–1415. The refining of argentiferous copper continued, even if at a diminutive level, at Venice and Nuremberg, the surviving *Saigerhütte* (Saiger hut=*smelting plant, where by means of the 'Saiger' process silver was extracted from the argentiferous copper ores, P. R.*) at the latter centre drawing raw copper during the 1430s from Kuttenberg (Bohemia), Zwickau and Meissen (Saxony and Thuringia) and lead from the Erzgebirge market town of Eger.[8] The new technology remained exotic and production small however as long as existing reserves of ore allowed production to continue based on prevailing smelting and refining techniques.

It was only in the 1450s, therefore, when conjunctural and structural changes within the existing European silver industry, which obtained the precious metal by the cupellation of argentiferous lead, hastened an acute general crisis on international specie markets, that conditions were propitious for the diffusion of the new technology. This, moreover, could not take place before the medieval industry had succumbed to its final death throws. Thus in the short-term from ca. 1442–1462, as the European industry underwent the transition to the new resource base of 8–12.5 ounce silver-lead ores, production by the old methods continued but the situation in which producers found themselves was a highly precarious one. High silver prices coupled with low lead prices minimised the opportunity cost of the lead lost in the refining of low-grade ores, for a moment. This permitted production to continue by traditional methods in old English mining centres (Bere Ferrers, Devon) and the newer workings of the Lyonnais and Beaujolais. With the emergence of resource depletion problems at these centres and rising lead prices in the 1460s, however, they were doomed.[9] The onus of maintaining European silver production now, during the 1460s, shifted elsewhere as rising copper prices, engendered by embargoes on the export of the Balkan product and the collapse of eastern Slovak production, combined with enhanced silver prices to encourage the diffusion of the previously exotic *Saigerprozess*.

A new age was dawning in the history of the European silver industry. The foundations were laid for an entirely new production complex applying the new technologies, including the *Saigerprozess*, to an entirely new resource base of polymetallic ores (argentiferous tin, bismuth, nickel, cobalt and above all copper) in the Saxon and Bohemian Erzgebirge, Thuringia, Slovakia and the lands of the Tyrol. A seemingly never ending flood of silver now from ca. 1460–1540 dominated international precious metal markets and even thereafter from 1540–1560, as decline set in, was not without significance (Figure 1.1/15.1).

In Nuremberg, where interest in the new technology had been sustained during the difficult years 1415–1450, activity was frantic as the new crisis transformed market conditions, the years 1455–1466 witnessing the construction of at least half a dozen

---

8   H. SCHENK, Nürnberg und Prag, in: Giessener Abhandlung zur Agrar- und Wirtschaftsforschung des europäischen Ostens, XLVI (1969).

9   I. BLANCHARD, The British Silver-Lead Industry and its Relations with the Continent 1470–1570. An Outline of Research, in: W. KROKER / E. WESTERMANN (eds.), Montanwirtschaft Mitteleuropas vom 12. bis 17. Jahrhundert. Stand, Weg und Aufgaben der Forschung, Bochum 1984, p. 179s.

Saigerhütten in or about the city.[10] It was the Nurembergers, moreover, who now played a major role in the diffusion of the new technology as they attempted to vertically integrate their concerns by buying into the principal production regions – the Erzgebirge, Tyrol and Thuringia – of their traditional supply networks. Initially from ca. 1460–1477, the primary focus of their activity was the Schneeberg mine in the Saxon Erzgebirge where production rose to ca. 120,000 marks in 1477.[11] When, how-

---

10   E. WESTERMANN, Die Bedeutung des Thüringer Saigerhandels für den mitteleuropäischen Handel an der Wende vom 15. und 16. Jahrhundert, in: Jahrbuch für die Geschichte Mittel- und Ostdeutschlands, XXI (1972), p. 70. Until 1453 the solitary town *Saigerhütte* was under the direction of a number of scribes – Georg Madach (–1436), Fritz Tyrolf (1436–40), Lutz Steinlinger (1440–6) and Sebald Groland (1446–53) – and a single smelter, Eberhard Funck. Then it was leased for six years to the brothers Hans and Leinhardt von Plauen. During the 1430s *Rohkupfer* (=*"raw copper"*, *P. R.*) was bought for this works from Hans von Moren, the Baumgartner, from Albrecht Koch from Zwickau, Poklein from Meissen and from the Stokker and Sebald Tuchenschmid out of Eger, as well as from Kuttenberg through Prague. The lead required was obtained from the Gartner and Haller out of Eger. Subsequent years saw the construction of a number of new works: 1455 by Burkhart Semler, "near the garden of the Erkel"; 1456 by Hans Gresel "am Sandt"; 1457 by a corporation formed by Sebald Groland Jr., Heinrich Meischner, Hans Gartner, Hans and Leinhardt von Plauen and Burkhart Semler. On the Groland family see A. GÜMBEL, Die Nürnberger Goldschmiedfamilie der Groland, in: Mitteilungen aus dem Germanischen Nationalmuseum (1921). Martin Semler, a relative of Burkhart, had since 1445 been a participant in the *Ilmenauer Bergwerkgesellschaft* supplying Thuringian raw copper to the city. In 1460 a works was built by the Tucher at Mögeldorf near the city. On the Tucher see L. GROTE, Die Tucher, Munich 1961. To these works was added in the years to 1465 another hut of Thomas Zyngel and one of Wilhelm Moliter and Ruprecht Haller. Each works, moreover, saw an extension of its corporate capital by the bringing in of new partners like Peter and Hans Tetzel who entered into partnership with Sebald Rothan and Hans Gresel or Leinhardt Ebner, who also joined this corporation. On the Tetzel family see T. G. WENER, Das Kupferhüttenwerk des Hans Tetzel aus Nürnberg auf Kuba, in: Vierteljahrschrift für Sozial- und Wirtschaftsgeschichte, XLVIII (1961), pp. 294–6. Jobst, in partnership with Andreas Harsdorfer, in 1466 built the works at Enzendorf bei Rupprechtstegen. The details of company and family histories used here are derived from E. WESTERMANN, Das Eislebener Garkupfer und seine Bedeutung für den europäischen Kupfermarkt 1460–1560, Cologne / Vienna 1971, App. I–II, pp. 176–185, and C. NORDMANN, Nürnberger Grosshändler im spätmittelalterlichen Lübeck, University of Kiel PhD Thesis, Kiel 1933, supplemented with the individual family histories referred to above.

11   In Saxony at FREIBERG production, which had amounted to ca. 500 marks a year in 1453, thereafter grew steadily, though expansion came not from the working of silver-lead ores but from the exploitation of bismuth-cobalt-nickel-silver formations. On output figures 1450–1510, see J. KÖHLER, Die Keime des Kapitalismus im sächsischen Silberbergbau (1168 bis um 1500), in: Freiberger Forschungsgeschichte, D13 (1955), pp. 113, 120; 1511–1540: W. GOERLITZ, Staat und Stände unter den Herzögen Albrecht und Georg 1485–1539, Leipzig 1928, p. 300; 1540–1568: M. F. GÄTSCHMANN, Vergleichende Übersicht der Ausbeute und des wieder erstatteten Verlages, welche vom Jahr 1530 an bis mit dem Jahr 1850 im Freiberger Revier verteilt wurden, Freiberg 1852. The SCHNEEBERG-SCHLEMA district, covering an area of 400 square kilometres, is mainly made up of crystalline slates and granite with a wide diversity of ores – silver, mercury, cobalt, nickel, tin, lead, iron and manganese – often of considerable richness. The silver bearing ores fall into two main groups: the older with tin, copper, quartz and lead formations includes low grade lead ores, the younger baryt-cobalt and iron formations with rich silver ores and lower grade silver-lead ores. The richest ores were found in the mica and clay-slate districts of the Schneeberg which overlay granite extending from Schlema and falling to the south-west. On output here see for the years 1470–1503: K. HAHN, Die ältesten Schneeberger Zehntrechnungen, in: Neues Archiv für Sächsische Geschichte, NF 53 (1932), p. 32, and 1504–1539, when additional production of high-grade argentiferous copper, containing 3–4 marks of silver per cwt (*Zentner*) in comparison with 18–19

ever, output here collapsed (in 1478–1479, 1481 and 1485) other centres attracted their attention. From ca. 1479–1486, production in the Tyrol and Slovakia increased to compensate for Saxon decline. Neither was capable of replacing the old production centre, however, and these years saw the beginnings of the downswing of the industrial production-cycle. Moreover, when Slovak and Tyrolean production declined during the years 1486–1489, slow decline gave way to collapse as the new industry experienced the first great mining crisis of the new age.[12]

---

with 18–19 lots from Mansfeld, 20 lots from Bohemia and only 9 from Hungarian, from Schlema was included in the statistics: GOERLITZ, Staat und Stände, p. 300. Finally on output 1540–68, see C. MELTZER, Erneuerte Stadt- und Bergchronik der [...] Bergstadt Schneeberg, Schneeberg 1716, p. 690ss. A minor field, production at GEYER was dominated by tin output, though there were also finds of argentiferous copper. Unfortunately data on neither of these products is available, but on silver production see J. FALKE, Geschichte der Bergstadt Geyer, in: Mitteilungen des königlichen sächsischen Vereins für Erforschung und Erhaltung vaterländischer Geschichts- und Kunstdenkmale, XV (1866), p. 34, in which the methodology employed is at Schneeberg-Schlema. The major ore field of ANNABERG with Buchholz and Scheibenberg covered an area of 56 square kilometres situated in a region of upper shales where the bismuth-cobalt-nickel formation yielded the highest grade silver-bearing ores in a cobalt silver structure. On silver production see A. LAUBE, Studien über den erzgebirgischen Silberbergbau von 1470–1546, Berlin 1976, p. 268s., whilst the produce of the tin-silver formations of MARIENBERG is the subject of: W. BOGSCH, Der Marienberger Bergbau in der ersten Hälfte des 16. Jahrhunderts, Schwarzenberg 1933 and ID., Der Marienberger Bergbau seit der zweiten Hälfte des 16. Jahrhunderts, Cologne / Graz 1966, as well as H. KELLENBENZ, Sächsisches und böhmisches Zinn auf dem europäischen Markt, in: ID. / H. POHL (eds.), Historia Socialis et Oeconomica. Festschrift für Wolfgang Zorn zum 65. Geburtstag, Stuttgart 1987, p. 239.

12 The metalliferous zone of the ALPENLANDS comprising the Tyrol, Bixen, Trentino, Salzburg, Steiermark and Kärnten, as well as the Venetian Alps encompassed an enormous number of mines of both precious and base metals. Amongst their number, however, one – the *Falkenstein* mine near Schwaz – reigned supreme in the sphere of silver production. Activity here commenced in ca. 1420 but for slightly less than half a century the argentiferous copper deposits of the Falkenstein mine remained subordinate to the silver-lead ones of Brixen (Gossensass, Sterzing, Klausen, Terlen and Schneeberg). With the diffusion of the new techniques, however, it went from strength to strength, already in ca. 1500, when the industry organized into twenty corporations each with its own smelter employed 7,000 miners, producing 40,000 marks of *Brandsilber* a year and subsequently rising to 55,800 marks a year in 1523 before decline set in. On production at Falkenstein during these years, see for 1470–91: S. WORMS, Schwazer Bergbau im 15. Jahrhundert. Ein Beitrag zur Wirtschaftsgeschichte, Vienna 1905, p. 173, the data in this study being derived from Register 3078 in the K.u.K. Court Library, Vienna, and presented on the basis of an accounting year beginning at Christmas; for 1491–1536: A. JÄGER, Beiträge zur Tirolisch-Salzburgischen Bergwerks-Geschichte, in: Archiv für Österreichische Geschichte, Vol. LIII (1875), pp. 431–6, duplicating and extending Worm's series. These series of silver output may also be supplemented with regards to silver and copper by reference to E. EGG, Das Wirtschaftswunder der silbernen Schwaz. Der Silber- und Fahlerzbergbau am Falkenstein im 15. und 16. Jahrhundert, in: Leobener Grüne Hefte, XXXI, Vienna 1958, pp. 12, 20, 24 and 26 which provides decennial averages of silver and copper production derived from two registers in the Innsbruck *Landesregierungsarchiv*: Leopoldina Litt. S. Nr. 102 (register of total silver and copper production delivered by the mining corporations, 1470–1605) and Pestarchiv XIV, Nr. 897 (register of yearly production of silver delivered by the mining corporations, 1470–1623). The studies of Worms, Jäger and Egg, together with that of M. VON ISSER GAUDENTHURM, Schwazer Bergwerksgeschichte, in: Berg- und Hüttenmännisches Jahrbuch der kk. Montanistischen Hochschule zu Leoben und Pribram, LII (1904) & LIII (1905), have, however, now been superseded by the critical edition of the production data by E. WESTERMANN who, by carefully collating all copies of the production figures and subjecting them to critical scrutiny in E. WESTERMANN, Zur Brandsilber- und Kupferproduktion des Falken-

After the mining crisis of 1486–1492 the European silver industry entered upon a new developmental stage under a new industrial management. The second production-cycle of the European silver industry, which ran its course during the years 1492–1522/6, witnessed a major structural change as output, within the existing industrial base, recovered to, and stabilised at previous peak levels of ca. 120,000 marks of silver a year. Within what had previously been the principal mining centres – Saxony and the Tyrol – there was a counter-cyclical movement of production between the two centres but about the debased combined output levels of about 1480, namely ca. 75,000 marks a year or about three-quarters of the 1477 peak. The previously minor Slovak and Thuringian production centres[13], however, now came into their own, out-

---

steins bei Schwaz 1470–1623. Eine Kritik bisheriger Ermittlungen von Produktionsziffern, in: Tiroler Heimat, L (1986), pp. 109–125, ID., Sammlung 'Stephan Worms' im Haus-, Hof- und Staatsarchiv Wien. Eine Fundgrube für Montanhistoriker, in: Der Anschnitt, XXXVIII, 1 (1986) and ID., Über Beobachtungen und Erfahrungen bei der Vorbereitung der Edition einer vorindustriellen Produktionsstatistik. Zur Brandsilberproduktion des Falkenstein bei Schwaz/Tirol von 1470–1623, in: E. WESTERMANN (ed.), Quantifizierungsprobleme bei der Erforschung der Montanwirtschaft des 15. bis 18. Jahrhunderts, St. Katharinen 1988, pp. 27–42, has produced what must be the definitive edition of the production statistics: ID. Die Listen der Brandsilberproduktion des Falkenstein bei Schwaz/Tirol von 1470–1623. Kommentar und Edition, in: Leobener Grüne Hefte, VII, Vienna 1987. Far less satisfactory is the data on the other mines of the *Schwazer Revier* – the *Alte Zeche* and *Ringenwechsel* – contained in E. EGG, Schwaz ist aller Bergwerke Mutter, in: Der Anschnitt, XVI, 3 (1964), pp. 21, 25s., or on the new mining regions opened up after 1540 including *Röhrerbichl bei Kitzbühel*, a deposit 4 kilometres long by 100 metres wide, yielding argentiferous copper ores, whose output is recorded in M. WOLFSTRIGL-WOLFSKRON, Der Tiroler Erzbergbau, 1321–1665, Innsbruck 1902, p. 193; the Steiermark workings at Schladming and Öbarn – H. KUNNERT, Die Silberversorgung österreichischer Münzstätten durch den Schladminger Bergbau im XVI. und Anfang des XVII. Jahrhunderts, in: Numismatische Zeitschrift, LXI (1928), p. 23 and ID., Beiträge zur Geschichte des Bergbaues im Berggerichtsbezirk Schladming in den Jahren 1304 bis 1616, Diss. Vienna 1927, p. 81 and M. WENGER, Ein Beitrag zur Statistik und Geschichte des Bergbaubetriebes in den österreichischen Alpenländern im 16. Jahrhundert, in: Montanische Rundschau, XXIII (1931), pp. 225ss., 239ss. and 247ss. – and Radmer – K. A. REDLICH, Der Kupferbergbau Radmer an der Hasel, in: Berg- und Hüttenmännisches Jahrbuch, LIII (1905), or the Kärnten workings described by H. WIESNER, Geschichte des Kärntener Bergbaus, 2 Vols., Klagenfurt 1951, II, p. 276ss.

13   THURINGIA: Information concerning *Rohkupfer* production is derived from two sources. First, contemporary accounts of total production, detailing the output of individual smelters, together with details of the tenth and fifth (of the tenth) due the lord, such as are presented in WESTERMANN, Garkupfer, pp. 192–5, and ID., Hans Luther und die Hüttenmeister der Grafschaft Mansfeld im 16. Jahrhundert. Eine Forschungsaufgabe, in: Scripta Mercatura, 9 (1975), pp. 68–86. Second there are the accounts of the lordly fifth, collected from each corporation with occasionally particular accounts detailing the quantity and quality of the copper collected as presented in WESTERMANN, Garkupfer, pp. 217–8. Indirect evidence is provided by accounts and contracts of the sale of the lordly tenth. In each case the total amount of money collected is recorded with the price per cwt (*Zentner*). From 1522 the price quoted is that of a *Zentner* containing 16 lots of silver and for each lot of silver above or below this norm half a florin was added or subtracted (WESTERMANN, Garkupfer, pp. 201–10). The total figure is thus a composite and surviving particulars from 1547–61 reveal the quantities and qualities of copper delivered (WESTERMANN, Garkupfer, pp. 198–200). These data provide the basis for the statistics employed in Figure 1.1/15.1. Copper: WESTERMANN, Garkupfer, pp. 236, 251, and silver: ibid., pp. 247, 251. It should be noted, however, that many of these figures (e.g. 1506–9, 1514, 1522, 1526–7) are estimates involving the conversion of renders into production statistics, a process involving Professor Westermann in a number of assumptions: (1) that the composition of the production mix remained

put therein rising during the years from 1492 to 1503–6/1509–12 to some 35,000 marks a year and thereby stabilising aggregate industrial output during the years 1503–1526 at previous peak levels. Long-term stabilisation of silver output between 1503 and 1526, however, was also associated with periodic short-term destabilisation. The industry became subject to successive crises (in 1503–1506/1509–1512, 1514–1515 and 1519–1522) during which output declined in the older mining centres of Saxony and the Tyrol and growth in Thuringia and Slovakia was insufficient to compensate. Particularly during the years 1503–1526, therefore, a new production pattern had emerged within the European industry associated with the rise of new production centres, as the Tyrol and Thuringia rose to a position of supremacy in the industry totally eclipsing Saxony.

No less significant were the changes also taking place at this time in the managerial structure of the industry. That group headed by Nurembergers, who had dominated operations during the first, Saxon mining boom, culled of some of their numbers during the crisis of 1486–1492, continued to control activity in the North. This was only achieved, however, through an internal transformation of their operations as from 1492–1526 they severed their ties with the declining Saxon industry and transferred the focus of their activity to Thuringia. From 1492–1503 this process was a slow one, as alternative investment opportunities in the Saxon tin industry[14] and a revival in silver production associated with the development of the Annaberg deposits 1498–1504[15] continued to hold many of their number in thrall. Thus that old link between Nuremberg, Saxony and all points East was maintained whilst their peers engaged in the Thuringian industry and its supply systems re-orientated their activities towards the Frankfurt Fairs and Antwerp beyond. From 1503 and particularly during the years 1503–1506/1509–1512 and 1519–1526, however, the movement gained strength. By the latter date the second-generation entrepreneurs of the original Leipzig and Nuremberg families undertook a wholesale abandonment of their old Saxon interests which now became but a minor adjunct of what were essentially Thuringian enterprises. Nor was this pattern of local control other than replicated in the South where Tyrolean cor-

the same as that of the years 1547–61, viz. 16–7 lots per *Zentner* throughout the period; (2) that the price deflator was that of 16-lot copper; (3) that the tenth of Hettstedt production, which was included in the composite sale, was related to the tenth of Eisleben-Mansfeld production in the ratio 1:14 and that relative prices of the two coppers were in the ratio 2:3; (4) that in the period to 1514 when the tenth was only collected on the *Erbfeuer* works, the *Herrenfeuer* works paying a fixed tax, the former contributed 48% of production (WESTERMANN, Garkupfer, pp. 197–203). Moreover, it must be borne in mind that in the three years (1508, 1522 and 1527) when the estimate can be checked against direct evidence there is an increasing divergence between the two. As the third and fourth assumptions above may be checked against near contemporary direct evidence and prices are contemporary ones for 16-lot copper, it is thus possible that assumption (1) is in error and that the silver content of the copper was falling over the period under consideration. *If* this is the case, then between 1506–27 estimated silver production (estimated by multiplying copper production by a constant yield of 1.053 marks per *Zentner*) markedly overestimates actual silver production derived from copper of declining silver content (1508=15.5, 1522=10, and 1527=4 lots/*Zentner*).

14   See chapter 16 below
15   See note 11 above.

corporations had assumed an industrial hegemony in the 1480s.[16] They continued to dominate activity at Schwaz in recession, crisis and boom alike between 1492 and 1526, only ceding ground during the early 'twenties as successive crises wracked the industry.

Yet whilst the long-established merchant houses, through their constant movement of funds, continued to maintain their positions in the essentially local foci of regional trading systems a new force emerged which particularly during the years 1492–1526 would weld these elements into an international trans-continental network. Indeed even during the *Gründerzeit* of the industry there are indications that such changes were underway. At this time, in the 1470s, the Nuremberg Rummel laid the foundations of an enterprise spanning each of the major production regions – Erzgebirge (Freiberg), Tyrol (Rattenberg and Schwaz) and Thuringia – which subsequently became an element in an even more extensive Nuremberg family group network.[17] It was, however, during the second production-cycle of the industry (1492–1526) that such enterprises became common. During these years Augsburg houses, and most notably the Fugger, began to forge trans-regional production links.[18] In the context of

---

16 See note 12 above.

17 C. SHAPER, Die Ratsfamilie Rumel – Kaufleute, Finanziers und Unternehmer, in: MVGN, LXVIII (1981). A series of articles by L. SUHLING, Innovationen im Montanwesen der Renaissance. Zur Frühgeschichte des Tiroler Abdarrprozesses, in: Technikgeschichte, XLII (1975), pp. 119–36; ID., Herzog Ludwig der Reiche als Montanunternehmer am Inn. Versuch eines Technologietransfers von Nürnberg nach Brixlegg in den Jahren 1467/8, in: Veröffentlichungen des Museum Ferdinandeum, LVII (1977), pp. 119–36 and ID., Bergbau, Territorialherrschaft und technologischer Wandel. Prozessinnovationen im Montanwesen der Renaissance am Beispiel der mitteleuropäischen Silberproduktion, in: U. TROITZSCH / G. WOHLAUF (eds.), Technikgeschichte. Historische Beiträge und neuere Ansätze, Frankfurt-on-the-Main 1980, pp. 139–79, and WESTERMANN, Garkupfer, pp. 267ss. and E. WESTERMANN, Zur den verwandtschaftlichen und geschäftlichen Beziehungen der Praun, Frohler und Muhlich vom Nürnberg, Erfurt und Lübeck in der zweiten Hälfte des 15. Jahrhunderts, in: Wirtschaftsgeschichte und Personengeschichte. Festschrift für Wolfgang von Stromer, Trier 1987 provide much information on the diffusion of the Saigerprozess from Nuremberg to the Tyrol and on the close technological links, provided by the Rummel and associated family of Fasolt, between the works of Rattenberg and Schwaz and those of Thuringia, the available evidence being drawn together in a valuable diagram in: E. WESTERMANN, Zur Silber- und Kupferproduktion Mitteleuropas vom 15. bis zum frühen 17. Jahrhundert. Über Bedeutung und Rangfolge der Reviere vom Schwaz, Mansfeld und Neusohl, in: Der Anschnitt, XXXVIII, 5/6 (1986), p. 194, which supplements the information on the family's activities in Nuremberg and Saxony in WERNER, Kupferhüttenwerk, pp. 326–7.

18 SLOVAKIA. On the enterprise during the period of the *Fugger-Thurzo Gesellschaft* 1494–1547, see VLACHOVIC, Slovenská Med, pp. 53, 58, 101 and ID., Die Kupfererzeugung und der Kupferhandel in der Slowakei vom Ende des 15. bis zur Mitte des 17.Jahrhunderts, in: H. KELLENBENZ (ed.), Schwerpunkte der Kupferproduktion und des Kupferhandels in Europa 1500–1650, Cologne / Vienna 1977, pp. 170–1 on ore, copper and silver production. Data on total sales from the Neusohl, Hohenkirchen and Fuggerau works, together with information on sales at Venice, Stettin and Danzig is presented in H. VAN DER WEE, The Growth of the Antwerp Market and the European Economy, Fourteenth–Sixteenth Centuries, The Hague 1963, I, Appendix 44/1, pp. 522–3. Information on direct sales from Hohenkirchen is provided by E. KOCH, Das Hütten und Hammerwerk der Fugger zu Hohenkirchen bei Georgenthal in Thüringen, 1495–1549, in: Zeitschrift des Vereins für Thüringische Geschichte und Altertumskunde, NF, XXVI (1926), pp. 322–7 and NF, XXVII (1927), pp. 5–40. Part of the Thuringian output was distributed, however, via Leipzig and as such was the responsibility of the Fugger factor there. For a summary of such sales see T. SOMERLAD, Die Faktorei der Fugger in Leipzig, in: Schriften des Vereins für die Geschichte Leip-

reorganising with Jan Thurzo the Slovak industry and in response to problems in the Tirolean industry, the Fugger took the first steps in this direction creating a great trans-regional mining and metallurgical enterprise. This was centred on Neusohl but with works, utilising Slovak "black" copper, in Thuringia (Hohenkirchen) and Kärnten (Fuggerau). Nor did this new system solely introduce intrusive independent elements into existing production centres. A supporting raw material supply system was created. This combined the old trading network to Venice and Nuremberg with a new one through Leipzig to Thuringia. A commercial network distributing refined copper to markets from the North Sea to the Mediterranean, served also to link the regional systems to those of the wider world. Building on the foundations laid by the Rummel, the Fugger thus during the years 1492–1504 afforded the participants in the regional systems access to an international network which during the years 1504–1526 was steadily strengthened as other Augsburg houses – notably the Paumgartner and Hörwart – emulated the Fugger creating trans-regional enterprises. By 1526, the previously autonomous regional trading systems, associated with central European silver production, had been welded into an integrated international network.

Then in 1527/8 the whole system collapsed. In part, as during the crisis of 1477/8, this marked the end of the prevailing production-cycle, subsequent crises in 1530/1 and 1536–1538 (as in 1480/1 and 1486–1492) pushing output in existing production centres to lower and lower levels. On this occasion, however, there was no inter-cyclical crisis like that of 1486–1492. The third production-cycle, based upon the exploitation of the Bohemian deposits of Joachimsthal and the Saxon ones of Marienberg and upon the redevelopment of the Freiberg, Schneeberg and Annaberg mines, had already commenced in 1516. Overlapping with the second production-cycle this served to push aggregate output levels once again upwards to ca. 140,000 marks a year at the end of the first developmental stage in 1527.[19] It then increased again to ca. 180,000 marks at the end of the second in 1540 before output declined and the production-cycle closed in the acute crises of 1541–1542 and 1545–1547.[20] During the course of this third production-cycle, in 1540, therefore the European silver producer attained the pinnacle of his achievement, output rising to a level which would never be surpassed again in the sixteenth century. Paradoxically, however, it was at

---

zigs, XXII, (1938), p. 45 which may be amplified by reference to G. PÖLNITZ, Jakob Fugger, Tübingen 1949–51, II, pp. 285–6, 297, 431. The works of J. VLACHOVIC should also be consulted regarding subsequent lessees, 1548–68. Further information on the organization of production may be gleaned from: F. DOBEL, Der Fugger Bergbau und Handel in Ungarn, in: Zeitschrift des historischen Vereins für Schwaben und Neuberg, VI (1879), pp. 33–50; M. JANSEN, Jakob Fugger der Reiche (Leipzig, 1926), pp. 287–327; L. SCHICK, Un grand homme d'affaires au début du XVI siècle: Jakob Fugger, Paris 1957; J. VLACHOVIC, Hutnícke spracúvanie medenych rúd v Banskej Bistrici v druhej polovine 16 storice, in: Historické Stúdia, V (1960), pp. 110–48. The latter two studies are particularly valuable on production techniques.

19 BOHEMIAN ERZGEBIRGE: K. STERNBERG, Umrisse einer Geschichte der böhmischen Bergwerke, Prague 1836–8, Vol. 1/2, pp. 415–27; G. W. SCHENK, Über die Anfänge des Silberbergbaues von St. Joachimsthal, in: Der Anschnitt, XX, 5 (1968), p. 21 and ID. Strucny nástin dejin hornického dobyvání v Jáchymové, in: Rozpravy Narodniho Technickeho Muzea v Praze, XL (1970), pp. 4–36; H. STURM, Skizzen zur Geschichte des Obererzgebirges im 16. Jahrhundert, in: Forschungen zur Geschichte und Landeskunde der Sudeten, V (1965), pp. 105ss.

20 See note 11 above.

this time that the previously highly integrated trans-continental system of industrial production began to disintegrate. Following the crisis of 1527/8 the existing group of merchant-industrialists was split asunder. Those Augsburgers and Nurembergers who had dominated the industry during the second production-cycle and who survived the crash of 1527/8 now displayed very little interest in developments in the Erzgebirge. In relation to their European operations, they concentrated on the manipulation of copper markets rather than involving themselves in the new centres of silver production and trade.[21] These operations now became the preserve of the Nuremberg Welser, Schütz and their associates.[22] Even as European silver production reached peak output levels the group of merchant-industrialists who had controlled the industry's destiny to 1527/8 showed signs of disintegrating. When, during the fourth production-cycle of the industry (1537–1568), expansion gave way to decline, this tendency towards disintegration became even more pronounced.

Relentlessly, during the course of the fourth production-cycle (1537–1568) European output of argentiferous copper declined. This had disastrous effects on silver production which fell during the years 1540–1547 from 180,000 to 120,000 marks a year before stabilising at that level to 1561 when a further phase of rapid decline reduced output to 80,000 marks a year in 1568. The long-cycle, that with the diffusion of the *Saigerprozess*, had begun a century before in the 1460s, was coming to its end. The tail of the production-curve might be a long one, three more production-cycles running their course before the industry was finally extinguished, but to all intents, the fourth production-cycle marked the end of the central European silver industry. It also witnessed the final disintegration of that group of entrepreneurs whose fortunes had rested upon their central European mining interests. Of the great houses who had presided over the industry during its hey-day only the Fugger remained and they witnessed the gradual attrition of the lesser houses who had once been the clients of the great. One by one, these houses fell, their assets in many cases being taken over by state-owned enterprises. In their place came others, notably the Haug and their associates[23] and the Manlich[24], but they and the Fugger were more concerned with the

21   See studies concerning these companies in n. 10 above; WESTERMANN, Garkupfer, pp. 266–83; E. EGG, Hans Auslasser, in: Schwazer Weihnachtsbote, 1954 and on the Fugger: PÖLNITZ, Jakob Fugger, ID., Anton Fugger, 3 Vols., Tübingen, 1958–67, as well as J. STRIEDER (ed.), Die Inventur der Firma Fugger aus dem Jahr 1527, in: Zeitschrift für die gesamte Staatswissenschaft, Ergänzungsheft XVII (1905), and G. PÖLNITZ, Die Fuggersche Generalrechnung von 1563, in: Kyklos, XX (1967), pp. 355–370. The phenomenon of the transition from silver to copper production has been described by Professor WESTERMANN in a number of places but most fully in: WESTERMANN, Zur Silber- und Kupferproduktion Mitteleuropas, pp. 188–194.

22   T. G. WERNER, Das fremde Kapital im Annaberger Bergbau und Metallhandel des 16. Jahrhundert, in: Neues Archiv für Sächsische Geschichte und Altertumskunde, LVII (1936) and LVIII (1937); R. KLIER, Zur Genealogie der Bergunternehmerfamilie Schütz in Nürnberg und Mitteldeutschland im 15. und 16. Jahrhundert, MVGN, LV (1967/8); E. STIMMEL, Die Familie Schütz, in: Abhandlungen des Staatlichen Museums für Mineralogie und Geologie zu Dresden, XI (1966).

23   J. HARTUNG, Aus dem Geheimbuche eines deutschen Handelshauses im 16. Jahrhundert, in: Zeitschrift für Sozial- und Wirtschaftsgeschichte, VI (1898), pp. 39–63; F. HASSLER, Der Ausgang der Augsburger Handelsgesellschaft Anton Haug, Hans Langnauer, Ulrich Link und Miterwandt Augsburg 1926; J. MEILINGER, Der Warenhandel der Augsburger Handelsgesellschaft Anton Haug, Hans Langnauer, Ulrich Link und Miterwandt, Univ. Diss. Leipzig 1911, and F. W. RING-

manipulation of copper markets than with the production of silver, which had become an affair of but little import.

Only briefly interrupted, the central European silver industry underwent during the years 1460–1560, a major long-cycle. This carried output to unprecedented heights. Production rose rapidly to ca. 120,000 marks in 1477 and then more slowly to ca. 180,000 marks in 1540 before decline commenced reducing output to ca. 80,000 marks in 1568. Even as this production long-cycle ran its course, moreover, there was superimposed upon it a pattern of medium term, resource-related production cycles which followed each other at about 30-year intervals and displayed a pattern of alternating spatial displacement. During the first (1460–1491) and third (1516/22–1542/7) production sub-cycles the bismuth-cobalt-nickel-silver mines of the Erzgebirge rose to a position of supremacy. During the second (1492–1522/6) and fourth (1537/42–1568) they were displaced by the argentiferous copper workings of the Thuringian-Slovak and Tyrolean production complex. Only for brief periods (1500–1513 and 1547–1560) did the constituent elements exist in a state of equilibrium.

On each of those occasions when the *Saigerhändler* (=*merchants involved in the organization and finance of the 'Saiger' process'*, P. R.) of the Thuringian-Slovak and Tyrolean production complex held centre stage (1492–1522/6 and 1537/42–1568) these entrepreneurs' insatiable demand for lead as a refining agent caused them to totally dominate the market within which English producers of that metal operated. In undermining at these times the competitive position of Saxon silver producers who exploited bismuth-cobalt-nickel-silver ores, moreover, they also caused this latter group of entrepreneurs to seek out new sources of silver supply including the argentiferous tins of the Saxon-Bohemian Erzgebirge. Thereby by their investments in these stanniferous deposits they created a major competitor to the English tin producer.

The English Trade and European Lead Supply Systems.[25] Large amounts of lead were required for the successful extraction of silver from argentiferous copper (probably amounting to about 0.4–0.55 cwt. of lead per cwt. of "black" copper) in the *Saigerhütten*. Both temporal and spatial changes within the central European silver industry, accordingly, exerted a major influence on the fortunes of the lead producer. During each production-cycle of the Thuringian-Slovak and Tyrolean mining and metallurgical complex (in 1492–1522/6 and 1537/42–1568) the *Saigerhändler* exploiting the argentiferous copper deposits of these regions evinced an almost insatiable demand for supplies of lead. At the height of the sectoral long-cycle, central European argentiferous copper production amounted to ca. 4,800 tonnes a year during the years 1525–1535.[26] At that time this sector of the industry consumed ca. 2,650 tonnes of

---

LING, Sixteenth-Century Merchant Capitalism: the Haug-Langnauer-Linck and Relatives of Augsburg as a case study, Unpubl. University of Rochester Ph.D thesis, Rochester 1979.

24 Apart from the studies of VLACHOVICH referred to in note 18 above, see F. ROTH, Zum Bankrott der Firma Melchior Manlich, in: Zeitschrift des historischen Vereins für Schwaben und Neuberg, XXXV (1908).

25 For a much fuller consideration of English lead production and trade in a European context the reader is referred to I. BLANCHARD, International Lead Production and Trade in the "Age of the Saigerprozess," 1460–1560, Stuttgart 1995, upon which the following section is based.

26 R. HILDEBRANDT, Augsburger und Nürnberger Kupferhandel, 1500–1619, in: Zeitschrift für Wirtschafts- und Sozialwissenschaften, XCII/1 (1972), p. 3.

lead a year or about two-thirds of European annual lead output. It is thus clear that the *Saigerhütten* of the area totally dominated the demand for the products of the European lead industry.

In the formulation of their supply responses to these alterations in demand the lead producers were no less influenced by other changes taking place within the silver industry. The diffusion of the *Saigerprozess* in the 1460s and the resultant expansion in the production of silver from argentiferous copper ores had transformed the situation of the silver-lead producer who had, particularly in continental Europe, previously been a major supplier of "sterile" lead to the market. The stabilization of silver prices in conditions of endemic resource depletion rendered the exploitation of low-grade silver-lead ores unviable. The returns from the sale of the precious metal were small and the losses of the by-product "sterile" lead, inherent in the refining of supplies of "fertile" lead smelted from low concentrate ores by the old methods, unacceptable. Everywhere the silver producer utilizing traditional techniques to exploit deposits of argentiferous lead ores was therefore in the years after 1460 in retreat in the face of competition from central European entrepreneurs employing the new *Saigerprozess*. Yet paradoxically, the new technology which posed such a threat to the old argentiferous lead mines in the 1460s and subsequently caused their displacement as major suppliers of the European silver market also provided the means for their survival, through the creation of a new market – for "fertile" lead. The works employing the new technology had an almost insatiable appetite for lead, which when mixed with argentiferous "black" copper in the *Saigerhütten* allowed the separation of the precious metal from the copper. That technology also set a premium on silver-bearing lead in comparison with the non-argentiferous product for when mixed in the hearth with the "black" copper the lead not only took up the silver contained in that metal but also combined it with the silver content of the lead. The "fertile" lead if processed on its own in a cupellation hearth could only be made to yield up a part of its silver content by the creation of a "hard" and totally unvendable "sterile" lead. When employed in a *Saigerhütte*, however, by combining its silver with that in the argentiferous copper, it could be made to yield up the whole. *Saigerhändler*, accordingly, able to secure this silver were prepared to pay a premium for "fertile" lead. Thereby they allowed the producers of argentiferous lead to offset enhanced mining costs and to continue production in the face of competition from the non-argentiferous sector of the lead industry.

Access to lead markets frequented by central European *Saigerhändler* thus became a major determinant in the fortunes of silver-lead producers. From the beginning of the central European silver boom, members of this group in the Harz and Poland participated in the creation of a commercial system to take advantage of the new situation.[27] From ca. 1460, Polish and Silesian producers normally smelted the ores of Olkusz, Tarnowitz, Beuthen and Schweidnitz. They sold the resultant "soft" lead unrefined. Output rose through a series of short-term booms (peaking in ca. 1470, 1512/3 and 1530–1536) to a level of some 3,170 tonnes a year in ca. 1536. Thereafter the industry commenced on a long-term decline again characterised by a series of short-term fluctuations (peaking in 1549–1558 and 1560–1565) but now also by a counter-

27   BLANCHARD, International Lead Production, Appendix 1/2a–b, pp. 209–16.

vailing production pattern between the minor (Olkusz) and major (Tarnowitz) sectors of the industry. Nor was the situation markedly different in Harz. Here production also increased in a series of production booms (peaking in ca. 1480, 1503–1506 and 1525–1527) to a peak level of 1,034 tonnes in ca. 1526/7 before again undergoing a protracted decline associated with a series of short-term production fluctuations (peaking in 1537/42--1548 and 1560–1565). From ca. 1460 the "fertile" lead or *frisches Blei* smelted in the works of Polish and Harz producers was thus normally dispatched in an unrefined state to the central European *Saigerhütten*, thereby creating a distinctive sector of an expanding lead trade. Output distributed through this trading network, moved counter-cyclically between the two centres. First, from 1490–1525/7 Harz assumed a dominant position. Then from 1527/8–1565, Poland displaced it. Total production in these centres, steadily increased, rising to ca. 3,673 tonnes a year on average in the early 1530s before declining thereafter to 1,630 tonnes in the early 1560s (Figure 15.2). Conditions in the lead trade now largely determined the fortunes of Polish and Harz lead producers even dictating when and if they could refine the metal they produced. In normal circumstances, they vended the metal in an unrefined state. It was only when the lead trade from these regions was interrupted and prices fell that the losses of the base metal inherent in refining were rendered acceptable, allowing producers to revert to their earlier role as extractors of silver from the argentiferous lead. Thus in Harz it was predominantly during that period, ca 1531–1547 when the industry's products were subordinated to those of Poland on international markets that refining of the fertile lead was undertaken. Some 5,600 marks of silver a year were produced during the years 1531–1535 before increasing lead sales from 1537/42–1547 caused a reduction of refining and silver production. In Poland it was only when intersectoral shifts in production caused a reduction of local lead prices (at Krakow in 1536–1538, 1562–1564 and at Olkusz in 1549–1551, 1558–1561) in conditions of enhanced silver prices that producers in Silesia and Little Poland undertook the refining of argentiferous lead. The initial high production levels of 17,000 marks a year in Tarnowitz during 1536-1538 soon fell to about 3,000 marks a year during subsequent slumps in the lead trade at Olkusz (in 1549–1551 and 1558–1561) and Tarnowitz (1562–1564).

The English mine which had enjoyed a central position amongst European silver producers in the 1450s underwent similar fundamental changes during the following century but was rendered marginal in relation to the newly created "fertile" lead trade network.[28] Throughout the period from ca. 1460–1560, in spite of the decline in silver and lead production and the displacement from the 1540s of activity from Bere Ferrers to Treworthie, mining activity in the workings of the south-western peninsula continued unabated. Moreover, when disruptions in European silver markets caused the price of the white metal to rise, as in 1527/8 or 1550/1 this basic output was augmented as marginal deposits of silver-lead ore were exploited. On no occasion, however, was more than 25–50 "bolls" (1 boll = ca. 7 cwt. of ore) a year produced from these marginal deposits, output of argentiferous lead ore continuing at ca. 2,300 "bolls" a year from ca. 1460–1560. Nor in "normal" circumstances was the silver extracted from the lead after smelting. Only in the most exceptional circumstances of

---

28   Ibid., Appendix 1/2c, pp. 217–219.

low lead prices, in 1538–1539 and 1552–1563, were attempts made to obtain silver from English "fertile" lead and then with only very meagre results. Usually, the unrefined product was delivered to the market. Given the high cost of Devon lead, the product of deep-mining operations, on only one occasion in 1519–1523/1527–1530 did it briefly come to the fore. On this occasion, 44 and 15 tons of "fertile" lead respectively were shipped to the Netherlands. Here the true character of the metal may well have been recognised by a young factor of the house of Höchstetter. He subsequently, during his British visit of 1526–1529, utilized the knowledge when he tried to secure control of the Devon mines as part of his attempt to garner supplies for the central European industry. At other times, the product was virtually unvendable. Even in the most favourable of circumstances (in 1486–1492 and 1503–1506) the Devon industry supported only small local sales on the Exeter market and an export trade amounting to 2.5–5 tons a year. For a brief moment, however, during the 1520s, the English industry had been integrated into the marketing system from which the Harz and Polish producer had for so long benefited, and production and exports of Devon "fertile" lead had briefly increased.

Figure 15.2: "Fertile" Lead Production, 1470–1570

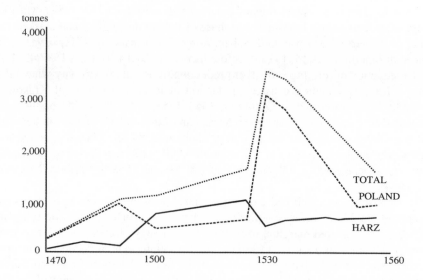

Elsewhere in Europe in those silver-lead mines where producers lacked any access to central European lead markets the situation was very different.[29] Their story was one of an unrelenting struggle to exploit by traditional means low-grade ores. Even in favourable circumstances (in 1486–1492, 1501–1508, 1516/9–1522 and 1527–1530, 1539–1542 and 1549–1552/62) these could be made to yield only small quantities of silver. This was obtained, moreover, only with enormous lead losses and the production of "hard" leads totally unvendable and in "normal" circumstances not worth working at all. Such production centres did not contribute to the international lead trade.

In a host of enterprises, exploiting argentiferous lead deposits the "Age of the *Saigerprozess*" was thus one of gloom and despondency. As the new technology was assimilated and the production of silver from argentiferous copper ores rapidly increased, the resultant stabilization of silver prices in conditions of endemic resource depletion rendered the exploitation of low-grade silver-lead ores unviable. The returns from the sale of the precious metal were small and the losses of the by-product "sterile" lead, inherent in the refining of supplies of "fertile" lead smelted from low concentrate ores by the old methods, unacceptable. Accordingly, across Europe silver producers utilizing traditional techniques to exploit deposits of argentiferous lead ores were in the years after 1460 in retreat, assuming the role of price takers in a market dominated by Central European producers. In "normal" circumstances, production came to a halt. Only in periods of high silver prices, occasioned by major mining crisis in central Europe, was production restarted as increasing quantities of silver-lead ores were raised and smelted and the resultant "fertile" lead was driven hard to yield up its meagre silver content. The results on these occasions were usually disappointing but to achieve even these diminutive levels of silver production a highly enriched "fertile" lead had to be made which was resistant to refining and produced a hard "sterile" lead which was totally unvendable. The contribution of producers in this sector of the argentiferous lead industry to both silver and lead markets was thus negligible during the years from ca. 1460–1560.

Only where such producers could find an alternative outlet for their wares could they undertake that organizational transformation of their enterprises, which was necessary for their survival in the new age. Thus in Harz, Poland and, during the years 1519–1523/1526–1529, England such producers finding that they could dispose of "fertile" lead on markets catering to the requirements of central European *Saigerhändler* abandoned the refining of this metal and began to provision an entirely new and rapidly expanding "fertile" lead trade.

The ability of the "fertile" lead smelter to sell in this new market was constrained, however, by the existence of an alternative source of lead supply – the English non-argentiferous lead producer. These producers, due to their unique form of industrial organization, operated at relatively low-cost levels. Production in this sector of the lead industry had in the mid-fifteenth century, because of acute resource depletion problems and a secular and cyclical decline in demand for lead amongst its aristocratic consumers, been reduced to low ebb.[30] As from ca. 1468 the central European

---

29   Ibid., Appendix 1/3, pp. 219–229.

30   Ibid., Appendix 2, pp. 231–288.

Saigerhändler commenced on that path which would ensure their hegemony over the continent's silver production, however, the English non-argentiferous lead producers' market situation was transformed. Henceforth during the course of the first two great production-cycles of the new central European copper-silver industry (ca. 1456–1486 and 1492–1522/6) the products of the English non-argentiferous lead industry passed almost exclusively to the export trade. The production and export of English lead increased during each successive trade boom (in 1470–1486, 1493–1503/1506–1509 and 1531–1534) from 80 tons in 1464 to 311 tons in 1473, 625 tons in 1508 and 750 tons in 1518. Thereafter it declined in conditions of acute resource depletion to 625 tons in 1531 (Figure 15.3).[31]

Year after year, in "normal" trading conditions the merchants of Hull carried northern English lead as ballast in the ships of the wool fleet to Netherlands marts. Their Bristol counterparts exported the Mendip product to southern France and Spain. The greater part of English lead production entered international trade. It not only dominated the markets of the continental seaboard but also penetrated deep inland. When financial-monetary crises or commercial embargoes at the Netherlands marts (in 1486–1493, 1503–1506, 1509–1513, 1519–1523 and 1527–1530) disrupted the important east-coast lead trade, moreover, at least initially, the growth of this commerce was not seriously impeded. During the crises of 1486–1493 and 1503–1506, an "alternative" commercial network centred on London emerged. Hanseatic, Spanish and French merchants drove a direct trade to the sources of English lead thereby allowing market stabilization. Only during the subsequent crises in 1509–1513 and 1519–1523 with their withdrawal from the capital was the lead trade seriously disturbed, before in 1527/8 exports once more rose to some 800 tons a year.[32] Then during the years after 1535 this 'old', carefully organized lead trade, which had formed a vital element in that commercial network serving the needs of the silver and copper producers – the *Saigerhändler* – of central Europe, was virtually destroyed by a new competitor emanating from an unexpected source. Monastic lead, the accumulated product of generations of English ecclesiastical building, stripped from its centuries-long resting-place by the rapacious hand of an iconoclastic king, suddenly from 1536 entered the market.[33] Henceforth when unimpeded by restrictions arising from either the vagaries of royal fiscal policy or financial-monetary disorders across the Channel, in 1536–1538 and 1542–1549, monastic lead flooded domestic and foreign markets for the metal. Exports increased, rising to ca. 2,850 tons a year at the close of the 1540s. English production of non-argentiferous lead fell. Only when royal export embargoes in 1541–1542 and 1553–1563 staunched the flow of monastic lead, and technological innovation in the form of the ore hearth transformed the resource base exploitable by the English industry, did domestic production recover. Output rose from about 400 tons a year in 1541–1542 to 735 tons a year again during the course of the years 1553–1563.

---

31   Ibid., Appendix 3, pp. 289–313.

32   Ibid., pp. 38–146.

33   Ibid., pp. 168–186.

Figure 15.3: English Lead Production and Trade, 1461–1561

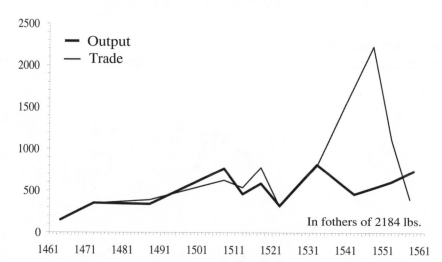

Before a flood of English monastic lead threw the whole European market for the metal into total disarray non-argentiferous lead from that nation thus provided a vital element in that commercial network serving the needs of the silver and copper producers – the *Saigerhändler* – of Central Europe. It co-existed alongside the argentiferous lead produced in Harz, Poland and England, which maintained its position only because of the willingness of consumers to pay a premium for the silver-bearing metal (Map 15.2). From ca. 1460 production and trade within this network increased, output fluctuations in one sector of the industry, engendering a countervailing response in the other about an upward trend. As the industrial long-cycle ran its course, output rose to a peak of about 4,500 tons a year in ca. 1525–1535 before European producers of the metal experienced a severe reversal of their fortunes, and production fell to ca. 2,350 tons a year in 1560–1565. Even as European lead production declined from 1536, however, alternative supplies of the metal were available to consumers. The quantities of monastic lead exported rapidly increased to ca. 2,850 tons years in 1548–1549, sustaining the amount of lead entering European markets at, or even above the levels of 1525–1535. From 1553, however, the importance of this English monastic lead within the prevailing trade network was revealed for the embargo imposed in that year on its export precipitated an acute crisis on European lead markets as consumers became once again dependent upon producers of the metal to meet their requirements. Severe shortages occurred and prices rose. The crisis was, however, ephemeral as the European lead industry underwent a fundamental transformation. The introduction of a new technology, in the form of the ore hearth, caused English production, which may have fallen to as little as 200 tons a year in the late 1540s, to rapidly increase. It reattained pre-Reformation levels of output, viz. 735 tons a year, during the period of the embargo, 1553–1564. Then it grew to ca. 12,300 tons a year in 1635. Viewed in a long-term perspective therefore, the crisis of the 1550s marked only a brief hiatus in a long-term expansion of the European lead industry. Market supplies of the metal increased from ca. 300–400 tons a year during the 1460s to ca. 4,000–5,000 tons a year in the period 1530–1550 and 14,000–15,000 tons a year in 1625–1635.

Map 15.2: Lead Trade, 1542

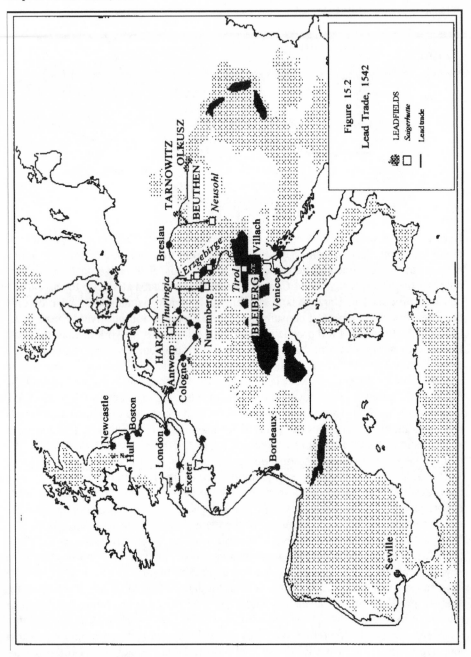

Until ca. 1530, most of this lead had passed to the *Saigerhändler* of central Europe. The industry at the height of its fortunes consumed about two-thirds of current lead production during the years 1525–1535. The subsequent decline of this sector of the European silver industry, however, caused a corresponding reduction in its requirements for lead, which fell to 1,950 tons in the 1540s and 1,750 tons in the 1560s. Even in crisis conditions, occasioned during the years 1553–1564 by the English lead embargo, therefore, the central European silver industry absorbed no more of contemporary lead production than it had twenty-five years earlier. At this time, however, the price of the metal was markedly enhanced. Between 1536 and 1553 a new range of consumers had entered the market. When after 1564 production again increased to new and higher levels, it was their demand that sustained the industrial boom. Lead prices, which had remained stable to ca. 1530, thereafter, save during the years 1553–1564, had in "real" terms fallen. The demand for the metal had steadily widened as new products, from the construction industry (paint, window glass, pipes), utensil and armaments fabricators, pottery glaziers, type manufacturers and even the medical profession, reached an ever greater proportion of the population.

During the years of this study (ca. 1500–1540) the fortunes of both English lead mining-metallurgical entrepreneurs and the merchants handling their wares was thus intimately bound up with those of European silver producers. As Central European silver-copper production increased to 1526 before declining to the low levels of 1538/42 the *Saigerhändler* of the Thuringian-Slovak and Tyrolean mining and metallurgical complex dominated the European lead market. It was their changing demand for the metal, which determined market conditions. In responding to these autonomously determined changes in demand the lead merchants' role was a largely passive one, conditioned by the supply determined decision-making of English producers. Until ca. 1520 the English merchants' competitive position within European markets rested almost entirely on the ability of those involved in the industry to maintain low and stable prices. This was achieved largely by prospecting new deposits, and smelting the ores obtained by means of the classic "bole"/"black work" oven technology complex ores, which would yield a tonne of lead for every 3.73 tonnes of ore (15 loads per fother). Then from ca. 1520–1536, the English industry was subject to general depletion problems, which reduced average industrial yields to 9 tonnes of ore per tonne of lead (1520–1536) and 10.25 tonnes of ore per tonne of lead (after 1536). In these conditions, the merchant's ability to withstand the onslaught of Harz and Polish lead again rested on the English producers' ability to reduce costs – but this time by wage reductions. In autonomously determined demand conditions the amount of English lead carried by merchants, usually as a ballast cargo, was almost entirely conditioned by the price at which they could be supplied by producers of the metal.

CHAPTER SIXTEEN

THE METAL TRADES: THE ENGLISH TIN TRADE AND ITS COMPETITORS

Producers in the English alluvial tin industry during the 1470s were embroiled in a
resource depletion crisis of European-wide dimensions which was directly analogous
to those which had affected the silver and lead industries two decades earlier. They
operated on an open mining frontier. The alluvial tinners of Devon and Cornwall had
throughout most of industry's quarter millennial history opened up new fields during
successive production-cycles – Climsland (ca. 1195–1245); Foweymoor and Black-
more (ca. 1295–1345); Penwith and Kirrier (1380–1420). This had allowed them to
expand production at constant mineral yields of 2 tonnes of ore per tonne of tin. During the last of these production-cycles (1380–1420), with the relocation of mining activity beyond the river Fal in the stannaries of Penwith and Kirrier production had expanded rapidly[1] and with the lower work intensity patterns, concomitant upon the
smaller cash requirements of the peasant workers, employment had increased. At the
height of the boom perhaps as many as 3,000 workers were employed in the two west
Cornish stannaries. Productivity per man-day re-attained the levels of the 1330s and
extraction costs were enhanced only by the necessity of maintaining daily rewards at a
level commensurate with those obtainable in outside employment.[2] The third English
industrial production-cycle was running its course but this time in a truncated form.
During the second decade of the fifteenth century, depletion problems once more became overt. The possibilities of further English expansion at constant levels of labour
productivity no longer existed and the resultant rise in English prices during the years
1405–1412 opened up new opportunities for central European producers, which were
not slow to be exploited. By the end of the first decade of the new century *Waschen*
were established on the Saxon alluvial deposits of Ehrenfriedersdorf and Geyer. Prices
once more stabilised and the English industry declined as its workforce, unable to sustain its earnings without increases in the level of work intensity, dispersed into occu-
pations that were more remunerative. From 1410–1430 the pace at which these
changes took place was slow, being dependent on the rate of decrease in English productivity, but with the, as yet unexplained, fall in Saxon production costs and resultant
decline in prices during the 'thirties it accelerated. From 1430, Saxon supremacy

---

1   All data on English production is derived from J. HATCHER, English Tin Production and Trade
    before 1550, Oxford 1973, Appendix A, pp. 152–163, and G. R. LEWIS, The Stannaries: A Study
    of the Medieval Tin Miners of Devon and Cornwall (=Harvard Economic Studies, III), Cambridge,
    Mass. 1903.

2   I. BLANCHARD, Labour Productivity and Work Psychology in the English Mining Industry 1400–
    1600, in: Economic History Review, Second series, XXXI, 1 (1978).

seemed secure but in reality during the years 1440–1450, the whole pattern was reversed. Production at Ehrenfriedersdorf and Geyer declined.[3] Prices once more rose
and English production rallied. All seemed set for yet another migration of the industry – back to England – to re-establish it in an old locale on the basis of a low produc-
tivity/high cost industrial organisation. In the event, the Saxon frontier proved not to
be closed. The discovery of alluvial tin deposits at Altenburg and Zinnwald and their
exploitation by the burgers of Freiberg and Graupen set the stage for a final migration
of the industry and for the re-assertion of Saxon hegemony. Production expanded rapidly, attaining during the 'fifties at Altenburg alone some 500 tons a year.[4] Prices fell
back to the levels of the 1430s and English output collapsed to about 350 tons. England was now eclipsed. Production reached its nadir in the 1460s. The protracted decline in exports[5] which had commenced at the beginning of the century now culminated in a total collapse. The English product was virtually excluded from European
markets in the 1460s and early 1470s. As the story of the stream-tin industry approached its close Saxony reigned supreme. For a period of almost one hundred and
fifty years a continuous process of migration to new deposits had allowed the industry
to expand at levels of productivity which, if lower than those prevailing in the thirteenth century, were at least constant over time. With the collapse of Saxon tin mining
in the 1470s, an epoch had ended.[6] Even the resultant massive rise in prices – at their
height in the 1470s they were almost three times greater than in the 1460s – engendered only a minimal response amongst the stream workers of Europe. Short-term
downswing had merged into a general crisis, which was directly analogous to those,
which had affected the silver and lead industries two decades earlier.

Succour came from an unexpected quarter, however, as the mining-metallurgical
entrepreneurs of the Erzgebirge evolved a distinctive business strategy with respect to
their operations as silver producers. As has been suggested above, during the course of
the silver industry's long-cycle, Saxon producers exploiting bismuth-cobalt-nickel-
silver ores on occasion (1480–1500/1509–1527 and 1537–1547/1560–1568) experienced difficulties and were displaced by the *Saigerhändler* of the Thuringian-Slovak
and Tyrolean production complex. At these times, the Nuremberg and Leipzig mining
entrepreneurs attempted to diversify their investment portfolios. This involved them in
fund allocation not only to the Thuringian copper industry and to those involved in its
lead supply system but also to those who on these occasions attempted to exploit the
argentiferous tin deposits of the Erzgebirge. Accordingly during the years 1480–1500
a whole new metallurgical complex came into existence as the German houses who
flocked to enter the argentiferous-tin industry of the Erzgebirge applied a new, though
as yet unexplained, technology to both existing and new ore deposits. Old centres of

---

3   On production at this time at in the Saxon alluvial deposits of Ehrenfriedersdorf and Geyer, see J.
     FALKE, Geschichte der Bergstadt Geyer, Dresden 1866, and E. REYER, Beiträge zur Geschichte
     des Zinnbergbaues in Böhmen und Sachsen, in: Österreichische Zeitschrift für Berg- und Hütten-
     wesen, XXVIII (1880), p. 349.

4   REYER, Beiträge, pp. 374–375.

5   Data on English exports is derived from HATCHER, Tin Production, Appendix B, pp. 164–200.

6   REYER, Beiträge, p. 375.

vein working, like Graupen[7] and Schönfeld, were revitalised as previously un-utilisable ores were exploited. At the old stream-works of Altenburg, Geyer and Ehrenfriedersdorf the new mining and smelting technology was introduced in the 1480s whilst during the next decade new mines were opened up at Eibenstock.[8] The tin corporations of the Saxon and Bohemian Erzgebirge were thus integrated into the second expansionary phase of the new European silver industry and thereafter they shared in successive booms – in 1509–1527, 1537–1547 and 1560–1568.[9] Yet, the production pattern of the industry differed significantly from that of the larger and more famous copper-silver industry. The reasons, however, lay not in differences in their respective raw material bases but rather were due to divergences in their market structures.

---

7   H. HALLWICH, Geschichte der Bergstadt Graupen, Prague 1868, and J. SCHWAZER, Der Zinnberg-bau in Graupen, in: Erzgebirgs-Zeitung, V (1884), pp. 161–166.

8   S. SIEBER / M. LEISTNER, Die Bergbaulandschaft von Schneeberg und Eibenstock, Berlin 1967, p. 132.

9   Unless otherwise indicated Bohemian production data is henceforth largely derived from J. MA-JER, Tezba cínu v Slavkovském lese v 16. století, Prague 1970, and Saxon data from H. WILSDORF (in collaboration with W. QUELLMALZ), Bergwerk and Hüttenanlagen der Agricola-Zeit, Berlin 1971, in the series H. PRESCHER (ed.), Georgius Agricola – Ausgewählte Werke, 10 Vols., Berlin 1955–1974.

Map 16.1: Tin Production: Erzgebirge, Kaiserwald, Fichtelgebirge and Oberpfalz

Map 16.1 Tin Production: Erzgebirge, Kaiserwald, Fichtelgebirge and Oberpfalz

1. Zinnwald
2. Graupen
3. Seiffen
4. Freiberg
5. Altenberg
6. Geising
7. Thum
8. Ehrenfriedersdorf
9. Marienberg
10. Sebastiansberg
11. Eibenstock
12. Fletzmaul
13 Graslitz
14. Oelsnitz
15. Hof
16. Konigswart
17. Barringen
18. Schlaggenwald
19. Schonfeld
20. Lauterbach
21. Neudeck
22. Gottesgab
23. Hengst
24. Fruhbuss
25. Sanderberg

● Tin workings
□ Tin Manufactory

The characteristic production-cycle of the tin-silver industry is clearly revealed in the cycle spanning the years 1480–1500. Chasing the seemingly insatiable demand of the European consumer for silver, the tin corporations expanded output with great rapidity. Yet, growth at such a pace was something of a mixed blessing. If the silver market would absorb all the precious metal that the industry could produce, the tin market was not so resilient. For more than a century (ca. 1460–1560) continental European consumption stagnated at about eight hundred tons per annum. Prices accordingly slumped and unable to dispose of his by-products the tin-silver producer experienced acute cash flow problems during the 1490s. Output regulation, necessitated not by resource depletion but by market saturation, was required. Impossible for producers, operating in an environment of near perfect competition, it was now undertaken by the *Zinnhändler* (=*merchants involved in tin production and trade, P. R.*). The crisis of the 1490s opened the way for the formation of the Mordeison-Probst purchasing organisation which was endowed with monopoly powers over Saxon production for three years by the ducal tin purchase of 1500.[10] Primarily concerned with maximising income from tin-sales, however, the interests of the monopolists conflicted with those of the producers who operated in both silver and tin markets. Having acquired monopoly powers the Leipzig consortium regulated prices to producers to curtail output in order to force up market prices. How successful they were is revealed by the events of 1500–1509. Output fell and prices rocketed up. England could offer no significant competition. Production stagnated and the English merchant community was reduced to the short-term expedient of denuding the domestic market and exporting scrap. Given high enough prices the Portuguese might import from the Indies, but the only real threat to the monopoly was the opening up of new deposits in the Erzgebirge. In this instance, threat became reality with the discovery in 1507 of new deposits at Schlackenwald.[11] Perhaps this event made the duke more than usually responsive to the complaints of the mining corporations. For whatever reason – the monopoly was abolished.

From the latter part of 1513, the cycle began all over again. This time, however, that tin emanating from the new Bohemian field augmented the output of the original Saxon producing centres, uninhibited by depletion problems because of the truncation of the preceding cycle. The result was that the market was flooded that much quicker. By 1521, prices had fallen back to the level of the 1490s and central European producers although engrossing some two-thirds of the continental European market, again suffered from cash flow problems. Accordingly, aided by ducal willingness to grant a tin purchase, the industry was again brought under the control of a monopolistic consortium. This time, however, the Welser and Fugger ensured there would be no recurrence of the events of 1503–1508. Both Bohemian and Saxon fields were brought within the ambit of the monopoly. Little wonder then that – when in 1521 ill feeling amongst the tin corporations expressed itself in Altenburg in riots, causing "the merchants and their kind" to be "driven out with threats and menaces" – the rioters got

---

10 J. STRIEDER, Studien zur Geschichte kapitalistischer Organisationsformen, Kartelle und Aktiengesellschaften im Mittelalter und in der Neuzeit, 2nd ed. Munich / Leipzig 1925.

11 On the Schlackenwald mine see V. PRÖKL, Geschichte der königlichen Bergstadt Schlaggenwald und Schönfeld, Eerg 1887; A. GNIRS, Eine Schlaggenwalder Bergchronik, in: Elbogener Zeitung (1926) and REYER, Beiträge, p. 399s.

short shrift from Duke George.[12] The monopoly held firm, but not for long and when
the threat to its existence did emerge it came not from within the Central European
industry but from without. An exogenously determined rise in English exports shattered the monopoly and resulted in the English industry increasing its market share.
The trend was most pronounced when commercial crises, by disrupting the marketing
of Central European tin brought production there to a halt (1522–1523 and 1525–
1526), but continued unabated when (in 1521, 1524 and 1527) the Central European
producer was not hamstrung by such problems. In such circumstances, the central
European production-cycle was interrupted. Only an abatement of English competition would allow its re-commencement. This occurred in the summer of 1527 as stan-
nary production declined and a Saxon-Bohemian tin purchase was negotiated as part
of the *Leipziger Monopolprojekt*.[13] The path abandoned in 1521 was resumed. The
second tin production-cycle was again running its course but now in an environment
of foreign competition. The monopoly formed in 1527 controlled only about a quarter
of the market. Monopoly pricing was accordingly only possible within marked constraints. Yet, even if the monopolists were limited in the exercise of their power, there
still remained an incentive for producers to break the grip of the consortium. The
search for new deposits thus continued and when in 1528 tin ore was found at *Heng-
stererben*, on the lands of the Lord of Plauen, the tin purchase, organised during the
previous year, collapsed.[14] Prices fell and the English share of the market was reduced. On the completion of the second tin production-cycle capacity had once more
been augmented, thereby endowing the industry, at the commencement of third cycle,
with a greater productive potential than ever before.

The new cycle began abortively in 1533. Attempts at monopoly and countervailing attempts to break such a monopoly[15] by opening up new deposits at Gottegab and
Platten[16] created boom conditions. Prices fell, coincident with a retreat in English
production and trade, resulting in central European producers recapturing the continental market and even penetrating the English market.[17] Yet, this conjuncture of circumstances was exceptional. When during the years 1534–1539 successive crises disrupted the central European tin trade, whilst new and more profitable investment opportunities in the Erzgebirge silver industry deflected funding elsewhere, activity was
suspended. Producers had to wait until 1539/40 for a re-commencement of the cycle.
Then from 1539–1542, output once more expanded and prices again fell before the
commercial crisis and resultant production stoppage of 1542–1544 briefly stayed the

---

12 STRIEDER, Studien, p. 237s. and A. DIETZ, Frankfurter Handelsgeschichte, Frankfurt-on-the-Main
    1921, II, pp. 174–178.

13 STRIEDER, Studien, pp. 243s., 247s.

14 A. CHLUPSA, Das Zinnvorkommen im böhmischen Erzgebirge, in: Montanistische Rundschau.
    Zeitschrift für Berg- und Hüttenwesen, XXI, 16 (1929), p. 319s.

15 STRIEDER, Studien, p. 250.

16 On the Platten mine, see E. MATTHES, Die Anfänge der Bergstadt Platten, in: Bohemia. Jahrbuch
    des Collegium Carolinum, I (1960); Vierhundert Jahre Bergstadt Platten, Platten 1932; JANTSCH,
    Ueber das Vorkommen des Zinns in Böhmen, in: Jahrbuch der Geologischen Reichsanstalt, IV
    (1853), and CHLUPSA, Zinnvorkommen, p. 321s., whilst on Gottesgab, see WILSDORF, Bergwerk,
    pp. 149ss.

17 HATCHER, Tin Production, p. 122.

process. In 1545, however, producers were once more ready to resume production and as output increased, prices again fell to 1548. In 1548 in Saxony only five corporations remained capable of operating at the new price level. In Bohemia stabilisation was only achieved by the monopolisation of output by the Mair-Fugger consortium[18] who, with the support of king Ferdinand were able to exclude Saxon and English competition and sustain prices at a level some forty per cent higher than those prevailing on the free market. Even if only on a limited basis, however, the third production-cycle was running its course. Yet the old conflict between producer and monopolist remained, and when in 1549 production at St Wolfgang am Plattenberg expanded, the consortium collapsed, inflicting losses of some ten thousand florins on the unfortunate Mair.

A distinctive production pattern thus revealed itself amongst central European tin producers as cycle followed cycle during the years 1480–1550. Price downswings of steadily shortening duration – from twenty years during the first cycle, to eight during the second and five during the third – were followed by periods of monopoly. Output restriction thus characterised long periods in the industry's history and as production was also subject to a series of dislocations – in 1509–1512, 1522–1523, 1525–1526, 1529–1532 and 1542–1544 – occasioned by commercial crises which brought production there to a halt, the market often only received limited supplies of central European tin. The impact on the market, however, was dependent upon the availability of other sources of tin and an analysis of market conditions reveals the existence of a long-cycle of production from non-central European sources.

As has already been noted, the monopoly of 1500–1509 revealed the absence of such alternative sources of supply, the market mechanism being capable of generating only a limited supply of scrap. In such circumstances, the stoppage of 1509–1512 proved to be catastrophic. English production stagnated and exports fell as scrap reserves were exhausted. Prices rocketed upwards, attaining a level in 1512 a third higher than that prevailing during the monopoly. Even the arrival of the Portuguese East Indies fleet with Malacca tin had little effect.[19] The crisis continued unabated, to be relieved only with the revival of central European production in 1513. From the 'twenties, however, the pattern changed. The impact of dislocations was dampened, whilst the effects of monopoly power were limited. Prices might rise above the level of 1521 but never re-attained that of 1512. A competitor had emerged who steadily challenged the position of the central European producer. Curiously, as has been shown, that competitor was England, whose industry had been steadily ousted from international markets since 1410. From 1515, its output began to recover and its products to secure an increasingly important share of continental markets. The reasons for this unexpected revival, however, lay not in the discovery of previously unexploited mineral reserves but in a fall in the opportunity cost of labour, resulting from renewed demographic pressure. As the rewards from mining increased with rising prices and employment opportunities outside the industry declined, labourers, necessitous of earning more cash in an environment of rising prices, found the previously unconge-

---

18 On the activities of this consortium see H. KELLENBENZ, Sächsisches und böhmisches Zinn auf dem europäischen Markt, in: H. KELLENBENZ / H. POHL (eds.), Historia Socialis et Oeconomica. Festschrift für Wolfgang Zorn zum 65. Geburtstag, Stuttgart 1987, pp. 246–250.

19 Calendar of State Papers. Venetian, 1509–19, p. 144.

nial low productivity work attractive. Employment and output grew, but the problems of the English industry remained. Continuing resource depletion of the alluvial deposits meant that the raw material base of the expanding industry, which on occasion during the 'twenties rose to a position of European dominance, was unstable. The crisis came in 1527 when, in spite of the availability of more and cheaper labour than ever before, production declined. Thereafter, each subsequent challenge (in 1534–1539 and 1548–1560) to the central European industry was weaker than the one before, as production declined. Even the export boom of the late 1530s took place on the basis of declining output as supplies were diverted from domestic consumption which, as in the 1500s, fell to less than a third its "normal" level of 300 tons a year. Whether in expansion to 1527 or decline, however, the fortunes of the industry rested entirely on the willingness of the labourer to spend more and more time on increasingly arduous and unrewarding work. When therefore in 1556/7 the mortality concomitant upon the influenza epidemic transformed the labour market and freed him from his bondage, the industry, already in decline, collapsed. The European market, denuded of central European tin, because of declining production caused by successive commercial crises and more profitable investment opportunities in the *Erzgebirge* silver industry which from 1547–1560 deflected funding elsewhere, was thrown into turmoil as its last source of supply was removed. A crisis, even worse than that of 1509/12, emerged and a phase in the history of the tin industry closed.

Henceforth in England, rising incomes ensured that the home market would engross an increasing proportion of a declining domestic production and that the nation's contribution to the European market would be minimal. Continental Europe, accordingly, became the preserve of the Saxon and Bohemian producers but in very different circumstances to before. Their ability to exploit these opportunities now depended on supply conditions, which had dramatically changed. Returns from silver sales continued to make a diminishing contribution to costs. Accordingly, as from 1560 the fourth production-cycle ran its course it did so on the basis of a high level of minimum operating price. Initially this posed no problems as central European production expanded at a slower rate than the decline of English exports. In 1560 output in existing centres, was still maintained at 325 tons per annum at Schlackenwald-Schönfeld and 125 tons at Altenburg. This output was now, however, augmented by supplies from the newly discovered deposits at Hirschenstand and Sauersack, opened in 1560 and 1561 respectively.[20] Prices accordingly fell, reaching their minimum operating level in 1569, when the Harrer-Jenitz "great monopoly" was formed.[21] By 1571, however, it had collapsed. Production thus now once more expanded but in an environment of free trade for previously suppressed depletion problems now became overt and prevented the industry from ever saturating the market. By 1570, first-generation producers began to experience diminishing returns as production commenced on the downswing of their 60-year yield related cycle. By 1578, the same fate befell the second-generation producers. From 1578–1592, therefore, the new producers of the 1560s held pride of place in the industry. When their production declined during the 1590s, the days of the central European industry were over. Production, which had risen to some 535 tons a

---

20   WILSDORF, Bergwerk, pp. 177ss., and CHLUPSA, Zinnvorkommen, p. 323.

21   STIEDER, Studien, pp. 280 ss.

year in the 1570s, had thereafter steadily declined to 275 tons annually in the 1600s. At no point during the course of this production-cycle could they provide sufficient supplies to a European market. That market, accordingly, experienced acute shortages and rising prices.

Map 16.2: The Commerce in Tin, ca. 1470–1570

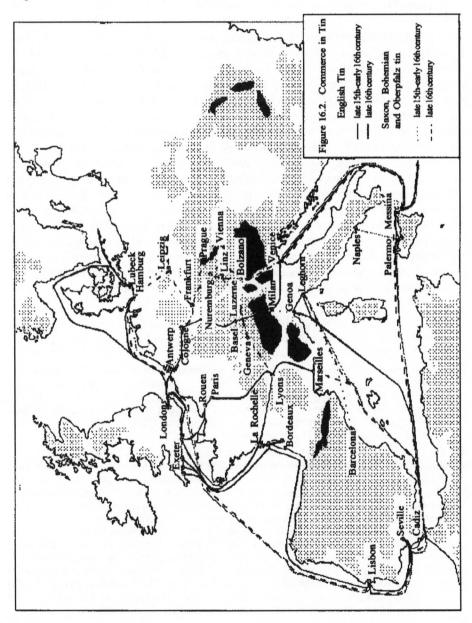

Figure 16.2. Commerce in Tin

English Tin
— late 15th-early 16th century
— late 16th century

Saxon, Bohemian and Oberpfalz tin
···· late 15th-early 16th century
-·- late 16th century

Still able in the 1450s to maintain a place on the Cologne and Antwerp markets[22], English tin thereafter had been forced to cede ground to the products of the Saxon and Bohemian Erzgebirge.[23] By 1500, it became confined to the periphery of continental European-trading systems. Throughout the period of this study (ca.1500–1540), those merchants who carried this high-cost product of a depleted mineral resource base, by either the "normal" or "alternative" trades, on accessing the continental market always found there Erzgebirge tin whose price determined how much of the English product they could sell.[24] In conditions of unfettered competition (in 1513–1521, 1529–1533 and 1539–1548) with their central European rivals, about 400 tons of English tin could be sold annually, predominantly on French, Iberian and Mediterranean markets.[25] The amount increased to 500–50 tons when (in 1500–1509 and 1534–1539) central European production was impeded by a lack of funding as new and more profitable investment opportunities in the Erzgebirge silver industry deflected funding away from the tin industry of the region. Such was the parlous state of the English industry, however, that on each of these occasions the increased quantities of English tin required for export could only be obtained by denuding the domestic market of supplies.

The English Metal Trades, 1492–1542: An Overview. During the years from 1492–1538/42 the fortunes of both English mining-metallurgical entrepreneurs and the merchants handling their wares were intimately bound up with those of central European silver producers. As central European silver-copper production increased from 1492 to 1523/6 before declining to the low levels of 1538/42 the *Saigerhändler* of the Thuringian-Slovak and Tyrolean mining and metallurgical complex dominated the European lead market. The Saxon merchant-finance houses who during the previous production-cycle had dominated activity in the central European silver industry, by diversifying their investments portfolios and encouraging (in 1492–1500, 1509–

---

22 DIETZ, Frankfurter Handelsgeschichte, II, pp. 174–178 and H. VAN DER WEE, The Growth of the Antwerp Market and the European Economy. Fourteenth–Sixteenth Centuries, 3 Vols., The Hague 1963, I, pp. 70, 73 and 80.

23 On the penetration of the Cologne market by the central European product: F. IRSIGLER, Die wirtschaftliche Stellung der Stadt Köln im 15. Jahrhundert. Strukturanalyse einer spätmittelalterlichen Exportgewerbe- und Fernhandelsstadt, Stuttgart 1979, pp. 114s., 127, 131, 175 and 311. About 1500 the product accomplished its conquest of the Antwerp market: see ibid., pp. 485 and 487, and H. POHL, Köln und Antwerpen um 1500, in: Mitteilungen aus dem Stadtarchiv von Köln, LX (1971), pp. 485–487.

24 On competition between English and central European tin on the markets of Antwerp – KELLENBENZ, Zinn, p. 250 and ID., Handelsbräuche des 16. Jahrhunderts. Das Medersche Handelsbuch und die Weserschen Nachträge (=Deutsche Handelsakten des Mittelalters und der Neuzeit, Vol. 15), Wiesbaden 1974, pp. 11, 41, 50, 136, 138, 144s., 213, 233 – Lyons and Marseilles from whence the central European product was despatched to North Africa and the Levant – T. G. WERNER, Bartholomäus Welser, Werden und Wirken eines königlichen Kaufmanns der Renaissance, in: Scripta Mercatura, 1 (1967), pp. 71–87; 1 (1968), pp. 89–109 and 2 (1968), pp. 75–101; R. COLLIER (ed.), Histoire de Marseilles, Vol. III: De 1480 à 1515, Paris 1951, and J. BILLIOURD (ed.), Histoire de Marseilles, Vol. IV: De 1515 à 1599, Paris 1951 – Spain – KELLENBENZ, Zinn, p. 250 – and Italy – A. SCHULTE, Geschichte der Großen Ravensburger Handelsgesellschaft (=Deutsche Handelsakten des Mittelalters und der Neuzeit, Vol. 1), Wiesbaden 1964, p. 334, and K. O. MÜLLER, Welthandelsbräuche 1480–1540 (=Deutsche Handelsakten des Mittelalters und der Neuzeit, Vol. 5), Berlin / Stuttgart 1934, pp. 26s., 31s., 34, 56ss., 59, 145, 159, 182 and 193.

25 HATCHER, Tin Production, pp. 120–135.

1522 and 1527–1531) the growth of Saxon-Bohemian tin production, had similarly come to dominate markets for the stanniferous metal. It was the activities of these central European entrepreneurs, which thus determined market conditions for those engaged in the English metal trades. In responding to these autonomously determined changes in market conditions the English metal traders' role was a largely passive one, conditioned by the supply-determined decision making of English producers. Until the 1520s, the merchants' competitive position within European markets rested almost entirely on the ability of those involved in the tin and lead industries to maintain low or at least stable prices. Miners undertook the exploitation of existing or new deposits, which in the lead industry at least allowed them for sixty years (1460–1520) to increase output by extending the mining frontier. Smelters eliminated the effects of local resource depletion problems through a process of technological assimilation and innovation. When from ca. 1520–1544 the English industries were subject to general depletion problems, which reduced average industrial yields, the merchants' ability to withstand the onslaught of the central European producer also rested on the English industrialists' ability to reduce costs. On this occasion, however, this was achieved by either wage reductions or in the case of the lead industry upon the merchants' ability to acquire cheap alternative supplies – from 1536 monastic lead. In autonomously determined demand conditions the amount of English lead and tin carried by merchants, usually as a ballast cargo, was almost entirely conditioned by the price at which the metal could be obtained from either producers or from other suppliers of these wares.

CONCLUSION

SUPPLICATIONS BEFORE THE ROOD

For about half a century, from ca. 1470–1520, European merchants watched every turn of events on the Antwerp market. As far as the English were concerned, the importance of the mart was neatly encapsulated in that near contemporary quotation which has been noted above:

> If English men's fathers were hanged at Andwerpes gates their children to come into that towne woulde creepe betwixt their legges.[1]

At that city the merchants disposed of most of their wares – woollen cloth, lead and tin – which had been the staples of their trade for more than a quarter of a millennium. It was also there that they could obtain those import wares to which all members of English lay and ecclesiastical society from the king right down the social scale to the members of the upper echelon of peasant society enjoyed access. In the new-fashioned shops of the English metropolitan centres or from the stalls located at the long-established annual or bi-annual fairs, such individuals were able (if they had the necessary cash) to obtain a wide range of wares. They secured them from merchants who had gained access to an international economy of truly global dimensions through Antwerp.

At the fairs of the city on the Scheldt and those of neighbouring Bergen-op-Zoom the English could both dispose of their export staples and acquire a whole range of such import wares. Their fleets, carrying cloth, lead and tin from England, arrived each year at fair time, and the wholesale unloading of these wares took place, and the settlement of financial transactions – above all bills of exchange – ran from one fair to the next. Even the English cloth, though it could only be displayed at the fairs, could be ordered throughout the year.[2] Most of the business carried on at the Old Bourse, founded in 1460, was in English cloth. The bourse at this time, however, was also a place where, on every working day of the year, merchants of Antwerp or Bruges, of Cologne or Nuremberg or other German towns, Italians, Portuguese, Spaniards and many others including occasional exotics such as Greeks or Armenians, would meet to

---

1   TNA, SP. D. Eliz. XXXVI, 34 (1565?) as quoted in F. J. FISHER, Commercial Trends and Policy in Sixteenth Century England, in: Economic History Review, X, 2 (1940), reprinted in E. M. CARUS-WILSON (ed.), Essays in Economic History, London 1954, I , p. 154.

2   R. DAVIS, The Rise of Antwerp and its English Connection, 1406–1510, in: D. C. COLEMAN / A. JOHN (eds.), Trade, Government and Economy in Pre-Industrial England. Essays presented to F. J. Fisher, London 1976, p. 11.

bargain over the enormous variety of products that could be bought there by sight, by sample or by individual order.[3]

From the rapidly developing mines of central Europe a flood of silver poured forth, much of which was spent in Italy, further intensifying the traffic with southern Germany.[4] Much was also spent on South German produce, expanding the fustian, metal working and linen industries to such a degree that it caused them to become highly efficient producers, sending some of their manufactures to the Antwerp market. Devaluation of the Burgundian currency in 1465, which heavily overvalued silver, was also a major attraction. As early as 1474 15,000 ounces of that metal were minted in Antwerp. Great quantities of silver and copper came to the Low Countries and a most important return product was English cloth, which could only be bought in Antwerp. Yet during these years, this was only one trade amongst many as a variety of branches of trade and finance coalesced at Antwerp about the pre-existing Anglo-German exchange. In the first place, the continuing role of Antwerp in supplying the towns of the Rhine valley with provisions, fish and salt, should not be overlooked, nor its substantial imports of Rhenish wine. Although the relative importance of this trade was declining, it remained in volumetric terms significant, providing much the largest element in the city's trade.[5] This trade route along the Rhine also provided an outlet to Europe for Netherlands cloths, for the tapestries of Brussels, Arras and Tournai, and for the growing metal industry of Liège.[6] South German merchants now also settled at Antwerp in increasing numbers. They had re-appeared there in about 1470, selling fustians and metals and buying cloth, and as the wealth of the Augsburg and Nuremberg merchants increased they established their own houses there. Initially their purpose was to handle trade alone. By the 1490s, however, as bullion and metal supply and profits continued to rise beyond the absorptive capacity of commercial investment, they moved into financial business. Here they gradually displaced the Italians as financiers of traders, municipalities, princes and from 1512 the Emperor himself, all of whom now benefited from a dramatic fall in interest rates on the Bourse.

The further strengthening of the links between South Germany and Italy, bringing more Italian goods into Frankfurt gave an impetus to through-traffic overland between the Mediterranean and the North Sea. Italy was by far the most important producer of silks of every kind, along with the finest metal wares – especially armour and weapons. Until just before 1500, it was also the sole source of spices and drugs and fabrics from Asia. Because Antwerp was a growing market in these wares, it also attracted Portuguese goods. The early produce of Portuguese colonization and trade in the Atlantic islands and the African coast had passed to Bruges. When, in the 1470s, the Portuguese reached the most densely populated part of the African coast, however, they

---

3   R. EHRENBERG, Capital and Finance in the Age of the Renaissance, London 1928, pp. 237–239.

4   Unless otherwise indicated the following three paragraphs draw heavily upon materials in DAVIS, Rise of Antwerp, pp. 12–15.

5   R. DOEHAARD, Études anversoises, 2 Vols., Paris 1963, I, pp. 62–5; W. BRULEZ, Brugge en Antwerpen in de 15 en 16 Eeuw: een Tegenstelling, in: Tidjschrift voor Geschiedenis, LXIII (1970), p. 23s.

6   J. A. VAN HOUTTE, La Genèse du grand marché international d'Anvers à la fin du Moyen Age, in: Revue belge de philologie et d' histoire, XIX (1940), pp. 116–8; E. SABBE, Anvers, métropole de l'occident, 1492–1566, Brussels 1952, p. 21.

experienced a big trade demand for copper bars and manufactures and for cotton goods. Germany was the obvious source to obtain such wares and Antwerp the place where they were most readily bought.[7] In return Antwerp became the principal northern outlet for ivory and African pepper and from 1488 on Madeiran sugar.[8] Similarly, when the Portuguese opened trade with India in 1498 they learned of Asia's insatiable demand for silver. This in addition, they sought at Antwerp, which they made the centre for Asian spices and drugs.[9]

Trade flooded into Antwerp. Apart from the English, German, Portuguese and Italian goods already mentioned, Antwerp had long been a market for local textiles. The recovery of the Flemish textile industry, as falling interest rates encouraged the distribution of its "heavy draperies" throughout Europe brought a large trade to Antwerp from the local production centres of Lille, Armentière and Valencienne.[10] France sent wine, woad and corn and salt for Netherlands consumption, taking English cloth, sugar, spices and German metal wares, particularly through Rouen for the great consumption centre of Paris.[11] Spanish merchants[12] still kept their most important business – wool and iron – at Bruges, but they took fruit and skins to Antwerp and bought German goods there. The Baltic Hanseatic merchants and the Dutch, who concentrated their grain trade on Amsterdam, brought many of their other products to Antwerp – skins, wax, potash, flax and linen, and iron – for they were buyers of most of the goods sold there.[13]

At the Brabant fairs English merchants thus mingled with merchants of Antwerp or Bruges, Cologne or Nuremberg, or traders from other German towns, Italians, Portuguese, Spaniards and many others including occasional exotics such as Greeks or Armenians. Amidst the stalls and exchange shops, they would meet to bargain over the enormous variety of products that could be bought there by sight, by sample or by individual order. They also in their peregrinations gained first-hand knowledge of everything that might concern their businesses. They listened attentively for those rumours of apocalyptic disaster – war, famine and disease – which perennially circulated on the commodity exchanges. These not only augured an enhancement in finance costs, as monarchs were forced to raise money to deal with the effects of such catastrophes. They also heralded major changes in conditions on those markets where

---

7   E. W. HERBERT, The West African Copper Trade in the 15th and 16th Centuries, in: H. KELLENBENZ (ed.), Precious Metals in the Age of Expansion. Papers of the XIVth International Congress of the Historical Sciences. Introduced and edited on behalf of the International Economic History Association, 2 Vols., II, Nuremberg 1981, pp. 119–130.

8   J. DENUCE, L'Afrique au XVIe siècle et le commerce anversois, Antwerp 1937, II, p. 39; BRULEZ, Brugge en Antwerpen, p. 30s.

9   W. A. HORST, Antwerpen als Specerijenmarkt, in: Tidjschrift voor Geschiedenis, LI (1936), pp. 334–6; V. MAGALHÃES-GODHINO, L'économie de l'empire portugaise au XVe et XVIe siècles, Paris 1969, p. 335.

10   E. COORNAERT, Les français et le commerce international à Anvers, Paris 1961, pp. 158–61, 184s.

11   Ibid., pp. 220–3.

12   J. A. GORIS, Les colonies marchandes méridionales à Anvers de 1488 à 1567, Louvain 1925, p. 138.

13   P. JEANNIN, Les relations économiques les villes de la Baltique avec Anvers au XVIe siècle, in: Vierteljahrschrift für Sozial- und Wirtschaftsgeschichte, XLIII (1956), pp. 202–6.

the commodities they traded were ultimately sold or acquired and signified enhanced transportation costs as carriers were forced to seek alternative routes or pay protection money to ensure safe passage. Thereby they thus gained access to an extended world of knowledge encompassing information garnered from the length and breadth of a commercial system of global dimensions. Here they heard rumours of Chinese famines or of civil wars in central Asia. Having circulated amongst the Arab, Greek or Persian merchants at Alexandria or Caffa, these rumours had been overheard by Italian traders. The Italian merchants immediately sent the news to Venice or Genoa. From thence, it was passed rapidly by pony-express riders to Antwerp. They also appraised themselves of how Sicilian and Neapolitan silk producers were responding to the resultant cessation of eastern supplies. They accordingly were able to assess the likely impact of these changes on the prices they would have to pay for the silk desired by peasant and lord alike in England. It was here also that during the years ca. 1500–1520 they received the first news each year of the number of gold-laded ships which had arrived in the Guadelquavir from the recently discovered Americas. This news not only portended the success of sales of their goods in Spain but forewarned them of the potentially disruptive impact of these specie flows on international monetary systems. Every day such items of mercantile gossip circulated on the Antwerp bourse to become part of that informational flow which would be transmitted by the English residents of that city to their masters and agents across the Channel in the city on the Thames. Sifted, structured and layered from a functional as well as a spatial perspective these fragments of information were gradually formed into a corpus of knowledge. This was then combined with further news, gleaned from traders visiting their counting houses or the various cloth halls of commodity supply conditions, to allow the merchants to formulate their business strategies. Yet encyclopaedic as it was, this information suffered from the fact that it had been gathered from within a temporally and spatially extended trade network. By the time news reached London from distant lands, it had passed through numerous hands. Each person along the way perceived and interpreted it in terms of his own particular religious, political and economic pre-conceptions, until it perhaps bore no more than a passing relationship to reality. Such distortions were an inevitable consequence of the temporal and spatial dimensions of the merchants' extended informational network. They were also an integral and very real element with his world-view.

On their trips to the Bourse, they dutifully each day made their supplications before the *plakaten* attached to the board recording rates of exchange. They then carefully recorded the quotations and diligently gathered any news of wars, bankruptcy or monetary disorder, which might upset the delicate balance of rates at that institution. On returning home almost their first act was to compose succinctly this varied information into an epistle to their masters or agents who eagerly awaited news of the day's events. The singular importance attached to this intelligence by the international merchant community is not hard to understand, for, in large measure, upon the movement of the Antwerp exchange depended the fortunes of their trade through that city. Dear money augured badly for commerce. Those merchants who borrowed money to buy wares would find their costs enhanced. Fearing lest their goods be overpriced on distant markets, they would cut back on their purchases. In such circumstances the mart was likely to be slack and those bringing their wares thence would not easily vent them. Cheap money, on the other hand, opened up the prospect of buoyant business. By reducing the foreign exchange price of commodities at their final point of sale, it increased their competitiveness and sales potential. Merchants thus flocked to buy such wares at the mart where sellers found plentiful takers for their produce. Throughout the years 1470–1570 mercantile correspondence passing between Antwerp and London revealed the intimate connection between the price of money at the western metropolis and the level of commercial activity there. Moreover, with finance costs comprising in normal circumstances ten to twenty per cent of the final wholesale price of commodities even relatively small movements in interest rates on the exchange could significantly affect prices. In the highly competitive markets of the international economy such price movements could make or mar sales of a particular product. Merchants at Antwerp thus watched every movement of the exchange with interest, for upon it depended their very livelihood.

During the period 1500–1529, English merchants thus received either by letter from their agents and factors at Antwerp or from their servants who visited the London cloth halls in search of suitable export wares a deluge of information concerning all aspects of their business. This data they sifted, structured and layered from a functional as well as a spatial perspective, forging these fragments of information into a corpus of relevant knowledge for the formulation of their business strategies. Amongst the information received at this time, however, that gathered at the London cloth halls relating to domestic price changes played a decidedly subordinate role in comparison with exchange movements in influencing merchant decision making. Both Low Countries' and English cloth prices followed a basically similar long-run path, rising from 1500/5–1514, stabilizing thereafter to 1523 and then falling to 1529 when they settled at a slightly higher level than in 1500/5. In terms of long-term domestic price changes, therefore, both groups of producers lost ground in third party markets to indigenous producers who could maintain stable prices; whilst neither gained any overall advantage at the expense of the other. In the short-run the emergence of price differentials might temporarily offset these trends, stemming for an instant the inflation or swinging the advantage for a brief interval in favour of either the Netherlands (1514–22 and 1526–8) or English (1524–5) product. In both the long- or short-run, however, the impact of these changes was slight when compared with that of exchange movements. Any short-term advantage enjoyed by the English producer before 1526 or by his Low Countries' counterpart thereafter was offset by the rise and subsequent fall of the English exchange. Any disadvantages both producers might suffer, through domestic inflation, in relation to third party competitors, between 1500/5–1523 was offset (during the years 1500–8, 1515, 1518–9 and 1524–6) by the fall in the cost of money on the Antwerp Bourse. Exchange influences during the years 1500–1529 reigned supreme. It was as though the English merchants viewed the international economy through a screen or rood, before which they made their supplications and had revealed to them that ultimate truth which they regarded as being of prime importance for the success of their businesses – the price of money on the Antwerp exchange. In an international economy, which was characterised by near perfect market conditions, of paramount importance to the merchant communities was the long-term fall in interest rates from 1492–1526 which, reducing transaction costs and the foreign exchange price of their wares, paved the way for a major trade boom through Antwerp. Of no less concern were the periodic exchange crises. These in 1513, 1517(1518–9) interrupted that trade boom. In 1521 and 1522–3, when direct Habsburg intervention into the Antwerp bill market "crowded out" private borrowers enhancing the general bill rate level and increasing the amplitude of crisis-induced fluctuations, they crippled it.

In these circumstances, the English merchants from 1524/9–1539/42 were forced to suspend their visits to the city on the Scheldt and had to forge new "direct" links with the markets in which they could either vend their wares or acquire the import wares required by their customers at home. By the 1530s, these English merchants for the first time began to establish their personal presence within the interstices of the world commercial system. During that decade, "direct" English commerce began to establish itself as a permanent feature of the nation's trade. Merchants certainly for the first time in half a century started to locate branches of their businesses at the markets where the commodities they traded were ultimately sold or acquired. On this occasion, moreover, such activities were not confined to continental Europe. Following in the wake of the original explorers and the South German and Netherlands merchants trading to the new worlds, they also trans-shipped on Spanish and Portuguese vessels to the Americas and India. As a result of this spatial extension of the "Merchants' World" its denizens were thus now able to observe directly market conditions in the places where their goods were sold to final consumers or where the commodities they required could be bought from producers. With the publication of the explorers' original journals and the receipt of mercantile intelligence in factors' letters, layer after layer of misconception about market conditions was removed. Lacking a contextual framework, which would allow them to locate their descriptions of local trading conditions in an analysis of indigenous extra-European commercial systems and business strategies, however, they merely substituted one body of misinformation for another. Both distance and time might have distorted the original rumours, which had circulated at Antwerp about extra-European trade. They were, however, rooted at least in the knowledge of Islamic merchants who operated on the basis of advanced business practices and possessed an intimacy with trading conditions in commercial networks which extended by land and sea between the Near East and China and from the Tell to the Bilad-al-Sudan. The new reports, arriving from the extra-European worlds to the South, East and West, possessed that veracity born of direct observation in relation to conditions at the points where the Europeans accessed prevailing systems. In being conceived in terms of an atavistic cultural viewpoint and lacking in such perspectives, they were, however, no less distorted. As a result of the "Discoveries" the English "Merchants' World" may have undergone a process of topographical extension, but their understanding of that world remained as restricted as before and continued to be limited by constraints of time and space.

In organizing their "direct" voyages, moreover, the merchants found that the mercantile-financial facilities available to them in the ports from which they dispatched their ships were somewhat lacking. Shipping freights out of London fell between 1524/9–1539/42 as better forms of commercial organisation were adopted. At best, however, the shipping interest could only create by the latter date a trading environment in which the English merchants could operate as efficiently as had the Antwerp merchants in their hey-day. Similarly before 1542 those English merchants who visited Lombard Street, tendering their bills of exchange to raise the finance for their ventures, secured funds at a steadily falling rate of interest. That rate, however, although moving countervailingly, always in the long-term remained above that prevailing in Antwerp.

Between 1524/9–1539/42 therefore English merchants ventured forth, participating in the "Age of Discovery" and fostering "direct" trades, which established their personal presence within the interstices of the world commercial system. That comprehensive multilateral "world view" to which they had previously subscribed at Antwerp now fragmented, however, into a series of atomistic elements, to each of which they only gained access on a bi-lateral basis. Nor in fitting out their "direct" voyages did they enjoy any better mercantile-financial facilities than had been to their predecessors who had ventured no further than Antwerp. Yet at this time, and particularly when the "direct" commerce was in the ascendant, English trade expanded rapidly, not only absolutely but also relatively to that commerce which continued to pass to Antwerp.

Operating on the basis of inferior informational flows and at best neutral mercantile-financial costs, which enhanced international transactions costs, the English merchants' competitive position in world markets no longer rested on their participation in the mechanisms of the international economy. Rather the onus of maintaining the merchants' competitive position now rested with English manufacturers. By assimilating new production techniques appropriate to the prevailing factor market situation, of rising wool prices and falling labour costs, both merchants and manufacturers not only survived but indeed prospered. Thus in England it was those who were able to assimilate the techniques involved in the production of the "new" kersey that now came to the fore. By mastering the labour-intensive techniques involved in fabricating the extra-strong warp thread, they were able to almost halve the amount of wool used in the production of the fabric and were able to stabilize the price of their cloth when elsewhere they were rising. The rapidity with which manufacturers responded to the new conditions, which emerged during the crisis of 1532–1534, was stunning. Production within established centres manufacturing these "light" cloths increased massively and as success followed success others emulated. During the late 1530s manufacturers in many of the decayed centres of the "heavy" drapery took up the production of these "light" stuffs. The day of the kersey had arrived and the manufacturer, by orientating his production about these "light" stuffs, had once more by 1541 provided the trader with a cheap product which allowed him to re-establish his position at the very centre of international cloth markets. When in 1542 analogous crisis conditions to those prevailing a decade earlier re-asserted themselves, moreover, they proved that their responses had not been a flash in the pan and that they were once more able to respond with similar rapidity to the new situation then emerging. As the whole market once more equilibrated upward in price and traders, dealing in "heavy" and even "light" draperies, experienced difficulties in selling their wares, manufacturers responded as before by the creation of a new product. Mixed cloths – serges and bays – utilising a mixture of combed and carded wools, which were able to attain approximately the limit of the prevailing technology to produce a light cloth purely from wool, now came to the fore.

The manufacturers' ability to create these new and highly saleable products, however, depended entirely on their ability to obtain ever-increasing amounts of cheap labour, which they could bend to their will. Within some two decades, 1520–1540, they achieved just this. As labour markets weakened in conditions of increasing population pressure, in the cloth industry the position of the master weaver and that of his peer group was totally transformed. A petition of the weavers of Ipswich, Hadleigh,

Lavenham and Bergholt in 1539 reveals the new situation prevailing at that time only too clearly when they declared that

> Clothiers have their own looms and weavers and fullers in their own houses so that master weavers are rendered destitute for the rich men, the clothiers, have concluded and agreed amongst themselves to pay only one price for weaving, which is too little to sustain the household even by working night and day, holiday and workday.[14]

Presented in an extreme and rather dramatic form the fate of the Suffolk weavers was representative of the lot of many English workers in manufactory during the fateful 1520s and 1530s. As their neighbours' command over landed resources weakened, and they were forced to adopt a more farinaceous diet, supplies of wool delivered to the master weavers declined and customers were loathe to have it made up into the wool-intensive "heavy" draperies. The weavers' "private" business, which had allowed them to keep the clothier at arm's length and had secured for them returns to capital and enterprise as well as to labour, was thus eroded. Increasingly during these two decades, they found themselves with only their labour to sell and the only groups who were in a position to hire them were those clothiers who found a market for their wares abroad. By 1540 the master weavers, at least in the "heavy" drapery trades, could no longer maintain an independent position. As the Suffolk weavers indicated they no longer possessed their own tools but rather were forced to labour at looms provided by their employers. They also now worked with raw materials provided by those employers. Given the contemporary low wage rates and high price of wool, in order to prevent the work-force stealing and selling the wool to augment their meagre earnings, clothiers concentrated "weavers and fullers in their own houses" where every aspect of their activity could be supervised. The erstwhile independent master weavers had been reduced to the position of highly supervised wage-labourers. They had also, in conditions of resurgent population growth and falling real wages, been "rendered destitute." Continuing to adhere to the work-norms of village society, as the clothiers "agreed amongst themselves to pay only one price for weaving" in accord with prevailing low market wage rates, the weavers, like other members of peasant society, were constrained to increase their labour intensity. This they did in order to maintain their household consumption at the levels required of them by their peers in peasant society. As the Suffolk weavers declared in 1539, however, even "by working night and day, holiday and workday" at prevailing piece rates they had only a forlorn hope of earning the cash they required to pay their rents and buy those packages of consumer goods which were the material embodiment of their position in society. The lot of these Suffolk weavers, or others labouring in the production of "heavy" draperies, might well not be entirely representative of that of workers in the cloth industry as a whole. It is probable that those engaged in the manufacture of "light" draperies felt only the muted effects of these changes but certainly these textile workers' experience was shared by others employed in the export industries of this period.

---

14 "The History of the Cloth Industry in Suffolk", in: R. H. TAWNEY (ed.), Studies in Economic History: The Collected Papers of George Unwin, London 1927, reprinted from Victoria County History, Suffolk, II, pp. 254–271.

During the 1520s and 1530s, those engaged in the lead and tin industries felt the impact of exactly the same forces at work in their labour markets. Increasingly during these two decades as smelters bought into the resource base of their industries becoming, particularly after 1536, owners of the miners' "meers," the previously independent miners who, like the master weavers, had received returns to capital and enterprise as well as to labour, were reduced to the position of wage labourers.[15] They were also, in the prevailing conditions of resurgent population growth and falling real wages, impoverished. Previously able to indulge their high leisure preference by spending only some 54 "man-days" each year on extractive work they were now forced to increase their levels of labour intensity to 84 "man-days" in order to maintain their household consumption at the levels required of them by their peers in peasant society.[16] Unfortunately in the case of these miners it is now impossible to determine whether this increase in labour intensity was achieved by changes in the numbers of hours worked per day or by alterations in the number of days worked per year but perhaps they adhered to the behavioural patterns, later recalled by Harrison in the 1570s as characteristic of the period of his youth forty years before, when he declared that

> [h]eretofore there has been much time spent in eating and drinking than commonly is in these days, for whereas of old we had breakfasts in the forenoon, beverages or nuncheons after dinner, and thereto reresuppers (i.e. second or late suppers) generally when it was time to go to rest. [...] Now these odd repasts [...] are very well left and each one in manner [...] contenteth himself with dinner and supper only [...].[17]

Clearly already in the 1530s peasant-workers were established on that path which during the next forty years would force them to work harder in order to maintain their state of material prosperity and would make them secure the time for this extra work by abandoning breakfast and afternoon drinking. Whether engaged in the export industries or other sectors of the economy, peasant-workers seemingly were already, when first observed by the young Harrison in the second quarter of the sixteenth century, altering the ritual elements of their flexible time in order to increase overall labour intensity levels so that they could maintain status-related consumption and leisure time differentials within village society in difficult times. In the process, they were also transforming England into a low-wage economy.

Since Hakluyt first chronicled the achievements of those Englishmen who during the years 1520–1540 undertook "direct" voyages to new climes within Europe and beyond, historians have lauded praise on their feats in the "Age of Discovery." The discoverers' letters and accounts have afforded successive generations of readers with a sense of the excitement that these men felt as they had "new" worlds opened to view before them. The misery of those English workmen whose labours provided them with

---

15 See the unpublished paper of I. BLANCHARD, La loi minière anglaise 1150–1850. Une étude de la loi et de son impact sur le developpement économique, 2e partie: Mythe, 1550–1850, presented at the École des Hautes Études en Sciences Sociales, Paris 1985.

16 I. BLANCHARD, Labour Productivity and Work Psychology in the English Mining Industry 1400–1600, in: Economic History Review, Second Series, XXXI, 1 (1978), pp. 1–15.

17 Quoted and analysed in I. BLANCHARD, Introduction, in: ID. (ed.), Labour and Leisure in Historical Perspective, Thirteenth to Twentieth Centuries, Stuttgart 1994, p. 22–23s.

the cheap woollen, cloth tin, and lead, which, when sold funded and made possible these voyages of discovery, has received far less attention. Nor has it been asked, whether these costly voyages, measured in terms of both money and human misery, provided useful mercantile information when compared with that which had previously been obtained from listening to the down-the-line gossip which had circulated in the alley-ways and vennels of the Antwerp fair.

APPENDIX

ANGLO-NETHERLANDS TEXTILES: TOWARDS A NEW NOMENCLATURE

In 1974 at an Economic History Society Conference held at Bristol I was privileged to attend a fascinating paper given by Professor Herman van der Wee on the process of structural change within the textile industries of the southern Netherlands during the years 1100-1600.[1] The discussion which followed the paper was equally fascinating but for a completely different reason. It revealed one of the barriers dividing international scholarship – a barrier of words. Terms like "old drapery" and "new drapery" were used with gay abandon, each participant in the debate attaching his or her own particular meaning to the terms, and as a result, everyone talked at crossed purposes with everyone else. Nor in the intervening twenty-five years has the situation been clarified much. In 1988 a conference was held at Leuvan to define the nature of just one of these cloth types, the "new drapery," with no more conclusive results.[2] Accordingly, in the following pages an attempt will be made to make a new classification of the products of the Anglo-Netherlands textile industry utilising a new nomenclature.

Before this new classification is outlined, however, yet another historical typology employed by Netherlands historians (and on occasion in the text above) needs to be considered. This divides Low Countries textile production between a "grande" and "petite draperie." Such nomenclature, unlike either the traditional one or indeed the new one employed here, is not based on technological criteria but on market ones. The "grande draperie" was produced for the export market whilst sales of the "petite draperie" were restricted to the domestic market. For reasons explained in the text this categorization has no relevance to the English experience. Also in the Netherlands whilst the heavy cloth industry may be classified as a "grande draperie" in the case of light cloth production, although normally it falls into the category of the "petite draperie", on occasion these products were also elevated into the ranks of the "grande draperie."

Thus there are two basic typologies employed in this study. The first is based on market criteria and applies only to the Netherlands industry which is divided into a "grande draperie," orientated towards the requirements of export markets, and a "petite draperies", catering for consumers in the domestic market. The second, applicable

1   H. Van der Wee, Structural Changes and Specialization in the Industry of the Southern Netherlands, 1100–1600, in: Economic History Review, Second Series, XXVIII, 2 (1975), pp. 203–221.

2   N. B. Harte (ed.), The New Draperies in the Low Countries and England, 1300–1800, Oxford 1997.

to the whole of the Anglo-Netherlands textile industry, is based on technological criteria and in this context an attempt is made below to provide a new classification of its products utilising a new nomenclature.

GLOSSARY OF ANGLO-NETHERLANDS TEXTILE TYPES

HEAVY DRAPERY (1.25–1.75 lbs / square yard)

This category encompasses those cloths which are referred to in the historiography of the Netherlands industry as both "old" and "new draperies" and which in the English literature are encompassed under the single generic term "old draperies." The term "old draperies" is applied by Dutch and Belgian historians only, and very specifically, to the traditional luxury product of the great Flemish cloth towns – Ghent, Bruges and Ypres – which utilised only the highest quality English wools. This cloth had enjoyed a dominant position amongst Netherlands textile products in the late thirteenth and early fourteenth centuries but thereafter in both its original form and a debased one (produced in both Brabant and Flanders outside the great towns) it lost ground until by the beginning of the sixteenth century it had virtually ceased to exist. During the course of the later Middle Ages it was displaced by a product specifically referred to in the Netherlands as a "new drapery" which, although aimed at imitating the traditional product and, initially at least, using the same raw materials, was characterised by a deliberate simplification of the production process. This product was dominant in the Netherlands industry on the eve of the sixteenth century, although from the second quarter of the fifteenth century Spanish wools had begun to be used in place of English in its manufacture.

A similar development pattern took place in the English textile industry with the displacement of a traditional luxury product, manufactured in the great cloth towns of eastern England (Lincoln, Stamford and Beverley being the most renowned), by a new cloth, similar in form to the traditional product but made from a wider variety of wools and fabricated by a greatly simplified production process. In ca. 1500 the luxury cloth produced by the old urban industry had, long ago, disappeared and was all but forgotten. The new cloth reigned supreme in a luxury variant, made from the finest quality wools, which was analogous to the Netherlands "new drapery", and in the form of a more mundane product, which in size and weight had no Netherlands equivalent. In the historiography of the English industry, however, both the old luxury cloth and new one, in either of its forms, are referred by the generic term "old draperies." To avoid confusion, therefore, in the text above all of these cloths have been grouped under a single name derived from their dominant characteristic – the "heavy draperies." Within this broad grouping, however, two major sub-divisions may perhaps be usefully distinguished:

A. That group of textiles weighing between 1.6 and 1.75 lbs per square yard, which were the most luxurious and costly woollen textiles produced within the Anglo-Netherlands industry during the early sixteenth century.[3] Supreme within this group were **English long cloths**: produced predominantly in Kent and Worcestershire and in the town of Coventry from the very highest quality English wool. 28–31 yards long by 1.75 yards wide, dyed and undyed, they weighed 80–90 lbs each.[4] Comparable in weight, if not in quality, were the products of the **Draperie de Lys** (Leysche lakene): produced in Commines, Warneton, Wervique, Courtrai, Menin together with the neighbouring regions of Bousbecque and Halluin in Flanders and the towns of Armentières and Leiden. These cloths, usually 1.5 yards wide, were fabricated in a variety of lengths[5] and seem, on the basis of the evidence provided by the surviving *keures*, to have weighed 1.6–1.7 lbs per square yard. Originally these cloths had been made from the same high quality wool (e.g. Cotswold) as their English equivalents but during the late fifteenth and early sixteenth centuries this had been replaced by various mixtures in which Spanish and even Scottish wool was combined with English wools of varying quality.[6] The resulting product accordingly sold at about two-thirds of the price of the English long cloth or at a level roughly comparable with the second group of heavy draperies.

B. This group of English cloths, weighing between 1.3 and 1.6 lbs per square yard, encompasses most products of the English industry which entered into international trade and for which there is no direct Netherlands equivalent. They were made in a variety of sizes and used an equally wide variety of wools. The **English short cloth**: 23–25 yards long and 1.75 yards wide, produced in Wiltshire, Gloucestershire, Norfolk, Essex, Suffolk, Kent and Worcestershire from a variety of wools and weighing 60–64 lbs each. **English half-cloths or "dozens"**: 12–13 yards long by 1.75 (63 inches) wide made in the same areas as the short cloth but with some specialisation, notably in two areas. In Yorkshire the northern "dozen" of the above specification was produced in the area about Leeds whilst in the area of Penistone a white "dozen" was produced which was only six and a half quarters (of a yard) wide. Similarly in the Bridgewater-Taunton area "dozens" were the characteristic product of manufacture. **English narrow-cloths or "straights"**: produced in varying lengths from 17 to 25 yards but only one yard wide. Again of widely dispersed manufacture but with some specialisation in Yorkshire, Hampshire and East Anglia.[7]

---

3   For relative sale prices of these products in the Netherlands during the years 1538–44 see F. ED-LER, The Van der Molen, Commission Merchants of Antwerp: Trade with Italy, 1538–44, in: Medieval and Historiographical Essays in Honour of James Westfall Thompson, Chicago 1938, pp. 94–9.

4   Statutes of the Realm, IV, 1 (London, 1819), p. 136s.

5   H. E. DE SAGHER / J.-H. DE SAGHER / H. VAN WERVEKE / C. WYFFELS, Receuil de documents relatifs à l'histoire de l' industrie drapière en Flandres. 2e partie. Le sud-ouest de la Flandre depuis l' époque Bourguignonne, Bruxelles 1951–66, I, Nr. 36, pp. 102–117; II, Nr. 231, p. 50, Nr. 265/1, p. 276 and Nr. 275, p. 306; III, Nr. 586/318, p. 577.

6   IBID., I , Nr. 36, pp. 102–117; II , Nr. 275, p. 306.

7   Statutes of the Realm, IV, 1 (London, 1819), p. 136s.

LIGHT DRAPERY (0.5–1.25 lbs. per square yard)

This group encompasses a wide variety of types, weights and shapes of cloth, known by Dutch and Belgian historians as "light" or "slight" draperies. There is no equivalent category in the historiography of the English industry. The products in this group are accordingly called by English historians either "old draperies," a term used to describe for instance kerseys, or "new draperies," for such products as bays and says. Moreover, whilst the products of the heavy drapery were all woollens, light cloth manufactory employed all three techniques of woollen cloth production – woollen, worsted and mixed cloths.

1. WOOLLENS. Like all the categories of the heavy drapery these cloths were produced from yarn spun on the wheel (either large or small) from carded wool. The cloth once woven was then thickened by fulling to produce a heavy blanket-like fabric which did not (like the worsted) reveal its weave. Such cloths, distinguished by their weight from the products of the heavy drapery, may be divided into various groups. **Doucken**: essentially these cloths, weighing between 1.0 and 1.1 lbs per square yard, were debased heavy draperies utilising either

> (a) the cheapest varieties of wool, or
> (b) the refuse of the clip and inferior fells – flocks, thrums, lentynware, morlings or shorlings.[8]

Manufactured in England predominantly in Norfolk, in Holland in the textile towns about Naarden and in the southern Netherlands in the region south and south-west of Ypres these cloths represent the bottom end of the heavy drapery market.[9] **Kersey**: a small English cloth. It was narrow (1.25 yards or 45 inches) and varied in length between the 12 yards of the Devon "dozen" and the normal 17–18 yards.[10] Manufactured in the sixteenth century in most English textile centres it was distinguished from the doucken by the use of the same range of wools as the heavy drapery. Its evolution is obscure and identification of the process of change in this product, which underwent a profound transformation in the period under consideration, is made no easier by the retention of an obsolete nomenclature for a new product. During the fifteenth century and the first quarter of the sixteenth the kersey seems, apart from its size, to have been indistinguishable from such heavy drapery products as the long cloths of Kent,

---

8   *Flocks* and *thrums* are the waste ends of wool and yarn; *lentynware* is the skin of lambs that have died shortly after being dropped in the spring; *morlings* are the fells of sheep that have died of disease and *shorling* is broken wool.

9   For a classic instance of the deterioration of a product of the heavy drapery into a doucken see the successive *keures* of the Dixmude industry: DE SAGHER et al. (eds.), Documents, II, Nrs. 243–251.

10 On the length of the kersey see the Statute 5/6 Edward VI c. 6 referred to in note 7 above. No width is given there. On widths see for instance R. P. CHOPE, The Aulnager in Devon, in: Transactions of the Devon Association, XLVI (1912), p. 594.

Worcestershire and Coventry weighing some 1.7 lbs per square yard.[11] It was certainly heavier and perhaps of a better quality than the renowned English short cloth (which weighed 1.3–1.6 lbs per square yard). Yet in the second quarter of the sixteenth century, throughout England and without any deterioration in the quality of the wool utilised, it seems to have been transformed into a light cloth, weighing only 0.9 lbs. per square yard.[12] How this metamorphosis took place is unclear but it may be associated with some change in the nature of the warp thread (which if made stronger allowed less wool to be used per square yard of product). Certainly kersey (or carsey) yarn seems to have been sufficiently distinctive that it was not only used in the fabrication of the eponymous cloth but was sold independently under is own name[13] to be utilised in the production of various other materials whenever strength in the warp threads of the fabric was required.[14] If the origins of this new cloth remain obscure, however, its impact on English commerce was not as from the second quarter of the sixteenth century it swept all before it, displacing the earlier, dominant forms of light drapery in England's export trade.[15] Paramount amongst these had been **Cottons and Freizes**: these cloths were produced during the early sixteenth century in Wales and such northern English counties as Cheshire and Lancashire from coarse local wools. The former product is shrouded in mystery but seems to have been distinguished from other coarse cloths in the finishing processes.[16] The name of the cloth is perhaps derived from the process of raising the nap with teasels to give a softer, fluffy appearance like true cotton.[17] In the case of the latter cloth the nap, instead of being shorn like most woollens, was left to naturally form itself into curls and tufts. These cloths were made in a variety of sizes and seem to have weighed about 0.75–0.8 lbs. per square yard.[18] Apart from these products of the Anglo-Netherlands industry there was a whole range of coarse local woollens produced throughout Europe which entered on

---

11 The weight of the fifteenth-century kersey may be derived from information contained in E. M. CARUS-WILSON, Trends in the Export of English Woollens in the Fourteenth Century, in: Economic History Review, Second Series, III, 2 (1950), p. 169, n. 4.

12 Statute 5/6 Edward VI, c. 6.

13 There is a great need for a study of the independent yarn trades.

14 On the use of kersey (carsey) yarn in worsted products see K. J. ALLISON, The Norfolk Worsted Industry in the Sixteenth and Seventeenth Centuries. I. The Traditional Industry, in: Yorkshire Bulletin of Economic and Social Research, XII, 2 (1960), p. 76. The author's identification (ibid., p. 82, n. 19) of this yarn with "Jarsey or Garnesey" (Jersey or Guernsey?) yarn seems, however, to be improbable. Perhaps some light may be thrown on the nature of the yarn by an analysis of the kersey and broadcloth samples preserved in BL, Lansdowne C IV, 24 fos. 92^v–93^r.

15 It is noticeable that when conditions favoured the export of the light draperies during the years down to the 'twenties, singularly few kerseys will be found amongst exports. Under such circumstances the favoured light drapery seems to have been the Chester or northern "cotton", together with some freizes (see e.g. Hengrave Hall MSS., 78/1). Only during the 'twenties were such wares gradually displaced by the kersey.

16 A. P. WADSWORTH / J. DE LACY MANN, The Cotton Trade and Industrial Lancashire, 1600–1780, Manchester 1931, pp. 14–23.

17 T. C. MENDELHALL, The Shrewsbury Drapers and the Welsh Wool Trade in the XV and XVI Centuries, London 1953, p. 4s.

18 The sizes of Welsh cloth quoted in the Statute of 5/6 Edward VI are somewhat obscure and accordingly that of 34/5 Henry VIII, c. 11 has been used for the calculations here.

occasion into international trade. The characteristics of many of these cloths as yet remain obscure.

2. WORSTEDS. Of as great an antiquity as the woollen this group of textiles was distinguished by the use of combed long-staple wool, rock-spun on the distaff, and normally not fulled but calendared thereby exposing the weave to view. Within this range of cloths which, like the woollens, became progressively lighter in weight during the early sixteenth century three major types may be identified, all of which were represented in the East Anglian industry of the late fifteenth century. **Pure Worsteds** found in England predominantly in Norfolk and in the Netherlands in Hainault (Valencienne) and south-eastern Flanders (Lille) these cloths, like all worsteds were produced from the cheapest wools. 1.25 yards (in England) and 1.5 yards (in the Netherlands) wide they were made in various lengths – ten, fifteen and twenty five yards - and were comparable in weight with the other products of the light drapery, ca. 0.9 lbs per square yard.[19] **Says**: similar in size and weight to the worsted (0.9 lbs per square yard), the say was distinguished from the pure worsted by the use of the *filé de sayette* for the warp. This was a particularly strong thread made of 2 or 3 double strands, prepared dry and spun on the small wheel. The variety of uses to which this yarn was put was, however, legion and far beyond the scope of this brief note to describe. The interested reader should accordingly consult the classic study of the principal centre of the Netherlands industry: E. COORNAERT, Un centre industriel d' autrefois. La draperie-sayetterie d' Hondschoote (XIVe–XVIIIe siècles), Paris 1930. **Étamettes** (staﾠmyns, staminett or rasse, étamines, tammies, stammets). Again worsted cloths of similar weight to the above categories. Cloths of this type were widely produced in Italy, France, the Netherlands and England. Its distinguishing characteristics are, however, uncertain although they may be in some way related to the nature of the loom used. For a careful analysis of the tangled evidence on this point the reader is referred to D. C. COLEMAN, An Innovation and its Diffusion: the 'New Draperies', in: Economic History Review, Second Series, XXII, 3 (1969), p. 420.

3. MIXED CLOTHS. Utilising a mixture of combed and carded wools these were hybrids which assumed the character of both worsteds and woollens. Only two types of this cloth, however, need concern us here. **Serges**, which were produced during the period of this study in French Flanders. **Bays**, which began to take root on both sides of the Channel in the late 1530s and early 1540s.[20] This was again a mixed woollen-worsted, fulled and accordingly not showing its pattern. All varieties known in England were some 34 yards long and were distinguished by the number of warp threads used which affected both the weight and width of the cloth:

---

19   On the size of worsteds see ALLISON, Norfolk Worsted Industry, p. 76 and their weight J. JAMES, History of the Worsted Manufacture in England, London 1857, p. 118s.

20   The following description of the bay is based upon J. E. PILGRIM, The Rise of the 'New Draperies' in Essex, in: University of Birmingham Historical Journal (subsequently re-named *Midland History*), VII (1959/60), p. 41. The weights have been transposed from the more accurate TNA, Fine Rolls, 394, as quoted in N. J. WILLIAMS, Two Documents concerning the New Draperies, in: Economic History Review, Second Series, IV, 3 (1952), p. 354, rather than from the corrupt BL. Lansdowne MS., Vol. 27, Nr. 265 quoted by Pilgrim.

Single bay: 54–60 threads, 1 yard wide, 19.5–20 lbs each.
Double bay: 100 threads, 1.37 yards wide, 29–30 lbs each.

The double bay was not only a larger cloth but also a heavier and denser one. With the bay, however, we have reached approximately the limit of the prevailing technology to produce a light cloth (in this case weighing 0.58–0.64 lbs per square yard) purely from wool. Subsequent development took the form of mixtures of wool with other – lighter, cheaper and more price elastic – materials.

NEW DRAPERY (less than 0.5 lb. per square yard)

Under this heading are included cloths which historians in the Netherlands would refer to as "light draperies" and which in England would be categorised as "new draperies." What is referred to here as "new draperies" is synonymous with neither of these historiographical groupings in their entirety and refers only to textiles made from wool and other materials. The adoption of the light drapery to incorporate other, even lighter, raw materials, as in the production of the silk and woollen say weighing only 0.25 lbs per square yard, took place outside the period of this study.[21] Yet the industries which subsequently provided the model for this transformation did in their own right become directly competitive with the woollen industry in the years about 1540. They fall into two broad categories.

1. CLOTHS BASED UPON THE USE OF YARN SPUN FROM MATERIALS OF VEGETABLE FIBRE. Predominant amongst these were fabrics made from linen and cotton.[22] These had been long domiciled in western Europe and during the fifteenth century the focus of production had shifted from Italy to South Germany where under the market conditions prevailing during the early sixteenth century **fustians** (cotton-linen mixtures) and **bombazines** (cotton-silk mixtures) became, because of their cheapness, competitive with the products of the light drapery.

2. CLOTHS BASED UPON THE USE OF YARN SPUN FROM ANIMAL HAIR. Paramount amongst these during the early sixteenth century were the products of Anatolia, **mohair cloths** made from the hair of the Angora goat and **camlets** a cloth made from a silk and camel-hair mixture.

---

21 On the size of the silk-say see PILGRIM, Rise, p. 44 and WILLIAMS, Two Documents, p. 354 for its weight.

22 For an invaluable introduction to the medieval cotton and barchant manufactory see N. J. G. POUNDS, An Economic History of Medieval Europe, London 1974, pp. 310–317, whilst an exhaustive study of this industry is provided by M. F. MAZZAOUI, The Italian Cotton Industry in the Later Middle Ages 1100–1600, Cambridge 1981, which is much more wide-ranging than its title implies.

A NOTE CONCERNING CERTAIN AMBIGUITIES ARISING FROM THE EVIDENCE OF THE ENGLISH CUSTOMS ACCOUNTS

When textile products were exported from England during the late-fifteenth and early-sixteenth centuries they were subject to certain specific customs duties which varied according to the type of cloth : cloths "in grain" (i.e. dyed with kermes, a scarlet colorant made from a crushed beetle found on the Mediterranean oak), cloths "in half grain", cloths "without grain" and worsteds. The classification was, however, by this time totally obsolete. Few cloths indeed were finished with the luxuriant dye and accordingly the overwhelming mass of textiles paid the duty under the classification "cloth without grain". This has frequently been interpreted as meaning that English cloth was exported undyed in the form of "whites" to be finished off at the continental mart. Even taken at its face value, however, the customs house classification merely indicates that the cloths exported were not dyed with kermes, used either straight or in an admixture with other dye-stuffs. They could certainly have been dyed with other materials and still classified as cloths "without grain". This moreover can be confirmed by a comparison of shipping manifests contained in contemporary merchant account books and the particular accounts of the customs officials. Certainly on occasion "whites" were exported, particularly to the Low Country marts, but even in these instances they shared passage with dyed cloths classified, for customs purposes, as cloths "without grain". In the English "direct" trades these latter cloths were absolutely dominant, barely a single "white" being carried.

Another ambiguity arising from the use of the evidence provided by the customs accounts relates to the type of cloth exported. Duties were levied in terms of the cloth of assize – 28 yards long and five quarters (of a yard) wide – but this was nothing more than an administrative abstraction which, as may be gauged from the evidence presented above, bore no relationship to any of the cloths being exported from England in the late fifteenth or early sixteenth centuries. Yet it has become a commonplace of historians, interpreting the evidence of "cloth" exports recorded in the customs accounts that, at this time, English exports were made up overwhelmingly of "broadcloths". Contemporary customs officials would not have made so brash a statement, if only because it fell to them to resolve the problem of classifying the myriad types of cloths, delivered to their customs houses, in terms of the basic taxable unit. Few succeeded and at best they made rough approximations, reckoning in the mid-sixteenth century, for instance, 3 kerseys or 4 "dozens" to the cloth of assize. They also were very well aware of why their task was such a difficult one for whilst they attempted this exercise in relation to cloths exported by denizen and Hanseatic merchants, who paid the specific cloth duty, they also had to assess the value of cloths exported by other aliens who paid an *ad valorem* tax – poundage – and, at least before their valuations became ossified, kept very detailed lists of types of cloth and their price. Had historians examined this minor trade, recorded in the particular accounts, or the officials' memoranda concerning types and prices of cloth with the same attention they have given to the engrossed records recording total English "cloth" exports, they perhaps would not have been so sanguine about their statements concerning the dominance of "broadcloth" exports. Contemporary customs officials were certainly aware that this was not the case, as a brief note attached to the Sandwich customs accounts of 1465/6[23], which was written before officials gave up the task of making accurate valuations, reveals:

Short cloths of Northampton without grain	£3. 6s. 8d.
Cloths of Coksale (Coggeshall in Essex)	£2. 13s. 4d.
Short cloth "Vilag'" (?), diverse colours without grain	£2. 0s. 0d.
Narrow cloth of Suffolk, diverse colours without grain	5s. 0d.the doz.
Cloths of Wynchestr' (Winchester, Hants.)	£2. 0s. 0d.
Narrow cloths of diverse colours	6s. 8d.
Short cloths of Colchester (Essex) without grain	£2. 0s. 0d.
Narrow cloths of Southampton	5s. 0d. the doz.
Cloths bastardes	£1. 6s. 8d.
White cloths of Wostr' (Worcester)	£1. 0s. 0d.
Kerseys	13s. 4d.
Short cloths without grain	£2. 6s. 8d.
Short cloths without grain of diverse colours	£2. 0s. 0d.
Short cloths of Colchester without grain	£2. 13s.4d.
Narrow cloths of Essex	6s. 0d. the doz.
Short cloths without grain	£2. 0s. 0d.
Violets "in dimidio grano"	£3. 0s. 0d. the doz.
"Skarletts" in grain	£4. 0s. 0d. the doz.

In no way can the evidence of the English customs accounts be interpreted to present a picture of a monolithic English trading system, characterised in the late fifteenth and early sixteenth centuries by the export of undyed "white broadcloths."

---

23   TNA, E122/128/8, as quoted in: D. BURWASH, English Merchant Shipping 1460–1540, Toronto 1947, p. 203.

BIBLIOGRAPHY

A. MANUSCRIPT BRITISH NATIONAL

Customs Records

ENGLAND: The National Archives (formerly Public Record Office/P.R.O), Kew, London. Exchequer, *Particular Customs Accounts* (E122), *Enrolled Customs Accounts* (E356) and *Port Books* (E190). The English overseas trade can, because of the remarkable survival of the national customs records, be charted in some detail for the years ca. 1460–1560, although (because of the nature of the levies imposed on the products) the documentary coverage is more comprehensive for those wares – wool and woollen cloth – which were subject to specific taxes than for those – tin and lead – which paid the petty custom and poundage on a pro-rata basis. The accounts relating to the national customs, large numbers of which are still extant in The National Archives, Kew, London, are of two kinds – *Particular Accounts* (E122) and from 1558 onwards *Port Books* (E190) and *Enrolled Accounts* (E356). In each port it was the duty of royal officials to record day by day every ship arriving from foreign lands or departing thence, noting its name and port of registration, its master, and every item of its cargo, and giving for each item the name and status (denizen, alien or hansard) of the merchant responsible and the amount of duty payable. These details were then entered into *Particular Accounts*, written sometimes in books and sometimes on parchment rolls. Short summaries were also compiled in each port, recording total quantities shipped in the case of export goods, such as wool and cloth, which paid specific customs but only total values in the case of those miscellaneous import and export goods, like lead and tin, which paid the petty custom and poundage on a pro-rata basis, together with the customs due in each case. These summary *Particular Accounts* for each port were sent up annually to the royal Exchequer. From them the Exchequer clerks made their own yearly statements, port by port, entering them on long membranes which were ultimately sewn together to form bulky rolls. These *Exchequer Enrolled Customs Accounts* (E356) survive almost completely intact and because of the separate identification of wool and cloth exports[1] they provide a continuous series of figures for the overseas trade in these commodities. Export commodities, like lead or tin, which paid the petty custom and poundage on a pro-rata basis, however, were all engrossed together with other miscellaneous wares in a single entry giving the total value of these goods and accordingly cannot be distinguished the one from the other. In these cases recourse must therefore be made to the surviving *Exchequer Particular Accounts* (E122) and *Port Books* (E190), of which large numbers, though only a very small proportion of the whole, survive for statistical information concerning the course of overseas trade.[2]

The collection, computer storage, manipulation and analysis of the vast amount of data concerning English trade in the period 1500–1540, abstracted from these national customs records has been greatly facilitated by the use of the RAPPORT and INGRES data-base systems developed at Edinburgh since

---

1   Data concerning these latter products is recorded in E. M. CARUS-WILSON / O. COLEMAN (eds.), England's Export Trade, 1275–1547, Oxford 1963.

2   Information from these records has been extracted for tin from J. HATCHER, English Tin Production and Trade before 1550, Oxford 1973, Appendix B; for lead: I. BLANCHARD, International Lead Production and Trade in the "Age of the Saigerprozess," 1460–1560, Stuttgart 1995; furs: E. VEALE, The English Fur Trade in the Later Middle Ages, Oxford 1966; salt: A. R. BRIDBURY, England and the Salt Trade in the Later Middle Ages, Oxford 1955.

1982–1985 with financial assistance provided by the SSRC–ESRC (Project HR8205/1–B 000 23 2, "The Anglo-Netherlands Bill Market and English Export Finance: 1440–1740" and R 000 23 2851: "England and the International Economy, 1544–1561").

SCOTLAND: National Archives of Scotland / NAS), Register House, Edinburgh, E71/1/1, published as *Rotuli Scaccarii Regum Scotorum* (Edinburgh, 1889–1897), Vols. XII–XVIII. I should like to express my thanks to Dr Martin Rorke for affording me access to the critical edition of the Scottish customs records which he has completed.[3]

B. MANUSCRIPT NON-BRITISH

Customs Records

DENMARK: Rigsarkivet, København. Sundtoldreguskab[4] 1497, 1503, 1528, 1536–1542.

SWEDEN: Stockholm Kammerarkivet, Tull och accis. Stockholms Tullrakenskaper Vol. 291 for the year 1533–4. I am grateful to Professor K. Ullenhag of the University of Uppsala for assisting me in acquiring microfilms of this document.

FINLAND: Valtionarkisto, Hensinki. Räkenskaper rörande tullen i Finland i 16: de och 17: de århundradenia. Nr. 233a–c. Åbo 1549, 1556, 1559.

POLAND.Wojewodskie Archiwum Panistwowe w Gdansku, Komora palowa, Pfahlkammerbuch Wojéwodzkie Archiwum Panstwowe w Gdansk, Komora Palowa, Pfahlkammerechnung 300, 19/7–11, 19.

C. OTHER MANUSCRIPT SOURCES FOR THE HISTORY OF MANUFACTORY AND TRADE

(i) Merchants' Accounts and Correspondence

Notarial Registers

ENGLAND

Bristol Record Office, Ashton Court MSS., AC/B63[5]

---

3   M. RORKE, Scottish Overseas Trade, 1275/86–1597, Unpubl. University of Edinburgh PhD Thesis, Edinburgh 2001.

Birmingham Public Library, William Mucklow's Ledger.

Cambridge University Library, Hengrave Hall MSS, 78/1–2.

Drapers' Company, London. Howell's Ledger, 1522–7.

Ipswich and East Suffolk Record Office, C/13/15/1, C5/12/8.

Mercers' Company, London. Gresham's Day Book.

The National Archives, Kew, London:

Johnson Papers (1534–1552), of which only the letters have been edited by B. WINCHESTER (ed.), The Johnson Letters, 1542–1552, Unpublished London PhD Thesis, London 1953, whilst the accounts (SP1/185, 196 and 244; SP 46/5–7) remain amongst the manuscript State Papers.

ITALY

Archivio di Stato, Ancona, II, ASA 11, 13–18, 21, 31. Information kindly provided by Dr Peter Earle.

NETHERLANDS

Antwerp Town Archives, Fonds Insolvente Boedelkamer, IB 2039

(ii) English Urban Government Records

Corporation of London Record Office, Guildhall, Repertories 7–8

D. PRINTED PRIMARY AND SECONDARY WORKS

"A Treatise concerning the Staple and the Commodities of this Realm", in: R. H. TAWNEY / E. POWER (eds.), Tudor Economic Documents, London 1924, III, p. 108.

"Extract from the state paper", quoted in: R. H. TAWNEY, The Agrarian Problem in the Sixteenth Century, London 1912

"A relation or rather a true account of the Island of England about 1500", ed. by C. A. SNEYD (London: Camden Society, Old Series, XXXVII, 1847)

O. STAVENHAGEN / L. ARBUSOW Sr. / L. ARBUSOW Jr. / A. BAUER (eds.), Akten und Recesse der Livlandischen Ständetage, Riga 1907–38

---

4   N. E. BANG / K. KORST (eds.), Tabeller over Skibsfart og Varetransport gennem Øresund 1661–1783 og gennem Storebælt 1701–1748: Vol. 1.1, Copenhagen / Leipzig 1939; Vol. 1.2, Copenhagen / Leipzig 1945

5   Published as J. VANES (ed.), The Ledger of John Smythe 1538–1550, London: Joint publication Bristol Record Series, Vol. XXVIII & HMC JP19. 1974).

ALLISON, K J., Flock Management in the Sixteenth and Seventeenth Centuries, in: Economic History Review, Second Series, XI (1958)

————, The Norfolk Worsted Industry in the Sixteenth and Seventeenth Centuries, I: The Traditional Industry, in: Yorkshire Bulletin of Economic and Social History, XII, 2 (1960)

AMMANN, M. H., Der Hessische Raum in der mittelalterlichen Wirtschaft, in: Hessisches Jahrbuch für Landesgeschichte, VIII (1958)

ARNOULD, M.-A., La ville de Chièvres et sa draperie, in: Bulletin scientifique de l' institut supérieur de commerce de la province de Hainault, II (1954)

————, Les créations de draperies en Hainault à la fin du moyen âge, in: Revue du Nord, LX (1969)

ATTMAN, A., The Russian and Polish Markets in International Trade, 1500–1650, Gothenburg 1973

BANG, N. E. / KORST, K. (eds.), Tabeller over Skibsfart og Varetransport gennem Øresund 1661–1783 og gennem Storebælt 1701–1748: Vol. 1.1, Copenhagen / Leipzig 1939; Vol. 1.2, Copenhagen / Leipzig 1945

BARKAN, O., Les mouvements des prix en Turquie entre 1499 et 1655, in: Mélanges en l' honneur de Fernand Braudel: histoire économique du monde mediterranéen, 1450–1650, Toulouse 1973

BERG, L. P. C. van den, Correspondance de Marguerite d' Autriche avec ses amis sur les affaires des Pays Bas, 2 Vols., La Haye 1842–1847

BERTHE, J.-P., Las minas de oro del Marqués del Valle en Tehuantpec, in: Historia Mexicana, VIII (1958)

BILLIOURD, J. (ed.), Histoire de Marseilles, Vol. 4: De 1515 à 1599, Paris 1951

BISCHOFF, J. P., Fleece Weights and Sheep Breeds in Late Thirteenth- and Early Fourteenth Century England, in: Agricultural History, LVII, 2 (1982)

BLANCHARD, I. (ed.), The Duchy of Lancaster Estates in Derbyshire 1485–1540 (=Derbyshire Archaeological Society Record Series, Vol. 3 for 1967), Kendal 1971

————, Population Change, Enclosure and the Early Tudor Economy, in: Economic History Review, Second Series, XXIII, 3 (1970)

————, The Miner and the Agricultural Community in Late Medieval England, in: Agricultural History Review, XX, 2 (1972)

————, Commercial Crisis and Change: Trade and the Industrial Economy of the North-East, 1509–32, in: Northern History, VIII (1973)

————, Stannator Fabulosus, in: Agricultural History Review, XXII, 1 (1974)

————, English Lead and the International Bullion Crisis of the 1550s, in: D. C. COLEMAN / A. H. JOHN (eds.), Trade, Government and Economy in Pre-Industrial England. Essays presented to F. J. Fisher, London 1976

————, Labour Productivity and Work Psychology in the English Mining Industry 1400–1600, in: Economic History Review, Second Series, XXXI, 1 (1978)

————, Consumption and Hierarchy in English Peasant Society, 1400–1600, in: Chicago Economic History Workshop Papers, XX (1980)

————, Konsumpcja ne wsi angielskiej, 1580–1680, in: Kwartalnik Historii Kultury Materialnij XXX, 1 (1982)

————, The British Silver-Lead Industry and its Relations with the Continent 1470–1570. An Outline of Research, in: W. KROKER / E. WESTERMANN (eds.) Montanwirtschaft Mitteleuropas vom 12. bis 17. Jahrhundert. Stand, Weg und Aufgaben der Forschung, Bochum 1984

————, Le marché égyptien des espèces et la crise d'or au quinzième siècle, Unpubl. Paper presented at the École des Hautes Études en Sciences Sociales, Paris, April 1985.

————, La loi minière anglaise 1150–1850. Une étude de la loi et de son impact sur le developpement économique" 2e partie. "Mythe, 1550–1850", Unpubl. Paper presented at the École des Hautes Études en Sciences Sociales, Paris 1985.

————, The Continental European Cattle Trades, 1400–1600, in: Economic History Review, Second Series, XXXIX, 3 (1986), reprinted in D. IRWIN (ed.), Trade in the Pre-Modern Era, 1400–1700 Oxford 1995

————, Introduction, in: I. BLANCHARD (ed.), Labour and Leisure in Historical Perspective, Thirteenth to Twentieth Centuries, Stuttgart 1994

————, International Lead Production and Trade in the "Age of the Saigerprozess," 1460–1560, Stuttgart 1995

————, Credit and Commerce: from the Mediterranean to the North Sea Economies in the Early Sixteenth Century, in: H. DIEDERIKS / D. REEDER (eds.), Cities of Finance: Proceedings of the colloquium. Amsterdam (May 1991), Amsterdam 1996

————, Northern Wools and Netherlands Markets at the Close of the Middle Ages, in: G. G. SIMPSON (ed.), Scotland and the Low Countries 1124–1994, East Linton 1996

————, English Royal Borrowing at Antwerp, 1544–1574, in: M. BOONE / W. PREVENIER (eds.), Finances publiques et finances privées au bas moyen âge. Actes du colloque tenu à Gand le 5–6 mai 1995, Garant, Leuven-Apeldoorn: Studies in Urban Social, Economic and Political History of the Medieval and Modern Low Countries, IV (1996)

BOGSCH, W., Der Marienberger Bergbau in der ersten Hälfte des 16. Jahrhunderts, Schwarzenberg 1933

————, Der Marienberger Bergbau seit der zweiten Hälfte des 16. Jahrhunderts, Cologne / Graz 1966

BOISSONNADE, P., L' industrie languedocienne pendant les soixante, premières années du XVIIe siècle, in: Annales du Midi (1909)

————, Le mouvement commerciale entre la France et les îles Britanniques, in: Revue Historique, CXXXV (1920)

BOONE, M., Nieuwe teksten over de Gentse draperie: Woolaanvoier, productiewijze en controlepraktijken (c. 1456–1468), in: Bulletin de la commission royale d'histoire, XIV (1988)

BOWDEN, P., Statistical Appendix, in: H. P. R. FINBERG (ed.), The Agrarian History of England and Wales, Vol. IV: 1500–1640 (series ed. by J. THIRSK), Cambridge 1967

BOYCE, H., The Mines of the Upper Harz from 1514–1589, Menasha, Wisconsin 1920

BRAND, H., A Medieval Industry in Decline: The Leiden Drapery in the Early Sixteenth Century, in: M. BOONE / W. PREVENIER (eds.), La draperie ancienne des Pays Bas: débouchés et stratégies de survie (14e–16e siècles), Leuven /Appeldorn 1993

BRAUDEL, F. / BELLART, G., Les emprunts de Charles Quint sur la place deAnvers, in: Charles Quint et son temps. Colloques internationaux du centre national de la recherche scientifique, sciences humaines (Paris 30. 9.– 3. 10. 1958), Paris 1959

BRAUDEL, F. / SPOONER, F., Prices in Europe from 1450 to 1750, in: E. E. RICH / C. H. WILSON (eds.), The Cambridge Economic History of Europe, Vol. IV: The Economy of Expanding Europe in the Sixteenth and Seventeenth Centuries, Cambridge 1967

BRAUDEL, F., La Méditerranée et le monde mediterranéen à l'epoch de Philippe II, 2 Vols., 2nd ed. Paris 1966

BRAURE, M., Etudes économiques sur les Châtellenies de Lille, Douai et Orchies, in: Revue du Nord, XV (1928)

BRULEZ, W., Lettres commerciales de Daniel et Antoine de Bombergen à Antonio Grimani 1532–43, Bulletin de l' Institute Historique Belge de Rome, XXXI (1958)

————, L' exportation des Pays-Bas vers Italie par voie de terre au milieu du XVIe siècle, in: Annales, XIV (1959)

————, Les routes commerciales d' Angleterre en Italie au XVI siècle, in: Studi in onore di Amintore Fanfani IV, Milan 1962

————, Brugge en Antwerpen in de 15 en 16 Eeuw: een Tegenstellung, in: Tidjschrift voor Geschiedenis, LXIII (1970)

BRUNS, F. / WECZERKA, H., Hansische Handelsstraßen (Quellen und Darstellungen zur Hansischen Geschichte, NF XIII, 1–3), Weimar 1962–8

BURWASH, D., English Merchant Shipping 1460–1540, Toronto 1947

BYRNE, M. S. C. (ed.), The Lisle Correspondence, 6 Vols., Chicago / London 1981

CALENDAR OF STATE PAPERS. Venetian, 1509–19

CALONNE, S., Un bourg drapant du Ferrain, in: A. LOTTIN (ed.), Histoire de Tourcoing, Dunkirk 1986

CARMONA, M., Sull' economia toscana del '500 e del '600, in: Archivio storico italiano, CXX (1962)

CARUS-WILSON, E. M., The Overseas Trade of Bristol, in: E. POWER / M. M. POSTAN (eds.), Studies in English Trade in the Fifteenth Century, London 1933

————, Trends in the Export of English Woollens in the Fourteenth Century, in: Economic History Review, Second Series, III, 2 (1950)

————, The Expansion of Exeter at the Close of the Middle Ages, Exeter 1963

CARUS-WILSON, E. M. / COLEMAN, O., England's Export Trade, 1275–1547, Oxford 1963

CAU, C., (ed.), Groot Placaet-Boek vervattende de Placaten, Ordonantien ende Edicten vande Doorluchtige, Hoogh Mog. Herren Staten Generael, The Hague 1658

CHALLIS, C. E., Currency and the Economy in Mid-Tudor England, in: Economic History Review, Second Series, XXV, 2 (1972)

————, The Tudor Coinage, Manchester 1978

CHAUNU, P., Séville et l' Atlantique, 1504–1650, Paris 1959

CHILDS, W. R., Anglo-Castilian Trade in the Later Middle Ages, Manchester 1978

CHLUPSA, A., Das Zinnvorkommen im böhmischen Erzgebirge, in: Montanistische Rundschau. Zeitschrift für Berg- und Hüttenwesen, XXI, 16 (1929)

CHOPE, R. P., The Aulnager in Devon, in: Transactions of the Devon Association, XLIV (1912)

CIRKOVIC, S., The Production of Gold, Silver and Copper in the Central Parts of the Balkans from the 13th to the 16th Century, in: H. KELLENBENZ (ed.), Precious Metals in the Age of Expansion, Stuttgart 1981

CLASEN, C. P., Die Augsburger Weber. Leistungen und Krisen des Textilgewerbes um 1600, Augsburg 1981

CLAUZEL, D. / CALONNE, S., Artisant rural et marché urbain: la draperie à Lille et dans ses campagnes à la fin du moyen âge, in: Revue du Nord, LXXII (1992)

COLEMAN, D. C., An Innovation and its Diffusion: the New Draperies, in: Economic History Review, Second Series, XXII, 3 (1969)

COLLIER, R. (ed.), Histoire de Marseilles, Vol. 3: De 1480 à 1515, Paris 1951

CONNELL SMITH, G., The Ledger of Thomas Howell, in: Economic History Review, Second Series, III, 3 (1951)

————, Forerunners of Drake: A Study of English Trade with Spain in the Early Tudor Period, London 1954

COORNAERT, E., La draperie de Leyde du XIVe au XVIe siècle, in: Vierteljahrschrift für Sozial- und Wirtschaftsgeschichte, XII (1914)

————, Un centre industriel d' autrefois. La draperie-sayetterie de Hondschoote (XIVe–XVIIIe siècles), Rennes 1930

————, Une capitale de la laine: Leyde, in: Annales: économies, sociétés, civilisations (1946)

————, Draperies rurales, draperies urbaines: l' évolution de l'industrie flamande au moyen âge et au XVIe siècle, in: Revue belge de philologie et d'histoire, XXVIII (1950)

————, Les français et le commerce international à Anvers, 2 Vols., Paris 1961

COUSSEMAKER, I. de, Keures de la ville de Bailleul, in: Annales du Comité Flamand de France, XIII (1875–7)

DALLE, J., Histoire de Bousbecque, Wervicq 1880

DAVIDSON, J. / GRAY, A., The Scottish Staple at Veere, London 1909

DAVIS, R., The Rise of Antwerp and its English Connection, 1406–1510, in: D. C. COLEMAN / A. H. JOHN (eds.), Trade, Government and Economy in Pre-Industrial England. Essays Presented to F. J. Fisher, London 1976

DAY, J., The Great Bullion Famine of the Fifteenth Century, in: Past and Present, LXXIX (1978)

DELAPIERRE, O. / WILLEMS, M. F. (eds.), Collection de keuren ou statuts de tous les métiers de Bruges, Ghent 1842

DENUCÉ, J., L'Afrique au XVIe siècle et le commerce anversois, Antwerp 1937

DEYON, P., Amiens, capitale provinciale: étude sur la société urbaine au XVIIe siècle, Paris 1967

————, Variations de la production textile au XVIe et XVIIe siècles, in: Annales, XVIII (1963)

DEYON, P. / LOTTIN A., Évolution de la production textile à Lille aux XVIe et XVIIe siècles, in: Revue du Nord, XLIX (1967)

Die Recesse und andere Akten der Hansetage, series I, edited by W. JUNGHANS (Vol. 1) and K. KOPPMANN (Vols. 2–8), Leipzig 1870–97; Series II, Vols. 1–7 ed. by G. ROPPE, Leipzig 1876–92; Series III, ed. by D. SCHÄFER (Vols. 1–7) and D. SCHÄFER, / F. TESCHEN (Vols. 8–9), Leipzig 1881–1913; Series IV, Vol. 1 ed. by G. WENTZ, Weimar 1941

DIETZ, A. Frankfurter Handelsgeschichte, 5 Vols., Frankfurt-on-the-Main 1910–1925

DOBEL, F., Der Fugger Bergbau und Handel in Ungarn, in: Zeitschrift des historischen Vereins für Schwaben und Neuberg, VI (1879)

————, Ueber den Bergbau und Handel des Jakob und Anton Fugger in Kärnten und Tirol, 1495–1560, in: Zeitschrift des historischen Vereins für Schwaben und Neuberg, IX (1882)

DOEHAARD, R., Études anversoises, 2 Vols., Paris 1963

DRUMMOND, D., The Famine of 1527 in Essex, in: Local Population Studies, XXVI (1981)

DUBOIS, M. (ed.), Textes et fragments relatifs à la draperie de Tournai au moyen âge, in: Revue du Nord, XXXII (1950)

DUPLESSIS, R., The Light Woollens of Tournai in the Sixteenth and Seventeenth Centuries, in: E. AERTS / J. H. MUNRO (eds.), Textiles in the Low Countries in European Economic History (=Proceedings of the Tenth International Economic History Congress), Leuven 1990

EARLE, P., The Commercial Development of Ancona, 1497–1551, in: Economic History Review, Second Series, XVII, 2 (1969)

EDLER, F., Winchester Kerseys at Antwerp, 1538–1544, in: Economic History Review, First Series, VII (1936)

————, Le commerce d' exportation des says d' Hondschoote vers l' Italie, d' après la correspondence d' une firme anveroise, entre 1538 et 1544, in: Revue du Nord, XXII (1936)

————, The Van der Molen, Commission Merchants of Antwerp: Trade with Italy, 1538–44, in: Medieval and Historiographical Essays in Honour of James Westfall Thompson, Chicago 1938

EDWARD, J. H., El comercio lanero en Córdoba bajo los Reyes Católicos, paper presented at the I Congreso de Historia de Andalusía in December 1976 and subsequently published in the Acta of the Congress, Madrid 1978, I, pp. 423–8

EGG, E., Hans Auslasser, in: Schwazer Weihnachtsbote (1954)

————, Das Wirtschaftswunder der silbernen Schwaz. Der Silber- und Fahlerzbergbau am Falkenstein im 15. und 16. Jahrhundert, in: Leobener Grüne Hefte, 31, Vienna 1958

————, Schwaz ist aller Bergwerke Mutter, in: Der Anschnitt, XVI, 3 (1964)

EHRENBERG, R., Hamburg und England im Zeitalter der Königin Elisabeth, Jena 1896

————, Capital and Finance in the Age of the Renaissance, London 1928

————, Das Zeitalter der Fugger. Geldkapital und Creditverkehr im 16. Jahrhundert, 2 Vols., reprint Hildesheim 1963

ELSAS, M. J., Umriss einer Geschichte der Preise und Löhne in Deutschland, 3 Vols. in 2, Leiden 1936–49

ENDREI, W., English Kerseys in Eastern Europe with Special Reference to Hungary, in: Textile History, V (1974)

ESPINAS, G., La vie urbaine de Douai au moyen âge, 4 Vols., Paris 1913

——, La draperie dans la Flandre française au moyen âge, 2 Vols., Paris 1923

—— (ed.), Documents relatifs à la draperie de Valenciennes au moyen âge, Paris 1931

ESPINAS, G. / PIRENNE, H. (eds.), Receuil de documents relatifs à l' histoire de l' industrie drapière en Flandre, Ie partie: Des origines à l' époque bourguignonne, 4 Vols., Brussels 1906–1924

FABIUNKE, G., Martin Luther als Nationalökonom, Berlin 1963

FALKE, J., Geschichte der Bergstadt Geyer, in: Mitteilungen des königlichen sächsischen Vereins für Erforschung und Erhaltung vaterländischer Geschichts- und Kunstdenkmale, XV (1866)

FEAVERYEAR, A. E., The Pound Sterling: A History of English Money, Oxford 1931

FINBERG, H. P. R., (ed.), The Agrarian History of England and Wales, Vol. IV: 1500–1640 (series ed. J. THIRSK), Cambridge 1967

FINK, E., Die Bergwerksunternehmungen der Fugger in Schlesien, in: Zeitschrift des Vereins für Geschichte und Alterthum Schlesiens, XXVIII (1894)

FINOT, J., Etude historique sur les relations entre France et la Flandre au Moyen Age, Paris 1894

——, Relations commerciales et maritimes entre la Flandre et l' Espagne au Moyen Age, in: Annales du Comté flamand de France, XXIV (1898)

——, Etude historique sur les relations commerciales entre la Flandre et l' Espagne au moyen age, Paris 1899

FISCHER, G., Aus zwei Jahrhunderten Leipziger Handelsgeschichte, 1470–1650. Die kaufmännische Einwanderung und ihre Auswirkung, Leipzig 1929

FISHER, F. J., Commercial Trends and Policies in Sixteenth Century England, in: Economic History Review, First Series, X, 2 (1940), reprinted in E. M. CARUS-WILSON (ed.), Essays in Economic History, London 1954

FLAMMERONT, J., Histoire de l'industrie à Lille, Lille 1897

FLECK, A., Beiträge zur Geschichte des Kupfers, Jena 1908

FOURDIN, E., Privilèges des drapiers de la ville d'Ath, in: Bulletin de la commission royale d'histoire (1867)

FUDGE, J. D., The German Hanse and England: Commercial and Political Interaction at the Close of the Middle Ages, Unpubl. University of Edinburgh Ph.D. Thesis, Edinburgh 1988

——, Cargoes, Embargoes, and Emissaries. The Commercial and Political Interaction of England and the German Hanse, 1450–1510, Toronto 1995

GASCON, R., Grand commerce et vie urbaine au XVIe siècle. Lyon et ses marchands, Paris 1971

GÄTSCHMANN, M. F., Vergleichende Übersicht der Ausbeute und des wieder erstatteten Verlages, welche vom Jahr 1530 an bis mit dem Jahr 1850 im Freiberger Revier verteilt worden, Freiberg 1852

GELDER, H. E. van, De Draperye van den Haage, The Hague 1907

GILLIODTS-VAN SEVEREN, L. (ed.), Inventaire des Archives de Bruges: Série 1: Treizième au seizième siècle, 6 Vols., Introduction and 2 Indices, Bruges 1878–1885

GNIRS, A., Eine Schlaggenwalder Bergchronik, in: Elbogener Zeitung (1926)

GOERLITZ, W., Staat und Stände unter den Herzögen Albrecht und Georg 1485–1539, Leipzig / Berlin 1928

GORIS, J. A., Etude sur les colonies marchandes méridionales à Anvers, 1477–1567, Louvain 1925

GOULD, J. D., The Great Debasement. Currency and the Economy in Mid-Tudor England, London 1970

GROTE, L., Die Tucher, Munich 1961

GÜMBEL, A., Die Nürnberger Goldschmiedfamilie der Groland, in: Mitteilungen aus dem Germanischen Nationalmuseum (1921)

GUNTER, F., Die älteste Geschichte der Bergstadt St. Andreasberg, in: Zeitschrift des Harzer Vereins für Geschichte (1909)

HAEPKE, R., Niederländische Akten und Urkunden zur Geschichte der Hanse und zur deutschen Seegeschichte, Munich / Leipzig / Lübeck 1913–1923

HAHN, K., Die ältesten Schneeberger Zehntrechnungen, in: Neues Archiv für Sächsische Geschichte, NF, LIII (1932)

HAKLUYT, R., The Principall Navigations, Voyages and Discoveries of the English Nation, London 1589

————, The Principal Navigations, Voyages, Traffiques and Discoveries of the English Nation, 3 Vols. in 2, London 1599–1600

HALL, E., Chronicle […], London 1809

HALL, H., The English Staple, in: Gentleman's Magazine, CCLV (1883)

HALLWICH, H., Geschichte der Bergstadt Graupen, Prague 1868

HAMILTON, E. J., American Treasure and the Price Revolution in Spain, 1501–1650, Cambridge, Mass. 1934

HANHAM, A., Foreign Exchange and the English Wool Merchant in the Late Fifteenth Century, in: Bulletin of the Institute of Historical Research, XLVI (1973)

———— (ed.), The Cely Letters, 1472–1488, London 1975

————, Profits on English Wool Exports, 1472–1544, in: Bulletin of the Institute of Historical Research, LV (1982)

————, The Celys and their World. An English Merchant Family of the Fifteenth Century, Cambridge 1985

Hansisches Urkundenbuch, edited by K. HÖHLBAUM (Vols. 1–3), J. KUNZE (Vols. 4–6), H.-G. Von RUNDSTEDT (Vol. 7) and W. STEIN (Vols. 8–11), Halle 1876–96; Leipzig 1899–1907; Munich 1916; Weimar 1939

HARING, C. H., American Gold and Silver Production in the First Half of the Sixteenth Century, in: Quarterly Journal of Economic History, XXIX, 3 (1915)

HARLEY, C. K., Ocean Freight Rates and Productivity, 1740–1913: The Primacy of Mechanical Invention Reaffirmed, in: Journal of Economic History, XLVIII (1988)

HARRISON, C. J., Grain Price Analysis and Harvest Qualities, 1465–1634, in: Agricultural History Review, XIX, 2 (1964)

HARTE, N. B. (ed.), The New Draperies in the Low Countries and England, 1300–1800, Oxford 1997

HARTUNG, J., Aus dem Geheimbuche eines deutschen Handelshauses im 16. Jahrhundert, in: Zeitschrift für Sozial- und Wirtschaftsgeschichte, VI (1898)

HASSLER, F., Der Ausgang der Augsburger Handelsgesellschaft Anton Haug, Hans Langnauer, Ulrich Link und Miterwandt, Augsburg 1926

HATCHER, J., English Tin Production and Trade before 1550, Oxford 1973

HEATON, H., The Yorkshire Woollen and Worsted Industries, 2nd ed., Oxford 1966

HERBERT, E. W., The West African Copper Trade in the 15th and 16th Centuries, in: H. KELLENBENZ (ed.), Precious Metals in the Age of Expansion (=Papers of the XIVth International Congress of the Historical Sciences), Nuremberg 1981

HILDEBRANDT, R., Augsburger und Nürnberger Kupferhandel, 1500–1619, in: Zeitschrift für Wirtschafts- und Sozialwissenschaften, XCII, 1 (1972)

HILLEBRAND, W., Der Goslarer Metallhandel im Mittelalter, in: Hansische Geschichtsblätter, LXXXVII (1969)

HORST, W. A., Antwerpen als Specerijenmarkt, in: Tidjschrift voor Geschiedenis, LI (1936)

HOSHINO, H., L'arte della lana a Firenze nel Basso Medioevo, Florence 1980

HOSHINO, H. / MAZZAOUI, M., Ottoman Markets for Florentine Woollen Cloth in the Late Fifteenth century, in: International Journal of Turkish Studies, III (1985–6)

HOSKINS, W. G., Harvest Fluctuations and English Economic History 1480–1619, in: Agricultural History Review, XII, 1 (1964)

HOUTTE, J. A. van, La Genèse du grand marché international d'Anvers à la fin du Moyen Age, in: Revue belge de philologie et d' histoire, XIX (1940)

————, Quantitative Quellen zur Geschichte des Antwerpener Handels im 15. und 16. Jahrhundert, in: H. AUBIN et al. (eds.), Beiträge zur Wirtschafts- und Stadtgeschichte. Festschrift für Hektor Amman, Wiesbaden 1965

————, De Draperie van Leidse Lakens in Brugge, 1503–1516, in: Album Viaene (1970)

HUDSON, W. / TINGAY, J. C., Records of the City of Norwich, Norwich 1910

INNES, C. (ed.), The Ledger of Andrew Halyburton, Conservator of the Privileges of the Scotch Nation in the Netherlands, 1492–1503, Edinburgh 1867

IRSIGLER, F., Die wirtschaftliche Stellung der Stadt Köln im 15. Jahrhundert. Strukturanalyse einer spätmittelalterlichen Exportgewerbe- und Fernhandelsstadt, Stuttgart 1979

ISRAEL, J., Spanish Wool Exports and the European Economy, 1610–1640, in: Economic History Review, Second Series, XXXIII, 2 (1980)

ISSER GAUDENTHURM, M. von, Schwazer Bergwerksgeschichte, in: Berg- und Hüttenmännisches Jahrbuch der kk. Montanistischen Hochschule zu Leoben und Pribram, LII (1904) & LIII (1905)

JÄGER, A., Beiträge zur Tirolisch-Salzburgischen Bergwerks-Geschichte, in: Archiv für Österreichische Geschichte, LIII (1875)

JAMES, J., History of the Worsted Manufacture in England, London 1857

JANSEN, M., Jakob Fugger der Reiche, Leipzig 1926

JANSMA, T. S., L'industrie lainière des Pays Bas du Nord et spécialement celle de Hollande (XIVe–XVIIe siècles): production, organisation, exportation, in: M. SPALLANZI (ed.), Produzione, commercio e consumo dei panni di lana (nei secoli XII–XVII), Florence 1976

JANTSCH, Ueber das Vorkommen des Zinns in Böhmen, in: Jahrbuch der Geologischen Reichsanstalt, IV (1853)

JEANNIN, P., Les relations économiques des villes de la Baltique avec Anvers au XVIe siècle, in: Vierteljahrschrift für Sozial- und Wirtschaftsgeschichte, XLIII, 2 (1956)

JOHNSON, A. H., The History of the Worshipful Company of Drapers of London, Oxford 1914–22

KAULAK, J., (ed.), Correspondance politique de MM de Castillon et de Marillac, ambassadeurs de France en Angleterre, 1537–42, Paris 1882

KELLENBENZ, H., Handelsbräuche des 16. Jahrhunderts. Das Medersche Handelsbuch und die Weserschen Nachträge, Wiesbaden 1974

————, The Fustian Industry of the Ulm Region in the Fifteenth and Early Sixteenth Century, in N. B. HARTE / K. G. PONTING (eds.), Cloth and Clothing in Medieval Europe. Essays in Memory of Professor E. M. Carus-Wilson, London 1983

————, Sächsisches und böhmisches Zinn auf dem europäischen Markt, in: H. KELLENBENZ / H. POHL (eds.), Historia Socialis et Oeconomica. Festschrift für Wolfgang Zorn zum 65. Geburtstag, Stuttgart 1987

KLIER, R., Der Konkurrenzkampf zwischen dem böhmischen und dem idrianischen Quecksilber in der ersten Hälfte des 16. Jahrhunderts, in: Bohemia, VIII (1967)

————, Zur Genealogie der Bergunternehmerfamilie Schütz in Nürnberg und Mitteldeutschland im 15. und 16. Jahrhundert, in: MVGN, LV (1967/8)

KLOEK, E., Vrouwenarbeid aan banden gelegd? De arbeidsdeleing naar sedse volgens de keurboeken van de oude draperie van Leiden, c. 1380–1580, in: Tijdschrift voor Sociale Geschiedenis, XIII (1987)

KOCH, E., Das Hütten- und Hammerwerk der Fugger zu Hohenkirchen bei Georgenthal in Thüringen, 1495–1549, in: Zeitschrift des Vereins für Thüringische Geschichte und Alterthumskunde, NF, XXVI (1926) & NF, XXVII (1927)

KÖHLER, J., Die Keime des Kapitalismus in sächsischen Silberbergbau (1168 bis um 1500), in: Freiberger Forschungsgeschichte, D13 (1955)

KOVACEVIC, D., Dans la Serbie et la Bosnie médiéval: les mines d'or et d'argent, in: Annales. E.S.C., II (1960)

KUNNERT, H., Beiträge zur Geschichte des Bergbaues im Berggerichtsbezirk Schladming in den Jahren 1304 bis 1616, Univ. Diss., Vienna 1927

————, Die Silberversorgung österreicher Münzstätten durch den Schladminger Bergbau im XVI und Anfang des XVII Jahrhunderts, in: Numismatische Zeitschrift, LXI (1928)

LADURIE, E. Le Roy, Les Paysans de Languedoc, Paris 1966

LANE, F. C., Venetian Bankers, 1496–1533, in: Journal of Political Economy, XLV (1937), repr. in Venice and History. The Collected Papers of Frederick C. Lane, Baltimore 1966

LANZ, K., Correspondenz des Kaisers Karl V, Aus dem königlichen Archiv und der 'Bibliothèque de Bourgogne' zu Brüssel, 3 Vols., Leipzig 1844–1846

LAUBE, A., Studien über den erzgebirgischen Silberbergbau von 1470–1546, Berlin 1976

LE GLAY, Correspondance de l' Empereur Maximilien Ier et de Marguerite d' Autriche sa fille, Gouvernante des Pays Bas, 2 Vols., Paris 1845

A. LOUANT (ed.), Le Journal d' un Bourgeoisie de Mons, 1505–1536, Bruxelles 1969

LEPEYRE, H., Le commerce des laines en Espagne sous Philippe II, in: Bulletin de la société d' histoire moderne, série II, XIV (1955)

————, Les exportations de laine de Castille sous le regne de Philippe II, in: M. SPALLANZI (ed.), La lana come materia prima. I fenomeni della sua produzione e circulazione nei secoli XIII–XVII, Florence 1974

————, El comercio exterior de Castillo a través de la aduanas de Felipe II, Valladolid 1981

Letters and Papers, Foreign and Domestic, of the Reign of Henry VIII. Edited by BREWER, J. S. (Vols. III–IV); (Vols. V–XI); GAIRDNER, J. (Vols. XII–XIV); GAIRDNER, J. / BRODIE, R. H. (Vols. XV–XIX), London, HMSO, 1867–1905.

LEWIS, G. R., The Stannaries: A Study of the Medieval Tin Miners of Devon and Cornwall, Cambridge, Mass. 1903 (=Harvard Economic Studies, III)

Liv-, Est- und Curländisches Urkundenbuch ed. by F. G. von BUNGE, (Series I, Vols. 1–6), H. HILDEBRAND (Series I, Vols. 7–9), P. SCHWATZ (Series I, Vols. 10–12), L. ARBUSOW (Series II, Vols. 1–3), Reval 1853–9; Riga 1867–73; Riga / Moscow 1881; Riga / Moscow / Leipzig 1884–1914

LLOYD, T. H., The Movement of Wool Prices in Medieval England, Cambridge: Economic History Review Supplement, 6 (1973)

————, The English Wool Trade in the Middle Ages, Cambridge 1977

MAGALHÃES-GODHINO, V., L'économie de l'empire portugaise au XVe et XVIe siècles, Paris 1969

MAJER, J., Tezba cínu v Slavkovském lese v 16. století, Prague 1970

MALANIMA, P., La decadenza di un'economia cittadina – l'industria di Firenze nei secolo XVI–XVII, Bologna 1982

MALDEN, H. E. (ed.), The Cely Papers: Selections from the Correspondence and Memoranda of the Cely Family, Merchants of the Staple, AD 1475–1488 (=Camden Society, Third Series, I) London 1900

MARECHALL, J., La colonie espagnole de Bruges du XIVe au XVIe siècle, in: Revue du Nord, XXXV (1953)

MARTÍN, F. Ruiz, Lettres marchandes échangées entre Florence et Medina del Campo (=Ecole pratique des hautes études – VIe section, centre de recherches historique, Affaires et Gens d' Affaires, XXVII), Paris 1965

MATTHES, E., Die Anfänge der Bergstadt Platten, in: Bohemia, I (1960)

MAUGIS, E., La saieterie à Amiens, 1480–1587, in: Vierteljahrschrift für Sozial- und Wirtschaftsgeschichte, V (1907)

MAZZAOUI, M. F., The Italian Cotton Industry in the Later Middle Ages 1100–1600, Cambridge 1981

MEILINGER, J., Der Warenhandel der Augsburger Handelsgesellschaft Anton Haug, Hans Langnauer, Ulrich Link und Miterwandt, Univ. Diss., Leipzig 1911

MELTZER C., Erneuerte Stadt- und Bergchronik der […] Bergstadt Schneeberg, Schneeberg 1716

MENDELHALL, T. C., The Shrewsbury Drapers and the Welsh Wool Trade in the XV and XVI Centuries, London 1953

MICKWITZ, G., Aus Revaler Handelsbüchern. Zur Technik des Ostseehandels in der ersten Hälfte des 16 Jahrhunderts, Helsingfors 1938

————, Die Hansakaufleute in Wiborg, 1558–9, in: Historiallinen Arkisto, XLV (1939)

MITTENZWEI, I., Der Joachimsthaler Aufstand 1525 – Seine Ursachen und Folgen, Berlin 1968

MOLLAT, M., Affaires et infortunes de Gaspar Centurione en Normandie, 1522–32, in: Mélanges en l' honneur de Fernand Braudel: histoire économique du monde mediterranéen, 1450–1650, Toulouse 1973

MOZZATO, A., Circulation, Production, Quality and Retail of Raw Wool and Woollen Cloth in Venice and the Mediterranean World during the Fourteenth and Fifteenth Centuries, Unpubl. Paper presented at Ester Seminar, held at Jyvaskyla, October 1998.

MÜLLER, K. O., Welthandelsbräuche 1480–1540 (=Deutsche Handelsakten des Mittelalters und der Neuzeit, Vol. 5), Berlin / Stuttgart 1934

MUNRO, J. H., Wool Price Schedules and the Qualities of English Wools in the Later Middle Ages, c.1270–1499, in: Textile History, IX (1978)

————, The Origins of the English 'New Draperies': The Resurrection of an Old Flemish Industry, 1270–1570, in: N. B. HARTE (ed.), The New Draperies in the Low Countries and England, 1300–1800, Oxford 1997

MURRAY, A., The Exchequer and the Crown Revenue of Scotland, 1437–1542, Unpubl. University of Edinburgh Ph.D Thesis, Edinburgh 1961

MUS, O., De verhouding van der waard tot de drapier in de Kortrijkse draperie op het einde van 15e eeuwe, in: Annales de la Société d' Emulation de Bruges, XCVIII (1961)

NOORDEGRAAF, L., Textielnijver in Alkmaar, 1500–1850, in: Alkmaarse Historische Reeks, V (1982)

NORDMANN, C., Nürnberger Grosshandler im spätmittelalterlichen Lübeck, Diss. Phil., Kiel 1933

NORTH, D. C., Ocean Freight Rates and Economic Development, 1750–1913, in: Journal of Economic History, XVIII (1958)

————, Sources of Productivity Change in Ocean Shipping, 1600–1850, in: Journal of Political Economy, LXXVI (1968)

NORTH, D. C. / THOMAS, R. P., An Economic Theory of the Growth of the Western World, in: Economic History Review, Second Series, XXIII, 1 (1970)

OUTHWAITE, R. B., The Trials of Foreign Borrowing: the English Crown and the Antwerp Money Market in the Mid-Sixteenth Century, in: Economic History Review, XIX, 2 (1966)

PAGART, F. de Hermansart, Les anciennes communautés d'arts et métiers à St Omer, in: Mémoires de la société des antiquaires de la Morinie, XVII (1881)

PEETERS, J. P., Het verval van de lakennijverheid te Mechelen in de 16de eeuw en het experiment met de volmolen (1520–1580), in: Handelingen van de koninklijke Kring voor Oudheidkunde, Letteren en Kunst van Mechelen, LXXXIX (1985)

———, Bouwstoffen voor de geschiedenis der laatmiddeleeuwse stadsdraperie in een klein Brabants produktiecentrum: Vilvoorde (1357–1578), in: Bulletin de la commission royale de l'histoire, CLI (1985)

———, Sterkte en zwakte van Mechelse draperie in der overgang van middeleeuwen naar nieuwe tijd (1470–1520), in: Handelingen van de koninklijke Kring voor Oudheidkunde, Letteren en Kunst van Mechelen, CX (1986)

———, De-industrialization in the Small and Medium-size Towns in Brabant at the End of the Middle Ages. A Case Study: The Cloth Industry of Tienen, in: H. VAN DER WEE (ed.), The Rise and Decline of Urban Industries in Italy and the Low Countries: Late Medieval–Early Modern Times, Leuven 1988

PELC, J., Ceny w Gdansku w XVI i XVII wieku (=Badania z dziejów spolecznych i gospodarczych, Nr. 21), Lwów 1937

PHILLIPS, C. R., The Spanish Wool Trade, 1500–1780, in: Journal of Economic History, XLII, 4 (1982)

PHYTHIAN-ADAMS, C., Desolation of a City. Coventry and the Urban Crisis of the Late Middle Ages, Cambridge 1979

PICKL, O., (ed.), Das älteste Geschäftsbuch Österreichs. D. Gewölbereg. d. Wiener Neustädter Firma Alexius Funck (1516–ca.1538), in: Forschungen zur geschichtlichen Landeskunde der Steiermark, XXIII (1965)

PIKE, R., Enterprise and Adventure: The Genoese at Seville and the Opening of the New World, Ithaca / New York 1966

PILGRIM, J. E., The Rise of the 'New Draperies' in Essex, in: University of Birmingham Historical Journal (subsequently re-named *Midland History*), VII (1959/60)

POHL, H., Köln und Antwerpen um 1500, in: Mitteilungen aus dem Stadtarchiv von Köln, LX (1971)

PÖLNITZ, G. (Freiherr von), Jakob Fugger, 2 Vols., Tübingen 1949–51

———, Anton Fugger, 3 Vols., Tübingen 1958–67

———, Die Fuggersche Generalrechnung von 1563, in: Kyklos, XX (1967)

POOS, L. R., The Rural Population of Essex in the Later Middle Ages, in: Economic History Review, Second Series, XXXVIII, 4 (1985).

POSTAN, M. M., Credit in Medieval Trade, in: Economic History Review, First Series, I, 2 (1928), reprinted in E. M. CARUS-WILSON (ed.), Essays in Economic History, London 1954

POSTHUMUS, N. W., Geschiedenis van de Leidsche Lakenindustrie, 3 vols in 2, 's Gravenhage 1908–39

——— (ed.), Bronnen tot de geschiedenis van der leidsche textielnijverheid, 1333-1795, 6 Vols., 's Gravenhage 1910–1922

———, De Uitvoer van Amsterdam 1543–5, Leiden 1971

POUNDS, N. J. G., An Economic History of Medieval Europe, London 1974

POWER, E., The English Wool Trade in the Reign of Edward IV, in: Cambridge Historical Journal, II, (1926–8)

———, The Wool Trade in the Fifteenth Century, in: E. POWER / M. M. POSTAN (eds.), Studies in English Trade in the Fifteenth Century, London 1933

———, The Wool Trade in English Medieval History, Oxford 1941

PRÖKL, V., Geschichte der königlichen Bergstädte Schlaggenwald und Schönfeld, Eerg 1887

QUINSONAS, E. de, Materiaux pour servir a l'histoire de Marguerite d' Autriche Duchesse de Savoie, Regente des Pays Bas, Paris 1860

RAMSEY, G. D., The Undoing of the Italian Mercantile Community in Sixteenth-century London, in: N. B. HARTE / K. G. PONTING (eds.), Textile History and Economic History. Essays in Honour of Miss Julia de Lacy Mann, Manchester 1973

RAMSEY, P., Overseas Trade in the Reign of Henry VII: The Evidence of Customs Accounts, in: Economic History Review, Second Series, VI, 2 (1953)

REDLICH, K. A., Der Kupferbergbau in Radmer an der Hasel, in: Berg- und Hüttenmännisches Jahrbuch, LIII (1905)

REUTHER, O., Die Entwicklung der Augsburger Textilindustrie, Univ. Diss, Munich 1915

REYER, E., Beiträge zur Geschichte des Zinnbergbaues in Böhmen und Sachsen, in: Österreichische Zeitschrift für Berg- und Hüttenwesen, XXVIII (1880)

RICH, E. E. (ed.), The Ordinance Book of the Merchants of the Staple, Cambridge 1937

RICHARDSON, W. C., Stephen Vaughan, Financial Agent of Henry VIII. A Study of Financial Relations with the Low Countries, Baton Rouge 1953

RINGLING, F. W., Sixteenth Century Merchant Capitalism: the Haug-Langnauer-Linck and Relatives of Augsburg as a Case Study, Unpubl. University of Rochester PhD Thesis, Rochester 1979

ROBINSON, H. (ed.), Zurich Letters, London 1842–5 and 1846–7

ROMANO, R., A Florence au XVIIe siècle. Industries textiles et conjuncture, in: Annales E.S.C., VII (1952)

ROOSEBOOM, M. P., The Scottish Staple in the Netherlands, The Hague 1910

ROSHAINER, F., Die Geschichte des Unterharzer Hüttenwesens, in: Beiträge zur Geschichte der Stadt Goslar, XXIV (1968)

ROTH, F., Zum Bankrott der Firma Melchior Manlich, in: Zeitschrift des historischen Vereins für Schwaben und Neuberg, XXXV (1908)

ROTULI SCACCARII REGUM SCOTORUM (Edinburgh, 1889–1897), Vols. XII–XVIII

RUDDOCK, A., London Capitalists and the Decline of Southampton in the Early Tudor Period, in: Economic History Review, Second Series, II, 2 (1949)

————, Italian Merchants and Shipping in Southampton, 1270–1600, Southampton 1951

RUWET, J., L'agriculture et les classes rurales au Pays de Herve sous l'Ancien Régime, Liège: Bibliothèque de la faculté de philosophie et lettres de l' université de Liège, Fasc. C. (1943)

RYE, W. (ed.), Calendar of the Freemen of Norwich, 1317–1603, Norwich 1888

SABBÉ, E., Anvers, métropole de l'occident, 1492–1566, Brussels 1952

SAGHER, H. E. DE, Une enquête sur la situation de l' industrie drapière en Flandre à la fin de XVIe siècle, in: Etudes d' histoire dédiées à la memoire de Henri Pirenne par ses anciens éleves, Brussels 1937

————, SAGHER, J.-H. DE / WERVEKE, H. VAN / WYFFELS, C., (eds.), Receuil de documents relatifs à l' histoire de l' industrie drapière en Flandre. 2e partie, Le sud-oeust de la Flandre depuis l' époque Bourguignonne, Bruxelles 1951–66

SAMSONOWICZ, H., Über Fragen des Landhandels Polens mit Westeuropa im 15. und 16. Jahrhundert, in: K. FRITZE et al., Neue Hansische Studien (=Forschungen zue mittelalterlichen Geschichte, Vol. 17), Berlin 1970

SCARISBRICK, J. J., Henry VIII, Penguin ed., London 1971

SCHANZ, G., Englische Handelspolitik gegen Ende des Mittelalters mit besonderer Berücksichtigung des Zeitalters der beiden ersten Tudors Heinrich VII und Heinrich VIII, 2 Vols., Leipzig 1881

SCHENK, G. W., Über die Anfänge der Silberbergbaues von St. Joachimsthal, in: Der Anschnitt, XX, 5 (1968)

————, Strucny nástin dejin hornického dobyvání v Jáchymové, in: Rozpravy Narodniho Technicke-ho Muzea v Praze, XL (1970)

SCHENK, H., Nürnberg und Prag, in: Giessener Abhandlungen zur Agrar- und Wirtschaftsforschung des europäischen Ostens, XLVI (1969).

SCHICK, L., Un grand homme d'affaires au début du XVI siècle: Jakob Fugger, Paris 1957

SCHMEDT, O. de, De Engelse natie te Antwerpen in de XVIe eeuw, 1496–1582, 2 Vols. Antwerp 1950–4

SCHMID, U., Die Bedeutung des Fremdkapitals im Goslarer Berghau um 1500, in: Beiträge zur Geschichte der Stadt Goslar, XXVII (1970)

SCHREMMER, E., Antwerpen als Warenhandelsplatz im 15. und 16. Jahrhundert und seine wirtschaftlichen Beziehungen zu Mitteleuropa, in: Jahrbücher für Nationalökonomie und Statistik, CLXXVIII (1965)

SCHULTE, A., Geschichte der Großen Ravensburger Handelsgesellschaft (=Deutsche Handelsakten des Mittelalters und der Neuzeit, Vol. 1), Wiesbaden 1964

SCHWAZER, J., Der Zinnbergbau in Graupen, in: Erzgebirgs-Zeitung, V (1884)

SELLA, D., Commerci e industrie a Venezia nel secolo XVII, Venice / Rome 1961

————, The Rise and Fall of the Venetian Woollen Industry, in: B. PULLEN (ed.), Crisis and Change in the Venetian Economy of the Sixteenth and Seventeenth Centuries, London 1968

SHAPER, C., Die Ratsfamilie Rumel – Kaufleute, Finanziers und Unternehmer, in: MVGN, LXVIII (1981)

SHARPE, R. R., London and the Kingdom, 3 Vols., London 1894

SHAW, B., "The Devil's Disciple" from "Three Plays for Puritans," The Bodley Head Bernard Shaw. Collected Plays and Prefaces.

SHAW, W. A., The History of Currency, 1252–1894, London 1895

SIEBER, S. / LEISTNER, M., Die Bergbaulandschaft von Schneeberg und Eibenstock, Berlin 1967

SLOOTSMAN, K., Brabantse kooplieden op de Bergse jaarmarkten, in: Oudheidkundige Kring "De Ghulden Roos" Roosendaal, Jaarboek, XXIII (1963)

SNELLER, Z. W. / UNGER, W G., Bronnen tot de Geschiedenis van den Handel met Frankrijk (=Rijk Geschiedkundige Publicatien, G. Ser. LXX), s'Gravenhage 1930–42

SOIL, E., Les tapisseries de Tournai, in: Mémoires de la société historique et littéraire de Tournai, XXII (1891)

SOLANO, T. Mazo, El comercio de lanas por el puerto de Santander con Flandes y Francia en los años 1545–1551, in: Aportación al estudio de la historia económica de la Montaña, Santander 1957

SOMERLAD, T., Die Faktorei der Fugger in Leipzig, in: Schriften des Vereins für die Geschichte Leipzigs, XXII (1938)

SPOONER, F. C., L' économie mondiale et les frappes monétaires en France, 1493–1680, Paris 1956

SPRANDEL, R., Zur Tuchproduktion in der Gegend von Ypern, in: Vierteljahrschrift für Sozial- und Wirtschaftsgeschichte, LIV (1967)

STATUTES OF THE REALM (London, 1819)

STERNBERG, K., Umrisse einer Geschichte der böhmischen Bergwerke, Prague 1836–8

STIMMEL, E., Die Familie Schütz, in: Abhandlungen des Staatlichen Museums für Mineralogie und Geologie zu Dresden, XI (1966)

STRIEDER, J. (ed.), Die Inventur der Firma Fugger aus dem Jahr 1527, in: Zeitschrift für die gesamte Staatswissenschaft, Ergänzungsheft XVII (1905)

————, Studien zur Geschichte kapitalistischer Organisationsformen, Kartelle und Aktiengesellschaften im Mittelalter und in der Neuzeit, 2nd ed., Munich / Leipzig 1925

STROMER, W. von, Nürnberger Unternehmer in Karpetenraum. Ein oberdeutsches Buntmetall-Oligopol 1396–1412, in: Kwartalnik historii kultury materialnej, XIV, 4 (1968)

————, Das Zusammenspiel oberdeutscher und Florentiner Geldleute bei der Finanzierung von König Ruprechts Italienzug 1401–1402, in: Öffentliche Finanzen und privates Kapital im späten Mittelalter und in der ersten Hälfte des 16. Jahrhunderts, Stuttgart 1971

STURM, H., Skizzen zur Geschichte des Obererzgebirges im 16. Jahrhundert, in: Forschungen zur Geschichte und Landeskunde der Sudeten, V (1965)

SUHLING, L., Innovationen im Montanwesen der Renaissance. Zur Frühgeschichte des Tiroler Abdarrprozesses, in: Technikgeschichte, XLII (1975)

————, Der Seigerhüttenprozess. Die Technologie des Kupferseigerns nach den frühen metallurgischen Schriften, Stuttgart 1976

————, Herzog Ludwig der Reiche als Montanunternehmer am Inn. Versuch eines Technologietransfers von Nürnberg nach Brixlegg in den Jahren 1467/8, in: Veröffentlichungen des Museum Ferdinandeum, LVII (1977)

————, Bergbau, Territorialherrschaft und technologischer Wandel. Prozessinnovationen im Montanwesen der Renaissance am Beispiel der mitteleuropäischen Silberproduktion, in: U. TROITZSCH / G. WOHLAUF (eds.), Technikgeschichte. Historische Beiträge und neuere Ansätze, Frankfurt-on-the-Main 1980

SZÉKELY, G., Niederländische und englische Tucharten im Mitteleuropa des 13.–17. Jahrhunderts, in: Annales Universitatis Scientiarum Budapestinensis de Rolando Eötvas Nominatae. Sectio Historica, VIII (1966)

TAWNEY, R. H., The Agrarian Problem in the Sixteenth Century, London 1912

TAWNEY, R. H. / POWER, E. (eds.), Tudor Economic Documents, 3 Vols., London 1924

———— (ed.), Studies in Economic History: The Collected Papers of George Unwin, London 1927

TOUCHARD, H., Le commerce maritime breton à la fin du moyen age, Paris 1967

TRAVERS, A. P., The Practice of Usury in Mid-Sixteenth Century England, Unpublished University of Edinburgh PhD Thesis, Edinburgh 1975

TRENARD, L., Roubaix, ville drapant entre Lille et Tournai, 1496–1776, in: Revue du Nord, LI (1969)

UNGER, M., Die Leipziger Messen und die Niederlande im 16. und 18. Jahrhundert, in: Hansische Geschichtsblätter, LXXXI (1963)

UNGER, W. S., De Tol van Iersekerood, 1321–1572 (=Rijks Geschiedkundige Publicatien, Kl. Ser. XXIX), s' Gravenhage 1939

UNWIN, G., The History of the Cloth Industry in Suffolk, in: R. H. TAWNEY (ed.), Studies in Economic History: The Collected Papers of George Unwin, London 1927, reprinted from Victoria County History, Suffolk, Vol. 2.

UYTVEN, R. van, Een rekening betreffend Edmond Claysson, handelaar te Antwerpen (ca. 1518–1520), in: Bijdragen tot de geschiedenis, inzonderheid van het oud hertogdom, Brabant, 42 (1959)

————, La Flandre et le Brabant, 'Terres de Promission' sous les Ducs de Bourgogne?, in: Revue du Nord, XLIII (1961)

————, 'Hierlandsche' wol en lakens in Brabantse documenten (XIIIde–XVIde eeuw), in: Bijdragen tot de geschiedenis inzonderheid van hey oud hertogdom Brabant, LIII (1970)

————, La draperie brabanconne et malinoise du XIIe au XVIIe siècle: grandeur éphémère et décadence" in M. SPALLANZI (ed.), Produzione, commercio e consumo dei panni di lana (nei secoli XII–XVII), Florence 1976

VANHAECK, M., Histoire de la sayetterie à Lille, 2 Vols., Lille 1910

VERHULST, A., De inlandse wol in de textielnijverheid van de Nederlanden van de 12e tot de 17e: produktie, handel en verwerking, in: Bijdragen en Mededelingen betreffende de Geschiedenis de Nederlanden, LXXXV, 1 (1970)

VERLINDEN, C., A propos de la politique économique des ducs de Burgogne à l' égard de l' Espagne, in: Hispania, X (1950)

VERRIEST, L., Étude d'histoire économique et sociale. La draperie d'Ath, des origines au XVIIIe siècle, in: Annales du cercle royale archéologique d'Ath et de la région, XXIX (1943)

VIERHUNDERT JAHRE BERGSTADT PLATTEN, Platten 1932

VLACHOVIC, J., Hutnícke spracúvanie medenych rúd v Banskej Bistrici v druhej polovine 16 storice, in: Historické Stúdie, V (1960)

————, Slovenská Med v 16 a 17 storoci, Bratislava 1964

————, Die Kupfererzeugung und der Kupferhandel in der Slowakei vom Ende des 15. bis zur Mitte des 17. Jahrhunderts, in: H. KELLENBENZ (ed.), Schwerpunkte der Kupferproduktion und des Kupferhandels in Europa 1500–1650, Cologne / Vienna 1977

VRANKRIJKER, A. C. J. de, De textielindustrie van Naarden, in: Tijdschrift voor Geschiedenis, LI (1936)

WADSWORTH, A. P. / MANN, J DE LACY, The Cotton Trade and Industrial Lancashire, 1600–1780, Manchester 1931

WAESBERGHE, W. van, De Invoering van de nieuwe Textiel-nijverheden te Brugge en hun Reglementering (einde 15e–16 eeuw), in: Appeltjes van het Meetjesland (1969)

WALTON, G. / SHEPHERD, J. F., Shipping, Maritime Trade, and the Development of Colonial North America, Cambridge 1972

WATSON, A. M., Back to Gold – and Silver, in: Economic History Review, Second Series, XX, 1 (1967)

WEBB, J., Great Tooley of Ipswich. Portrait of an Early Tudor Merchant, Ipswich 1962

WEE, H. van der, The Growth of the Antwerp Market and the European Economy (Fourteenth–Sixteenth Centuries), 3 Vols., The Hague 1963

————, Structural Changes and Specialization in the Industry of the Southern Netherlands, 1100–1600, in: Economic History Review, Second Series, XXVIII, 2 (1975)

———— / AERTS, E., The Lier Livestock Market and the Livestock Trade from the Fourteenth to the Eighteenth Century, in: E. WESTERMANN (ed.), Internationaler Ochsenhandel, 1350–1750 (=Akten des 7th International History Congress, Edinburgh 1978), Stuttgart 1987

———— / BLANCHARD, I., The Habsburgs and the Antwerp Money Market: the Exchange Crises of 1521 and 1522–3, in: I. BLANCHARD et al. (eds.), Industry and Finance in Early Modern History. Essays Presented to George Hammersley on the Occasion of his 74th Birthday, Stuttgart 1992

WENGER, M., Ein Beitrag zur Statistik und Geschichte des Bergbaubetriebes in den österreichischen Alpenländern im 16. Jahrhundert, in: Montanische Rundschau, XXIII (1931)

WERNER, T. G., Das fremde Kapital im Annaberger Bergbau und Metallhandel des 16. Jahrhunderts, in: Neues Archiv für sächsische Geschichte und Alterthumskunde, LVII (1936) and LVIII (1937)

————, Das Kupferhüttenwerk des Hans Tetzel aus Nürnberg auf Kuba, in: Vierteljahrschrift für Sozial- und Wirtschaftsgeschichte, XLVIII (1961)

————, Bartholomäus Welser, Werden und Wirken eines königlichen Kaufmanns der Renaissance, in: Scripta Mercatura, I (1967) and II (1968)

WERVEKE, H. VAN, Die Stellung des hansischen Kaufmanns dem flandrischen Tuchproduzenten gegenüber, in: H. AUBIN et al. (eds.), Beiträge zur Wirtschafts- und Stadtgeschichte. Festschrift für Hektor Ammann, Wiesbaden 1965

WESTERMANN, E., Das Eislebener Garkupfer und seine Bedeutung für den europäischen Kupfermarkt, 1460–1560, Cologne 1971

————, Das 'Leipziger Monopolprojekt' als Symptom der mitteleuropäischen Wirtschaftskrise um 1527/8, in: Vierteljahrschrift für Sozial- und Wirtschaftsgeschichte, LVIII, 1 (1971)

————, Der Goslarer Bergbau vom 14. bis zum 16. Jahrhundert […], in: Jahrbuch für die Geschichte Mittel- und Ostdeutschlands, XX (1971)

————, Die Bedeutung des Thüringer Saigerhandels für den mitteleuropäischen Handel an der Wende vom 15. zum 16. Jahrhundert, in: Jahrbuch für die Geschichte Mittel- und Ostdeutschlands, XXI (1972)

————, Hans Luther und die Hüttenmeister der Grafschaft Mansfeld im 16. Jahrhundert. Eine Forschungsaufgabe, in: Scripta Mercaturae, IX (1975)

———— (ed.), Internationaler Ochsenhandel (1350–1750) (=Akten des 7 International Economic History Congress, Edinburgh 1978), Stuttgart 1979

————, Zur Silber- und Kupferproduktion Mitteleuropas vom 15. bis zum frühen 17. Jahrhundert. Über Bedeutung und Rangfolge der Reviere von Schwaz, Mansfeld und Neusohl, in: Der Anschnitt, XXXVIII, 5/6 (1986)

————, Sammlung 'Stephan Worms' im Haus-, Hof- und Staatsarchiv Wien – Eine Fundgrube für Montanhistoriker, in: Der Anschnitt, XXXVIII, 1 (1986)

————, Zur Brandsilber- und Kupferproduktion des Falkensteins bei Schwaz 1470–1623. Eine Kritik bisheriger Ermittlungen von Produktionsziffern, in: Tiroler Heimat, L (1986)

————, Zur den verwandtschaftlichen und geschäftlichen Beziehungen der Praun, Frohler und Muhlich vom Nürnberg, Erfurt und Lübeck in der zweiten Hälfte des 15. Jahrhunderts, in: Wirtschaftsgeschichte und Personengeschichte. Festschrift für Wolfgang von Stromer, 3 Vols., Vol. I, Trier 1987

————, Die Listen der Brandsilberproduktion des Falkensteins bei Schwaz/Tirol von 1470–1623. Kommentar und Edition, in: Leobener Grüne Hefte, VII, Vienna 1987

————, Über Beobachtungen und Erfahrungen bei der Vorbereitung der Edition einer vorindustriellen Produktionsstatistik. Zur Brandsilberproduktion des Falkenstein bei Schwaz/Tirol von 1470–1623, in: E. WESTERMANN (ed.), Quantifizierungsprobleme bei der Erforschung der Montanwirtschaft des 15. bis 18. Jahrhunderts, St. Katherinen 1988

WIESNER, H., Geschichte des Kärntner Bergbaus, 2 Vols., Klagenfurt 1951

WILLEMSEN, M. G. (ed.), Le réglement général de la draperie malinoise de 1544, in: Bulletin du cercle archéologique de Malines, XX (1910)

————, La technique et l'organisation de la draperie à Bruges, à Gand et à Malines au milieu du 16e siècle." Annales de l'académie royale de archéologie de Belgique, VI série, VIII–IX (1920–1)

———— (ed.), Le réglement sur le draperie brugeoise du 20 septembre 1544, in: Annales de l'académie royale de archéologie de Belgique, LXIX (1921)

WILLIAMS, N. J., Two Documents concerning the New Draperies, in: Economic History Review, Second Series, IV, 3 (1952)

WILSDORF, H. (in collaboration with W. QUELLMALZ), Bergwerk and Hüttenanlagen der Agricola-Zeit, Berlin 1971 (= H. PRESCHER [ed.], Georgius Agricola – Ausgewählte Werke, 10 Vols., Berlin 1955–1974)

WINCHESTER, B. (ed.), The Johnson Letters, 1542–1552, Unpubl. University of London PhD Thesis, London 1953

WOLFSTRIGL-WOLFSKRON, M., Der Tiroler Erzbergbau, 1321–1665, Innsbruck 1902

WORMS, S., Schwazer Bergbau im 15. Jahrhundert. Ein Beitrag zur Wirtschaftsgeschichte, Vienna 1905